Liberating People, Planet, and Religion

RELIGION IN THE MODERN WORLD

Series Editors

Kwok Pui-lan, Emory University, and Joerg Rieger, Vanderbilt University

This series explores how various religious traditions wrestle with the dynamic and changing role of religion in the modern world and examines how past changes reflect on today's critical issues. Accessibly and engagingly written, books in this series will look at secularization, global society, gender, race, class, sexuality, and their relation to religious life and religious movements.

Titles in the Series

Liberating People, Planet, and Religion: Intersections of Ecology, Economics, and Christianity, edited by Joerg Rieger and Terra Schwerin Rowe
The Seven Deadly Sins of White Christian Nationalism: A Call to Action by Carter Heyward
The Hong Kong Protests and Political Theology, edited by Kwok Pui-lan and Francis Ching-wah Yip
Race, Religion, and Politics: Toward Human Rights in the United States by Stephanie Y. Mitchem
Modern Muslim Theology: Engaging God and the World with Faith and Imagination by Martin Nguyen
The Politics of Jesús: A Hispanic Political Theology by Miguel A. De La Torre
The Food and Feasts of Jesus: The Original Mediterranean Diet, with Menus and Recipes by Douglas E. Neel and Joel A. Pugh
The Food and Feasts of Jesus: Inside the World of First Century Fare, with Menus and Recipes by Douglas E. Neel and Joel A. Pugh
Occupy Religion: Theology of the Multitude by Joerg Rieger and Kwok Pui-lan
Not God's People: Insiders and Outsiders in the Biblical World by Lawrence M. Wills

Liberating People, Planet, and Religion

Intersections of Ecology, Economics, and Christianity

Edited by Joerg Rieger and
Terra Schwerin Rowe

ROWMAN & LITTLEFIELD
Lanham • Boulder • New York • London

Published by Rowman & Littlefield
An imprint of The Rowman & Littlefield Publishing Group, Inc.
4501 Forbes Boulevard, Suite 200, Lanham, Maryland 20706
www.rowman.com

86-90 Paul Street, London EC2A 4NE

Copyright © 2024 by The Rowman & Littlefield Publishing Group, Inc.

All rights reserved. No part of this book may be reproduced in any form or by any electronic or mechanical means, including information storage and retrieval systems, without written permission from the publisher, except by a reviewer who may quote passages in a review.

British Library Cataloguing in Publication Information Available

Library of Congress Cataloging-in-Publication Data

Names: Rieger, Joerg, editor. | Rowe, Terra Schwerin, editor.
Title: Liberating people, planet, and religion : intersections of ecology, economics, and Christianity / edited by Joerg Rieger and Terra Schwerin Rowe.
Description: Lanham : Rowman & Littlefield Publishers, [2024] | Series: Religion in the modern world | Includes bibliographical references and index.
Identifiers: LCCN 2024002696 (print) | LCCN 2024002697 (ebook) | ISBN 9781538194027 (cloth) | ISBN 9781538194034 (paperback) | ISBN 9781538194041 (ebook)
Subjects: LCSH: Climatic changes—Religious aspects—Christianity. | Ecology—Religious aspects—Christianity. | Environmental justice
Classification: LCC BT695.5 .L527 2024 (print) | LCC BT695.5 (ebook) | DDC 261.8/8—dc23/eng/20240312
LC record available at https://lccn.loc.gov/2024002696
LC ebook record available at https://lccn.loc.gov/2024002697

Contents

Acknowledgments   vii

Introduction   1
Joerg Rieger and Terra Schwerin Rowe

PART I: GLOBAL HISTORICAL AND CONTEXTUAL APPROACHES   15

Chapter 1: "Energizing Human Development"? Humanity, Divinity, and Climate Change   17
Terra Schwerin Rowe

Chapter 2: Liberation Theologies and Grassroots Education in Latin America and the Caribbean: The Complex Path to Restore Human and More-than-Human Worlds   43
Nathalia Hernández Vidal

Chapter 3: *Moana* Eco-Theology: Toward an Eco-Theology of Commoning   65
George Zachariah

PART II: ALTERNATIVE FRAMEWORKS   83

Chapter 4: The Peculiar Agency of People and the Planet: On the Need to Rethink Everything, Including Religion   85
Joerg Rieger

Chapter 5: Capitalism's Incompatibility with Christianity: The Churches' Deep Solidarity with Labor   109
Jeremy Posadas

Chapter 6: Christian Animist Economics: The Intimate
   Re-enchantment of Creation for a Regenerative Eco-Socialism 137
   Timothy Reinhold Eberhart

Chapter 7: Planetary Economies 155
   Whitney Bauman

PART III: PRACTICAL ENGAGEMENTS 173

Chapter 8: Resistance as Healing: Disrupting the Spiritual
   Foundations of Capitalism 175
   Gabriella Lettini

Chapter 9: Corporate Confession: The Presbyterian Church (USA)
   and Fossil Fuels 193
   abby mohaupt

Chapter 10: Engaging the Climate Crisis through Spiritual
   Nonviolence 211
   Daniel Joranko

Chapter 11: Distorted Imagination: Land, Food, and Economies 235
   Tim Van Meter

Index 255

Contributor Biographies 261

Acknowledgments

This volume had its roots in another world—or so it sometimes seems. Joerg envisioned and planned a conference on Christianity, ecology, and economics for the Wendland-Cook Program at Vanderbilt Divinity School that should have met shortly after the spring break in 2020 that turned into pandemic shutdowns. When we couldn't meet in person, Joerg and Aaron Stauffer shifted gears to offer a series of webinars on the topics related to those we had planned to discuss in person (https://www.religionandjustice.org/liberating). The editors would like to express our thanks to Aaron Stauffer, Jeremy Posadas, and Francisco Garcia who helped with planning the original meeting and then organizing and hosting the webinars.

While much has changed since early 2020, too much of the established world remains the same. The problems we had sought to meet and discuss—climate change; social-environmental-economic injustice; ongoing colonial oppressions; and religious inaction, quietism, or contribution to these problems—have only intensified since then. The editors would like to express our profound gratitude to the participants in this discussion and contributors to this volume, including Elaine Nogueira-Godsey, Annika Rieger, Rosetta Ross, and Upulo Luma Vaai. We would especially like to thank our editor, Richard Brown, whose initial support of this project has been tested by pandemic-related delays and who has tenaciously advocated for and supported the project. We would also like to thank our blind reviewers who offered helpful insights, suggestions, and support for the vision. Finally, we would like to express our gratitude for all those whose labor has directly or indirectly supported the project: our families and childcare workers, Francisco Garcia for preparing our index, Geran Lorraine for editing and formatting assistance, supportive administrators and colleagues at our institutions, farm workers, and others who have provided sustenance and care work.

We dedicate this project to human and other-than-human laborers struggling and organizing for a better world.

Introduction

Joerg Rieger and Terra Schwerin Rowe

Life on the planet is in peril, with innumerable humans and other-than-humans at stake. Climate change is currently affecting humans in unequal measure, and, despite pervasive experiences of worsening climate catastrophes around the planet, many can hardly fathom the devastating consequences of a rise in temperature of two degrees Celsius or more for multispecies flourishing. While the lives of multitudes are increasingly rendered precarious, climate change will not spare the few who have resources to protect themselves. In this context, religion will have to decide whether it will continue to be a justification for the status quo and a source of tranquility for the few or a mode of agitation and solidarity for the many. Christianity, in particular, is implicated as its adherents have often neglected other-than-human nature if not the material world as a whole. Yet, predominant economic systems are not off the hook, as they are pervasively marked by exploitation and extraction. As authors, we emphasize the need for both fresh analyses and creative alternatives at the nexus of religion, economics, and ecology.[1] We offer these contributions as a way of supporting movements that are already bearing fruit and contributing to their momentum.

ECOLOGY, ECONOMICS, AND RELIGION

It remains common to think of economy and ecology as being at odds with one another: Do we save the environment or create new jobs? Do we care more about polar bears or exploited people? Yet, separating each of these realms of planetary life into separate spheres creates false dichotomies, abstracts life in consequential ways, and reinforces political and ideological polarization. In this volume, we aim to think them together and thus make a contribution to emerging alternatives. We take this up as a strategy to highlight common problems—beginning with the often-ignored fact that both people and more-than-humans are often exploited by the same forces. We also believe that thinking them together opens possibilities for new cooperatives and collaborations, new ways of organizing, new ways of feeling and being in the world. This, we argue, is where the value and importance of religious communities can come to the fore and where scholarship addressing religious, ecological, and economic perspectives can be broadened. At their best, religions have helped people organize themselves to meet challenges—embodying, imagining, and feeling a way into new realities and developing new agencies that would otherwise be dismissed as impossible but still altogether rooted in this material life.

RESISTING ECOLOGICAL AND ECONOMIC OPPRESSION

The most original ecological, economic, religious thought has not sprung forth from brilliant minds in ivory towers but has been squeezed out of the pressure cookers of urban neighborhoods, desperate farming communities, and the exploitation of increasingly diverse working majorities where a way had to be made out of no way. Complex theories, rigorous scholarship, new terms or concepts all become important to constructing new ways of living and relating. However, often economic or ecological thought has not started here but in the experiences of exploitation, colonization, impoverishment, environmental racism, and toxic exposure. Economic exploitation and ecological devastation meet in the bodies of the working majority, specifically in "sacrifice zones" where experiences are marked by systemic marginalization and colonization. This is where thinking/living/feeling ecology, economy, and even religion otherwise become a necessity of life; it is from here that we seek to situate scholarly ecological and economic religious reflection.

Since colonization in the broadest sense refers to land-based processes of control for the economic benefit of a group of people often far removed from the environmental effects of resource extraction, there have likely been environmental and ecological justice thinkers as long as there has been colonization. From this perspective, as George Zachariah emphasizes in this volume, we cannot merely link people and land—or people and planet for that matter—romantically. The nexus of people and planet must first be seen in the context of colonization and its various iterations in globalization, which are marked by the exploitation and extraction of what people and planet produce. More specifically, extracting profit from labor and land requires controlling the means of production, whether in the form of direct ownership or in the form of the ownership of shares and stocks (the majority of which are held by the few rather than the many). For centuries, extractive and colonizing capitalists have understood these dynamics well: to control profit, you need to control resources; to control resources, you need to control land; and control of land and the people who inhabit it—through exploitation, enslavement, or elimination—go hand in hand. This is also not a newfound insight for resistance movements. For example, in the context of extraction in colonial Peru, centuries ago Felipe Guaman Poma de Ayala linked the exploitation and elimination of his fellow Andeans with a Christianized redefinition of relation to land and extractive practices.[2] Similarly, North American abolitionists like Black radical David Walker were already explicitly linking extractivist exploitation of the land with the extraction of labor from human bodies in slavery. In his excoriating analysis of the systems of US enslavement, Walker does not fail to also rail against the hypocrisy of this self-proclaimed "Christian nation."[3]

Liberation movements engaging with various forms of exploitation and liberation theologies, too, have by necessity engaged the nexus of economic and ecological justice because of the interlinkage of exploitation of land and people. This is true in Latin America as well as in many other places around the world during the past four or five decades.[4] As Nathalia Hernández Vidal emphasizes in her chapter on Latin American liberation theologies, the relationship between ecological and economic struggles and Christianity—even in liberation movements—has surfaced ever ambiguously.

The control of land and people for economic exploitation also became the focus of the North American environmental justice movement. Since early advocates of environmental justice have focused more on areas of toxic exposure and the racialization of urban space rather than on conserving "wild" or "untouched" spaces in national parks, this movement has consistently focused on the interlinkages of economic exploitation, labor exploitation, and land exploitation.[5] By contrast, most mainstream US conservation or eco-theology movements have, until relatively recently, failed to adequately account for the exploitation of economic systems—or, for that matter, racialization—in their environmentalisms.[6] The ongoing patterns of racialized colonialism and capitalism become foregrounded in the environmental justice movement, which coined the term "environmental racism." In this volume, we seek to build on and further expand analysis of the parallels between human and environmental exploitation, offering both critical and constructive reflections.

The environmental justice movement has, from early on, maintained key religious influences as well. The term environmental racism traces back to 1982 when the US state of North Carolina chose to place a landfill that would collect soil contaminated with illegally dumped PCBs in an impoverished, predominantly Black community in Warren County. A group of mothers from the neighborhood organized to block the construction of the site by laying their bodies on their road in front of the proposed site. Residents of Warren County also reached out to United Church of Christ pastor Dr. Ben Chavis, then executive director of the United Church of Christ (UCC) Commission for Racial Justice (CRJ), to help organize their campaign of civil disobedience.[7]

As the actions of citizens of North Carolina gained public attention, it became widely recognized that Warren County was not alone. Across the United States, the UCC CRJ heard from communities inhabited predominantly by minoritized populations and the working poor that they were suffering from health effects as a result of living in close proximity to toxic sites. In response, the CRJ published the first study on the correlation between race and toxic waste sites in 1987, concluding that members of minority races in the United States were more likely to live in close proximity to environmental toxins. This study, produced by a religious body, referred to the intentional selection of communities of color for sites of waste disposal as "environmental racism," and it is often credited with initiating the North American environmental justice movement.[8]

ECOLOGY AND ECONOMY AMONG RELIGION SCHOLARS

While embodied alternative ecological and economic relations have materialized in the urgency of resistance movements on the ground, some religion scholars have also recognized the imperative of thinking of alternative ecological and economic relations. In 1994, theologian John B. Cobb Jr. and economist Herman Daly published *For the Common Good: Redirecting the Economy toward Community, the Environment, and a Sustainable Future*.[9] While Cobb had sparked early theo-ethical interest in environmental issues with his pathbreaking, *Is It Too Late?*,[10] Daly challenged conventional economics when he began the field of ecological economics.[11] The interdisciplinary work of Cobb and Daly marked the first text cowritten by an economist and environmentalist from a religious perspective.

Like Cobb, feminist theologian Sallie McFague was already a leading thinker on environmentalism and Christianity when she recognized the crucial importance of engaging the ways environmental destruction was being driven by economic interests. McFague made an early and influential case for the importance of engaging economics among those who were taking up environmental concerns from a Christian perspective.[12] While McFague's critique of consumption and Cobb and Daly's emphasis on an economy with limited growth are significant, they fail to address deeper questions of capitalist exploitation of people and planet and the role of economic production as a site of resistance and struggle[13]—both of which will be addressed in this volume.

Cobb, Daly, and McFague have also not explicitly addressed the ways that racism infuses and directs structural economic-ecological violence. This is a key contribution of Christian ethicist Cynthia Moe-Lobeda. Her 2013 text *Resisting Structural Evil: Love as Ecological-Economic Vocation* emphasizes this key missing locus of analysis.[14] What her work highlights are the ways that common Christian moral practices like "mission work," hunger ministries, and many gestures toward sustainability merely reinforce rather than challenge existing structural injustices like racism, poverty, and environmental destruction. All these insights call for further examinations of the relations of race, class, and ecology, including the role of religion.[15]

More recently and with a significantly more global audience, Pope Francis became the first Roman Catholic pope to address economic environmental issues in a papal encyclical, the highest form of papal authority. Pope Francis's *Laudato Si'* is written to explicitly address the social and ecological injustices of climate change. In the encyclical, he highlights the importance of thinking in terms of an "integral ecology": of recognizing interconnections of environmental and social injustice and pressing the importance of framing economics within ecological realities.[16] At the same time, the so-called "Economy of Francesco" is a mix of proposals that would benefit from the more particular alternatives to exploitative and extractive capitalism that many of the authors in this book are developing.[17]

Continuing and extending the interdisciplinary focus of Cobb and Daly, the Drew University Transdisciplinary Theological Colloquium (TTC) has brought sustained scholarly energy and discourse to the ecological-economic nexus of the commons. The 2012 conference and edited publication, *Common Goods*, considers the crucial importance of the imagination of the political—along with religious difference in this sphere—if efforts to transition from extractivist economies are going to be mobilized. Crucially, the voices at the 2015 conference, and the corresponding edited volume, *Assembling Futures*, emphasized that, given continued growth of religious adherence worldwide rather than its continual decline, it will be critical to rethink common views of the political and secular. Rather than marking religiously vacuous space, these contributors emphasize the importance of imagining a political sphere that teems with religious difference—a space where solidarity can be employed to work toward goods that are common to multiple religious and nonreligious populations. Yet political engagement is not necessarily engagement in the economy and its dynamics, and so the most recent TTC conference and edited volume move one step further by drawing attention to the importance of sustained reflection on religion, economy, and ecology in the assemblages of liberating democratic spaces.[18] The present volume further expands this conversation.

Together, the contributions of these religion scholars to the study of ecology and the economy—as well as the voices and perspectives they do not yet address—suggest that the time has come for more sustained engagement of ecology, economics, and religion.

DISTINCTIVE PERSPECTIVES AND APPROACHES OF THIS VOLUME

The contributors to this volume are standing on the shoulders of many who have come before, marking embodied spaces of ecological or economic injustice and imagining alternative modes of relation and investigating problems and promise. We have been in conversation with these actors and thinkers and many more, sometimes building on and continuing their work, sometimes differing from their views and distinguishing a variant approach. For example, as Rieger has emphasized, most twentieth-century religious engagements with ecology and economy in the United States have aimed to resist reductive materialism but, in so doing, have often shied away from fully accounting for the ways economic systems can and have influenced religious ideals, values, practices, and symbols.[19] Resonating with Rieger and others like Ulrich Duchrow, Franz Hinkelammert, Jung Mo Sung, Devin Singh, Karen Bray, and Terra Schwerin Rowe, in this volume we develop the importance of analyzing not just how religion influenced economic systems in the past and how it continues to do so in the present but also how systems of practice, belief, ritual, institution, and power resonate all the way down.[20] We are interested in accounting for the ways in which dominant economic practices have influenced religious trends and how religious faith has infused and informed extractive practices—sometimes supporting them by granting them transcendent or even apocalyptic meaning.

We are interested in accounting for the ways capitalism can take on a religious character and how religious and economic values resonate on symbolic, rational, and unconscious affective levels. In short, as Keri Day emphasizes in her study of womanist resistance to neoliberalism, we too are interested in the way "religious ideas and practices both fuel neoliberal logics and subvert these logics," often with possibilities for alternatives emerging first within marginalized communities where ecological, economic, religious engagement becomes a necessary way of life.[21] In other words, if religion and material relationships are linked, then economic, ecological, and religion alternatives will not fall from the sky but will have to be developed in conjunction.

This shift in focus is crucial, we argue. Clearly, it requires a more complete accounting of the ways dominant religion has developed in relation to extractivist and exploitative activities and how it has supported them.[22] But, by analyzing the nexus of religion and economic practice, we can also see how these points of connection have been producing new expressions of religion toward both unjust and more just materializations. As Rieger has emphasized, for example, accounting for the ways economic systems have influenced religion can also highlight how "subaltern structures such as worker cooperatives and forms of organized labor might contribute to religious alternatives."[23] Similarly, as mohaupt, Eberhart, Bauman, and Van Meter emphasize in this volume, the intersection of environmental and economic concerns has also produced new forms of Christian liturgical practice, communal living, and theology.

This shift to focusing on the kinds of religion produced in interaction with ecology and economy also signals a second differentiating feature of the voices gathered in this volume. The majority of ecological-economic theologies have focused critical attention on and taken as their locus the agency of consumer behaviors.[24] This reflects a shared approach among many economic and ecological theologians of diagnosing modern problems as modes of disenchantment. Various theorists from ecological, economic, and religious as well as sacred perspectives view modern social and environmental crises as an extension of a modern loss of meaning or the sacred, leading to a compulsion to fill that void with consumptive behaviors. While there are elements of truth to this diagnosis, an exclusive focus on consumption tends to focus the locus of agency and transformative activity on the individual rather than on systems. Furthermore, the pervasive narrative of disenchantment obscures the ways that many industries, resources, technologies, and extraction practices continued to be enchanted—and pushed for enchantment—well into modernity.[25] Identifying consumption as driven by a compulsive need to fill the void left by an absence of meaning misses the ways that many consumer behaviors have not been driven by an innate human need but by the systemic imperative of production in capitalist economies.

Take, for example, the case of the dramatic increases in fossil fuel consumption in the twentieth century. Petroculture scholars have emphasized that, with oil, unlike gold or coal, the main problem was not how to find it but how to contain it once it was struck. Once tapped, oil could geyser for days—and, even once controlled, many oilmen struggled to find sufficient space to hold it. Especially in the early days when oil was used primarily as an illuminant and lubricant, the supply of oil often exceeded existing market demand. When faced with this issue, founder of BIOLA University, Presbyterian Lyman Stewart, would not be satisfied with existing markets and set out to create new markets, new demand for oil. In particular, he funded the design of new petroleum-burning locomotives and asphalt.[26] In terms of petro patterns of consumption, as with many other consumer behaviors, overconsumption has not necessarily been driven by a gradual increase in consumer demand or a human drive to fill a void of modern meaning; rather, it has been driven by surplus production, leading to the creation of new markets, consumer desires, and high-consuming ways of life.

As a result, production needs to be understood as one of the drivers of capitalist exploitation and extraction as well as of religious ratification. At the same time, this means that production can be approached as the battleground where resistance emerges and alternatives develop. As Posadas, Rieger, and Rowe explicitly emphasize in their chapters, when production becomes the focus of ecological-economic religious engagement, rather than consumption or distribution—new imaginaries of agency transpire that can lead to solidarity and symbiotic partnerships between religious communities and labor, agricultural, and divestment movements. In the process, economics, ecology, and religion are transformed together. The chapters of this volume give accounts of what is already happening, with an eye toward sparking new symbiotic struggles and coalitions for the future.

OVERVIEW OF CHAPTERS

The following chapters will unfold around three organizing themes. The first section includes chapters that take a historical and contextual approach. Narrowing in on the economic-ecological intersection of energy, Terra Schwerin Rowe analyzes the history of energy developmentalisms in Greco-Roman philosophical and Christian traditions, which have contributed to an exuberant energy culture driving ecological, economic, and social catastrophe. Nathalia Hernández Vidal contextualizes her engagement with Latin American liberation theologies, analyzing their historical and ongoing materializations in Columbian peasant farming movements as they resist the globalized industrial farming complex. George Zachariah takes up the ecological and economic theme of the commons, placing the enclosure of the commons within the scope of religious colonial histories in the Pacific.

The chapters in part 1 all point to or give indications of a theme taken up in earnest by contributors to part 2: Alternative Frameworks. These authors seek to disrupt and rewrite common narratives or analyses of Christianity, ecology, and the economy. Rieger, for example, identifies the possibility of consolidating agencies for change among populations whose agencies are often overlooked: exploited humans—the majority of humanity—and the mass of other-than-human creatures. In so doing, he identifies these agents as the locus of production and reproduction, which become the locus of necessary reforms of relationships and systems. Posadas flips the common script of alliances between Protestantism and capitalism to demonstrate a basic incongruence between Christianity and capitalism—a proposal that highlights the importance of building alliances between churches and labor movements. Timothy Reinhold Eberhart disrupts common oppositions between Christianity and animisms, identifying an emerging "Christian animism" and arguing that it provides crucial perspectival and affective shifts necessary for an alliance between Christianity and various eco-socialist projects. Anchoring this section, Bauman articulates a queer "home economics" that makes a multiplicitous and interconnected planetary the context for all human working, thinking, playing, desiring, relating, and meaning making.

Authors contributing to our final section, part 3, frame their chapters in terms of the practical engagements of particular groups at the nexus of Christianity, ecology, and economy. Gabriella Lettini begins with the realities of so-called essential workers during the COVID-19 pandemic and draws conclusions for new relationships along the lines of race, class, gender, and the environment. abby mohaupt outlines current church-body divestment movements in the context of an entangled history of oil and Christianity in the United States. In this context, mauhaupt proposes the importance of the Christian liturgical practice of corporate confession as a mode of action accompanying fossil fuel divestment. Daniel Joranko draws on his rich experience of organizing communities and nonviolent resistance movements in the context of dealing with climate change. Finally, Tim Van Meter describes the community-transforming process of creating a working sustainable farm and local food movement on the grounds of a mainline seminary campus.

A commonality among all of these chapters is the sense that alternatives are emerging in many—if often unheralded—places. As a result, the work of theology and religious study is not conjuring up ideas and theories that would subsequently be put into practice. Our work is investigating what is going on in response to the challenges people and planet are facing and reinforcing the most promising alternatives in light of the creative openings they provide for the flourishing of life everywhere, "on earth as it is in heaven." In the process, both praxis and scholarship are transformed.

NOTES

1. *Ecology* can refer to the diverse insights supplied by the ecological sciences specifically or, more broadly, to environmental practices that take into account human and more-than-human relations and systems. We are using the term *ecology* here in the broader sense to refer to interdependent relations among human and more-than-human beings and systems.

2. Felipe Guaman Poma de Ayala, *The First New Chronicle and Good Government*, trans. David Frye (Indianapolis: Hackett, 2006). See also Willie James Jennings, "Binding Landscapes: Secularism, Race, and the Spatial Modern," in *Race and Secularism in America*, ed. Jonathon S. Kahn and Vincent W. Lloyd (New York: Columbia University Press, 2016), 205–38.

3. David Walker, *Appeal to the Colored Citizens of the World* (Boston: 1829). See J. Insko, "Extraction," in *The Cambridge Companion to Environmental Humanities*, ed. J. Cohen and S. Foote (Cambridge, UK: Cambridge University Press, 2021), 170–84 for further reflection on Walker's remarkably early analysis of human enslavement and resource extraction.

4. From Latin America writers, see Leonardo Boff, *Cry of the Earth, Cry of the Poor* (Maryknoll, NY: Orbis, 1997); Ivone Gebara, *Longing for Running Water: Ecofeminism and Liberation* (Minneapolis: Fortress Press, 1999); and Marcella Althaus-Reid, *Indecent Theology* (New York: Routledge, 2000). From North American writers, see Rosemary Radford Ruether, *Gaia and God: An Ecofeminist Theology of Earth Healing* (San Francisco: HarperSanFrancisco, 1992); and Frederick Herzog, *Theology from the Belly of the Whale: A Frederick Herzog Reader*, ed. Joerg Rieger (Harrisburg, PA: Trinity Press International, 1999). From German writers, see Ulrich Duchrow and Gerhard Liedke, *Biblical Perspectives on Creation, Justice, and Peace* (Geneva: WCC Publications, 1989). From a group of international scholars comes *Decolonizing Ecotheology: Indigenous and Subaltern Challenges*, eds. S. Lily Mendoza and George Zachariah (Eugene, OR: Pickwick, 2022).

5. Robert Bullard and Benjamin Chavis Jr., *Confronting Environmental Racism: Voices from the Grassroots* (Boston: Southend Press, 1999); Robert Bullard, *Dumping in Dixie: Race, Class, and Environmental Quality* (New York: Routledge, 2000); Dorceta Taylor, *Toxic Communities: Environmental Racism, Industrial Pollution, and Residential Mobility* (New York, NYU Press, 2014).

6. Carolyn Finney, *Black Faces, White Spaces: Reimagining the Relationship of African Americans to the Great Outdoors* (Chapel Hill: University of North Carolina Press, 2014); Dorceta Taylor, *The Rise of the American Conservation Movement: Power, Privilege and Environmental Protection* (Durham, NC: Duke University Press, 2016).

7. United Church of Christ, "Environmental Racism," accessed September 29, 2022, https://www.ucc.org/what-we-do/justice-local-church-ministries/justice/washington-dc-office/washington-dc/environmental-ministries_environmental-racism/.

8. Commission for Racial Justice, "Toxic Wastes and Race in the United States: A National Report on the Racial and Socio-Economic Characteristics of Communities with Hazardous Waste Sites" (New York: United Church of Christ, 1987), https://www.nrc.gov/docs/ML1310/ML13109A339.pdf. This context is also where the work of Frederick Herzog got further inspiration for engaging the intersectionalities of race, class, and ecology.

9. Herman E. Daly, John B. Cobb, and Clifford W. Cobb, *For the Common Good: Redirecting the Economy toward Community, the Environment, and a Sustainable Future* (Boston: Beacon Press, 1994).

10. John B. Cobb, *Is It Too Late? A Theology of Ecology*, rev. ed. (Denton, TX: Environmental Ethics Books, 1995).

11. Herman E. Daly, *Beyond Growth: The Economics of Sustainable Development* (Boston: Beacon Press, 1996); Robert Costanza, John Cumberland, Herman Daly, Robert Goodland, and Richard B. Norgaard, *An Introduction to Ecological Economics* (Boca Raton, FL: St. Lucie Press, 1997).

12. Sallie McFague, *Life Abundant: Rethinking Theology and Economy for a Planet in Peril* (Minneapolis: Fortress Press, 2000); Sallie McFague, "New House Rules: Christianity, Economics, and Planetary Living," *Dædalus* 130, no 4 (Fall 2001): 125–40; Sallie McFague, *A New Climate for Theology: God, the World, and Global Warming* (Minneapolis: Fortress Press, 2008); Sallie McFague, *Blessed Are the Consumers* (Minneapolis: Fortress Press, 2013).

13. Is consumption primarily an ethical issue for consumers or is it linked to the capitalist imperative to increase production, on which the need to entice production rests? See Joerg Rieger, *Theology in the Capitalocene: Ecology, Identity, Class, and Solidarity* (Minneapolis: Fortress Press, 2022), chapter 1.

14. Cynthia D. Moe-Lobeda, *Resisting Structural Evil: Love as Ecological-Economic Vocation* (Minneapolis: Fortress Press, 2013).

15. A thorough examination of these relations goes beyond what can be done in this volume. For the relation of ecology, race, and gender, see Melanie Harris, *Ecowomanism: African-American Women and Earth-Honoring Faiths* (Maryknoll, NY: Orbis, 2017). For the relation of ecology, race, and class, with some reference to gender, see Rieger, *Theology in the Capitalocene*, chapter 4.

16. Pope Francis, *Laudato Si'*: Encyclical Letter of the Holy Father Francis on Care for Our Common Home," retrieved June 18, 2015, https://www.vatican.va/content/francesco/en/encyclicals/documents/papa-francesco_20150524_enciclica-laudato-si.html.

17. See "The Economy of Francesco," accessed September 29, 2022, https://francescoeconomy.org.

18. Melanie Johnson-DeBaufre, Catherine Keller, and Elias Ortega-Aponte, eds., *Common Goods: Economy, Ecology, and Political Theology* (New York: Fordham University Press, 2015), and the forthcoming volume, Catherine Keller and Jennifer Quigley, eds., *Assembling Futures: Economy, Ecology, Democracy* (New York: Fordham University Press, forthcoming). Rieger's work might be considered one of the connectors between these projects as he has a contribution in each.

19. Rieger, "Capitalism and Christian Theology," *Religion Compass* 14 (2020), https://doi.org/10.1111/rec3.12350.

20. Devin Singh, *Divine Currency: The Theological Power of Money in the West* (Redwood City, CA: Stanford University Press, 2018); Karen Bray, *Grave Attending: A Political Theology for the Unredeemed* (New York: Fordham University Press, 2019); Terra Schwerin Rowe, *Of Modern Extraction: Experiments in Critical Petro-theology* (London: T&T Clark, 2023).

21. Keri Day, *Religious Resistance to Neoliberalism: Womanist and Black Feminist Perspectives* (New York: Palgrave Macmillan, 2015). Also see Bray, *Grave Attending*, for an analysis of modes of redemption within neoliberalism.

22. See, for instance, Rowe's account of the Protestant Reformation of the sixteenth century in this light, "Capital," *Of Modern Extraction*.

23. Rieger, "Capitalism and Christianity," 4, and his chapter in this volume.

24. See, for example, McFague, *Blessed Are the Consumers*; William Cavanaugh, *Being Consumed: Economics and Christian Desire* (Grand Rapids, MI: Eerdmans, 2008); and Pope Francis, *Laudato Si'*.

25. Cf. Rowe, "Introduction," *Of Modern Extraction*.

26. B. M. Pietsch, "Lyman Stewart and Early Fundamentalism," *Church History* 82, no. 3 (Sept 2013): 617–46.

REFERENCES

Althaus-Reid, Marcella. *Indecent Theology*. New York: Routledge, 2000.

Boff, Leonardo. *Cry of the Earth, Cry of the Poor*. Maryknoll, NY: Orbis, 1997.

Bray, Karen. *Grave Attending: A Political Theology for the Unredeemed*. New York: Fordham University Press, 2019.

Bullard, Robert. *Dumping in Dixie: Race, Class, and Environmental Quality*. New York: Routledge, 2000.

Bullard, Robert and Benjamin Chavis Jr., *Confronting Environmental Racism: Voices from the Grassroots*. Boston: Southend Press, 1999.

Cavanaugh, William. *Being Consumed: Economics and Christian Desire*. Grand Rapids, MI: Eerdmans, 2008.

Cobb, John B. *Is It Too Late? A Theology of Ecology*. Rev. ed. Denton, TX: Environmental Ethics Books, 1995.

Commission for Racial Justice. *Toxic Wastes and Race in the United States: A National Report on the Racial and Socio-Economic Characteristics of Communities with Hazardous Waste Sites*. New York: United Church of Christ, 1987. https://www.nrc.gov/docs/ML1310/ML13109A339.pdf.

Costanza, Robert, John Cumberland, Herman Daly, Robert Goodland, and Richard B. Norgaard. *An Introduction to Ecological Economics*. Boca Raton, FL: St. Lucie Press, 1997.

Daly, Herman E. *Beyond Growth: The Economics of Sustainable Development*. Boston: Beacon Press, 1996.

Daly, Herman, John B. Cobb, and Clifford W. Cobb. *For the Common Good: Redirecting the Economy toward Community, the Environment, and a Sustainable Future*. Boston: Beacon Press, 1994.

Day, Keri. *Religious Resistance to Neoliberalism: Womanist and Black Feminist Perspectives*. New York: Palgrave Macmillan, 2015.

de Ayala, Felipe Guaman Poma. *The First New Chronicle and Good Government*. Translated by David Frye. Indianapolis: Hackett, 2006.

Duchrow, Ulrich and Gerhard Liedke. *Biblical Perspectives on Creation, Justice, and Peace*. Geneva: WCC Publications, 1989.

"The Economy of Francesco." Accessed September 29, 2022. https://francesco-economy.org.

"Environmental Racism." Accessed September 29, 2022. https://www.ucc.org/what-we-do/justice-local-church-ministries/justice/washington-dc-office/washington-dc/environmental-ministries_environmental-racism/.

Finney, Carolyn. *Black Faces, White Spaces: Reimagining the Relationship of African Americans to the Great Outdoors.* Chapel Hill: University of North Carolina Press, 2014.

Pope Francis. "*Laudato Si'*: Encyclical Letter of the Holy Father Francis On Care for Our Common Home." Retrieved June 18, 2015. https://www.vatican.va/content/francesco/en/encyclicals/documents/papa-francesco_20150524_enciclica-laudato-si.html.

Gebara, Ivone. *Longing for Running Water: Ecofeminism and Liberation.* Minneapolis: Fortress Press, 1999.

Harris, Melanie. *Ecowomanism: African-American Women and Earth-Honoring Faiths.* Maryknoll, NY: Orbis, 2017.

Herzog, Frederick. *Theology from the Belly of the Whale*, edited by Joerg Rieger. Harrisburg, PA: Trinity Press International, 1999.

Insko, J. "Extraction." In *The Cambridge Companion to Environmental Humanities*, edited by J. Cohen and S. Foote, 170–84. Cambridge, UK: Cambridge University Press, 2021.

Jennings, Willie James. "Binding Landscapes: Secularism, Race, and the Spatial Modern." In *Race and Secularism in America*, edited by Jonathon S. Kahn and Vincent W. Lloyd, 205–38. New York: Columbia University Press, 2016.

Johnson-DeBaufre, Melanie, Catherine Keller, and Elias Ortega-Aponte, eds. *Common Goods: Economy, Ecology, and Political Theology.* New York: Fordham University Press, 2015.

Keller, Catherine and Jennifer Quigley, eds. *Assembling Futures: Economy, Ecology, Democracy.* New York: Fordham University Press, forthcoming.

McFague, Sallie. *Blessed Are the Consumers.* Minneapolis: Fortress Press, 2013.

———. *Life Abundant: Rethinking Theology and Economy for a Planet in Peril.* Minneapolis: Fortress Press, 2000.

———. *A New Climate for Theology: God, the World, and Global Warming.* Minneapolis: Fortress Press, 2008.

———. "New House Rules: Christianity, Economics, and Planetary Living" *Dædalus* 130, no 4 (Fall 2001): 125–40.

Mendoza, S. Lily and George Zachariah, eds. *Decolonizing Ecotheology: Indigenous and Subaltern Challenges.* Eugene, OR: Pickwick, 2022.

Moe-Lobeda, Cynthia D. *Resisting Structural Evil: Love as Ecological-Economic Vocation.* Minneapolis: Fortress Press, 2013.

Pietsch, B. M. "Lyman Stewart and Early Fundamentalism." *Church History* 82, no. 3 (Sept 2013): 617–46.

Radford Ruether, Rosemary. *Gaia and God: An Ecofeminist Theology of Earth Healing.* San Francisco: HarperSanFrancisco, 1992.

Rieger, Joerg. "Capitalism and Christian Theology." *Religion Compass* 14 (2020). https://doi.org/ 10.1111/rec3.12350.

———. *Theology in the Capitalocene: Ecology, Identity, Class, and Solidarity* Minneapolis: Fortress Press, 2022.

Rowe, Terra Schwerin. *Of Modern Extraction: Experiments in Critical Petro-theology.* London: T&T Clark, 2022.

Singh, Devin. *Divine Currency: The Theological Power of Money in the West.* Redwood City, CA: Stanford University Press, 2018.

Taylor, Dorceta. *The Rise of the American Conservation Movement: Power, Privilege and Environmental Protection.* Durham, NC: Duke University Press, 2016.

———. *Toxic Communities: Environmental Racism, Industrial Pollution, and Residential Mobility.* New York: NYU Press, 2014.

Walker, David. *Appeal to the Colored Citizens of the World.* Boston: 1829.

PART I

Global Historical and Contextual Approaches

Chapter 1

"Energizing Human Development"?

Humanity, Divinity, and Climate Change

Terra Schwerin Rowe

Energy is a particularly fascinating locus of ecological-economic entanglement. From photosynthesis and the decomposition of plant life to the herbivore's consumption of sun energy to carnivorous consumption of sun-come-plant-come-animal sustenance to human consumption of decomposed organic material to fuel petro-modernity, energy emerges as a currency of ecological economics. As a mode of ecological economic exchange, energy has gained particular interest for its dualism disrupting character. Is energy biological or mechanistic? Is it natural or cultural? Energy and the history of its construction seem to defy any tidy modern delineations between nature and culture, biology and machine, and economy and ecology.[1]

Even the historical construction of modern energy science has long been entangled with economic theory. Economist Philip Mirowski has written a comprehensive study on the mutual influences of modern energy science and economics, concluding that, for disciplines that hold tightly to a sense of the independence of these sciences, the "history of physics and the history of economics are so intimately connected that it might be considered scandalous."[2] Looking more particularly at the case of the emergence of modern energy science among Scottish physicists like William Thomson (later Lord Kelvin), historians Crosbie Smith and M. Norton Wise emphasize that commercial interests didn't just influence or at times "contaminate" the science (as was charged of Thomson even during his lifetime); rather, the Scottish scientist's whole project of creating a modern science of energy was from the start fully immersed in commercial, industrial, and indeed imperial pursuits.[3] Energy consistently emerges at the nexus of the economic and ecological exchanges of the world.

While recognizing the historical imbrications of economics and energy, one might wonder what any of this has to do with the current study of religion. Clearly eco and social injustices emerge at the ecological-economic nexus of energy, and an ethic informed by religious justice traditions would seek to address such conditions.[4] Yet, this approach has generally left religion in a reactionary position focused on agency at sites of consumption and responding to existing technological and economic realities as if they were a given. This is the position much of Christian energy ethics has found itself in. From the pathbreaking work in energy ethics of Dieter Hessel,[5] the National Council of Churches, and US Catholic Bishops to the more recent work on energy science, religion, and ethics, religious energy ethicists have made significant contributions, but have generally taken energy technologies and sciences as a given, focusing on ethical deliberation in their employment.[6] This leaves the primary opening for agency and ethical action with consumption—after technology and economic drivers have produced whatever they will.

Rather than merely responding to a set of existing conditions, couldn't the tools of critical theological analysis begin to address such concerns in the material-conceptual construction of such conditions in the first place? Couldn't the skills of theologians as critical analyzers of value and meaning production, the human tendency to deify and sacralize what should not be deified or sacralized, also be applied to energy policy, practice, habits, and embodied rhythms? With energy so consistently associated with divinity and transcendence, this emerges as a locus of ecological, economic, and religious imbrication in particular need of critical religious reflection.

From ancient Greek and medieval Latin to modern philosophies and sciences, energy has been uncritically aligned not only with growth and life but also with divinity, perfection, stability in the midst of change, and masculinity. Into modernity, thermodynamics informed biological, evolutionary theories of full human and civilizational development. Seemingly natural or commonsensical conclusions about the necessity of economic growth and unlimited energy supplies find themselves in the wake of these long-standing values that today lead to unsustainable energy economies, expectations, and habits. Given these historical associations and their current unsustainable materializations, I explore the possibility of decoupling this particular view of energy from ideals of human fulfillment.[7] Drawing on recent insights from ecological economists whose studies on energy call into question long-standing assumptions that human fulfillment requires high energy production and consumption, I suggest that a key contribution religious scholars, activists, and communities can make to the climate crisis is in examining and rethinking the ways soteriological human fulfillment and divinity have contributed to the production of energy-exuberant values, habits, and expectations.

ENERGY, CULTURAL DEVELOPMENT, AND MODERNITY

Modern approaches to energy technologies and resources generally approach energy as a potentiality, something laying in wait to be discovered, pulled from beneath the surface in order to be actualized or put to its true purpose. Philosopher Martin Heidegger identified this as the idea of nature treated as "standing reserve"—as material that has potential for usefulness yet to be actualized.[8] In terms of energy, this is particularly true. Hydrocarbons like coal, petroleum, and natural gas are generally brought from beneath the surface where they are put to work for human purposes. This is condensed, powerful energy "stock" that has the benefit of yielding to human desires and temporalities. As opposed to "flow" sources like wind or sun, energy stock can be turned on and off, heated and cooled, activated, and set aside for another day.

Alongside the sense of energy as potentiality, a progressive directionality has meant moderns assume that more energy is better, that more energy leads to higher levels of civilization, or even that energy excess is necessary for human cultural development. Take, for example, Lewis Mumford's influential 1934 *Technics and Civilization*, which described four stages in the role of energy and societal development. Societies develop, he argued, according to the amount of energy they are able to activate. Only in the fourth stage, "Creation," when energy is no longer just sustaining civilization but available *in excess*, can societies create great works of art, literature, knowledge production, architecture, and meaningful symbols that characterize human fulfillment. Only at the point when "the human animal" is supplied with "more energy than he needs to maintain his physical existence" can a society help actualize human potential.[9]

Similarly, anthropologist Leslie White stated in his 1943 essay, "Energy and the Evolution of Culture," his law of cultural evolution: "[C]ulture develops when the amount of energy harnessed by man per capita per year is increased; or as the efficiency of the technological means of putting this energy to work is increased; or, as both factors are simultaneously increased."[10] Here, energy has a directionality—its aim is properly actualized when a society can properly harness sufficient energy to help a culture develop.

Mumford's and White's views anticipate what became identified as the Kardashev scale. Nikolai Kardashev proposed this method of measuring levels of a civilization's technological advancement in 1964. This scale defines a civilization according to the capacity it has to access and store energy for consumption from its surrounding environment. Like Mumford and White, it assumes a causative correlation between a civilization's level of development based on the amount of energy it has access to. It measures types of intergalactic civilizations based on the planet's ability to access all energy from the planet (type 1), all energy from the planet and surrounding stars (type 2), or all of the energy available in its galaxy (type 3). While this scale has played a key role in sci-fi narratives, it is something physicists take seriously as well. Carl Sagan, for example, calculated that earth has not yet reached level 1 but is at a level 0.7 on the Kardashev scale.[11] Physicist Michio Kaku remains hopeful about earth's ability to reach the level of a type 1 civilization in about one to two hundred years. Doing so, he emphasizes, would require a 3 percent increase in energy consumption per year for the next century or two.[12]

While Sagan and Kaku make plans for ramping up energy production and consumption for the next one to two hundred years, others articulate grave concerns about such aims. Energy humanities scholars, for example, emphasize that current climate change is inherently an energy crisis,[13] while recent studies fundamentally challenge White's and Mumford's conclusions by demonstrating an upper limit to the benefits of energy consumption for human well-being.[14] These studies do emphasize that low-to-moderate access to energy is indeed vital—thus reaffirming the need to retain a focus on unequal global energy access. However, they also demonstrate that moderate-to-high energy consumption shows diminishing returns and even negative effects for human well-being. For example, Vaclav Smil emphasizes that energy consumption and "human well-being appears to be correlated only up to a point—about 100 gigajoules (GJ) per year, per capita—and even appear to be counter-productive beyond about 200—GJ." To put these numbers in perspective, he notes that US residents have "far surpassed both markers, with energy consumption at 316 GT per year, per capita in 2017."[15] Such calculations radically call into question the aims and projections supported by the Kardashev scale and other views correlating energy enhancement and civilizational advance.

Contrary to the correlations Mumford, White, and others make between levels of energy consumption and increased cultural development, Smil sets out to demonstrate in *Energy and World History* (1994) that energy has no effect on cultural production. "The amount of energy at a society's disposal," he writes, "puts clear limits on the overall scope of action." But beyond limiting this scope, Smil asserts, energy has little to no effect on culture: "[T]imeless literature, painting, sculpture, architecture, and music show no correlation with advances in energy consumption."[16] I share Smil's concerns with energy intensive society for planetary well-being. I also share his concern with associations between higher levels of energy and increases in human cultural development. But, as energy humanities scholars like Fredrick Buell and other have emphasized, to say that there is no correlation between energy and cultural production dramatically obscures the ways cultural values, beliefs, and desires have infused and informed energy practices and pursuits.[17]

As Timothy Mitchell has persuasively demonstrated in *Carbon Democracy*, energy systems come with different distributions of capital and political power—each of which has profound implications for collective life. Mitchell demonstrates that the shift from coal to fossil fuels dramatically reduced the choke points—places of worker agency—in the energy economy. While acknowledging that labor conditions in coal production were often unjust and dangerous, he also highlights how the material conditions of coal production provided different opportunities for economic and political organization as compared to petroleum. Coal production was labor intensive and required laborers to work in close proximity to one another, often beyond the surveying ear of managers. This physical proximity of laborers created space to communicate and organize, while the labor-intensive nature of coal provided consistent opportunities to literally have their hands on coal and thus put a halt to production if their demands were not met. By contrast, petroleum can be extracted by a couple workers, remote from others, and its fluidity allows it to be transported in pipelines beyond the reach of striking workers. Mitchell argues that, while coal and urban, industrial society provided the conditions for modern democracy, fossil fuels have created its limit.[18] So, while it is important to contest energy-culture developmentalism, contra Smil it will be important to do this not by asserting a rupture between energy and culture, but by paying closer attention to the kinds of sociopolitical cultural dynamics energy makes possible.

Beyond the possibilities of democracy, Smil's separation of energy from culture widely overlooks the ways that modern concepts like freedom and nature have been shaped by energy systems. By contrast, therefore, energy humanities scholars analyze energy cultures—fusions of a particular kind of energy and cultural expression.[19] They have identified, for example, the ways that petroculture has helped produce modern subjectivities and gender performances through literature, art, pop culture, and music.[20] But, in spite of this broadly insightful and revealing scholarship on energy and cultural production, critical reflection on *religion* and energy cultures has been conspicuously absent among energy humanities scholars.[21] I think this is a particularly detrimental oversight when it comes to understanding where basic assumptions about energy come from, what drives such uniformly accepted conclusions about the increase of energy correlating with higher levels of human development, and, most importantly, being able to think about energy otherwise. As we will see, modern energy concepts and values have come from a certain philosophical perspective, with particular theological weight, and have consistently correlated high energy with human fulfillment.

ANCIENT ENERGEIA, MASCULINITY, AND HUMAN FULFILLMENT[22]

The idea of energy as potentiality waiting to be actualized as well as the idea that more energy leads to more human development are rooted in a long entangled history of theo-philosophical energy concepts. Modern energy synthesized an earlier science of "dynamics" with theories of heat, resulting in thermodynamics. Both dynamics and heat carried with them long cultural histories going back at least to Aristotle. What connects them, even before a scientific synthesis, is the way human fulfillment functions for each as a primary aim. Theological views of human fulfillment in redemption then play a key role in aiding this synthesis as well as a more general slippage between high energy, masculinity, and divinity.

Energeia

In the seventeenth century, German philosopher Gottfried Wilhelm Leibniz argued for the need of a new science of "dynamics," or of "power and action." In arguing for this new science, he made explicit reference to Aristotle's ancient distinction between *energeia* and *dunamis* (*potentia* in Latin).[23] Though "energy" wouldn't be a term used to describe this science until the nineteenth century, Aristotle's energeia clearly reverberates in the earliest articulations of what would become energy science.

Philosopher David Bradshaw has traced the development of Aristotle's neologism, which initially drew on Plato's distinction between the possession of a thing and the use of a thing. Bradshaw argues that, in Aristotle's earliest use of energeia, it is a form of activity and, more specifically, an activity that is the "exercise of a capacity in contrast to its mere possession."[24] In short, Aristotle's energeia represents the fulfillment or enactment of a capacity, as opposed to a potential or possibility that it could be done or used, but does not yet signify a substance or thing that could be found, discovered, or extracted.

Since energeia takes on this sense of the fulfillment or enactment of a capability, it eventually came to indicate, for Aristotle, a complete reality and was mapped onto the distinction between actuality and potentiality. Something that is possessed so that it *could* be used or exercised is a potentiality where that which is in use or being exercised is an actuality. In this sense, energeia also became synonymous for Aristotle with *entelecheia*, which indicates that which is complete or fully actualized.[25] Here, life and reality became associated with action and the fulfillment or actualization of potential.

As actualization, energeia also mapped onto Aristotle's definition of humanity. The philosopher concluded that thinking or reasoning is not just the exercise of any old capacity but the proper work of the soul. Where thinking registers as an actualization of the soul, the extent to which humans exercise this capacity registers their level of being: "Now if living is, alike for every animal, its true being, it is clear that the one who will be in the highest degree and the most proper sense is the thinker, and most of all when he is in action and contemplating the most knowable of all things."[26] For Aristotle, the use of the ability for reason is not only what distinguishes the human from other animals but also what is most fully realized in the male—and the male thinker above all else. In short, for Aristotle, when the male is exercising his capacity (energeia) for thought, he is the complete, fully actualized human. Therefore, energeia—even from ancient times—carries implications of full actualization or fulfillment of human potential most fully realized in male rational human form.

Energeia also accumulated ancient theological significance. Early Christian theologians embraced Aristotle's energeia, maintaining the original sense of an exercise of a capacity that results in a fulfillment or actualization, while adding distinctive emphases as well. St. Paul, in particular, drew on Aristotelian associations of energeia with full development of humanity and, in doing so, broadly influenced early Christian thinkers.

In an extensive survey of Aristotle's and early Christians' employment of energeia, philosopher David Bradshaw notes that St. Paul, in particular, applied Aristotle's energeia in a distinctive way. While Aristotle and later Hellenistic thinkers applied the term broadly, Paul restricted its use to the action of spiritual agents: God, Satan, Christ, angels, and demons. Bradshaw emphasizes the uniqueness of Paul's usage, noting that "there was no similar restriction [in the application of energeia to spiritual agents] in non-Biblical Greek or the Septuagint."[27] In short, Paul applied energeia in a way that David Bradshaw calls "unprecedented."[28] Bradshaw furthermore suggests that "Paul's restriction of *energeia* and *energein* to supernatural action was so striking that it apparently established a precedent for subsequent Christian literature."[29] Of the occurrences of the term in the writings of Apostolic Fathers—from the Shepherd of Hermas to the Epistle of Barnabas, First Clement, and Justin Martyr—all retained Paul's usage of the term restricted to spiritual agents.[30]

Despite this divergence from Aristotelian usage, Paul retained the association with human fulfillment, using the term to build on a key theology expressed in the Hebrew Bible. The sense of the human becoming fully human by embracing the divine is a belief expressed in the Hebrew Bible.[31] Paul took this belief and, in an entirely new way, applied the language of energeia to express this sense of human fulfillment through the embrace of the divine. Here the "*energeia* of a supernatural agent, when it is present in a human being, is most readily understood as a power or capacity for certain kinds of action."[32] For Paul, energeia took on a sense of "a capacity for action or accomplishment"[33] that was associated not only with divine action but also with divine presence. Again, Paul's usage of the term became widely influential for early Christians. Bradshaw notes, for example, that in the "Apostolic Constitutions, the author, speaking as one of the Apostles, states that on Pentecost 'the Lord Jesus sent us the gift of the Holy Spirit, and we were filled with His energy and spoke with new tongues'" (*Apostolic Constitutions* V.20.49). Clearly here, as Bradshaw emphasizes, energeia was not just the activity or the exercise of a capability, but now a corresponding sense of that capacity associated with the divine presence of the Judeo-Christian God. Therefore, while Paul did not seem to retain Aristotle's sense of masculinity as the full expression or development of humanity, this was primarily because, for Paul, energeia was not the work of males or humanity at all. Rather, for Paul, energeia became the exclusive work of divinity and, by associating it with divine presence, energeia becomes substantial, a kind of power or ability one can have or not have.

Heat

In contrast to the widely recognized influence of energeia, the lasting impact of Aristotle's understanding of heat on developmental biology and the ways this merged in the nineteenth century with modern thermodynamics is less widely understood even among energy humanities scholars. While the study of energy as a phenomenon including heat did not emerge until the nineteenth-century science of thermodynamics, Aristotle's theory of heat and the role it played in the full development of substances, including basic human physiology, retains a close connection to energeia, and these theories remained influential far into modernity.

Aristotle gave to vital heat not just the power of warming, but of in-forming, of giving form through concoction. For Aristotle, concoction is the process of heating a moist substance, making it more dense, compact, and dry, thereby transforming indeterminate, "passive," "feminine" matter into its "mastered" form.[34] Aristotle gives the example of the coagulation of milk by rennet.[35] In the same way, concoction works on a formless, fluid substance, "setting" it into its form. Here, Aristotle linked heat, masculinity, in-forming, mastery, and perfection. Semen, for example, has the capacity for mastery and formation, as evidenced in Aristotle's embryology: "'If [the male semen] gains the mastery, it brings [the material] over to itself; but if it gets mastered, it changes over either into its opposite [i.e., female] or else into extinction'" (*GA* VI. 1, 766b16 f).[36] Semen's capacity for mastery is due to its vital heat—its ability to concoct, and thus to give form.

With varying levels of vital heat come varying levels of concoction, formation, and thus perfection. For example, Aristotle theorized that semen was merely fully developed menstrual fluid on account of its higher heat.[37] Heat or lack thereof imbues bodies with active or passive characteristics that function in the development of an embryo, creating differentiation between sexes. Again, in the *Generation of Animals*, Aristotle concluded, "It will perhaps be now clearer for what reason one embryo becomes female and another male. For when the first principle does not bear sway and cannot concoct the nourishment through lack of heat nor bring it into its proper form, but is defeated in this respect, then must the material change into its opposite. Now the female is opposite to the male, and that insofar as the one is female and the other male." (*GA* IV, 1, 766a16–22). Greater amounts of vital heat lead to the actualization of the potential of matter in the form of the male. The female's lesser actualization is a direct result of inadequate heat.

From the formation of semen to the development of a male embryo, to the formation of organs, the impact of differing levels of vital heat continues throughout biological development in Aristotle's thought. In the end, for Aristotle, a feminine tendency toward passion, emotionality, and less rationality are due to a less developed rational soul in accordance with lower levels of vital heat.[38] In other words, for Aristotle, sexual difference is not primarily or fundamentally defined by biological organs. Rather, the distinguishing difference between the sexes depends on heat variance that then determines biological sex difference. In this sense, full human actualization requires high production and consumption of heat and only the male exercising his capacity (energeia) for rationality is a fully developed human.

Even as Aristotle's ancient methodology lost favor in modernity, rather than losing ancient associations between sex, heat, and energeia, these concepts only become further imbricated. The ancient Greek philosopher-physician Galen of Pergamon (130–210 CE) remained a leading medical authority in the West for the next fourteen hundred years and accepted Aristotle's conclusion that the female is less developed than the male on account of lower levels of heat.[39] In modern biological sciences, associations between energy, heat, and full development of humanity remained. Leading figures of biological sciences into the nineteenth century variously reiterated a gender distinction according to levels of heat.[40]

In the nineteenth century, thermodynamic and evolutionary theories often converged, resulting in a reframing of the ancient gender distinction based on heat—now explicitly articulated in terms of modern energy. Here, theorists concluded that reproduction results in an excessive draw on energy, thus stunting the full intellectual development of females. Darwinist Herbert Spencer (1830–1903), for example, applied the second law of thermodynamics to the human body. Spencer theorized that, with the body as a closed system of finite energy, an expenditure of energy for one function would necessitate a loss of energy for another. Spencer identified the reproductive organs and the brain as the most powerful organs in the human body and consequently concluded that they were in direct competition for energy. An excessive draw of energy for reproductive organs meant a lesser amount of energy for the full development of the brain.[41] Therefore, differences between males and females were due to the "somewhat earlier arrest of individual evolution in women than in men, necessitated by the reservation of vital power to meet the cost of reproduction."[42] Where a woman's reproductive organs necessitated an excessive draw of energy, her full development was impeded.

Such conclusions about a feminine lack of vital energy resulting in lower intellectual capacity and emotional stability became widely influential and explicitly employed in public debates on whether or not to accept women into universities.[43] Consequently, even as modern definitions of energy and gender are variously articulated, the value of high heat/energy production and consumption remains continuous with premodern associations of full human development or perfection.

With the emergence of modern "race science," theories of full human development were applied not just to gender but also to racial difference. Historian Jürgen Osterhammel, for example, emphasizes that nineteenth-century racism "classified the human 'races' on a scale of potential physical and mental energy."[44] Differences were delineated between intellectual energies characteristic of Anglo races necessary for producing fully developed civilizations and animal energies characteristic of Oriental races that made them suitable for labor but unable to adequately focus or organize their labors for civilizational development.[45] People of the "Orient" were consistently characterized in modern Euro-American scholarship as passive, lacking masculine vitality, action, and energy. As Edward Said has famously noted, African and Asian populations were denied full humanity on account of their apparent inability "to either mine their own resources or inventively use them."[46] This supposed biological lack of energy then was seen to have direct implications for the sociocultural development of their civilizations. Such feminine passivity, low energy, or lack of human development was used to justify colonialism and slavery. People of the Indus Valley, for example, were seen as politically and intellectually indolent, simply not interested in governing themselves, and so were thought to need British colonial rule.[47] Indians' supposed lack of energy for governance and the development of society merely indicated that Britain would be doing them a favor by stepping in to do the governing for them while assisting with the full development of their society.

In addition to the valuation of humans according to energy, the same associations also impacted the interpretation of energy resources in Euro-American contexts. Barbara Freese explains that coal was commonly associated with divine purpose, racial superiority, and full human development. Coal was interpreted both as "evidence of God's desire to elevate humanity" as well as "His longstanding plan to have Anglo-Saxon Protestants do the elevating."[48] In the nineteenth century, the vast majority of coal had been found in England and America. This fact did not go unnoticed and was interpreted as proof of the divine role God had granted to the world's most energetic peoples to bring about the full development of humanity. Freese, for example, cites an 1856 edition of the *Christian Review* wherein a US American writes of "A race of men energetic and enterprising; fitted by their natural characteristics, by their mental and moral culture, and by their hold on the pure gospel of Jesus Christ, to be leaders in the onward march of humanity, have had thrust into their hands, unlooked for and unexpected, a treasure, which if used aright, must secure to them a controlling influence on the affairs of the world."[49] Here, cultural, biological, racial, gendered, religious, and energy natural resources all converge to confirm a sense of divine purpose in contributing to the fulfillment of humanity.

This was the case not only for coal. When oil was "discovered," first as a seemingly exclusive gift to the United States, it was common to see oil as confirmation of earlier narratives of America as a "redeemer nation" with a central role to play in God's plans for human fulfillment.[50] From its discovery in Titusville, Pennsylvania, in 1859, oil was consistently hailed as a redemptive force, sometimes even emerging as a savior figure.[51] Eventually, once the mechanical and industrial applications of oil became apparent, America's gift of oil was also taken as confirmation of the nation's divine calling as a "city on a hill," an economic way to aid the full development of societies and peoples, thus fulfilling, as Woodrow Wilson articulated, "her destiny in saving the world."[52]

Electricity was also associated with divinity and a redemptive means to fulfill human potential. Historians Carolyn de la Peña, Carolyn Marvin, and Brett Michael Grainger describe what they have identified as an "electric theology" that developed in the eighteenth to twentieth centuries. Grainger, for example, identifies electrical theology as a key aspect of antebellum evangelical spirituality.[53] De la Peña defines electrical theology as a "belief that electricity was a spiritual triumph of mysterious power with unlimited potential,"[54] and Marvin emphasizes that electrical theology emerged at the interactions and overlaps of constructed concepts of electricity and bodies, connections smoothed over by particular religious assertions.[55] Marvin asserts that, for many, "electrical science was treated as an extension of religious revelation," a conclusion upheld by a belief that "electricity contained the divine power to bestow life."[56] In this sense, early Christian associations of energeia with human fulfillment exclusively associated with divine agency become applied in new ways to energy technologies of the nineteenth century.

Even though Aristotle's energeia was articulated as the opposing term of *potentia*, the consistent pairing of philosophical, theological, and scientific energy concepts with the aim of human fulfillment renders modern energy a kind of potentiality waiting to be actualized in the aid of actualizing humanity. Theological influences from ancient times and modern interpretations of energy and energy resources resonated with and in these energy concepts, resulting in a common sense that high levels of human individual and social development required high energy production and consumption.

DECOUPLING STRATEGIES IN CLIMATE-CHANGE MITIGATION

By taking in the long historical scope of energy associations with divinity and full development of humanity, we see just how deeply rooted current energy values and expectations are in the Euro-American psyche. Even into the twentieth century, secularized narratives of the role of energy in civilization retain a close alignment between full human development and high, even excessive, energy. Attending to this history of cultural influence makes a critical difference in how climate change is currently addressed. Several approaches focus on decoupling strategies.

For example, ecomodernists at the Breakthrough Institute released a report in 2014 titled *Our High-Energy Planet*. In the report, the authors highlight the material consequences of unequal energy access around the world while acknowledging the crucial importance of addressing climate change. Yet, they argue against positions that would address unequal energy access and climate change by limiting high, even excessive, energy production and consumption in countries like the United States. Instead, citing the importance of energy for meeting the needs of human development, they insist that twenty-first-century citizens of the world must embrace a "high-energy planet."[57] They propose that preserving human development through continued high energy practices while mitigating climate change can be accomplished by a strategy of decoupling deleterious ecological impacts from high energy production/consumption through technological advances.[58] In leaving the historical alignment between energy and human development unquestioned, the authors are left with a solution that would intensify techno-modernity.

As energy humanities scholar Cara Daggett emphasizes, ecomodernist strategies, in general, fully depend on the "unquestioned assertion that modernization and high-technology society can be trusted to produce widespread well-being."[59] In *The Birth of Energy*, Daggett argues that decoupling strategies like the one proposed by the Breakthrough Institute misplace the focus of what needs to be decoupled. Rather than decoupling environmental destruction from high energy consumption through technology as ecomodernists suggest, Daggett argues that adequately addressing the current energy-induced climate crisis calls for a decoupling of the modern epistemology of energy from the cultural valuation of work. Daggett outlines the way the Protestant work ethic infused the modern redefinition of energy as an ability to do work. She emphasizes that this alignment between energy, work, and productivity fortifies political economies that associate value and well-being with progressivism and productivism.[60]

Daggett's illuminating genealogy of the beginnings of modern thermodynamics emphasizes the key role Scottish Calvinist Presbyterianism played in framing modern energy science through a "geo-theology of work and waste." She emphasizes, for example, that "the urgency with which we burn fuel is tied to the urgency with which we pursue productivity and hard work."[61] Daggett's analysis thereby signals the crucial importance of analyzing the past and current religious dynamics of modern energy policy and practices, while proposing "an alternative vision of a society that decouples energy from work, and productivism from equality and well-being."[62] Drawing on feminist post-work theory, she concludes that an alliance between post-work and post-carbon movements would provide an alternative political vision where a person's productivity and work do not define the person's value in society.[63]

I agree with much of Daggett's analysis of problematic theological influences on the way energy has been conceptualized in modernity. However, as outlined above, I have found the problem to be much more ancient than the Protestant work ethic. From the time of Aristotle and St. Paul to the time of the nineteenth-century "discovery" of oil in the United States, ecomodernists, theologians, philosophers, and scientists have consistently aligned high heat/energy production and consumption with divinity and the fulfillment of human life. Frequently, this full development of humanity is identified with the form of an Anglo rational male and the height of civilization. In this broader historical scope, an infusion of the Protestant work ethic into thermodynamics is a particular modern materialization of a deeply rooted alignment of high energy with divinity and the height of human fulfillment.

Daggett also importantly points to the necessity of producing alternative understandings of energy or alternative energy imaginaries. She emphasizes that the Western modern understanding of energy is merely one energy epistemology among many, but then doesn't develop an alternative that would make her argument cohere. By acknowledging that modern energy has been defined by work, then emphasizing the need to decouple work from energy but leaving this alternative undeveloped or undefined, the reader is left with an unintelligible conclusion: We need to decouple the ability to do work (energy) from work. Furthermore, as Rieger has emphasized, while one can question the tendency in capitalism to define the inherent value of a person by his or her ability for work, a pure de-work approach typically focuses entirely on the quantity of work while leaving unexamined the quality of work, or how one's labor is valued.[64] And, if we are to contest extractive energy, human collectives will need to embrace and work out just ways of performing manual labor rather than exporting it to fueled machines. This all suggests, I would argue, that decoupling work from energy remains relevant but does not quite encompass the full scope of the problem.

Building from Daggett's emphasis on the problematic theological imaginaries infused in modern energy while shifting decoupling strategies, I would suggest that what really needs to be decoupled is the alignment between human fulfillment and high energy and that, more than pure idealism that may have no direct correspondence to material conditions, this kind of decoupling is empirically supported as well. Julia Steinberger is an ecological economist studying connections and correlations between energy use and markers for human well-being. Referring to evidence that Smil also points to of an upper limit to the coupling of increased energy use and human well-being, Steinberger and J. Timmons Roberts conducted a comprehensive analysis of correlations over the past seventy years between energy consumption, traditional markers for economic growth such as GDP, and markers for human development. Importantly, their analysis demonstrated an increasing separation or decoupling of these two factors during the study's time period.[65] Furthermore, they concluded that while energy consumption and human well-being were being decoupled, during the same period, economic activity, energy use, and carbon emissions became more tightly coupled. In other words, while economic growth continues to be highly dependent on ever-increasing energy consumption, it is not necessarily translating to markers of increased human well-being.[66] Such results not only support long-standing concerns over the inadequacy of GDP for measuring human well-being,[67] but also have key implications for the ways we account for potential impacts of climate-change mitigation.

Basing her report to the United Nations Development Programme on her research, Steinberger argues for a particular focus on energy as a nexus of ecological and economic analysis. She affirms the Intergovernmental Panel on Climate Change's concern for the unequal effects of climate mitigation on underdeveloped or developing countries as well as the United Nation's stance that access to energy up to a certain point is an important aspect of human well-being. Yet, she points out that most research and policy decisions aimed to mitigate climate change have assumed that human well-being is tied to economic growth which, in turn, depends on "cheap and plentiful energy,"[68] allowing for continued increases in energy consumption. Yet, if energy use is being decoupled from human well-being but not from economic growth, as Steinberger and Roberts's study concluded, continuing to make decisions about climate mitigation based on effects on economic growth will keep us chained to high-energy societies without necessarily equalizing markers for human well-being.

Steinberger and Roberts's research also identified places in the world where low or moderate energy-consumption habits correlate with high markers for human well-being. The researchers focused on countries like Costa Rica as examples of places where markers of high levels of human well-being are met with low-to-moderate energy consumption. Given these conclusions and the way they directly oppose such long-standing Western associations about human fulfillment and high levels of energy consumption, clearly more research needs to be done to identify characteristics of these societies and their systemic structures so that their lessons about achieving high levels of human well-being with low-to-moderate energy use might be applied in other contexts.

ENERGY, FLUX, RELATIONALITY

This demonstrated decoupling between high energy consumption and human well-being also indicates a need—as Daggett suggests—to reimagine what energy is and its relationship to planetary well-being. Yet, clearly removing work from a term so closely identified with it requires further nuance. Rather than a de-work articulation of energy, I would argue for a renewed emphasis on energy as flux.[69]

The prevalence of fossil fuel energy that functions like potentiality has obscured a broader understanding of the ways energy functions not just as potentiality but also as flux.[70] Some energies—those more prevalent in ancient times—are not waiting to be uncovered and put to use. Energies like wind catching a sail or sunlight hitting the face of a leaf ebb and flow. As these energies fluctuate, they have not easily been saved, set aside, and stored up for another day. They come and go according to natural flows. To pair their interests with these flows, humans must attune their daily habits and rhythms according to this flux rather than put forth a continual challenge to nature to meet human needs and desires.

Flux also assumes a different temporality than potentiality lying in wait for its actualization. Potentiality has a direction, an aim or telos: It must find its fulfillment, making it, as I have argued, particularly resonant with ideals of human development. Energy in this sense not only necessitates progress but also emerges as inherently a subsurface waiting for extraction. By contrast, flux does not obey a linear trajectory toward a final goal but meanders, ebbs and flows, or cycles.

Flux also characterizes energy but in a way that rarely gets identified or valued as such in modernity. Philosophers Robert-Jan Geerts, Bart Gremmen, Josette Jacobs, and Guido Ruivenkamp emphasize the importance of seeing energy as flux. They see it as an important step in a transition from "standing reserve" kinds of energy like fossil fuels to energy that waxes and wanes like wind and solar. Significantly, Geerts et al. emphasize the importance of flux energy production for changing consumer patterns: "[A]nother form of energy supply, perhaps one more sensitive to daily and seasonal rhythms, will induce different energy consumption practices."[71] Rather than leading with individual responsibility or consumer habits, these authors highlight a strategy where production changes initiate alterations in consumer habits.

But these authors also hint at a necessary change in imaginaries to accompany systemic material shifts. There is a danger, they emphasize, in merely swapping energy inputs without a simultaneous change in energy cultures and imaginaries. If consumers of flux energy, like sun or wind, are still thinking of and acting as though their electricity is a form of potentiality, then the change in energy production will not change energy-consumption patterns: "As long as users perceive electricity as potentiality they cannot be expected to change their behavior in order to cope with flux."[72] In other words, as many other energy humanities scholars have emphasized, solar panels and windmills do not necessarily result in more just distribution of power, capital, and voice.[73] These forms of flux can, especially with increasingly powerful battery storage, end up functioning like fossil fuels, resulting in a mere change of energy input into a socio-political-economic system that still consolidates power and capital.

So the production of energy as flux could, but does not necessarily, lead to more dispersed forms of political-economic power as well as a more symbiotic approach to the relationship between humans and other-than-human systems. Geerts et al. emphasize that this would only be the case if a corresponding cultural shift in human expectations of energy also took place. I would add that shifts in ideals of human fulfillment would also need to take place—and this is where theological anthropologies and theologies of redemption come into focus. In a 2017 study further examining possibilities of decoupling human well-being and energy, Steinberger and Brand-Correa emphasize that, "The meaning societies give to well-being will directly influence the pathways they choose to follow in order to improve it, and these pathways will necessarily have some sort of environmental consequences."[74] Given the role of religions in value and meaning production, along with the above demonstrated role of Western philosophy and Christianity in fostering alignments between divinity and Anglo-masculinity with high energy, a recalibration of these associations might be just the remedy needed.

Thankfully, this work is already well underway. Theologians informed by critical gender, race, and disability studies have long criticized normalized alignments between divinity and white masculinity.[75] The intersections of modern race and divinity are currently receiving renewed attention, while indigenous studies, postcolonial studies, and queer, trans, and crip theologies question what or who has been recognized as redeemable or in need of redemption as well as the consistent articulation of redemption as a static, totalized wholeness.[76] These theologies have emphasized the ways that redemption has served as a good capitalist investment, ensuring efficient, productive, and fully committed neoliberal workers and consumers.[77] What remains to be seen, though, is for the insights of these various critiques of theological anthropology and redemption to be brought to bear on energy policy and embodied energy values and practices.[78]

Critical analysis of theological anthropologies and theologies of redemption have mainly been approached within the scope of social concerns. I'm suggesting that their current impact can and should be extended to spheres of ecological economics through movements for energy justice. This would aid a shift also in religious energy ethics to move beyond its consumerist constraints to more powerfully analyze the production of energy values and how these intersect with the production of theological values. While flux successfully decouples energy from trajectories of fulfillment, a shift in energy imaginaries could be further enhanced if paired with theological anthropologies and theologies of redemption that also challenge capacitization, productivism, and hierarchies of humanity emerging from a universalized ideal of the rational male.

NOTES

1. Some insights and arguments from Rowe, *Of Modern Extraction: Experiments in Critical Petro-theology* (New York: T&T Clark, 2023), are summarized in this chapter.

2. Philip Mirowski, *More Heat than Light: Economics as Social Physics, Physics as Nature's Economics* (New York: Cambridge University Press, 1989), 3.

3. Crosbie Smith and Norton Wise, *Energy and Empire: A Biographical Study of Lord Kelvin* (New York: Cambridge University Press, 2009), xx.

4. Indeed, studies in religious energy ethics have been emerging since Dieter Hessel's *Energy Ethics: A Christian Response* (New York: Friendship Press, 1979).

5. Giovani Frigo suggests that Hessel was the first—among both religious and secular thinkers—to write of an "energy ethics." Giovanni Frigo, "Energy Ethics: A Literature Review," *Relations* 6 (2018), 194.

6. US Catholic Bishops, "Reflection on the Energy Crisis" (Washington, DC: United States Catholic Conference, 1981), and Pontifical Academy of Sciences, "Mankind and Energy: Needs, Resources, Hopes" in *Mankind and Energy: Needs Resources, Hopes*, ed. André Blanc-Lapieerre (Amsterdam: Elsevier, 1982). For a literature review of energy ethics, including religious perspectives, see Frigo, "Energy Ethics: A Literature Review." Larry Rasmussen, Normand Laurendaeu, and Dan Solomon organized what was likely the first US-based conference on energy science and religion. Papers from and reflections on the conference have been published in "The Energy Transition: Religious and Cultural Perspectives," *Zygon* 46 (2011). Jim Martin-Schramm, too, has been an important leader in energy ethics. See his *Climate Justice* (Minneapolis: Fortress Press, 2010) as well as his work with Christiana Peppard, Julia Watts Belser, and Erin Lothes Biviano, "What Powers Us? A Comparative Religious Ethics of Energy Sources, Power, and Privilege," *Journal of the Society of Christian Ethics* 35, no. 1 (2016): 3–25. See also Rowe and Larry Rasmussen, "An Interview on Energy, Christian Theology, and Ethics," *Dialog* (Summer 2023): 1–7.

7. For an approach to energy that does not revert to stasis or that which remains the same in the midst of change, see Clayton Crockett, *Energy and Change: A New Materialist Cosmotheology* (New York: Columbia University Press, 2022).

8. Martin Heidegger, "The Question concerning Technology," in *The Basic Writings*, ed. David Farrell Krell, trans. William Lovitt (London: Harper Perennial, 2009), 329.

9. Lewis Mumford, *Technics and Civilization* (New York: Harcourt, Brace and Company, 1934), 376. Mumford is here taking aim at capitalism in particular because, in the capitalist ethos and system, surplus energy does not get directed toward cultural creation but is instead reinvested for increased production.

10. Leslie A. White, "Energy and the Evolution of Culture" *American Anthropologist* 45, no. 3 (1943), 338.

11. Carl Sagan, *Cosmic Connection: An Extraterrestrial Perspective*, ed. Jerome Agel (New York: Cambridge University Press, 2000). Thanks to Evan Berry for suggesting I look into the Kardashev scale.

12. Michio Kaku, "The Physics of Interstellar Travel: To One Day, Reach the Stars," 2010, https://mkaku.org/home/articles/the-physics-of-interstellar-travel/, accessed September 26, 2022.

13. Imre Szeman and Dominic Boyer, *Energy Humanities: An Anthology* (Baltimore: John Hopkins University Press, 2017), 3.

14. A. D. Pasternak, *Global Energy Futures and Human Development: A Framework for Analysis* (Oak Ridge, TN: US Department of Energy, 2000); Vaclav Smil, *Energy at the Crossroads: Global Perspectives and Uncertainties* (Cambridge, MA: The MIT Press, 2003); D. M. Martinez and B. W. Ebenhak, "Understanding the

Role of Energy Consumption in Human Development through the Use of Saturation Phenomena," *Energy Policy* 36 (2008): 1430–35.

15. Vaclav Smil, "Science, Energy, Ethics, and Civilization," in *Visions of Discovery: New Light on Physics, Cosmology and Consciousness*, eds. R. Y. Chiao et al. (Cambridge, MA: Cambridge University Press, 2010), 725–26. See also Julia K. Steinberger's "Energising Human Development," in *UN Human Development Report*, last modified April 14, 2016, http://hdr.undp.org/en/content/energising-human-development: "Here we see a high correlation between lower energy and lower HDI [Human Development Index]: a small increment of energy use corresponds to a relatively large increase in HDI. As energy use increases, we witness what economists would call 'diminishing returns' in human development outcomes. And at higher energy use, there is no statistically significant dependency: the relationship shows evidence of saturation. The best-fit curve shows high human development (HDI above 0.7) was attainable at 50 GJ of primary energy per person in 2012."

16. Smil, *Energy in World History* (New York: Routledge, 2020), 252.

17. Frederick Buell, "A Short History of Oil Cultures: Or, the Marriage of Catastrophe and Exuberance," *Journal of American Studies* 46 (2012): 273–93.

18. Timothy Mitchell, *Carbon Democracy: Political Power in the Age of Oil* (New York: Verso, 2013).

19. Petrocultures Research Group, *After Oil* (Edmonton, AB: Petrocultures Research Group, 2016).

20. Buell, "A Short History of Oil Cultures"; Cara New Daggett, *The Birth of Energy: Fossil Fuels, Thermodynamics, and the Politics of Work* (Durham, NC: Duke University Press, 2019).

21. I make this case more expansively in Rowe, *Of Modern Extraction*.

22. See a fuller explication of this section in Rowe, "Energy," *Of Modern Extraction*.

23. Gottfried Leibniz, "On the Doctrine of Malebranche: A Letter to M. Remond De Montmort, Containing Remarks on the Book of Father Terte against Father Malebranche," in *The Philosophical Works of Leibniz* (New Haven, CT: Tuttle, Morehouse & Taylor, 1890), 233–37.

24. *Protrepticus*, B86. Translated in David Bradshaw, *Aristotle East and West: Metaphysics and the Division of Christendom* (New York: Cambridge University Press, 2004), 5.

25. Ibid., 13.

26. B86, cited in ibid., 5.

27. "There was no similar restriction [in the use of energeia to spiritual agents] in non-Biblical Greek or the Septuagint" (Bradshaw, "The Concept of the Divine Energies," *Philosophy & Theology* 18 [2006], 191). Passages with energeia in the New Testament—all in Paul: Eph 1:19–20, Eph 3:7, Eph 4:16, Phil 3:21, Col 1:29, Col 2:12, 2 Thess 2:9, 2:11 (ibid., 193).

28. Ibid., 101.

29. Ibid.

30. Ibid.

31. Bradshaw gives the examples of Psalm 1 and Psalms of repentance like 51.

32. Bradshaw, "The Concept of Divine Energies," 102.

33. Ibid.

34. See Gad Freudenthal, *Aristotle's Theory of Material Substance: Heat and Pneuma, Form and Soul* (New York: Oxford University Press, 1995) on this interpretation of the role of heat as concoction.

35. In *Generation of Animals*, IV, 8, 777a4–20, for example.

36. Cited in Freudenthal, *Aristotle's Theory of Material Substance*, 25.

37. Menstrual fluid is merely undeveloped semen: "semen not in a pure state, but in need of working up" (*GA* I, 20, 728a26).

38. Freudenthal, *Aristotle's Theory of Material Substance*, 59.

39. He differed from Aristotle in adding further anatomical explanation for female deficiency. "'The female is less perfect than the male for one, principal reason—because she is colder.'" (Galen, *On the Usefulness of the Parts of the Body*, 14.II.299, cited in Nancy Tuana, *The Less Noble Sex: Scientific, Religious, and Philosophical Conceptions of Woman's Nature* [Bloomington: Indiana University Press, 1993], 21).

40. A couple examples include Abroise Paré, Patrick Geddes, and John Arthur Thomson. See Nancy Tuana on heat and gender in *The Less Noble Sex*.

41. See Herbert Spencer, *Study of Sociology*, cited in Tuana, *The Less Noble Sex*, 47.

42. Spencer, "Psychology of the Sexes," 32, cited in Tuana, 47.

43. In the nineteenth century, obstetrician Charles Meigs and Edward Clarke, faculty member in the medical department at Harvard, drew on these concepts to argue that women should not be admitted to universities (see Tuana, *The Less Noble Sex*, 75–78).

44. Jürgen Osterhammel, *The Transformation of the World: A Global History of the Nineteenth Century* (Princeton, NJ: Princeton University Press, 2014), 658.

45. In 1799, English physician Charles White, for example, drew on the medieval great chain of being, adding races along this continuum with some races having characteristics closer to those of animals. (See Ibram X. Kendi, *Stamped from the Beginning: The Definitive History of Racist Ideas in America* [New York: Hachette Book Group, 2017], 132–33.)

46. Edward Said, *Orientalism* (New York: Vintage Books, 1979), 38.

47. Richard King, *Orientalism and Religion: Postcolonial Theory, India and "the Mystic East"* (New York: Routledge, 1999), 104.

48. Barbara Freese, *Coal: A Human History* (New York: Basic Books, 2003), 11.

49. Ibid., 12.

50. Oil had been known of for hundreds, if not thousands, of years by indigenous populations around the world. The Pennsylvania "discovery" therefore was seen as the first time oil could be collected in a way that was commercially viable. Historians still debate whether the Pennsylvania discovery was the first. The salient point here is that US Americans *thought* they were the first.

51. See my reading of John J. McLaurin's history of oil (*Sketches in Crude-Oil* [1998]) as a salvation history in *Of Modern Extraction*.

52. Cited as the epigraph for Ernest Lee Tuveson's *Redeemer Nation: The Idea of America's Millennial Role* (Chicago: University of Chicago Press, 1968).

53. Brett Malcolm Grainger, *Church in the Wild: Evangelicals in Antebellum America* (Cambridge, MA: Harvard University Press, 2019).

54. Carolyn Thomas de la Peña, *The Body Electric: How Strange Machines Built the Modern American* (New York: NYU Press, 2003), 105–6.

55. Carolyn Marvin, *When Old Technologies Were New: Thinking about Electric Communication in the Late Nineteenth Century* (New York: Oxford University Press, 1988). See also the ways electricity was interpreted in terms beyond Christian orthodoxy in spiritualisms: Darryl Caterine, "The Haunted Grid: Nature, Electricity, and Indian Spirits in the American Metaphysical Tradition," *Journal of the American Academy of Religion* 82 (2014): 371–97.

56. Marvin, *When Old Technologies Were New*, 127.

57. Mark Caine, Jason Lloyd, Max Luke, Lisa Margonelli, Todd Moss, Ted Nordhaus, Roger Pielke Jr., et al., "Our High-Energy Planet: A Climate Pragmatism Project," *The Breakthrough Institute* (2014), 4, https://thebreakthrough.org/articles/our-high-energy-planet, accessed May 21, 2019.

58. "Decoupling of human welfare from environmental impacts will require a sustained commitment to technological progress and the continuing evolution of social, economic, and political institutions alongside those changes" ("Ecomodernist Manifesto," *The Breakthrough Institute* [2015], 29).

59. Daggett, *The Birth of Energy*, 191.

60. Philosopher Michael Marder also suggests a decoupling of energy from productivity in *Energy Dreams: Of Actuality* (New York: Columbia University Press, 2017).

61. Daggett, *The Birth of Energy*, 206.

62. Ibid., 191.

63. Daggett, building on Kathi Weeks's post-work theory, calls for the creation of "'alternate mode[s] of valuation'" (199, citing Weeks). See my further engagement with Daggett and post-work approaches in chapter 3, "Capital," *Of Modern Extraction*.

64. Rieger, personal exchange.

65. Julia K. Steinberger and J. Timmons Roberts, "From Constraint to Sufficiency: The Decoupling of Energy and Carbon from Human Needs, 1975–2005" *Ecological Economics* 70 (2010).

66. Consistent with the United Nations, Steinberger and Roberts use the HDI (Human Development Index) to look for these markers.

67. Herman Daly and John B. Cobb Jr., *For the Common Good: Redirecting the Economy toward Community, the Environment, and a Sustainable Future* (Boston: Beacon Press, 1994).

68. Steinberger, "Energising Human Development."

69. Similarly and more recently, Clayton Crockett has made a compelling argument for energy not as that which remains the same over time but as change itself. Importantly, Crockett also explores the economic, theological, and ecological implications of this shift. See Crockett, *Energy and Change*.

70. Robert-Jan Geerts, Bart Gremmen, Josette Jacobs, and Guido Ruivenkamp, "Towards a Philosophy of Energy," *Scientiæ Studia* 12 (2014):105–27.

71. Ibid., 124.

72. Ibid., 125.

73. Shannon Elizabeth Bell, Cara Elizabeth Daggett, and Christine Elizabeth Labuski, "Toward Feminist Energy Systems: Why Adding Women and Solar Panels Is Not Enough," *Energy Research & Social Science* 68 (2020): 1–13.

74. Lina I. Brand-Correa and Julia K. Steinberger, "A Framework for Decoupling Human Needs Satisfaction from Energy Use," *Ecological Economics* 141 (2017), 44.

75. For just a couple examples of many: Rosemary Radford Ruether, *New Woman, New Earth: Sexist Ideologies and Human Liberation* (New York: Seabury Press, 1975); Delores Williams, *Sisters in the Wilderness: The Challenges of Womanist God-Talk* (Maryknoll, NY: Orbis, 1993); Ivone Gebara, *Longing for Running Water: Ecofeminism and Liberation* (Minneapolis: Fortress Press, 1999); Carol Wayne White, *Black Lives and Sacred Humanity: Toward an African American Religious Naturalism* (New York: Fordham University Press, 2016).

76. J. Kameron Carter, *Race: A Theological Account* (New York: Oxford University Press, 2008); Sharon Betcher, *Spirit and the Politics of Disablement* (Minneapolis: Fortress, 2007); Whitney Bauman, *Meaningful Flesh: Reflections on Religion and Nature for a Queer Planet* (Santa Barbara, CA: Punctum, 2018), Vine Deloria Jr., *God is Red: A Native View of Religion* (New York: Putnam Publishing Group, 1973).

77. Karen Bray, *Grave Attending: A Political Theology for the Unredeemed* (New York: Fordham University Press, 2020).

78. I've begun exploring this possibility in *Of Modern Extraction*, but much more work is called for.

REFERENCES

Aristotle. *Generation of Animals*. Loeb Classical Library 366. Edited by Jeffrey Henderson, translated by A. L. Peck. Cambridge, MA: Harvard University Press, 1942.

Bauman, Whitney. *Meaningful Flesh: Reflections on Religion and Nature for a Queer Planet*. Santa Barbara, CA: Punctum, 2018.

Bell, Shannon Elizabeth, Cara Elizabeth Daggett, and Christine Elizabeth Labuski. "Toward Feminist Energy Systems: Why Adding Women and Solar Panels Is Not Enough." *Energy Research & Social Science* 68 (2020): 1–13.

Betcher, Sharon. *Spirit and the Politics of Disablement*. Minneapolis: Fortress, 2007.

Bradshaw, David. *Aristotle East and West: Metaphysics and the Division of Christendom*. New York: Cambridge University Press, 2004.

———. "The Concept of the Divine Energies." *Philosophy & Theology* 18 (2006): 93–120.

Brand-Correa, Lina I. and Julia K. Steinberger. "A Framework for Decoupling Human Needs Satisfaction from Energy Use." *Ecological Economics* 141 (2017).

Bray, Karen. *Grave Attending: A Political Theology for the Unredeemed*. New York: Fordham University Press, 2020.

Buell, Frederick. "A Short History of Oil Cultures: Or, the Marriage of Catastrophe and Exuberance." *Journal of American Studies* 46 (2012): 273–93.

Caine, Mark, Jason Lloyd, Max Luke, Lisa Margonelli, Todd Moss, Ted Nordhaus, Roger Pielke Jr., et al. "Our High Energy-Planet: A Climate Pragmatism Project." *The Breakthrough Institute* (2014). https://thebreakthrough.org/articles/our-high-energy-planet. Accessed April 17, 2024.

Carter, J. Kameron. *Race: A Theological Account*. New York: Oxford University Press, 2008.

Caterine, Darryl. "The Haunted Grid: Nature, Electricity, and Indian Spirits in the American Metaphysical Tradition." *Journal of the American Academy of Religion* 82 (2014): 371–97.

Crockett, Clayton. *Energy and Change: A New Materialist Cosmotheology*. New York: Columbia University Press, 2022.

Daggett, Cara New. *The Birth of Energy: Fossil Fuels, Thermodynamics, and the Politics of Work*. Durham, NC: Duke University Press, 2019.

Daly, Herman and John B. Cobb Jr. *For the Common Good: Redirecting the Economy toward Community, the Environment, and a Sustainable Future*. Boston: Beacon Press, 1994.

de la Peña, Carolyn Thomas. *The Body Electric: How Strange Machines Built the Modern American*. New York: NYU Press, 2003.

Deloria Jr., Vine. *God Is Red: A Native View of Religion*. New York: Putnam Publishing Group, 1973.

Freese, Barbara. *Coal: A Human History*. New York: Basic Books, 2003.

Freudenthal, Gad. *Aristotle's Theory of Material Substance: Heat and Pneuma, Form and Soul*. New York: Oxford University Press, 1995.

Frigo, Giovanni. "Energy Ethics: A Literature Review." *Relations* 6 (2018): 173–214.

Galen. *Galen on the Usefulness of the Parts of the Body*. Translated by Margaret Tallmadge May. Ithaca, NY: Cornell University Press, 1968.

Gebara, Ivone. *Longing for Running Water: Ecofeminism and Liberation*. Minneapolis: Fortress Press, 1999.

Geerts, Robert-Jan, Bart Gremmen, Josette Jacobs, and Guido Ruivenkamp. "Towards a Philosophy of Energy." *Scientiæ Studia* 12 (2014): 105–27.

Grainger, Brett Malcolm. *Church in the Wild: Evangelicals in Antebellum America*. Cambridge, MA: Harvard University Press, 2019.

Heidegger, Martin. "The Question Concerning Technology." In *The Basic Writings*, edited by David Farrell Krell, translated by William Lovitt, 311–41. London: Harper Perennial, 2009.

Hessel, Dieter. *Energy Ethics: A Christian Response*. New York: Friendship Press, 1979.

Kaku, Michio. "The Physics of Interstellar Travel: To One Day, Reach the Stars." 2010. Accessed September 26, 2022. https://mkaku.org/home/articles/the-physics-of-interstellar-travel/.

Kendi, Ibram X. *Stamped from the Beginning: The Definitive History of Racist Ideas in America*. New York: Hachette Book Group, 2017.

King, Richard. *Orientalism and Religion: Postcolonial Theory, India and "the Mystic East."* New York: Routledge, 1999.

Leibniz, Gottfried. "On the Doctrine of Malebranche: A Letter to M. Remond De Montmort, Containing Remarks on the Book of Father Terte against Father Malebranche." In *The Philosophical Works of Leibniz*, 233–37. New Haven, CT: Tuttle, Morehouse & Taylor, 1890.

Marder, Michael. *Energy Dreams: Of Actuality*. New York: Columbia University Press, 2017.

Martinez, D. M. and B. W. Ebenhak. "Understanding the Role of Energy Consumption in Human Development through the Use of Saturation Phenomena." *Energy Policy* 36 (2008): 1430–35.

Martin-Schramm, James. *Climate Justice: Ethics, Energy, and Public Policy*. Minneapolis: Fortress Press, 2010.

Marvin, Carolyn. *When Old Technologies Were New: Thinking about Electric Communication in the Late Nineteenth Century*. New York: Oxford University Press, 1988.

Mirowski, Philip. *More Heat than Light: Economics as Social Physics, Physics as Nature's Economics*. New York: Cambridge University Press, 1989.

Mitchell, Timothy. *Carbon Democracy: Political Power in the Age of Oil*. New York: Verso, 2013.

Mumford, Lewis. *Technics and Civilization*. New York: Harcourt, Brace and Company, 1934.

Nordhaus, Ted, et al. "Ecomodernist Manifesto." *The Breakthrough Institute* (2015). http://www.ecomodernism.org. Accessed, April 17, 2024.

Osterhammel, Jürgen. *The Transformation of the World: A Global History of the Nineteenth Century*. Princeton, NJ: Princeton University Press, 2014.

Pasternak, D. *Global Energy Futures and Human Development: A Framework for Analysis*. Oakridge, TN: US Department of Energy, 2000.

Peppard, Christiana Z., Julia Watts Belser, Erin Lothes Biviano, James B. Martin-Schramm. "What Powers US? A Comparative Religious Ethics of Energy Sources, Power, and Privilege." *Journal of the Society of Christian Ethics* 35, no. 1 (2016): 3–25.

Petrocultures Research Group. *After Oil*. Edmonton, AB: Petrocultures Research Group, 2016.

Pontifical Academy of Sciences. "Mankind and Energy: Needs, Resources, Hopes." In *Mankind and Energy: Needs Resources, Hopes*, edited by André Blanc-Lapieerre. Amsterdam: Elsevier, 1982.

Rasmussen, Larry, Normand Laurendeau, and Dan Solomon. "Introduction to 'The Energy Transition: Religious and Cultural Perspectives.'" *Zygon* 46 (2011): 872–89.

Rowe, Terra Schwerin. *Of Modern Extraction: Experiments in Critical Petro-theology*. New York: T&T Clark, 2023.

Rowe, Terra Schwerin and Larry Rasmussen. "An Interview on Energy, Christian Theology, and Ethics." *Dialog* (Summer 2023): 1–7.

Ruether, Rosemary Radford. *New Woman, New Earth: Sexist Ideologies and Human Liberation*. New York: Seabury Press, 1975.

Sagan, Carl. *Cosmic Connection: An Extraterrestrial Perspective*, edited by Jerome Agel. New York: Cambridge University Press, 2000.
Said, Edward. *Orientalism*. New York: Vintage Books, 1979.
Smil, Vaclav. *Energy at the Crossroads: Global Perspectives and Uncertainties*. Cambridge, MA: The MIT Press, 2003.
———. *Energy in World History*. New York: Routledge, 2020.
———. "Science, Energy, Ethics, and Civilization." In *Visions of Discovery: New Light on Physics, Cosmology and Consciousness*, edited by R. Y. Chiao et al. Cambridge, MA: Cambridge University Press, 2010.
Smith, Crosbie and Norton Wise. *Energy and Empire: A Biographical Study of Lord Kelvin*. New York: Cambridge University Press, 2009.
Steinberger, Julia K. "Energising Human Development." In *UN Human Development Report*, last modified April 15, 2016. https://hdr.undp.org/content/energising-human-development.
Steinberger, Julia K. and J. Timmons Roberts. "From Constraint to Sufficiency: The Decoupling of Energy and Carbon from Human Needs, 1975–2005." *Ecological Economics* 70 (2010).
Szeman, Imre and Dominic Boyer. *Energy Humanities: An Anthology*. Baltimore: John Hopkins University Press, 2017.
Tuana, Nancy. *The Less Noble Sex: Scientific, Religious, and Philosophical Conceptions of Woman's Nature*. Bloomington: Indiana University Press, 1993.
Tuveson, Ernest Lee. *Redeemer Nation: The Idea of America's Millennial Role*. Chicago: University of Chicago Press, 1968.
US Catholic Bishops. "Reflections on the Energy Crisis." Washington, DC: United States Catholic Conference, 1981.
White, Carol Wayne. *Black Lives and Sacred Humanity: Toward an African American Religious Naturalism*. New York: Fordham University Press, 2016.
White, Leslie A. "Energy and the Evolution of Culture." *American Anthropologist* 45, no. 3 (1943).

Chapter 2

Liberation Theologies and Grassroots Education in Latin America and the Caribbean

The Complex Path to Restore Human and More-than-Human Worlds

Nathalia Hernández Vidal

MY PLACE-BASED ENCOUNTER WITH LIBERATION THEOLOGIES

I arrived to the National Gathering of Vegetable Seed Savers (*Encuentro Nacional de Guardianes de Semillas de Hortalizas*) at the Instituto Mayor Campesino (IMCA), in Buga, Colombia, in July 2017. Many delegations from across the country had already arrived. Some sat on the grass while others walked around. The spirit of the place was festive. People were smiling, laughing, and admiring the different plants, bugs, and animals that accompanied us in the space. Everyone greeted the newcomers as if they had known them forever, even if this was actually the first time they saw each other. The weather was warm and humid. After greeting a number of people, I entered the main house. There was a big patio in the center. Many gathered there to chat and work on the pedagogical materials for the next days.

I took some time to look at them. Some made drawings of different seed varieties and their companion species, others made tables classifying seeds by climate and altitude, and another group was putting together an exhibition of musical instruments and medicinal ointments made with seeds on a few tables. While they worked, I could hear all kinds of conversations. Sharp critiques to the politics of seeds and agriculture in Colombia, knowledge exchanges about planting and harvesting techniques, complaints about the long trip and the scarcity of resources ... They all mixed together in a loud tornado of voices.

I got lost for a little while in the deep sound while observing the infrastructure that was hosting us. Built with a common *colonial* style, the main house had white walls made of bahareque, Spanish tiles, and colorful wood beans. I thought to myself that that same *patio* must have served as a space of social connection between the aristocratic families during *La Nueva Granada*. These patios had lounges and dining rooms for criollos and Spaniards of high-class families to enjoy food, social, and political events. Some houses also had an exterior patio with a kitchen. There, Black and indigenous slaves and indigenous servants from the highlands cooked and were in charge of the property maintenance activities, including gardening and caring for farmyard animals.[1] It felt ironic that the same space that functioned as an infrastructure of oppression and racialized class division during the colonial period was being re-signified as a space of collective work to build just futures.

Indeed, the IMCA has been known as a center of Campesinxs[2] education and politics in Colombia for more than fifty years. It was founded by a Jesuit priest called Francisco Javier Mejía, who acquired the property in 1968. "El cura Mejía" (Mejia's priest), as many called him, saw in Campesino education a critical site to put liberation theology (LT) in action. With many ups and downs, the IMCA has been able to survive Colombia's armed conflict and difficult relationship with the Catholic Church while maintaining deep roots with LT's principles and praxis.

The IMCA and the National Gathering that I gave a glimpse of above are not the only examples of the interconnections between LT (or LTs, if one considers the diversity of perspectives within this approach) and grassroots rural education in Latin America and the Caribbean. LTs supported and influenced the Campesino a Campesino Movement (CCM) in Central and South America in the 1980s[3] and offered ideological, political, and material bases for creating peasant education centers. These spaces made visible their knowledge and fostered inter-epistemic exchanges among different actors.[4] Moreover, as I show in the following pages, the mutual influence of LTs and Campesinx cosmopolitics articulate a vision of the relation between human and more-than-human worlds that had long-lasting effects on Campesinx-based social movements across the region. Such vision is still important today. As agrarian capitalism and other forms of extractivism that maintain, feed, and reproduce the system advance, these movements continue to struggle against historical forms of precaritization, dispossession, exploitation, and annihilation while striving to restore human and more-than-human relationalities. In this chapter, I draw from my seven-year experience as a scholar-activist in Campesino-based movements in Colombia and in archival work to reflect on these issues.

In the first section, I provide a general overview of how LTs and agrarian politics have been entangled in the history of social mobilization in Latin America and the Caribbean. I discuss the contradictory role of Christianity within leftist politics and examine the importance of theological and social dissent in Christian nongovernmental organizations (NGOs) and within the Catholic Church. In the second section, I examine Colombia's political economy and social challenges at the time in which the IMCA was created (1960s–1970s). I reveal that a deep engagement with politics on the ground fueled the project and its influence in today's Campesino-based grassroots initiatives, such as national and local seed networks. I show how everyday practices of resistance and life-long community projects generate epistemic justice and open up spaces for restoring intergenerational and multispecies relationalities. I conclude by offering a series of questions and research paths that remain unexplored.

LIBERATION THEOLOGIES AND AGRARIAN POLITICS

Social mobilization in Latin America and the Caribbean has a long and complex history in which religion and the Catholic Church have often played diverse and sometimes problematic roles. These have tended to enforce and reproduce economic, colonial, and patriarchal domination. However, they have also promoted emancipatory projects. An example of these projects are LTs. As they arose and spread across the continent in the 1970s, they transformed the role of religion in social movements, their pedagogical praxis, and how knowledge was produced and circulated among oppressed communities.

Codina and other scholars have categorized the development of LTs in Latin America and the Caribbean in three phases. The first phase was in the years from 1957 to 1967, when theological, political, and ideological debates about the social doctrine of Catholicism were intensifying among all ranks of the church. The second period was marked by the Second Vatican Council (1962–1965) and the appearance of the *Encyclical Populorum Progressio* in 1967. And a third moment of consolidation occurred between 1968 and 1971, when LT became a praxis.[5]

LTs proposed to rethink Catholic theology and each of its treatises. "The poor" were their central subject. Latin America and the Caribbean were in enormous social turmoil, with both fascist dictatorships rising and taking over the continent and leftist guerrilla groups gaining traction. The Cold War was behind these ideological, political, economic, and social divisions, as were the emergence of neoliberalism and the pushes against it by dependency theory and communist/socialist movements. Amid these historical forces, rural and urban inhabitants faced increasing poverty and scarcity. LTs were born in this context as a Christian approach highly entangled with Marxist critics of capitalism. They were committed to transforming the social conditions that generated such precarity, violence, and suffering.

An important figure in Colombia was Cardinal Crisanto Luque. He thought that the Catholic Church had to be modernized to be able to respond to the social needs of the time. To do that implied exposing Colombian priests to European progressive universities. Thus, under his ordinance, many priests were paid to study sociology, philosophy, and other social sciences and humanities in universities with strong Marxist inclinations, such as Louvain in Belgium.[6] He also approved the creation of a center for socioreligious research and strengthened the parishes in marginalized neighborhoods in Bogotá, other cities, and rural areas. Later, he and other cardinals promoted "pastoral renewal movements" across the dioceses in the country.

From this perspective, the idea of liberation was closely tied to the idea of class-based justice, not the idea of freedom as it operates in the US discourse of nation-building. To be liberated implied the overcoming of historical systemic oppressions, echoing the Marxist understanding of emancipation. The result of such a process of liberation would be the flourishing of human dignity as a reflection of God. LTs became a social and political movement that expanded to various social movements, including the student movements and the many Campesinx-based movements of the '60s, '70s, and '80s.[7] They embraced the idea that their work would only be completed when the oppressed themselves could "freely raise their voices and express themselves directly and creatively in society."[8]

Both LTs and Campesinx-based movements worked in creating awareness about how the remaking of our biosocial worlds would imply long-term work. In this light, they articulated "Pedagogies of Liberation." These pedagogies were also focused on working with the poor in the development of knowledge and skills not only to advance communities' educational capabilities but also to foster class consciousness and political mobilization. Perhaps the most well-known representative of these pedagogies is Paulo Freire; his seminal work "The Pedagogy of the Oppressed" has influenced scholars and activists worldwide for several decades. He conceived "the oppressed" as the historical subject called to transform itself and society. By shifting the Marxist revolutionary subject from the proletariat to "the poor," Freire centers them in the pedagogical project of human emancipation.

Another important figure for liberation pedagogies at the time was Orlando Fals Borda, who created the approach of Participatory Action Research (PAR), today widely used across the world in universities, NGOs and multilateral organizations, and social movements. PAR was officially launched in Cartagena, Colombia, in 1977, in a world symposium for revolutionary research. The goal was to work on unified research and pedagogical principles to overcome poverty, exploitation, and oppression in the Third World. In Fals Borda's own words:

> PAR's aim is to achieve "power" and not merely "growth" for the grassroots population. This total process simultaneously encompasses adult education, scientific research and political action in which critical theory, situation analyses and practice are seen as sources of knowledge. PAR implies the acquisition of experience and valid data for the construction of a special kind of power—people's power—which belongs to the oppressed and exploited classes and groups and their organizations, and the defense of their just interests to enable them to advance towards shared goals of social change within a participatory political system.[9]

One of the centers of PAR implementation and experimentation was Colombia, particularly the department of Valle, precisely where the IMCA is located. Although PAR's revolutionary objectives have been watered down throughout the years due to several factors, including the general change in the geopolitics of power in the 1990s, it is still one of the most important methodologies and pedagogies for grassroots organizing and social-movement building.

An important feature of Freire's and Fals Borda's approach is the collective nature of teaching and learning. They saw knowledge as anchored in community-based dialogue. This implied the destabilization of preestablished social and epistemic hierarchies. Such destabilization was particularly challenging in the setting of the Catholic Church, which monopolized knowledge in the figure of the priest. However, the Church was going through a deep crisis at the time, reflected in a serious shortage of priests and the notable failure of traditional pastoral models to produce social change.[10] In that context, liberation pedagogies became a form for socially committed priests and nuns to work with the poor not only toward the transformation of systemic conditions of oppression but also, in some cases, toward revolution itself. This more radical approach was, in many cases, disapproved of by the Vatican. The censorship of the speech of Fernando and Ernesto Cardenal and Edgar Parrales, who were active Sandinista revolutionaries in Nicaragua, is an example. Another instance was Ratzinger's (later to become Pope Benedict XVI) statement about the incompatibility of Marxism and Christianity. He sought the condemnation of LT as an approach that put at risk the principles of the Church.[11]

Beyond these cases, most priests and nuns worked in small-scale projects, such as the Christian Base Communities and the Pastoral Land Commission (CPT), a nonprofit agrarian-based organization created in 1975 by the National Conference of Bishops of Brazil, or the IMCA in Colombia. Moksnes sheds light on how contemporary movements also have drawn from this legacy.[12] Focusing on the Zapatista movement, they show how Zapatistas have been highly influenced and supported by the Catholic diocese based in San Cristóbal, a big contemporary advocate of LTs. This influence recognizes the complex histories of relations between indigenous communities and the Catholic Church, both fostering and problematizing long-term articulations of indigenous identities with Catholicism, as in the case of the groups who identify as Maya Catholics. In a similar line, Pinehiro and Pinto have discussed how Freire's pedagogy has been highly influential for the Movement of Landless Workers in Brazil (MST).[13] They argue that grassroots education and itinerant learning gatherings have made the movement sustainable through time, supporting the creation of the collective identity of *landless workers* while promoting spaces for political education and interaction with other social movements, grassroots organizations, and institutional powers across the continent. Such work has not only made the MST one of the most known and powerful social movements in the world but also allowed the redefinition of rural education for political actors in Brazil and other places in South and Central America. Likewise, as I have shown elsewhere, Colombia LTs and liberation pedagogies have been critical for the IMCA, the National Network of Free Seeds of Colombia (RSLC), and many other grassroots organizations and projects.[14] Either using institutionalized spaces for such political programs of education to be carried out, or moving across itinerant and even clandestine spaces for gathering, Campesinxs epistemic and political power has been partly developed in these scenarios and in deep connection with these systems of thought and action.

SITUATED LIBERATION THEOLOGIES, CAPITALISM, AND EMANCIPATION

Colombia is an important site to study how LTs generated relevant reformations of the biosocial—and, in some ways, continue to do so, even as a good number of scholars have declared their fall. Colombia has been one of the centers of LTs' development on the continent, having a long history of social mobilization and grassroots struggles, both in urban and rural areas. Importantly, social mobilization has happened despite and amid a sixty-year-long armed conflict and the daily intensification of militarized extractivism, in which thousands of activists' and more-than-human lives have disappeared and been exterminated.

The rural population in Colombia faced drastic changes in the eighteenth and nineteenth centuries with the gradual incorporation of the capitalist system into the seignorial and colonial systems.[15] After independence from Spain, the project of nation-building included the homogenization of the population as Colombians, which promoted a process of invisibilization of ethnoracial identities, histories, and formations.

The elites, trained in racist liberal thought, believed that, to become modern, the Republic should foster individualism and private property. They saw as an impediment to such a project of nation-building the existence of special regimes of property for certain populations, such as the reservations granted to indigenous communities by royal decrees. Through constitutional and judicial reforms, collective properties were taken apart and sold.[16]

The formation of the modern Colombian nation also included the necessary demonstration of human domination of nature. Thus, the modern Colombian was portrayed as capable of dominating nature, of making it be at the service of modern human culture, which was to take place in urban centers, not in the countryside. Therefore, urbanization became a marker of modernity, and rurality a marker of backwardness, of nativism and primitivism.[17] Appelbaum examines how, for example, the displacement of indigenous and Black people from productive (or potentially productive) agricultural land and their replacement by colonos was utilized as a strategy of nation-building during the nineteenth century.[18] Colonos, she explains, were seen as mixed people from the region of Antioquia (called Antioqueños in local jargon). They were represented as a simile of the American Yankee, called to modernize agricultural work, whiten the unruly regions of the country (like Cauca, mainly populated by indigenous and Black people), and discipline local women to become reflections of the heterosexual bourgeois white women inhabiting urban areas such as Bogotá. As a result, land accumulation grew and racial inequalities became even more salient.

In environmental terms, this was a moment in which the ideology of development[19] saw biodiversity, or what was coded at the time as an unmanageable heterogeneity of ecosystems, as a problem.[20] Since the goal was to rapidly increase production and standardize agricultural processes, the diversity of biosocial worlds encountered in the countryside represented a challenge to achieve economic progress.[21] The project of constructing the modern Colombian nation (1850 to 1970) needed to privatize land and organize the space as rural, urban, or wild through Western science and technology.[22]

By the end of the nineteenth century, national and foreign agricultural corporations had found the perfect space for their growth and expansion in Colombia.[23] The model that was adopted was attuned with the environmental ideology of the time. The expansion of the agricultural frontier through monocropping exploded. Although the *hacienda*, a simile of the colonial plantation[24] used in Iberoamerica by the Spanish empire had died, a continuation of it was emplaced with the Green Revolution.[25] This model was (and still is) a militarized capitalist settler institution where resource monopoly, violence, and extreme gender, ethnic, and class polarization were embedded in the industrial complex of agricultural production. As a response to the increasing dispossession and proletarianization in rural areas, Campesinxs organized creating webs of solidarity between smallholders and the new Campesinx proletariat. For instance, during the '20s and '30s, Campesinx groups, such as the National Agrarian Party, the Campesinx Leagues, and the Rural Action Units, began to play important roles in the national political scene.

Such social, political, environmental, and spatial transformations generated a climate in which the Campesinx proletariat grew significantly. This meant that several ways of life coexisted in the rural countryside. There was "a peasant mode of production, in which the direct producers controlled the means of production and organized work themselves," a capitalist mode of production, in which peasants "controlled neither the material of labor nor its organization,"[26] and a gendered system in which women could not own property, had no control over their wage and reproductive labor, and had less than entire sovereignty over the use of their bodies.

This context encouraged Campesinx[27] labor organizing. Both the Communist Party and its factions (the National Left Revolutionary Union and the Socialist Revolutionary Party) and priests and nuns (who were, oftentimes, leftist too) focused on working closely with Campesinxs across the country in projects that could improve their situation. Those projects went from capitalist-oriented enterprises of Campesinx education that operated under the capitalist ideology that blames the poor for their own structural material condition, to radical revolutionary projects where, as opposed to what Marx thought, peasants would be the revolutionary subject.[28]

With the arrival of the time known as *La Violencia*,[29] the late 1940s and the entire 1950s were devastating for social movements in Colombia, particularly for movements located in the countryside.[30] The Catholic Church was active during this time in protecting the interests of the conservative party. However, priests and nuns on the ground, infused with a Marxist spirit, organized to help liberals and leftists hide and defend themselves from conservatives. Even though many forces were looking for ways to stop the violence, it took a decade more for rural grassroots organizations to be able to gain visibility and strength again.

The creation of the National Association of Campesino Users (ANUC)[31] in the mid-1960s restarted a cycle of Campesinx mobilization. It was during these times of Campesino organizing that the IMCA was born and LTs began to gain traction in the country. As I mentioned above, the expansion of the sugar-cane industrial agricultural production in Valle, the department where the IMCA was located, had modified the agrarian landscape, proletarianizing many Campesino communities while displacing others.

The proletarized peasantry looked for ways to organize, but the militarized attacks and surveillance of the sugar-cane industry quickly dismembered their unions. El Cura Mejía, the IMCA founder, realized that although the struggle for land was important, it could not be carried out under such difficult circumstances. Thus, he envisioned the IMCA as a space where Campesinxs could become agents of their own destiny. Such transformation was based on creating the conditions of possibility to practice liberation pedagogies as part of the LT agenda in the countryside.

Although this work was indeed revolutionary under the given circumstances, historians and sociologists underscore that it is not to be confused with a socialist agenda. El Cura Mejía was close to the Communist Party as it was one of the few parties that donated funds for the IMCA to operate. But he embraced many of the techniques of the financial sector to expand their power over the Campesinado, such as opening credit lines for them to be able to compete in the national and international markets. Thus, while advocating for small-scale agroecological farming, he also trained students at the IMCA to become disciplined members of the increasingly powerful financial system.

THE IMCA: BETWEEN EMANCIPATION AND COLONIALITY

The IMCA was born at a time when the rapid change of agrarian life was motivating the creation of educational institutions that could train and respond to the challenges of such transformations in the countryside. Most of these institutions were focused on teaching new knowledges demanded by the growing need for professionals trained in modern agro-industrial systems.

Although working as well with the purpose of using education as a dispositive of nation-building, the IMCA had a different epistemological agenda that reflected another imaginary of how the nation should look. The nation should be a modern project that could also work under democratic principles of government and wealth distribution. Moreover, they thought the means of production and production itself should be in the hands of Campesinxs.

Internally, things were complicated among students, "faculty,"[32] and staff. Some were articulated with the larger Campesinx movement and the growing weight of revolutionary Christianity represented by figures such as Camilo Torres. A former Catholic cardinal, cofounder of the department of sociology of the *Universidad Nacional de Colombia*, and future guerrilla member of the *Ejército de Liberación Nacional* (National Liberation Army, ELN), Torres embodied the radical wing of LT in Colombia and on the continent. Torres and others influenced grassroots organization across Colombia and infused a revolutionary spirit in the countryside.

A few members of IMCA worried about such spirit, fearing that it could become a center for the development of communism. They aligned more closely with the priests who ran Radio Sutatenza, another initiative of peasant-centered education that influenced thousands of Campesinxs across the country for more than thirty years. Radio Sutatenza was a public radio initiative founded by Father José Joaquín Salcedo in 1947. The Organization of American States, the United Nations, the World Bank, and other multilateral organizations were key funders. Its goal was twofold: to educate and evangelize peasants through radio courses. These included primary and secondary education, agricultural production, and catechism. Local parishes made available the materials used for the courses.[33]

Campesinxs did not learn in classrooms but in their homes, accompanied by neighbors who gathered to listen to the classes on the radio. This generated a collective learning environment and, unintentionally, created a political space where Campesinxs discussed a wide range of issues. To some extent, such spaces were plural, but nevertheless highly influenced by Catholic conservativism.

Similar to some of the IMCA members, Radio Sutatenza rejected the idea of the revolution,[34] embracing slow transformation as a methodology for social change. Both Radio Sutatenza and the more conservative members of the IMCA wanted to distance themselves from communism. Being associated with it represented a threat to their existence and survival due to the Cold War atmosphere that ran militarized politics in Colombia at the time. Thus, they adopted a more nuanced language and approach.

The internal tensions increased when, in 1975, three hundred peasants from the ANUC took over the headquarters of another institute directed by El Cura Mejía. ANUC members demanded the mutual administration of the institute. After a failed negotiation, the Jesuits had to cede the occupied facilities. Some members of the IMCA supported the ANUC and helped with the organization of the storming. The incident, apart from demonstrating the ANUC's impetuous desire to express its willpower and obtain political resonance, evidenced the conflictive situation that existed within the IMCA. It also increased the fear of those within the high ranks of the Catholic Church about communism's advancement in the region. Rumors about the IMCA being the next institute to be taken over by the ANUC spread.

El Cura Mejía, afraid to lose the Church's support, began a wave of censorship.[35] The more left-wing members of the IMCA were expelled, and soon the atmosphere of freedom of expression that was characteristic of it transformed. As a consequence, the dialogue between the social doctrine of the Church and Marxist philosophy slowly "went into hiding." However, the IMCA's library remained open for the general public. Unique at its time in size and availability, it was a powerful space for political education. Among its collections, it had a large set of texts on Marxist-Leninist canonical classics of communism, LT, and social Catholicism, among other subjects. People from across the country kept traveling to the IMCA to access the collection. And, although Marxism was no longer taught, the books stimulated readers' imaginations and seeded the ground for other kinds of peasant grassroots education to emerge outside the institute.[36]

Despite Mejia's efforts, the Jesuits removed him from the direction of the IMCA. Gustavo Jiménez replaced him. He was a pragmatic priest who envisioned the construction of an IMCA trademark to achieve self-sustainability. Its economic recovery plan was based on the adaptation of the university's infrastructure to a new production model. He created sheds for storage, bought land to augment cultivation and breeding, and transformed the student dining room into a textile workshop. He also turned from funding the IMCA with local and national money to focusing on obtaining international cooperation resources.[37]

In this scenario of tension, pedagogy was used not only as a channel for liberation but also as an instrument of social control and organization in the spirit of modernity. To that, left- and right-wing factions coincided in that literacy was the starting point to move toward social progress. In other words, whether communist or capitalist, there had to be development. Such development implied the codification of Campesinxs as effective producers and workers in the countryside. Thus, large-scale international development policies intersected with national and local projects where educational programs were key to transform rural subjectivities.

Since much of the knowledge filtered through these programs came from the US agricultural development interventions or the Union of Soviet Socialist Republics (USSR) approaches to agriculture, imperialism and the *coloniality of knowledge* were also at play here.[38] Both communists and capitalists moved through an epistemic linear temporal order in which indigenous, Black, ancestral, traditional, and popular knowledges were located in the realm of backwardness and underdevelopment, whereas development initiatives were seen as being intrinsically linked to modernity and, with this, to the future. The difference between capitalism and communism was then not given by their position toward development and modernity but in how they saw the power structure behind the control and distribution of the means of production and production itself.

This historical or situated perspective allows us to understand that digging where communism and capitalism align and diverge is a critical part of the generation of the agri-environmental transformation needed today to survive—and perhaps even overcome—the current moment of socio-ecological crisis. Influential scholars such as Moore have argued that environmental destruction is the product of capitalism.[39] Although the histories that intersect in the relationship between LTs and rural grassroots organizing in Colombia attest to that, they also reveal that the question about the kinds of relationality and power relations that other modes of production allow for must be at the forefront of the path to open up possibilities for socio-environmental justice and restoration. Indeed, a central issue at stake for more contemporary rural movements in Colombia and other places in Latin America and the Caribbean has been the deconstruction of the development model and the imperial colonial epistemology that it deploys. Parallel to this process, they have constructed their movements around indigenous, Campesinxs, and Black relationalities, cosmologies, and epistemologies that hold sharp critiques to exploitation, oppression, destruction, and genocide under capitalism, while at the same time promoting multispecies relations, temporalities, and spatialities that detour from the imaginaries of progress of both capitalism and communism alike.

In this path, LTs have also been transformed in significant ways, particularly in their incorporation of multispecies and gender justice in their agenda, two axes of justice that were problematic in approaches such as those of Camilo Torres and other former guerrilla members highly influenced by the first wave of LT. In the next section, I discuss how the IMCA's intended and unintended legacies have helped to encourage new articulations between LTs and grassroots rural movements. I reflect on the restorative paths that the interlinkage of alternative economies, regenerative agriculture, and feminist theology promote.

BEYOND THE IMCA'S VISION: MULTISPECIES CARING IN SMALL-SCALE CAMPESINX-OWNED FARMS

Although the IMCA imitated to a large extent the traditional model of the Western university, the curriculum included courses on agrarian unionism and other agrarian-rural organizational systems. Christian leadership courses also took place once a month in intensive five-day sessions. In the first years before el Cura Mejía was removed as director, lessons on the social doctrine of the Church, LTs, and rural emancipation were packed together. These lessons were complemented with field trips to communities in the region that had asked for the IMCA's support.

Priests and nuns walked or rode on the back of a mule or aboard a camper with el Cura Mejía and his students through the mountains in search of leaders interested in accepting the proposal of rural integral education. This project was based in building intergenerational epistemes and capacities, small-scale Campesinx-based and -controlled economies, and restorative and self-sustaining agricultural practices. To implement this model, students learned about the land tenure structure in the country and worked on projects of land redistribution, had several gardens available in which to learn agroecology, were encouraged to learn from wise elders in the community and pass their knowledge on to children, and ran their own weekly markets.

These nuns and priest also supported and embraced collective ways of farming and caring for the land and the territory. Such caring, as my own work on contemporary seed movements attests,[40] moves beyond an anthropocentric understanding of agriculture and connects with what social scientists today have called *multispecies care*.[41] Evidence of this was the explosion of the agroecological movement in Colombia, with hundreds of organizations proliferating across the country.[42]

Many of these organizations are working closely with the local dioceses or with national and international Christianity-based NGOs committed to agri-environmental justice. These organizations, it is important to underscore, are for the most part separated from the evangelical Christian NGOs that have proliferated in Latin America and the Caribbean, bringing with them a radicalization of conservative right-wing values and increasing class, gender, and racial inequalities in the country. On the contrary, they strive to restore not only the earth but also a different kind of Christianity, one that can face the errors of the past and work in the present toward human and more-than-human justice and liberation.

Drawing from the work of Leonardo Boff, many of these organizations saw emancipation not only as a human quest but also as a process that was based in relations of reciprocity between humans and more-than-humans. For Boff, the same political and ethical grounds that sustain the dehumanization of the poor allow and enforce the destruction of the more-than-human and its plurality of relations. Although Boff's work is more contemporary than many of the movements and grassroots organizations embracing LTs and pedagogies in the late '60s, '70s, and '80s, it is one of the most theologically driven developments showcasing the interconnections between the agrarian question, environmental justice, and human and more-than-human emancipation. The work of the IMCA, the Red Nacional de Semillas Libres de Colombia (National Network of Free Seeds of Colombia, RSLC), and other agrarian-based grassroots organizations on the continent, such as La Vía Campesina (LVC), are also good examples of these interconnections.

Velez points out that ecofeminist theology has contributed to strengthening some of these new perspectives both in the academy and on the ground.[43] In conversation with LTs, ecofeminist theology in Latin America has sought to frame eco-modern destruction as intersectional, considering not only issues of class oppression, but also of gender, ethnoracial, and inter-species (in)justice. In this light, the work of Ivone Gebara has contributed to expand the ecofeminist theology perspective positioned in poor urban contexts.[44] Moving away from the hierarchical and anthropocentric epistemology of colonial Christianity toward a nondualistic and interconnected epistemological approach, she articulates a feminist vision of religious biodiversity, a liberation theology that lives through plurality and relationality.

In conversation with Gebara, Salazar has proposed the recovery of the erotic to frame an LT for what she calls "abject bodies," that is, women and ecology.[45] As a scholar positioned in Mexico, her scholarship is traversed with the questions raised by *feminicidios* and the targeted killing of women in domestic violence and criminal activity. These women are, for the most part, poor and, in many cases, rural. Analyzing how similar the mechanisms to exercise violence against peasant, indigenous, and afro-Mexican women are to the ways the state, extractive industries, and drug cartels abuse the environment, she conceptualizes capitalist environmental and gendered violence as tied up in patriarchal systems of power.

Other scholars such as Federici and Merchant had already uncovered the pervasive relationship between capitalism and patriarchy.[46] However, Salazar's analysis shows the specificity of the workings of such relationships in the Latin American context and exposes the intricate role of Christianity in promoting it. An ecofeminist theology of liberation is then an embodied theology of everyday life that restores gender power relations within Christianity, radically transforming epistemic, territorial, and economic power relations within humans and among humans and more-than-humans. Thus, for ecofeminist theology, God's liberating action is no longer androcentric and patriarchal, as it was in the '70s and '80s, when most LTs were written. Very differently, it is based on the relationality implied by the image of the Trinity. This image is reworked under the presupposition that human and more-than-human relations are corporeal, sexual, and erotic. In this case, Salazar frames the erotic as a decolonizing political subversive force of abject bodies. The decolonizing power of the erotic resides in the recognition of corporality as territorial autonomy, as a tribute to the divine that uses the sensual as an affect-epistemology to contest the necrophilic relationships imposed by colonial capitalism into women's bodies and rural people's territories in the Americas.[47]

In addition to these contributions to the strengthening of popular rural social movements on the continent, the recent changes in the Catholic Church, with Papa Francisco's formulation of the *Laudato Si'*, have revived the traditions of LT as a theology that, despite its complicated history, has supported peasants' struggles for justice. Such struggles are intrinsically linked not only to the land, as much of the literature has pointed out, but also fundamentally to their relationships with the territory and the more-than-human worlds that cohabit with them.

CONCLUSION

There is sufficient evidence to demonstrate how Christianity, coloniality, patriarchy, and imperialism have been entangled in continuous processes of domination since 1492 in the Americas and other parts of the world. Such domination has fed capitalism and the ongoing destruction of human and more-than-human worlds. Much of this destruction has happened at the material, spiritual, affective, and epistemic levels. *Misioneros* (missionaries), for example, distorted and displaced ancestral knowledge and collaborated with the creation of dichotomies and binaries that estranged humans from nature.

However, Christianity has had a complex history in which it has not just taken the role of the oppressor. In Latin America and the Caribbean, the Catholic Church and Christian churches have replaced the weakened state institutions in many regions, becoming central for the provision of basic material needs to the communities. In other cases, as I have shown throughout this chapter, mostly priests and nuns at the bottom have articulated their religious practice with struggles for justice, even if that has created tensions and divisions in their own religious institutions.

I began this chapter describing my first impressions at the National Gathering of Seed Savers at the IMCA's house. I would like to close it by going back to my thoughts on the fourth and last day of that gathering. Then, I understood that the transformation of the house from a space of oppression to one of liberation was not simply "ironic." It was the materialization of centuries of social, political, economic, and epistemic struggle of a diverse and often contradictory array of social actors. Despite the terror and the horror of direct and slow violence, these actors have been able to survive and continue the struggle for justice. This conception of justice implies the construction of multispecies collective futures where dignity for humans and more-than-humans guides the horizons of action for mutual care and reciprocity. Historical memory and the everyday material, affective, and cognitive labor of Campesinxs in the Colombian countryside nurture these futures.

Regardless of the scale, liberation pedagogies have been the bridge that has united theology with liberation, sometimes even acting as a barrier for developmentalist approaches to alienate Campesinxs from their labor, bodies, and knowledge. However, such pedagogies have sometimes been used as methods of social control and indoctrination. Fortunately, in the past decades, we have been witnessing the revival of such pedagogies for the common good. Part of the result is the growth of diverse mass social movements that do not get tired of struggling for justice. This struggle has been happening in the form of protest and Campesinxs' everyday work in multispecies regeneration and care.

To finish, it is important to underscore the limitations and the challenges that still face new manifestations of LTs and peasant and agroecological movements. These include their still highly patriarchal organization and the epistemic dominance of expert knowledge that relegates locally based knowledge as complementary but not central to agri-cultural life. Many involved in these movements are aware of these limitations, as we also participate in the feminist movement that has significantly gained traction in Colombia, Argentina, and other Latin American and Caribbean countries in the past ten years. We are committed to continue to work for justice, for the memory of those killed and tortured by the past Colombian governments over so many decades, for those who have survived, and for the ones to come.

NOTES

1. I want to underscore that, under this system, plants and animals belonged to the racialized property system.
2. Peasant smallholders.
3. Eric Holt-Giiménez, *Campesino a Campesino: Voices from Latin America's Farmer to Farmer Movement for Sustainable Agriculture* (Oakland, CA: Food First Books, 2006).
4. Á. Acevedo and N. Jiménez, *Agroecología. Experiencias comunitarias para la agricultura familiar en Colombia* (Bogotá, Colombia: Corporación Universitaria Minuto de Dios-uniminuto; Editorial Universidad del Rosario, 2019); A. J. Echeverry Pérez, *Teología de la liberación en Colombia: Un problema de continuidades en la tradición evangélica de opción por los pobres* (Cali: Programa Editorial, Universidad del Valle, 2007); N. Hernández Vidal, "Pedagogies for Seed Sovereignty: Gendered, Territorial, and Epistemic Dimensions," *Agriculture and Human Values*, 2022, https://doi.org/10.1007/s10460-022-10310-9; N. Hernández Vidal and K. Moore, "Feminist Generative Dissent in Seed Schools in Colombia," in *Engaging Science, Technology and Social. Special Issue on Science and Dissent*, eds. K. Moore and B. Strasser (2022); D. Quilaqueo, S. Quintriqueo, and H. Torres, "Epistemic Characteristics of Mapuche Educational Methods," *Revista Electrónica de Investigación Educativa* 18, no. 1 (2016): 153–65.
5. V. Codina,*¿Qué es la Teología de la Liberación?* (Bogotá, Colombia: Centro de Investigación y Educación Popular, 1988), 5–6.
6. M. Cifuentes Transladiña, *Una mirada a la institución religiosa católica y su incidencia en la sociedad colombiana durante el siglo XX*, Ensayos críticos No. 4 (Bogotá, Colombia: Espacio Crítico, 2008).
7. Martínez Andrade, N. Hernández Vidal and K. Moore, "Feminist"; Hernández Vidal, "Pedagogies."
8. G. Gutiérrez, *Teología de la Liberación: Perspectivas* (Salamanca, Spain: Sígueme Editions, SA, 1972): 387–88, my translation.

9. O. Fals Borda, *Knowledge and People's Power. Lessons with Peasants in Nicaragua, Mexico, and Colombia* (New Delhi: Indian Social Institute, 1988), 10.

10. Mee-Ae Kim, "Libertation and Theology: A Pedagogical Challenge," *The History Teacher, Society for the History of Education* 46, no. 4 (2013), 607.

11. Ibid.

12. H. Moksnes, "Suffering for Justice in Chiapas: Religion and the Globalization of Ethnic Identity," *The Journal of Peasant Studies* 32, no. 3–4 (2005).

13. L. Pinheiro Barbosa, "Educação do Campo [Education for and by the countryside] as a Political Project in the Context of the Struggle for Land in Brazil," *The Journal of Peasant Studies* 44, no. 1 (2017); L. E. Pinto, "La influencia de la Comisión Pastoral de la Tierra (CPT) en la formación del Movimiento de los Trabajadores Rurales Sin Tierra (MST): breve análisis teórico-documental del papel de la religión en los conflictos sociales en Brasil (1954–1984)," *Revista de Estudios Sociales* 51 (2015).

14. Hernández Vidal, "Pedagogies"; Hernández Vidal and Moore, "Feminist."

15. Fals Borda, *Knowledge*; N. Appelbaum, "Whitening the Region: Caucano Mediation and 'Antioqueño Colonization' in Nineteenth-Century Colombia," *Hispanic American Historical Review* 79, no. 4 (1999): 631–67; Hernández Vidal and Moore, "Feminist."

16. Appelbaum, "Whitening."

17. Escobar, *Encountering*.

18. N. Appelbaum, *Mapping the Country of Regions: The Chorographic Commission of Nineteenth-Century Colombia* (Chapel Hill: University of North Carolina Press, 2016).

19. Escobar, *Encountering*.

20. G. M. Palacio, *Naturaleza en Disputa. Ensayos de Historia Ambiental en Colombia* (Bogotá, Colombia: Universidad Nacional de Colombia, 2001).

21. Ibid., 18.

22. Ibid., 19.

23. Fals Borda, *Knowledge*.

24. There are deep and complex discussions about the similarities and differences between both agrarian models of production, exploitation, and oppression. However, I do not have space to develop such an extensive body of work here.

25. Several scholars have elaborated critiques on the green revolution, which took place across the world and adjusted to the local conditions of the many places where it was implemented. Shiva (1991) analyzed the impact of the green revolution in India, showing how it destroyed nature and culture through the imposition of aggressive technoscience and Western scientific epistemes over local knowledges, economies, and ecologies. Other authors (McMichael 2013; Patel 2012; Holt-Giménez 2006; and Friedmann, 1982) have also shown those impacts in Latin America, Africa, and other parts of the world. They argue that the green revolution exported the US food regime, based on agrochemical inputs, hybrid seeds for increased yield production, and a neo-Malthusian philosophy, to the rest of the Third World, aiming to globalize corporate-centered and managed agricultural modernization.

26. M. Taussing, *The Devil and Commodity Fetishism in South America. Thirtieth Anniversary Edition* (Chapel Hill: University of North Carolina Press, 2010), 19.

27. Scholars of the history and sociology of social movements in Colombia, such as Archila (2006), agree that, in this scenario, those who worked the land identified with the mass of the Campesinado and peasantry, even if they were also subjected to or participated in the formation of regimes of ethnoracialization. However, in the decades of the 1940s and 1950s, this changed in important ways when the Campesinx and Indigenous Federation were born (Kalmanovitz 2006). This was the first national organization to separate indigenous peoples and Campesinxs as two different social and political subjects. However, their claims and discourse still centered on the problem of land access, distribution, and redistribution, keeping their narrative in terms of class struggle (Fajardo 2014]; Jaramillo and Cubides 1986).

28. Fajardo, *Las Guerras de la Agricultura Colombiana (1980–2010)* (Colombia: Siglo del Hombre Editores, CLACSO, Siglo XXI editores, 2014).

29. La Violencia was a ten-year period of civil unrest in Colombia (1948–1958) between the liberal and the conservative parties.

30. Fajardo, *Las Guerras,* 36–39.

31. ANUC was promoted by liberal president Carlos Lleras (1966–1970). As Bejarano (1991, 1994) and Zamosc (1992) show, Lleras was committed to carrying out an agrarian reform that had as one of its main objectives the redistribution of land, especially in those areas of the country dominated by the latifundista tenure structure. At the same time, the liberal president saw "the strengthening of the campesinado/peasantry as an essential element to expand markets for the national industry and slow down the pace of the rural-urban rapid migration" (Zamosc 1992, 28, my translation).

32. At the beginning, faculty at the IMCA were already trained as such in other places in the country but they joined it because they believed in the project and its transformative potential. Later on, as students finished the program of study, they became faculty members as well.

33. J. P. Angarita, *La música en el programa educativo de Acción Cultural Popular: Radio Sutatenza y sus usuarios (1955–1970).* Tesis de Maestría. Universidad de los Andes, Colombia, 2016.

34. As Gonzáles (2012) shows, the debate between Camilo Torres (later to become a guerrillero) and other factions of the Catholic Church about the right-wing inclinations of Radio Sutatenza can be found in Torres correspondence with Monseñor Salcedo.

35. Néstor Iván Mejçia Hincapié, *El Ser del Espíritu como Don: Teología Filosófica* (London: Editorial Académica Española, 2015).

36. Ibid.

37. N. E. Malagón Gómez, *Tiempos de Cosecha. Instituto Mayor Campesino: 52 años cultivando líderes y sostenibilidad* (Bogotá, Colombia: Universidad Javeriana, 2015).

38. A. Quijano, *Ensayos En Torno a La Colonialidad Del Poder*. 1a ed. El Desprendimiento (Buenos Aires, Argentina: Ediciones del Signo, 2019).

39. J. W. Moore, *Capitalism in the Web of Life: Ecology and the Accumulation of Capital.* First ed. (New York: Verso, 2015).

40. Hernández Vidal, "Pedagogies."

41. Diego Silva-Garzon, Nathalia Hernandez Vidal, and Christina Holmes, "Wounded Relational Worlds: Destruction and Resilience of Multispecies Relationality in the Age of Climate Change," *Alternautas* 9, no. 1 (2022): 129–62; Rowe, *Toward a Better Worldliness* (Minneapolis: Fortress Press, 2017); M. De la Cadena and M. Blaser, *A World of Many Worlds* (Durham, NC, and London: Durham University Press, 2018); D. Haraway, *Staying with the Trouble: Making Kin in the Chthulucene* (Durham, NC: Duke University Press, 2016); T. L. Miller, *Plant Kin: A Multispecies Ethnography in Indigenous Brazil*, 1st ed. Louann Atkins Temple Women & Culture; Culture Series (Austin: University of Texas Press, 2019); A. Tsing, *The Mushroom at the End of the World: On the Possibility of Life in Capitalist Ruins* (Princeton, NJ: Princeton University Press, 2015).

42. T. León-Sicard, M. Sánchez De Prager, and A. Acevedo Osorio, "Toward a History of Agroecology in Colombia," *Agroecology and Sustainable Food Systems* 41, no. 3–4 (2017): 296–310; Tarazona A. Acevedo and A. Delgado Díaz, "Teología de la Liberación y Pastoral de la Liberación: entre la solidaridad y la insurgencia," *Anuario de Historia Nacional y de las Fronteras* 17, no. 1 (2012): 245–68; J. A. Peña-Torres and J. D. Reina-Rozo, "Agroecology and Communal Innovation: LabCampesino, a Pedagogical Experience from the Rural Youth in Sumapaz Colombia," *Current Research in Environmental Sustainability* (2022).

43. C. Vélez, "Teología Feminista Latinoamericana de la Liberación: Balance y Futuro," *Horizonte* 11, no. 32 (2013): 1801–12.

44. I. Gebara, *Longing for Running Water* (Minneapolis: Fortress Press, 1999). Gebara, *Intuiciones ecofeministas. Ensayo para repensar el conocimiento y la religión* (Madrid: Trotta, 2000).

45. M. Salazar Rojas, "La pertinencia de la teología ecofeminista y su incidencia política ante el feminicidio y el ecocidio actual," *Revista Iberoamericana de Teología* 16, no. 30 (2020): 37–70.

46. Silvia Federici, *Caliban and the Witch*, 2nd, revised ed. (Brooklyn, NY: Autonomedia, 2014); Carolyn Merchant, *Death of Nature: Women, Ecology and the Scientific Revolution* (San Francisco: HarperCollins, 1980).

47. M. Salazar Rojas, "La pertinencia de la teología ecofeminista y su incidencia política ante el feminicidio y el ecocidio actual," *Revista Iberoamericana de Teología* 16, no. 30 (2020), 66.

REFERENCES

Acevedo, Á., and N. Jiménez (comps). *Agroecología. Experiencias comunitarias para la agricultura familiar en Colombia*. Bogotá, Colombia: Corporación Universitaria Minuto de Dios—uniminuto; Editorial Universidad del Rosario, 2019. doi.org/10.12804/tp9789587842326.

Acevedo, Tarazona A., and A. Delgado Díaz. "Teología de la Liberación y Pastoral de la Liberación: entre la solidaridad y la insurgencia." *Anuario de Historia Nacional y de las Fronteras* 17, no. 1 (2012): 245–68.

Angarita, J. P. *La música en el programa educativo de Acción Cultural Popular: Radio Sutatenza y sus usuarios (1955–1970)*. Tesis de Maestría. Universidad de los Andes, Colombia, 2016.

Appelbaum, N. *Mapping the Country of Regions: The Chorographic Commission of Nineteenth-Century Colombia*. Chapel Hill: University of North Carolina Press, 2016.

———. "Whitening the Region: Caucano Mediation and 'Antioqueño Colonization' in Nineteenth-Century Colombia." *Hispanic American Historical Review* 79, no. 4 (1999): 631–67.

Bejarano, J. A. *Historia económica y desarrollo. La historiografía económica sobre los siglos XIX y XX en Colombia*. Bogotá, Colombia: CEREC, 1994.

———. "Industrialización y política económica 1950–1976." *Colombia hoy* 14 (1991).

Cifuentes Transladiña, M. *Una mirada a la institución religiosa católica y su incidencia en la sociedad colombiana durante el siglo XX*. Ensayos críticos No. 4. Bogotá, Colombia: Espacio Crítico, 2008.

Codina, V.*¿Qué es la Teología de la Liberación?* Bogotá, Colombia: Centro de Investigación Educación Popular, 1988.

De la Cadena, M., and M. Blaser. *A World of Many Worlds*. Durham, NC: Duke University Press, 2018.

Echeverry Pérez, A. J. *Teología de la liberación en Colombia: Un problema de continuidades en la tradición evangélica de opción por los pobres*. Cali: Programa Editorial, Universidad del Valle, 2007.

Escobar, Arturo. *Encountering Development: The Making and Unmaking of the Third World*. Princeton, NJ: Princeton University Press, 2012.

Fajardo, Darío. *Las Guerras de la Agricultura Colombiana (1980–2010)*. Colombia: Siglo del Hombre Editores, CLACSO, Siglo XXI editores, 2014.

Fals Borda, O. *Knowledge and People's Power. Lessons with Peasants in Nicaragua, Mexico, and Colombia*. New Delhi: Indian Social Institute, 1988.

———. *Una sociología sentipensante para América Latina*. Buenos Aires: Siglo XXI Editores, 2015.

Fitting, Elizabeth. *Struggle for Maize: Campesinos, Workers, and Transgenic Corn in the Mexican Countryside*. Durham, NC: Duke University Press, 2011.

Federici, Silvia. *Caliban and the Witch*, 2nd, revised ed. Brooklyn, NY: Autonomedia, 2014.

Friedmann, Harriet. "The Political Economy of Food: The Rise and Fall of the Postwar International Food Order." *American Journal of Sociology* 88 (1982): S248–S286.

Gebara, I. *Intuiciones ecofeministas. Ensayo para repensar el conocimiento y la religión*. Madrid: Trotta, 2000.

———. *Longing for Running Water*. Minneapolis, MN: Fortress Press, 1999.

Gonzáles, F. "La correspondencia de Camilo Torres with Radio Sutatenza, 1962." *Boletín Cultural y Bibliográfico* 46, no. 82 (2012): 263–69. Accessed February 22, 2022. https://publicaciones.banrepcultural.org/index.php/boletin_cultural/article/view/240/244.

Gutiérrez, G. *Teología de la Liberación: Perspectivas.* Salamanca, Spain: Sígueme Editions, SA, 1972.

Haraway, D. *Staying with the Trouble: Making Kin in the Chthulucene.* Durham, NC: Duke University Press, 2016.

Hernández Vidal, N. "Pedagogies for Seed Sovereignty: Gendered, Territorial, and Epistemic Dimensions." *Agriculture and Human Values* 39 (2022): 1217–29.

Hernández Vidal, N., and Moore, K. "Feminist Generative Dissent in Seed Schools in Colombia." *Engaging Science, Technology and Social. Special Issue on Science and Dissent* (2022), edited by K. Moore and B. Strasser.

Holt-Giiménez, Eric. *Campesino a Campesino: Voices from Latin America's Farmer to Farmer Movement for Sustainable Agriculture.* Oakland, CA: Food First Books, 2006.

Jaramillo, Jaime Leonidas Mora, and Fernando Cubides. *Colonización coca y guerrilla,* 1a ed. Bogotá: Universidad Nacional de Colombia, 1986.

Kalmanovitz, S. *La agricultura colombiana en el siglo xx.* Centro de Cultura Económica, 2006.

Kim, Mee-Ae. "Libertation and Theology: A Pedagogical Challenge." *The History Teacher, Society for the History of Education* 46, no. 4 (2013): 601–12.

León-Sicard, T., M. Sánchez De Prager, and A. Acevedo Osorio. "Toward a History of Agroecology in Colombia." *Agroecology and Sustainable Food Systems* 41, no. 3–4 (2017): 296–310. doi: 10.1080/21683565.2017.1285843.

León, M., and C. D. Deere. "La mujer rural y la reforma agraria en Colombia." *Cuader–nos de desarrollo Rural.* Bogotá 38 & 39 (1997): 7–23.

Malagón Gómez, N. E. *Tiempos de Cosecha. Instituto Mayor Campesino: 52 años cultivando líderes y sostenibilidad.* Bogotá, Colombia: Universidad Javeriana, 2015.

McMichael, Philip. *Food Regimes and Agrarian Questions.* Halifax, Nova Scotia: Fernwood Press, 2013.

Mejçia Hincapié, Néstor Iván. *El Ser del Espíritu como Don: Teología Filosófica.* London: Editorial Académica Española, 2015.

Merchant, Carolyn. *Death of Nature*: *Women, Ecology and the Scientific Revolution.* San Francisco: HarperCollins, 1980.

Miller, T. L. *Plant Kin: A Multispecies Ethnography in Indigenous Brazil.* First ed. Louann Atkins Temple Women Culture; Culture Series. Austin: University of Texas Press, 2019.

Moksnes, H. "Suffering for Justice in Chiapas: Religion and the Globalization of Ethnic Identity." *The Journal of Peasant Studies* 32, no. 3–4 (2005): 584–607.

Moore, J. W. *Capitalism in the Web of Life: Ecology and the Accumulation of Capital.* First ed. New York: Verso, 2015.

Naranjo Mesa, J. F. *La Teología de la Liberación en el proceso histórico colombiano.* Siglo XX y XXI. Conferencia sobre el Papel de la Iglesia Católica a lo largo de los 200 años de historia nacional. Medellín, Colombia, 2010.

Ojeda, D. "Social Reproduction, Dispossession and the Gendered Workings of Agrarian Extractivism in Colombia." In *Agrarian Extractivism in Latin America,* edited by B. McKay, A. Alonso-Fradejas, and A. Ezquerro-Cañete. Oxfordshire, UK: Routledge, 2021.

Palacio, G. M. *Naturaleza en Disputa. Ensayos de Historia Ambiental en Colombia.* Bogotá, Colombia: Universidad Nacional de Colombia, 2001.

Patel R. C. "Food Sovereignty: Power, Gender, and the Right to Food." *PLoS Med* 9 no. 6 (2012): e1001223. https://doi.org/10.1371/journal.pmed.1001223.

———. "The Long Green Revolution." *The Journal of Peasant Studies* 40, no. 1 (2012): 1–63. https://doi.org/10.1080/03066150.2012.719224.

Peña-Torres, J. A., and J. D. Reina-Rozo. "Agroecology and Communal Innovation: LabCampesino, a Pedagogical Experience from the Rural Youth in Sumapaz Colombia." *Current Research in Environmental Sustainability.* 2022. https://doi.org/10.1016/j.crsust.2022.100162.

Pinheiro Barbosa, L. "Educação do Campo [Education for and by the countryside] as a Political Project in the Context of the Struggle for Land in Brazil." *The Journal of Peasant Studies* 44, no. 1 (2017): 118–43. doi: 10.1080/03066150.2015.1119120.

Pinto, L. E. "La influencia de la Comisión Pastoral de la Tierra (CPT) en la formación del Movimiento de los Trabajadores Rurales Sin Tierra (MST): breve análisis teórico-documental del papel de la religión en los conflictos sociales en Brasil (1954–1984)." *Revista de Estudios Sociales* 51 (2015): 76–88.

Quijano, A. *Ensayos En Torno a La Colonialidad Del Poder.* 1a ed. El Desprendimiento. Buenos Aires, Argentina: Ediciones del Signo, 2019.

Quilaqueo, D., S. Quintriqueo, and H. Torres. "Epistemic Characteristics of Mapuche Educational Methods." *Revista Electrónica de Investigación Educativa* 18, no. 1 (2016): 153–65.

Rowe, T. *Toward a Better Worldliness: Ecology, Economy, and the Protestant Tradition.* Minneapolis: Fortress Press, 2017.

Salazar Rojas, M. "La pertinencia de la teología ecofeminista y su incidencia política ante el feminicidio y el ecocidio actual." *Revista Iberoamericana de Teología* 16, no. 30 (2020): 37–70. https://doi.org/10.48102/ribet.16.30.2020.46

Silva-Garzon, Diego, Nathalia Hernández Vidal, and Christina Holmes. "Wounded Relational Worlds: Destruction and Resilience of Multispecies Relationality in the Age of Climate Change." *Alternautas* 9, no. 1 (2022): 129–62. https://doi.org/10.31273/an.v9i1.1172.

Taussing, M. *The Devil and Commodity Fetishism in South America.* Thirtieth Anniversary Edition. Chapel Hill: University of North Carolina Press, 2010.

Tsing, A. *The Mushroom at the End of the World: On the Possibility of Life in Capitalist Ruins.* Princeton, NJ: Princeton University Press, 2015.

Vélez, C. "Teología Feminista Latinoamericana de la Liberación: Balance y Futuro." *Horizonte* 11, no. 32 (2013): 1801–12. ISSN 2175-5841.

Zamosc, L. "Transformaciones agrarias y luchas campesinas en Colombia: Un balance retrospectivo (1950–1990)." *Análisis político* (1992): 75–132.

Chapter 3

Moana Eco-Theology
Toward an Eco-Theology of Commoning

George Zachariah

Eco-theologies are contextual theological reflections and praxis responding to the crisis of Mother Earth. However, in recent times, eco-theology has become a mainstream theology with "universal categories and metanarratives. Indigenous and subaltern social movements contest these dominant perceptions of the ecological crisis and offer us new insights and visions to engage in faith-based ecological activism. They invite us to go beyond our dominant feel-good eco-theological discourses and practices of romanticizing the earth, and to perceive ecological crisis in an intersectional way, privileging the voices of the communities that are disproportionally affected by different manifestations of ecological injustice.

The environmental history of Oceania and Aotearoa New Zealand is the history of the colonization of the commons perpetuated by settler colonialism, neoliberal capitalism, and institutional racism. *Moana* eco-theology problematizes mainstream eco-theologies and proposes alternative methodological standpoints from which to envision and initiate the liberation of the planet and the people. This chapter is an attempt to reflect upon *moana* eco-theology from the commons perspective, drawing from the struggles of the *tangata whenua* (people of the land) to liberate their *moana* (water bodies) and *whenua* (land).

COMMONS: AN ALTERNATIVE ECO-JUSTICE PARADIGM

The indigenous and subaltern engagement with the ecological crisis interprets the crisis as the colonization of the commons. The commons here signifies the commonwealth of the community of creation that births, sustains, and nurtures the movement of life—the land, water, forests, atmosphere, and commoners (members of the communities that live in communion with the commons from time immemorial) as well. This discernment calls for a new problematization of the current ecological crisis as ecological injustice and ecological racism. The crisis of the earth is more than the changes in the mercury level or the extinction of different species or the decrease in the natural green canopy over the earth. Rather, it is the colonization of the commons due to corporate appropriation of the commonwealth, which destroys the integrity of creation and uproots the commoners from their traditional abodes and livelihoods. Colonization of the commons is hence known as de-commoning.

Commons are nature's gift to the community of creation. They are spaces shared, protected, and nurtured by the community for mutual flourishing. Traditional commons signify an organic connection between land, water, forest, and the subsistence communities. This space is the locus of production and flourishing of life through nonexploitative planetary solidarity between humans and nature. The commons are also intimately and organically intertwined with the struggles and aspirations of these communities. Commons are therefore alternative spaces and socioeconomic and ecological relationships that contest the prevailing order through practicing and propagating the politics, ethics, and spirituality of a nonexploitative economy of life.

The British enclosure movement, which began in the twelfth century and peaked in the eighteenth century, was the precursor of de-commoning. The traditional communities in Britain used to have access to common lands for livestock grazing and collection of firewood. With the enclosure movement, these common lands became privatized (enclosed). Pastures, forests, and water bodies used by subsistence communities were stolen and declared to be private property by the kings, the aristocracy, and the land-holding nobility. From its monarchical beginnings, with the advent of capitalism, the enclosure movement evolved into a legitimized form of capitalist enclosure of the commons within the capitalist economy. The enclosure movement was perhaps the oldest attempt to convert the commons into commodity and capital, an example of "primitive accumulation." These commons were not just "resources" (land, water bodies, forests, etc.); rather, commons were constituted by commoners and their social practices and systems of planetary solidarity (commoning) that contested the logic of the market for the flourishing of life. The enclosure movement was an attempt to destroy this commons paradigm and the ethics of mutual flourishing of the flora and fauna through self-governance. The British enclosure movement, like its contemporary avatars, therefore, needs to be understood as a hegemonic and violent institution that erased the memory of relational and egalitarian social and ecological relations of the commoners.

Enlightenment rationality, combined with an anthropocentric Judeo-Christian theology, further contributed to the paradigm of de-commoning. Since the commons defies the logic of market control and state control, it embodies the potential to destabilize unjust systems and practices. Elevating the rational human being and considering it the crown of creation, endowed with the vocation to subdue the earth, invalidated the intrinsic worth of the working class, subaltern communities, and other-than-human persons. As a result, the indigenous and subaltern ethic of mutual respect and coexistence was replaced by an ethic of domination and alienation.

Colonialism further contributed to the destruction of the subsistence ethics of the commoners by alienating them from the commons. Colonial legal systems declared the commons as *terra nullius* and occupied them as the eminent domain of the colonial state. The doctrine of *terra nullius* was introduced for the first time by the bull issued by Pope Urban II in 1095, according to which the lands occupied by "pagans" were legally considered unoccupied and subsequently claimed by the Christian colonizing nations. The history of colonialism is also the history of the use of *terra nullius* to colonize the indigenous commons and to dispossess the commoners. For Christopher Columbus and several other colonizers, this act of occupation and dispossession involved naming the land by erasing the existing indigenous names. Alien legal and administrative systems were imposed and enforced, desecrating the commons by destroying the earth-healing sacred ethos and practices of the indigenous communities. For colonialists, nature was either a resource pile waiting to be plundered and engineered or wilderness needing to be fenced off from the traditional subsistence communities. This obsession with wilderness exposes the racial undertones of de-commoning. As Ramchandra Guha observes, enclosure of wilderness was "a form of environmentalism oblivious to both the legacy of slavery, colonialism, and imperialism and the voices, literatures, and imaginaries from people and communities embedded in struggles for postcolonial emancipation."[1]

A commons is more than a geographical space. Rather it is a paradigm—a paradigm of organic socioeconomic and ecological relationships, social ethics, shared socioeconomic practices, and a covenant of shared responsibility and obligation. This distinctive politics of the commons makes the commons an alternative economy of life in the neoliberal, market-driven world. "The ethos of the commons knit people together with their neighbors and with the land, plus the local fens, forest and bodies of water. Inhabitants and habitats are one inseparable whole."[2]

Mainstream Eco-Theologies and Religious Environmentalism: A Critical Review

The distress of the earth has inspired people of different faith traditions to engage theologically with the environmental crisis and to initiate ministries of creation care, informed by their scriptures and theological traditions. That has led to the emergence of religious environmentalism, and eco-theologies continue to challenge the faithful to engage in ministries of creation care for the restoration of creation. Roger Gottlieb's description of religious environmentalism summarizes the rationale for religious engagement with the ecological crisis:

> Religious environmentalism is a worldwide movement of political, social, ecological, and cultural action. As expressions of a particular religion, in ecumenical alliances with other traditions, through loose networks of spiritually committed activists, and in coalitions with secular environmental organizations, hundreds of groups have resisted global warming, destructive economic "development," dangerous toxic waste dumps, reckless resource extraction, mindless consumerism and simple waste. In a wonderful pattern of interfaith cooperation, believers have shown that they are capable of actively working with people whose theologies are quite different from their own. Contrary to the widespread secular liberal belief that religion is inherently antidemocratic, religious environmentalists have shown both a broad openness and a deep civic concern.[3]

The last two decades of the twentieth century witnessed the emergence of religious environmentalism and eco-theologies all over the world. They have been successful in inspiring the faithful to engage in ministries of creation care as expression of their faith. However, they tend to follow the politics of the mainstream liberal environmentalism, and, as a result, they have failed to identify the connection between ecological injustice and wider social and economic injustice. A methodological commitment to affirm the agency and the epistemological privilege of indigenous and subaltern communities, the primary victims of environmental injustice, seems to be missing in our mainstream eco-theologies and religious environmentalism. Their inability or, rather, reluctance to recognize the correlation between social location (race, gender, ethnicity, class, sexual orientation) and access to ecological wellness and well-being exposes the racial, patriarchal, and class bias of the dominant eco-theologies and ministries.

Along with its liberal environmentalist moorings, it is also important to recognize how the dominant strands of religious environmentalism are infected with the Religious Right and the fanatic and fundamentalist groups who propagate eco-fascism and supremacist ideologies. We see traces of eco-fascism and green nationalism in the manifesto of the perpetrator of the Christchurch, New Zealand, shooting. While resting on the backbone of fascism, this manifesto deploys the language of religious environmentalism to greenwash white supremacy and propagate hatred toward people of color. Bigotry, Islamophobia, and racism thus become means for ecological restoration. As the manifesto categorically suggests, the annihilation of a population (immigrants and people of color) is a prerequisite to ensure the well-being of the planet (white people and pristine nature).[4]

We see the same fascist and supremacist tendencies in the Zionist and Hindutva environmentalisms. Zionist environmentalism's greenwash of occupation is a major hurdle for the Palestinian struggles for self-determination and independence. Right from the beginning, environmental rhetoric has been part of the Zionist propaganda. The environmental campaign of the Zionist organizations to transform the desolate desert of Palestine into "a blooming green European terrain of forest" has resulted in the "planting of forests directly on sites where Palestinian Arab villages and mosques once stood, thus erasing the evidence of the Arab and Muslim presence in the name of environmental sustainability and Israeli Jewish sovereignty."[5]

Emma Tomalin's book, *Biodivinity and Biodiversity: The Limits to Religious Environmentalism*,[6] critically evaluates the dominant trends in Indian religious environmentalism. The environmental initiatives of the Hindu Right in India make it difficult to distinguish genuine concern for the environment from the broader politics of the Hindutva fanatics. In his analysis of "eco-casteism," Mukul Sharma observes that the history of caste has shaped the history of environment in India. Sharma elaborates two distinctive traits of eco-casteism. First, by glorifying the casteist ancient Indian culture, eco-casteism valorizes and legitimizes casteist traditions as organic and natural. Second, eco-casteism has "created a concept of natural and social order where people, place, occupation, and knowledge are characterized by pollution and ritual cleanliness; where bodies, behaviours, situations, and actions are isolated, 'out of place,' and 'untouched,' because of deep-down hierarchical boundaries."[7]

Eco-casteism perpetuates casteism by attributing ecological motifs and legitimizations to the ideology and structures of casteism. According to O. P. Dwivedi, "the Hindu caste system can be seen as progenitor of the concept of sustainable development."[8] Kailash Malhotra elaborates it further: "The caste system . . . was actually based on an ancient concept of sustainable development which disciplined the society by partitioning the use of natural resources according to specific occupations (or castes); and created the right social milieu in which sustainable patterns of resource use were encouraged to emerge."[9] Eco-casteism thus offers justification for the caste system through nature and perpetuates the caste system as an ecological model.

This critical review of mainstream religious environmentalism is not meant to discourage or reject faith-based eco-justice public ministries. Rather, it is an invitation to be suspicious of the politics of our theologies and faith-based public engagement in order to develop alternative eco-theologies and faith-based eco-justice ministries that are committed to creating a new world less contaminated with ideologies and practices of exploitation and exclusion.

CONTEXTUAL ECO-THEOLOGIES: METHODOLOGICAL STANDPOINTS

Contextual eco-theologies like *moana*[10] eco-theology are constructive and creative attempts from the margins to problematize the ecological crisis at the interface of interlocking systems and practices of oppression and marginalization and to develop alternative theological reflections and eco-justice ministries informed by their cosmologies, traditional wisdom, and community practices of resilience and planetary solidarity. Contextual eco-theologies explore how care of creation is integrally connected with the decolonizing life-flourishing struggles of indigenous and subaltern communities. They examine how dominant expressions of creation care are envisioned and practiced at the expense of the communities at the margins. They evaluate the racial, class, gender, and ethnic bias of various ecological worldviews, theologies, and projects. They uncover what has been stolen, commodified, thingified, and colonized through the colonization of the commons. Contextual and intersectional eco-theologies are therefore transgressive and transformative.

MOANA ECO-THEOLOGY: A BRIEF INTRODUCTION

Oceania is a region that consists of the islands of the Pacific Ocean and the seas around them. Unlike in other continental groupings, it is the *moana* that links the Oceania communities together. Colonialism not only plundered the *moana* and *moana* communities but also colonized the worldviews and the self-understanding of the region. Colonial narratives projected the smallness and the remoteness of the islands in the vast ocean. As Epeli Hau'ofa, the renowned Tongan and Fijian scholar rightly observed, the Pacific is not isolated "islands in the sea"; rather, the Pacific is a "sea of islands." For the Oceanic ancestors, *moana* was a large world in which they moved and mingled, unhindered by imperial boundaries—sailing, peddling, and weaving.[11]

For the colonialists and missionaries, the Pacific was "a paradise of noble savages living in harmony with nature." Pacific people were "simultaneously lost and degraded souls to be pacified, Christianized, colonized, and civilized."[12] Even today, we witness how legacies of colonialism continue the colonizing mission in the region. Development and globalization, the new waves of colonialism, have succeeded in keeping the Pacific as a region of neocolonial dependency and a region of importance for the security of economic and military interests of the West and China. But the Pacific people are determined to decolonize their minds, identities, *moana*, and land. The slogan of the Pacific Climate Warriors proclaims their resolve: "We are not drowning, we are fighting."[13] *Moana* eco-theology needs to be placed in this history of colonialism and neoliberal capitalism and in the courageous and creative resilience of the communities to decolonize themselves and their commons.

Winston Halapua, the retired archbishop of the Anglican Church in Aotearoa New Zealand and Polynesia, in his reflections on *theomoana*, begins with a foundational question: "Can theologies and ethics continue to work in isolation from each other at the cost of the extinction of most living species or all the earth?"[14] *Moana* eco-theology begins from this discernment of the signs of the times. The Pacific region is the ground zero of the climate crisis. Pacific nations like Kiribati and Tuvalu and their low-lying atolls are disappearing from the face of the earth because of sea-level rise due to climate change. Reflecting upon the experience of the Pacific islanders, Tuvaluan theologian and climate activist Maina Talia observes that, "relocation literally means our death, as it entails profound losses for us—loss of our land, loss of our culture, loss of our language and the loss of our identity."[15] Along with global warming, agribusiness, genetically modified foods, and corporate conversion of farmlands into real estate properties threaten the food sovereignty of the subsistence communities in the region. In the conflict between profit and guardianship, the rivers and waterways continue to decline from the pressure to export food. Confiscation and commodification of indigenous land not only colonizes the land but also desecrates this sacred space.

For the *moana* communities, the Pacific understanding of relationality is the hermeneutical key to decolonizing the commons and the commoners. We see the same logic of colonialism in the dominant practices of development, which is imposed upon the region in the name of progress and economic growth. As Upolu Luma Vaai rightly observes, development continues to desecrate the sacred value of relationality and colonize the *itulagi* (lifeworld).[16] In *moana* eco-theology, *moana* affirms this principle of relationality. According to Winston Halapua, "Moana as a dynamic metaphor is derived and energized from an inherent welling-up from within one's self and a yearning to be connected together with others. Yearning for interconnectedness is fundamental to life and is like the necessity of having an umbilical cord. The relationship of the individual to the placenta or the source of nourishment is imperative to the sustaining of life."[17]

Halapua identifies five Oceanic values, which are foundational for developing a *moana* eco-theology; *manakitanga* (hospitality), *tikanga* (identity), *kotahitanga* (unity), *talanoa* (sharing stories), and *taonga* (sharing of gifts). In the Polynesian worldview, *manakitanga* is the expression of deep love for the entire community of creation for their wellness and well-being. *Moana* eco-theology is rooted in the *moana tikanga*, which is an inclusive identity founded on *moana* ethics and customs. *Kotahitanga* signifies indigenous unity and solidarity. Engaging with one another always leads to mutual empowerment. *Talanoa* represents an open and safe space for sharing stories. *Moana* eco-theology emerges from the face-to-face encounter of diverse communities with deep and engaged listening. *Moana* is a *taonga*, a gift, commons; not a private property to occupy and colonize. *Moana* eco-theology, in short, is a *talanoa* founded on the ethical principles of relationality to celebrate unity and solidarity of all the children of *moana* so that they may flourish and celebrate life. These indigenous values and practices continue to inspire the Pacific communities, and their eco-justice witness testifies their attempt to reclaim these visions and practices and reformulate them relevantly in our times.

AOTEAROA NEW ZEALAND: COLONIZATION OF THE *MOANA* AND THE *WHENUA*[18]

"Colonisation is a *process* of dispossession and control rather than a historical artefact, and now it takes new forms. These forms may be less obviously violent, but they still deny Indigenous people the right to be fully free in their own lands."[19] This observation by Moana Jackson, a renowned lawyer, Māori-rights activist and teacher, summarizes the history of colonization and its continued impact on Māori and other indigenous communities in Aotearoa New Zealand.

Even though European voyages to Aotearoa began in the seventeenth century, the large influx of European settlers started only after 1840. By the end of the nineteenth century, the settler population surged to almost half a million people. According to historian Michael King, it was "the promise of prosperity and healthier environments, prospects for social advancement without the hurdles of a class system and, for investors, opportunities to enlarge capital"[20] that converted Aotearoa into a British settler nation, with its interlocking forms of oppression, namely, racism, white supremacy, heteropatriarchy, and capitalism. Colonial dispossession and capitalist plunder made the *tangata whenua* (people of the land) landless on their very land.

As Paul Tapsell rightly observes, "New Zealand is founded on extractive exploitation, depleting both *tangata* (indigenous people) and *whenua* (land)."[21] It is important here to understand the connection between colonialism and capitalism. The first half of the nineteenth century witnessed a growing crisis within the British capitalist economy, and the new colonies provided the British capitalist class opportunities to extract cheaper materials, create new markets for their products, and find cheap labor. To that end, the New Zealand Company, chartered in the United Kingdom, was established in 1841 for the systematic colonization of New Zealand. However, Māori society was not a fertile setting in which settler colonialism and capitalism could grow. Henry Sewell, a justice minister in the 1860s, observed that one of the objectives for introducing the 1865 Native Lands Act was "the detribalization of the Natives—to destroy, if it were possible, the principle of communism which ran through the whole of their institutions, upon which their social system was based and which stood as a barrier in the way of all attempts to amalgamate the Native race into our own social and political system."[22]

Settler colonialism unleashed its capitalist exploitation through "accumulation by dispossession." New laws were introduced to outlaw the indigenous practice of communal ownership of land, which led to large-scale industrial exploitation of natural resources. Māori land was confiscated and sold to individual settlers, and Māori were proletarianized. The original inhabitants of the land thus became landless laborers, dependent on settler capitalists for their survival. Māori resistance and resilience were met with violent retaliation by the government. This legacy of colonialism and capitalist development on stolen land continues in Aotearoa in this era of neoliberal capitalism.[23] Why did the Māori resist the ethos and institutions of settler colonialism and capitalism? For Māori, the *moana* and *whenua* are sacred, and, hence, colonizing the *moana* and *whenua* is nothing but desacralizing the sacred waters and land. In the Māori cosmology, creation is an intricate network of relationships in which all forms of life are mutually defined, linked, and animated by *hau* (wind, breath, life force). *Hau* drives the whole world, not just people. *Hau* emerged at the beginning of the cosmos. *Hau* binds their life journeys together. Colonization of the commons is therefore the destruction of the *hau*.

It is in this context that we need to revisit the Enlightenment notions of ocean and the cartography of Captain James Cook, keeping in mind that the Enlightenment was not only a product of capitalist development but also a supporter of its further expansion. The Enlightenment logic separates mind and matter, culture and nature. It objectifies and classifies things. Captain Cook's voyage was based on this logic of Enlightenment, and it shaped the laws of the sea and control over the ocean. Captain Cook's cartography reduced the *moana* into a static expanse, divided by lines of latitude and longitude, and mathematically partitioned and measured the *moana*. Scattered islands were depicted as vacant expanses, waiting to be explored, claimed, and ruled by European monarchs and settler capitalists.[24] And the rest is history. As Geoffrey Park observes, "When the smoke of the colonists' fires cleared at the end of the nineteenth century, New Zealand had become a different country . . . Huge slices of the ancient ecosystem were missing, evicted, extinguished."[25] However, the dominant ecological discourses and theologies tend to romanticize the landscape, forgetting the history of settler colonialism and capitalism. Today it has become normal to talk about ecology and eco-theology without reference to racism and white supremacy, ignoring *Te Tiriti o Waitangi*.[26] Colonization of the *moana*, the *whenua*, and the Māori is the environmental history of Aotearoa New Zealand. Bill Wallace exposes this brutal experience of de-commoning in his poems of resilience:

> Life fires that cremated irreplaceable flora and fauna,
> rage and guilt burn my heart but cannot rewrite history,
> shape bicultural futures or create indigenous spiritualities
> until earth becomes our placenta and this raped soil, our tabernacle:
> for liberation grows from the land,
> nurturing from the womb of nature
> and without beauty of feeling
> justice and wisdom are consumed by those incinerating gods of
> Profit, Power and Paternalism.[27]

This poem portrays the legacies of colonialism in the era of globalization and neoliberal capitalism. "The incinerating gods of Profit, Power and Paternalism" continue to devour the commons and the commoners. As Wallace opines, resilience against the colonizing forces should emerge from the Māori and indigenous worldviews and spiritualities. Māori identify themselves as *tangata whenua*, affirming that they belong to the *whenua* rather than that the *whenua* belongs to them. This also signifies kinship, the relationship between the Supreme Being, ancestors, people, and the land. *Whenua* also means placenta, and it symbolizes the organic relationship between people and the land. Land cannot be sold. Land provides the community with identity, sustenance, clothing, shelter, and the sacred space to perform their rituals.[28] These indigenous cosmological visions and practices are still respected and continued in Aotearoa New Zealand, and they inspire and inform contemporary initiatives of commoning contesting different manifestations of the colonization of commons.

Land as covenant is a foundational affirmation of the Māori. A landless Māori is a nonperson. Māori identity is integrally connected with one's canoe, tribe, ancestral mountain, ancestral river, and marae. *Te Tiriti o Waitangi* is understood as a covenant between the British Crown and *tangata whenua*, ensuring them land rights. *Whenua* as ancestral land (*papatipu*) is central to the Māori worldview and spirituality. Māori are traditionally buried in their ancestral land. Burying the placenta in the ancestral land signifies the link of the new life to the *whenua, Atua* (Supreme Being), *tipuna* (ancestors), and *tangata*. This notion of the *whenua* as ancestral land is a spiritual force that inspires the contemporary land struggles in Aotearoa.

Whenua as *papatuanuku* (earth mother) is a profound Māori eco-theological affirmation. Here, land is respected as an ancestor, a spiritual being, and an earth mother. Land is therefore *tapu* (sacred). It is the lifeline of the community. *Tikanga* (ethics) principles are in place for the use and treatment of land. *Rahui* (sacred ban) is used to reduce exploitation of the land to facilitate regeneration. Human vocation is to become the guardians (*kaitiaki*) of the treasures of the earth. The notion of land as kin makes it imperative on the community to decolonize the land.

COMMONING: DECOLONIZING ECOLOGICAL ACTIVISM

The commons paradigm challenges us to see the world through eyes that are not blinded by the logic of neoliberal market economy. It enables us to discern our vocation as commoning—to realize an economy that flourishes and celebrates life. Commoning is reclaiming our organic connectedness with nature and each other by coming out of the imperial and capitalist worldview of conquest and plunder. It is the ethical courage to denounce the morality of the market and to affirm the potential of planetary solidarity to transform the face of the earth. Commoning offers a credible alternative to the neoliberal development paradigm. It facilitates the flourishing of the commons and the commoners by reducing inequality and social exclusion and celebrating life in abundance.

A cursory analysis of the history of environmental activism in Aotearoa reveals that most of the mainstream campaigns and their ecological visions are rooted in the dominant colonial understanding of nature. As Amanda Thomas opines, "this position has often required the active denial of Māori sovereignty, and continues to underpin both national conservation policy and Pākehā nationalism."[29] Hence, it is imperative to draw from the *Te tiriti o Waitangi* and the courageous campaigns of the Māori and their allies to decolonize their *whenua* and the *moana*.

Te tiriti o Waitangi offers Māori "full, exclusive possession of their Lands and Estates, Forests, Fisheries and other properties so long as it is their wish and desire to retain in their possession."[30] However, this covenant was broken to continue the neocolonial aggression on the commons and the commoners. Māori movements of resistance and resilience against the colonization and commodification of the *moana* and *whenua* are the fertile land that can sprout a relevant eco-theology of commoning for Aotearoa. Te Whanau-a-Apanui's historic and symbolic resistance against offshore oil exploration in their ancestral waters and the ongoing struggle to protect *wahi tapu* and the *whenua* of Ihumatao are two significant epistemological sources for a Māori eco-theology.

In 2011, when the government issued to Petrobras a permit to explore for oil in the ancestral waters of the Te Whanau-a-Apanui, the Te Whanau-a-Apanui were outraged. They sailed *San Pietro*, their iwi fishing boat, into the path of *Orient Explorer*, Petrobras's oil exploration vessel. When the captain of the ship asked them to stay away, this was their response: "We will not be moving, we will be doing some fishing. We wish to reiterate that this is not a protest. We are defending tribal waters and our rights from reckless Government policies and the threat of deep-sea drilling, which our *hapu* have not consented to and continue to oppose. We have a duty to uphold the mana of our *hapu* here in our territorial waters."[31] However, the High Court issued a verdict, declining to overturn the permit given to Petrobras to drill for oil in the ancestral waters. In 2012, Petrobras announced its decision to quit its oil exploration in New Zealand for "economic" reasons.

As we gather from the Māori resistance against oil exploration in the ancestral waters, colonization of the *moana* has been the history of settler colonialism and neoliberal capitalism. In 1965, the government's sovereignty over the *moana* was extended out to three miles from the coast. In 1977, it was further extended out to twelve miles, and, in 1982, to two hundred miles, defining the oceanic Exclusive Economic Zone. This enclosure of the *moana* is a quantifying and commodifying cartography, alienating traditional communities from their *moana*. Settler colonialism and neoliberal capitalism are determined to commodify and privatize water flows, forests, flora and fauna, geothermal sources, the seabed, the foreshore, and minerals. Commons have become commodities for corporate plunder, and that has awakened indigenous and subaltern communities all over the world to protect and restore the commons. Ecological restoration is integrally connected with the self-determination and sovereignty of the indigenous communities over the commons.

Colonization of the land is an ongoing reality. Ihumatao, home for the Māori for more than eight hundred years, is a site of clash between two worldviews: the *whenua* as home and the *whenua* as commodity. "I am the

Whenua; the Whenua is me"; "This is our whakapapa, this is our identity, this is the thing that allows us to stand strong in this world."[32] These testimonies explain the politics, ethics, and spirituality of the Ihumatao movement. The premediated war initiated by the British Crown against the Kingitanga in 1863 was a war against the communities in Ihumatao as well. The very communities that fed and protected the settlers were driven out from their ancestral land. The land was confiscated and granted to the Wallace family from Scotland. In 2016, the Wallace family sold the land to Fletcher Building. In 2017, Fletcher Building decided to construct 480 houses on Ihumatao. This is the context in which the Save Our Unique Landscape (SOUL) movement came into being and started a historic struggle to reclaim the *whenua*. The movement's mission is to protect and reclaim the *whenua* from corporate takeover. Its vision is to restore the *whenua*, which is to be held for the benefit of all the people of Aotearoa to enjoy as an open, green, and historic reserve. And their values are *kotahitanga* (unity), *manaakitanga* (care for), *aroha* (compassion), *kaitiakitanga* (guardianship), *rangimarie* (peacefulness), and *whakapono* (belief, trust).

Our search for alternatives should lead us beyond a study of commons to the organic activity of commoning. Commoning is a verb, not a noun. We are surrounded with commoners all over the world who are involved in the politics of commoning. "Commoning is an attitude, an ethic, an impulse—a way of being that is deeply inscribed within the human species. But it is up to us to make it thrive. We must *choose* to practice commoning and reflect on the impact on our lives and the earth, the more consciously, the more better."[33] In the context of settler colonialism and neoliberal capitalism, this is the political responsibility of the indigenous and subaltern communities and their allies.

COMMONS AND COMMONING: AN ALTERNATIVE ECO-THEOLOGICAL STANDPOINT

Commons and commoning offer alternative eco-theological standpoints from which to reimagine our theologies and praxis of earth care and flourishing of life. Commons and commoning affirm the situatedness of our eco-theologies in the particularities of each commons. This paradigm privileges the perspectives and politics of the commoners by exposing the correlation between unjust social relations and ecological injustice. Commons challenges the Judeo-Christian, anthropocentric cosmologies by drawing from the panentheistic traditions and cosmologies of the indigenous communities.

Our exploration of the *moana* eco-theology offers an alternative standpoint from which to engage in eco-theological reflections and eco-justice ministries. Eco-theology originates from the pathos of the community, and hence the *moana* and *whenua,* the living and breathing commons at the margins, colonized, stolen, and occupied by settler colonialism, white supremacy and neoliberal capitalism are its loci. The *moana* and *whenua* are sites of contestation—contestation of different ecological visions, practices, virtues, ethics, projects, and policies. These contestations not only expose and challenge settler colonialism, white supremacy, and neoliberal capitalism but also propose alternative ecological visions, politics, and ethics. *Moana* eco-theology affirms that annihilation of racism and redemption of the earth are integrally connected.

A *moana* eco-theology begins with a deeper engagement with the indigenous traditions around the commons. Indigenous ecological visions emerge from their constant interaction with the commons. A deeper engagement with the commoners and their struggles for rights over the commons is a major epistemological source for *moana* eco-theology. Indigenous spirituality, rituals, and religiosity are resources that inform a *moana* eco-theology. Nevertheless, in pluralistic societies, there is also the danger of assimilation and integration of these traditions, which are always detrimental to the interests of indigenous and subaltern communities. It is in this context that biculturalism emerged as an alternative concept in Aotearoa New Zealand, affirming Māori sovereignty yet practicing deep solidarity between communities.

What is the meaning of this deep solidarity in *moana* eco-theology? Deep solidarity for *moana* eco-theology begins with the *talanoa* of sharing our stories. As we share the stories of corporate colonization of our commons and our resolve to contest them and to reclaim our commons through commoning, we practice deep solidarity. The testimony of Tina Ngata is an illustration of this *talanoa*:

> My story, as a Māori mother marching for land rights alongside my brothers and sisters of Ihumātao, is connected to the young Mohawk woman making a stand for her sacred ancestral waters being stolen from beneath her very feet by multinational corporations. My story is connected to that of a young man ripped away from his family in Ghana and transported by Portuguese slave runners to be sold to a plantation owner in the USA. It is connected to his descendant, being pulled over for no apparent reason on the streets of DC. My story is connected to the Berber woman in 15th century North Africa running for her life from Crusaders. It is connected to the African child whose mother cannot access healthcare because of US sanctions upon her country. My story is connected to my Kashmiri brother caged in his own home, staring out the window at his lands, wondering if his world will ever be the same again. It is connected to my sister in Hong Kong, on the ground, bleeding onto the tarmac out of her nose, cracked by the truncheon of enforced Chinese law. My story is connected to my brothers and sisters in Linwood Mosque who will never, ever recover from the entitlement of white supremacists to claim this land as theirs, with complete

rights to all who walk upon it. All of these stories are woven together by the Doctrine of Discovery, and we cannot wait another moment to dismantle it.[34]

An eco-theology of commoning, emerging from the crucible of indigenous and subaltern struggles to decolonize the commons, is an invitation to practice deep solidarity and to reweave our planetary mat.

NOTES

1. Ferdinand, "Behind the Colonial Silence of Wilderness," 183.
2. Menizes, *Reclaiming the Commons for the Common Good*, 27.
3. Gottlieb, *A Greener Faith*, 113.
4. Diwakar, "How White Supremacists Wield Environmentalism to Mask Racism."
5. Pellow, *What Is Critical Environmental Justice?*, 120.
6. Tomalin, *Biodivinity and Biodiversity*.
7. Sharma, *Caste and Nature*, xix.
8. O. P. Dwivedi, "Satyagraha for Conservation," 159.
9. Kailash Malhotra quoted in Sharma, *Caste and Nature*, 10.
10. *Moana* is a word used in Māori and other Polynesian languages to signify "ocean" or any water body.
11. Hau'ofa, "Our Sea of Islands," 7.
12. Hau'ofa, "The Ocean in Us," 398.
13. Wallace, "Regeneration," in *Singing the Circle*.
14. Halapua, "Theomoan."
15. Maina Talia, "We Have No Right to Be Silent," 17.
16. Vaai, "We Are Therefore We Live."
17. Halapua, "Theomoana," 24.
18. *Whenua* is the Māori word for land.
19. Jackson, "Where to Next? Decolonisation and the Stories in the Land," 134.
20. King, *The Penguin History of New Zealand*, 170.
21. Tapsell, *Kainga*, 175.
22. Quoted in Tapsell, *Kainga*, 71.
23. Rākete et al., "Settler-Colonialism in Aotearoa." Also see Rosamond, "Nation Destroying."
24. Salmond, "The Fountain of Fish."
25. Park, *Nga Uruora (The Groves of Life)*, 13.
26. *Te Tiriti o Waitangi* (the Treaty of Waitangi) is an agreement made in 1840 at Waitangi between representatives of the British Crown and more than five hundred Māori chiefs. This founding document of Aotearoa New Zealand is also the inspiration for biculturalism.
27. Wallace, "Regeneration," in *Singing the Circle*, 41.
28. Cadigan, "Land Ideologies that Inform a Contextual Māori Theology of Land."
29. Thomas, "Political Organisation and the Environment," in *New Forms of Political Organisation*.

30. "The Waitangi Tribunal and the Treaty," New Zealand Government Ministry of Justice.
31. Thomas, "Political Organisation and the Environment," in *New Forms of Political Organisation*.
32. Hurihanganui, "Ihumātao Protests Continue Despite PM's Assurances."
33. Bollier and Helfrich, "Finale," in *Patterns of Commoning*.
34. Ngata, "The Right to Conquer and Claim."

REFERENCES

Bollier, David, and Silke Helfrich. "Finale." In *Patterns of Commoning*, edited by David Bollier and Silke Helfrich, 393–94. Amherst, MA: The Commons Strategies Group, 2015.
Cadigan, Tui. "Land Ideologies that Inform a Contextual Māori Theology of Land." *Ecotheology* 6.1.6.2 (2001): 123–37.
Diwakar, Amar. "How White Supremacists Wield Environmentalism to Mask Racism." TRT World, 2019. https://www.trtworld.com/opinion/how-white-supremacists-wield-environmentalism-to-mask-racism-25376.
Dwivedi, O. P. "Satyagraha for Conservation: Awakening the Spirit of Hinduism." In *The Sacred Earth: Religion, Nature, Environment*, edited by Roger S. Gottlieb, 151–63. London: Routledge, 1996.
Ferdinand, Malcom. "Behind the Colonial Silence of Wilderness." *Environmental Humanities* 14:1 (March 2022): 182–201.
Gottlieb, Roger S. *A Greener Faith: Religious Environmentalism and Our Planet's Future*. Oxford, UK: Oxford University Press, 2006.
Halapua, Winston. "Theomoan: Toward an Oceanic Theology." In *Oceania and Indigenous Theologies*, edited by Elaine Wainwright et al., 23–33. London: SCM Press, 2010.
Hau'ofa, Epeli. "The Ocean in Us." *Contemporary Pacific* 10.2 (Fall 1998): 392–410.
———. "Our Sea of Islands." In *A New Oceania: Rediscovering Our Sea of Islands*, 2–16. Suva, Fiji: The University of the South Pacific, 1993.
Hurihanganui, Te Aniwa. "Ihumātao Protests Continue Despite PM's Assurances." Scoop, July 29, 2019. https://www.scoop.co.nz/stories/HL1907/S00158/ihumatao-protests-continue-despite-pms-assurances.htm.
Jackson, Moana. "Where to Next? Decolonisation and the Stories in the Land." In *Imagining Decolonisation*, edited by Biana Elkington et al., 133–55. Wellington, New Zealand: BWB Texts, 2020.
King, Michael. *The Penguin History of New Zealand*. Auckland, New Zealand: Penguin Books, 2003.
Menizes, Heather Menizes. *Reclaiming the Commons for the Common Good*. Gabriola Island, BC: New Society Publishers, 2014.
Ngata, Tina. "The Right to Conquer and Claim: Captain Cook and the Doctrine of Discovery." The Spinoff, October 3, 2019. https://thespinoff.co.nz/atea/03-10-2019/the-right-to-conquer-and-claim-captain cook-and the-doctrine-of-discovery.

Park, Geoffrey. *Nga Uruora (The Groves of Life): Ecology and History in a New Zealand Landscape*. Wellington, New Zealand: Victoria University Press, 1995.

Pellow, David Naguib. *What Is Critical Environmental Justice?* Cambridge, UK: Polity, 2018.

Rākete, Emilie et al. "Settler-Colonialism in Aotearoa." Organize Aotearoa, 2018. https://organiseaotearoa.nz/2020/01/30/settler-colonialism-in-aotearoa/.

Rosamond, Ben. "Nation Destroying: Sovereignty and Dispossession in Aotearoa New Zealand." *Economic and Social Research Aotearoa*, no. 9 (2018): 1–9. https://esra.nz/nation-destroying-sovereignty-dispossession-aotearoa-new-zealand/.

Salmond, Anne. "The Fountain of Fish: Ontological Collisions at Sea." In *Patterns of Commoning*, edited by David Bollier and Silke Helfrich, 309–29. Amherst, MA: The Commons Strategies Group, 2015.

Sharma, Mukul. *Caste and Nature: Dalits and Indian Environmental Politics*. New Delhi: Oxford University Press, 2017.

Talia, Maina. "We Have No Right to Be Silent: The Cry of a Climate Victim." *Theologies and Cultures* 12, no. 2 (December 2015).

Tapsell, Paul. *Kainga: People, Land, Belonging*. Wellington, New Zealand: Bridget Williams Books Ltd, 2021.

Thomas, Amanda. "Political Organisation and the Environment." In *New Forms of Political Organisation*, edited by Campbell Jones and Shannon Walsh, 36–45. Onehunga: Economic and Social Research Aotearoa, 2018. https://esra.nz/political-organisation-environment/.

Tomalin, Emma. *Biodivinity and Biodiversity: The Limits to Religious Environmentalism*. Farnham, England: Ashgate, 2009.

Vaai, Upolu Luma. "We Are Therefore We Live: Pacific Eco-Relational Spirituality and Changing the Climate Change Story." Toda Peace Institute, policy brief no. 56. https://toda.org/assets/files/resources/policy-briefs/t-pb-56_upolu-luma-vaai_we-are-therefore-we-live.pdf.

"The Waitangi Tribunal and the Treaty." New Zealand Government Ministry of Justice. Accessed May 2, 2024. https://waitangitribunal.govt.nz/treaty-of-waitangi/english-version/.

Wallace, William. "Regeneration." In *Singing the Circle*. Christchurch, New Zealand: Methodist Church of New Zealand, 1991. https://world.350.org/pacificwarriors/.

PART II
Alternative Frameworks

Chapter 4

The Peculiar Agency of People and the Planet

On the Need to Rethink Everything, Including Religion[1]

Joerg Rieger

What would most individuals do if they were diagnosed with a life-threatening condition? They would probably get a second opinion and perhaps a third. Suppose they got one hundred opinions and ninety-seven of them confirmed the existence of a life-threatening condition? Even if, for some reason, they chose to believe the three dissenting opinions, they would probably still take precautionary measures to mitigate harm.

It is now commonly known that 99 percent of scientists agree that human-caused climate change, driven by greenhouse gas emissions, like CO_2 and methane, is a reality.[2] Less well known may be the fact that in the confrontation of climate change science and climate change denial, we are not dealing with two ideas of equal value, not only because of a lack of scientific standards on the minority side of the debate but also because of firm ideological commitments and disproportionate funding on the side of those who deny climate change.[3]

Becoming aware of climate change amounts to the diagnosis of a life-threatening condition. What is threatened, to be sure, is not the future of life on planet Earth but the future of human life as we know it, along with the life of many other species. Earth, myriads of bacteria, cockroaches, and perhaps even some humans who have the means for survival will likely be fine for the time being; the majority of humanity, hummingbirds, and koalas probably will not. Inequalities along the lines of race, ethnicity, sexuality, gender, nationality, and class further exacerbate this scenario. Even if there were only a small chance that human-caused climate change was a problem, these issues would need to be addressed because of the magnitude of the problem, which amounts to matters of life and death for most people and many ecosystems.

Not all is lost just yet. As we take a deeper look at the causes of our current condition, a better grasp of possible solutions emerges as well. Social movements and the agency emerging from those not benefiting from prevailing developments have changed the world in the past and may well change it again. Neither should the agency of nature be dismissed out of hand, as nature is not just a victim but also has agency, even if its agency has for the most part been appropriated as a freebie by capitalism. How would another look at problems and solutions impact the work of theologians, economists, and social and natural scientists?

ANALYTICAL TASKS

Considering the sheer magnitude of the challenges, it would not be wise to limit our reflections to dealing with symptoms only. Yet, as we identify the core of these challenges and search for solutions, much of what we know must be rethought in one way or another, including dominant cultural assumptions and traditional academic disciplines. This chapter, therefore, seeks to address concerns for the environment as they have been registered at the grassroots level and picked up in theology, sociology, and economics, giving rise to what is now called eco-theology, environmental sociology, and ecological and environmental economics.

The role neoliberal capitalist economics has played in climate change is hard to dispute, although it often goes unrecognized. At present, 71 percent of CO_2 emissions are directly linked to the interests of only one hundred fossil fuel producers. According to the Intergovernmental Panel on Climate Change, between 1988 and 2016, the fossil fuel industry emitted as much greenhouse gas as in the previous 237 years, since the beginning of the Industrial Revolution. By comparison, according to some studies, if all Americans eliminated meat from their diet, this would reduce US greenhouse gas emissions by 2.6 percent.[4] While this is not an insignificant number, many concerned groups that include faith communities appear to be more aware of the problems of consuming meat than the role of capitalism in climate change. This lack of awareness is also supported by the fossil fuel industry, whose invention and promotion of fossil fuel calculators is designed to direct attention away from corporate interests.[5]

Evidence shows that, since the dawn of capitalism, things have gotten exponentially worse, and, although new technologies are being developed that limit some CO_2 emissions, capitalism's drive for expansion does not bode well for the future of the climate. Even if the environment were to register more in economic calculations (currently, the environment is still mostly considered an "externality" in capitalist economics), this would not be sufficient. In order to maximize profits for shareholders—the declared goal of capitalist economies, backed by legal precedents—environmental costs are pushed as low as possible, paralleling efforts to keep down the costs of labor.

Nature and labor are among the "seven cheap things" on which the history of the present-day world rests, along with cheap money, care, food, energy, and lives.[6] The labor of slaves—both past and present—and the reproductive labor of women provide the most severe examples of these dynamics, as these forms of labor have often been more closely identified with nature than with productive labor and, therefore, have gone mostly unpaid![7] Here, exploitation and extraction meet, and both continue to increase under the conditions of neoliberal capitalism, with no end in sight. In the process, capitalism keeps transforming the globe: No part of the so-called natural environment is left unaffected, and hardly any place in the world is left untouched by its reach. In the United States, only about 7 percent of old-growth forest is left, defined as areas that have not been used by humans in at least a century, and, since 1600, about 90 percent of the virgin forests that covered much of the United States have been cleared away.[8] The tropics, to give another example, now feature crops like sugar, tobacco, and coffee, which took over much of the natural vegetation with the help of the tools of the natural sciences.[9] The result is not just the transformation of nonhuman nature but also the transformation of traditional ways of life and labor.

Here lies a key to our analytical task, because the economic logic of exploitation and extraction is more foundational than it appears, affecting virtually everything else. It is not just a matter of accounting and bookkeeping but also lies at the heart of the histories of colonialism and neocolonialism, religion, culture, and politics, as well as of the histories of slavery and labor under the conditions of capitalism from the very beginning. This is also where the dynamics of race, ethnicity, gender, and sexuality find some of their most damaging expressions. Phenomena like environmental racism, when seen from this perspective, are not just about the dumping of toxic waste in racial minority neighborhoods; they are also about shaping people to the core, keeping in check their agency, the fruits of their labor, and any attempts to live in constructive relationships with the agency of nonhuman nature. This is why efforts at preservation and conservation are not sufficient and can often become complicit with oppression and exploitation: Preservationist John Muir's celebrated efforts, for instance, not only overlooked the existence of native populations; they also ignored the advances of capitalism that made the preservation of certain areas desirable in the first place.[10]

Another factor leading to climate change and ecological destruction more generally has, arguably, been religion, and Christianity in particular. As historian Lynn White argued in a now classic 1967 article in *Science*, Western Christianity in its Latin forms has been part of the problem of ecological destruction. According to White, Western Christianity is "the most anthropocentric religion the world has seen,"[11] playing off humanity and the natural world and leading to the devaluation and destruction of the latter on a grand scale. The problem, according to White, is not just with religion but also with other expressions of Western culture, including modern science. As a result, even post-Christian Western culture continues to be shaped by this overemphasis on humanity and related disregard for nonhuman nature. Much more could be said about this, as White is just scratching the surface. For our purposes, we might add the social sciences in this mix, whose very name indicates an emphasis on the human over the nonhuman, which emphasis is linked to the classical division of academic disciplines that is only gradually overcome today in areas like environmental sociology and postcolonial approaches to science and theology.

In the past five decades since White's clarion call, there have been various responses. In the natural sciences, the study of human-caused climate change is one example of how the results of an anthropocentric view of the world are being challenged. In the social sciences, the emergence of environmental sociology is an example not just for the expansion of a discipline but also for substantial changes in the conception of what counts as social relations, considering that society shapes nonhuman nature and that nonhuman nature shapes society.[12] In the study of religion and theology, some theologians have picked up White's critique and reclaimed alternative theological traditions that are less anthropocentric. After all, White challenged not only anthropocentrism but also the inability to conceive of positive relationships between the divine and nonhuman nature. In response, it was pointed out that such relationships are more common in the history of Christianity than White realized, and today these relationships are widely reclaimed by eco-theological circles. One of the most prominent examples is the late Vanderbilt theologian Sallie McFague's notion of the world as God's body.[13]

Having referenced the role of religion, another look at the bigger picture is called for. Scholars of religion and theology, although they might feel flattered that their subject matter is considered so important, also need to broaden their horizons. White's critique of modernity exemplifies the problem, as he missed important developments of the bigger picture, in particular the metamorphoses of capitalism. This topic often drops out also in the study of theology, religion, and even in some of the natural and social sciences.[14] The common descriptor of the current age—the "Anthropocene," found across various academic disciplines—signals the problem. A closer look at the relevance of capitalism for our topic suggests a change of terminologies: More appropriate might be the term "Capitalocene," given that capitalism pulls together capital, power, and nonhuman nature[15] as well as human productivity. Blaming humanity as a whole (or some generic notion of Western consumerism) for climate change and ecological destruction misses substantial flows of power that determine our age. The same would be true for blaming religion as such or blaming all the sciences, natural or social.

Key questions are, thus, (1) How are our various fields of study (natural and social sciences, economics, the study of theology and religion) tied to the realities of capitalism, for good and for ill? and (2) what might deeper encounters between these fields accomplish as we address climate change and ecological destruction more broadly?

CLASSICAL POSITIONS IN ENVIRONMENTAL ECONOMICS, ECOLOGICAL SOCIAL SCIENCE, AND ECOLOGICAL THEOLOGY[16]

While religious and theological studies often tend to employ the history of ideas, even when engaging environmental and economic concerns, a closer look at social scientific and economic paradigms is instructive. In theological studies in particular, the horizon of the social sciences and economics was initially introduced by various liberation theologies in the 1970s, but much is still to be learned, especially in conversation with ecological and environmental studies. In the social sciences, most ecological social science work has been developed since the 1960s. Two theoretical paradigms relevant to our discussion arose in the 1980s: the so-called "treadmill of production" (ToP)[17] and "ecological modernization" (EM).[18]

In both paradigms, economics is the central concern, as they recognize that the current capitalist economic system of production and consumption is the main contributor to ecological destruction culminating in climate change. Like efforts that seek to bring together ecology and religion, environmental social scientists have sought to bring together ecology and economics, based on the insight that economics that neglects ecology becomes destructive of it, just like religion that neglects ecology. Moreover, these positions share an understanding that the basic causes of ecological destruction and climate change are not anthropocentrism, as White argued, but the economic system of capitalism that organizes human action. In the so-called "Capitalocene," not all of humanity, and not even the majority of humanity, is driving and benefiting from the exploitation of the environment—just like the majority of humanity is hardly benefiting from the exploitation of nonhuman nature (and labor) or from the largely uncontrolled CO_2 emissions that are part of neoliberal capitalism.

Despite agreement on the importance of the economy, however, EM and ToP are often found in conflict with one another. After all, EM sees the current economic system as salvageable when modified, while ToP sees the current economic system as the source of the problem, so that the only solution is its overthrow and replacement with a new system. Similar disagreements about the role of economics can be found in theological approaches dealing with the environment, as we shall see.

EM theory argues that capitalism can become more "green" and that societies can become more sustainable and reduce their environmental impact by utilizing technology, supported by pressure from interest groups that push corporations and dominant institutions to prioritize the environment. EM theorists argue that, rather than thinking of the environment as external to economic concerns, it can be brought into economic equations and adequately accounted for, and that this process will force corporations to face the true costs of business and encourage them to invest in "greening" their production.[19] In this model, the political process is of special importance because the government is seen as the institution that is most likely to be able to implement pressure and encourage changes toward sustainability.[20] Sustainability is important to the theory in both senses—EM asks how economic institutions can become environmentally sustainable in order for the institutions themselves to be sustainable and continue their existence.

The positions of Christian mainline denominations often fit with this approach, as they share concerns for greening institutions while maintaining their existence—as well as institutionalized ideas of God. This can be seen, for instance, not only in common efforts to save energy and to install solar panels on the roofs of church buildings; it can also be seen in more courageous efforts to divest ecclesial endowments from funds linked to carbon emissions, when they fail to challenge the capitalist logic of growth. As a result, institutional stability and growth continue to be central values. The dynamics of EM also find parallels in theological approaches that support the principles of capitalism while trying to make it greener and perhaps a little more just. Images of God commonly found at work in these approaches typically envision God on the side of the institution, in terms of the sustainer and reformer of the status quo.[21]

The ToP theory, on the other hand, targets an institutional system that prioritizes profits and economic growth, encouraged by increasing productivity and industrialization, which results in environmentally detrimental outcomes.[22] At the root of ecological destruction is the economic system of capitalism, which requires increasing levels of production and consumption of material goods to maintain economic growth and ensure its existence.[23] Economic progress is likely to increase resource extraction, hazardous waste, pollution, and other forms of ecological destruction, eventually culminating in climate change. Sociologists like Richard York and others have weighed in on this topic, arguing that a new economic order is necessary to end the cycle of environmental harm. EM's hope of lowering environmental impact over time based on technological innovation is due to an increased variability across phenomena (like increased gas mileage of cars and even trucks) but overlooks that the overall situation continues to worsen (like the overall gas consumption of cars in the United States, which is getting heavier).[24] The same would be true for the adoption of self-driving electric vehicles, if savings result in more frequent or longer trips, and if better traffic flow results in increased traffic. ToP presents an encompassing critique of the economic status quo of capitalism since its beginnings, which makes solutions more difficult to identify. At the same time, it also opens up the possibility of cooperation with other social justice movements that present similar critiques and work toward shared goals.

While this approach finds fewer parallels in Christian communities, it finds kindred spirits in the work of some ecologically minded theologians who have engaged matters of economics for some time.[25] These approaches tend to envision images of God as presenting fundamental challenges to the logic of the capitalist economic status quo, linking them to emerging alternatives instead. Theologian John Cobb and economist Herman Daly, for instance, have promoted a so-called "steady-state economy," which does not require the constant growth that is a fundamental demand of capitalism. Unlike ToP, however, Cobb and Daly are not rejecting capitalism altogether and envision a capitalism with less growth.[26] Other theological approaches are more critical of capitalism (see below), but efforts to put together alternative economic and ecological thought is still in its beginnings in the field of theological studies.

Since their inception, the ToP and EM theories have clashed in various ways. The originator of ToP, Allan Schnaiberg, is critical of EM's faith in the capitalist system he sees as the source of environmental destruction. He also challenges EM's main solution, the idea that technological innovation is the key to environmental sustainability, arguing that no matter how much technology improves it will never be enough to balance out capitalism's need for the increase of production and consumption.[27] Another common critique of EM is that it cherry-picks case studies,[28] usually selecting industries from northern Europe that have implemented diverse technologies and instigated their own efforts at environmental protection. EM theorists acknowledge this focus, but they do not see it as a failing of their theory. They argue that the Netherlands and Germany, the countries from which most EM case studies are drawn, are simply the countries that are currently best implementing the ideals of EM and that they show potential ways in which capitalist industrialization can be environmentally beneficial.[29] ToP theorists respond that the case studies of EM theorists show no proof that modernization as a whole is encouraging sustainability at any level.[30]

The defense that EM theorists give for their theory of EM is that the ToP theory is more concerned with "academic debates" about "philosophy" than with the actual "questions raised by activists and policy makers."[31] They see ToP as having limited value because of what they see as idealist and utopian tendencies that do not produce real-world solutions.[32] EM theorists argue that their theory can provide practical and applicable solutions to environmental problems, solutions that utilize existing tools such as development, modernization, and innovation.[33] Focusing on reform rather than replacement, EM theorists believe that working within the economic system can solve the current environmental crisis.

Similar tensions between fundamental critiques of capitalism and efforts to ameliorate it can also be found in theological debates. Like ToP, liberation theologies of various proveniences have also often been accused of being idealistic and utopian, often without critics considering the actual struggles on the ground to which each of these approaches is linked. Too often, the charges of utopianism and idealism are leveled against those who are questioning the foundations of the system. At the same time, it cannot be denied that theologies of the mainline that are closer to the centers of the Capitalocene have had some influence on public matters like promoting efforts to recycle or to save energy and perhaps even to divest from fossil fuel. Nevertheless, these successes have given little indication of their ability to transform systemic problems and to turn things around at levels that would make much of a difference in the ongoing struggle against greenhouse gas emissions and climate change.

In sum, the urgency of climate change threatening human survival does not allow any of the positions to claim victory in the debates at this time, pushing instead for a closer look at the problems and more creative reflections. And, while each position has contributions to make, we do not suggest seeking the solution of a middle road, following the advice of seventeenth-century Germany poet Friedrich von Logau: "In situations of danger and great need, the middle road leads to death."[34]

PRODUCTION VERSUS CONSUMPTION

The divergence between the ToP and EM theories has to do with disagreements on the role of capitalism as solution or problem. This is linked to disagreements about what is identified as the source of ecological destruction and climate change and about whether more damage to the environment is done by the production or the consumption of material goods.

When theologians have engaged economic underpinnings of ecological destruction, consumption has often been the primary target. Sallie McFague, one of the early eco-theologians, has focused on consumerism, arguing that the problem is not a lack of love of nature (an earlier assumption of hers) but the temptations of consumption. Many other theologians have put forth similar arguments, and this logic can also be found in many mainline Christian communities.[35]

In my own work, by contrast, I have argued that theological critiques of capitalism need to pay more attention to production because consumption is directly tied to capitalism's need to grow production.[36] If consumption and consumerism are understood as closely related to the capitalist imperative to increase production, theologians' typical moral injunctions to consumers give way to a more profound analysis and critique of capitalism. Blaming consumers for consumerism not only fails to address what drives the production of consumers' desires but also covers up the mechanisms of growth of production that depend on creating demand leading to consumption.

The disagreement as to from which side of the production/consumption dynamic ecological destruction originates results in solutions targeting different sides of the dynamic. While EM theory recognizes that production has created ecological problems, proponents of EM see the further development of industry as the only path toward solving those problems.[37] This understanding of the problem encourages solutions that often focus on consumption: that is, the introduction of new technologies, changing consumer patterns to be more ecologically minded, and introducing environmental and sustainability values. Innovation—in the form of new regulations, industrial processes, technologies, and consumer demands—is seen as our best hope for dealing with ecological destruction, and capitalism is seen as the economic system best suited to encourage these innovations.

One of the solutions often proffered by EM theorists is implementing technology in as many realms as possible. Information and communication technologies, for instance, might have the potential to decouple consumption and material goods. This decoupling would allow for growth with limited environmental effects, because consumption levels would require fewer material resources. If consumption were decoupled from material goods, "developing" countries could adopt the consumption levels of "developed" countries without burdening the environment. Even without the possibility of dematerialization, the implementation of technology to increase the efficiency of production would enable more goods to be produced with fewer resources and less waste.

ToP theorists, on the other hand, see the suggestions offered by EM theorists as short-term solutions. ToP theorists focus on the production side rather than the consumption side of the dynamic because they argue, as I have in my own work, that production is not driven by consumer demand but rather by the demands of capitalism.[38] If this is correct, the only way to stop environmentally harmful practices would be to target the root of the problem: the capitalist production system. While, to their critics, the call for sweeping economic reforms seems unrealistic, ToP theorists see global social movements, such as the Landless Movement, the World Social Forum, and others, as offering a chance to enact solutions. Many of these social movements call for broad social change, especially economic change, and they have been able to mobilize people not only to demand change but also to enact it in particular situations. While these groups coalesce around different social problems, they have been able to wield bottom-up, democratic power by organizing larger groups of people, challenging the basis of the global capitalist ToP system that produces climate change.

In the study of theology, more profound critiques of capitalism and support for social movements can be found in approaches belonging to the diverse family of liberation theologies. While liberation theologies have often been considered to be primarily concerned with human oppression and exploitation, broader awareness of the range of oppression and exploitation, including in matters of ecology, has long been part of the conversation, including matters of ecology. The work of Brazilian liberation theologians Leonardo Boff and Ivone Gebara may serve as examples.[39] The ecofeminist work of Gebara, in particular, is deeply connected to poor people's movements, especially the everyday experiences of women in impoverished Brazilian neighborhoods, where she resides.[40] In my own work, I have addressed the importance of movements like Occupy Wall Street and the accomplishments of the labor movement, which have not only impacted economic relationships but also contributed to the fight against racism and sexism at work, where it often hurts people the most.[41] In these theologies, images of God develop in the midst of the struggle, with the divine inhabiting the world not only in general (as most ecological theologians would agree) but also in specific contexts, in solidarity with struggling humanity, the earth, and particular movements for liberation.

While the emphasis on production (and thus on people's agency) is crucial, attention to the dynamics of production still needs to be deepened. Where the goal is the generation of profits—the categorical imperative of the Capitalocene—production drives consumption, which results in ecological destruction and climate change. ToP theory would remind us that exploitation of the nonhuman world is part of production, but this dynamic is also manifest in the exploitation of human labor, both productive and reproductive. Here are significant connections that need to be explored further, not least since the labor of slaves and the reproductive labor of women is often considered as part of nonhuman nature and thereby further devalued.

Nevertheless, analysis and critique alone are insufficient and are open to the charge of idealism. Production, I would argue, pushing the conversation to the next level, is not only the location of the problem but also the place from which alternatives have emerged. Consequently, it should not be surprising that one of the most enduring social movements of modern times has been the labor movement. Even though this movement has faced many challenges and defeats, it is on the rise again today, with the potential to address the problems of production and transform them. The power of productive (and reproductive) labor as a revolutionary force also manifests itself today in an emerging worker cooperative movement that is global and highly diverse, with historical roots in minority communities, as we will see below.

Keep in mind, finally, also that capitalist production is never limited to economics but extends to the production of relationships between wealth, power, and nonhuman nature. If production is where these relationships are formed, this is also where they need to be reformed, including in matters of culture and religion. What difference can religion, when it is perceived as independent, be expected to make in an interconnected world determined by various flows of power?

RECONSIDERING AND RECLAIMING PRODUCTION AND AGENCY

If the topic of production and, therefore, the agency of working people and perhaps even of the planet is developed further, new possibilities emerge that push the conversations to the next level. As Jason Moore has argued, "if indeed capitalism is defined by its commitment to endless accumulation, then our starting point—and point of return—must be work."[42] To be sure, work includes not only industrial labor but all other forms of work, not least the reproductive and mostly unpaid labor of nonhuman nature and of women in patriarchal society. This observation is the foundation of a relational view of power. Moore puts it with unmistakable clarity: "Shut down a coal plant, and you slow global warming for a day; shut down the relations that made the coal plant, and you can stop it for good."[43]

In the fields of environmental sociology and economics, the work of Juliet Schor and others has made an important contribution, combining some traits of the ToP theory and EM theory. While Schor challenges consumerism (like EM), she is also attuned to the underlying economic challenges that come from capitalism (like ToP). Charting a way forward, Schor and her collaborators suggest a new economic model that takes its cues from both emerging grassroots movements and ecological models. Here, ecological thinking is not subordinated to economic thinking but put in conversation with it. These approaches resonate with the work of theologians like John Cobb and others who have added theological reflection to the conversation. Cobb, for instance, develops images of God not as powerful and transcendent overlord or in the image of economic elites but as caring for all creatures, suffering and rejoicing with them, and appreciating diversity.[44] Putting ecological, economic, and theological reflections in conversation is no longer optional because the problems leading to climate change are linked to all of these fields, and they mutually reinforce each other.

Juliet Schor and Craig Thompson make the interesting observation that the fathers of neoliberal capitalism, such as Friedrich von Hayek, also build their theories on certain ecological models. A specific interpretation of biological evolution provides the basis for the neoliberal economic emphasis of competition as natural and necessary for flourishing. Here, the often-referenced principle of "survival of the fittest" is taken to mean competition of all against all. In addition, the theological affinities of Hayek's economic thought have also been pointed out, envisioning a deity that requests sacrifices.[45] In contrast to this naturalization of capitalism, Schor and Thompson point out that more recent understandings of biological evolution contradict Hayek's social Darwinism, developing a sense of cooperation and symbiotic relationships instead.[46] This sort of cooperation does not diminish values like agency and diversity but supports them, as it is built on various specializations and adaptations to harsh environments.

While these alternative ecological models still seem to bear some resemblances with neoliberal economic thinking—decentralized rather than centralized approaches, appreciation for markets rather than planned economies—they also defy neoliberal economics by redefining success and emphasizing interconnectedness rather than individualism. Core elements of neoliberal economics are picked up and turned around: Markets in the new paradigm do not need to be defined by competition where winner takes all; instead, they can be defined by forms of "rhizomatic" cooperative networks. The trope of the rhizome, suggested by Schor and Thompson, signifies complex root systems that spread and thrive underground and are hard to uproot.[47] The decentralized nature of such rhizomes stands in stark contrast to neoliberal decentralization. Pushing beyond Schor and Thompson's argument, I would argue that what is overcome here is not neoliberalism's supposed individualism (which is but the myth of the powerful) but neoliberalism's own rhizomatic forms that connect the wealthy and powerful in ways that are highly effective but hardly noticed.

Developing the themes of rhizomes and connectedness, some scholars of religion and theology have gone even further, arguing that humans need to understand themselves as inextricable parts of the ecology. In the words of Whitney Bauman, humans need to think of themselves as "becoming plant, animal, mineral,"[48] because human bodies always include all these realities, whether we are aware of it or not. In such a model, the divine finds its place within ecology as well, as part of the world rather than separate from it. The technical term, commonly used in theological circles, is panentheism, which signals the presence of the divine in everything, without identifying God with everything.[49]

In these ecological models, alternative productivity and agency are found not in individuals (whether human, nonhuman, or divine) but in organized cooperatives that are interconnected at the roots rather than at the level of the elites. This is the precondition for broader connections with social networks that tie into social movements. Here, a very different kind of economy develops: The heart of ecological economics is not a kind of productivity or agency where supposedly individual actors are exponentially more significant than others (this is the illusion of capitalist economics, covering up the power differentials between individual buyers and sellers and multinational corporations). The heart of ecological economics is tied to collective forms of productivity and agency that shape up in worker and consumer cooperatives, community-supported agriculture, communal networks, and alternative communities that are often most vibrant in minority communities and led by women.[50] Added to that list should be various labor movements, both formal and informal, which also have a history of limiting the most destructive consequences of neoliberal capitalism for people and the planet.

These kinds of productivity and agency tend to go easier on the planet because destruction would directly affect communities where they live. Moreover, these kinds of productivity and agency have the potential to counteract ecological destruction because their primary goal is not infinite growth and the maximization of profits at all cost, but "a commitment to live within the limits of the biosphere."[51] This dynamic does not need to be based in ethereal moral values or abstract religious ideas but is rooted in the communal self-interest of people who live in specific ecological webs of life whose flourishing is the foundation for the flourishing of all.

In parallel, theologians also have argued for broadened notions of productivity and agency that resist the modern capitalist myth of the individual as the supreme economic agent. Bauman, for instance, talks about agency in relation to our "biohistories." In a different vein, the collective agency of working people has also been emphasized by a few theologians, including my own work, and it is at the heart of the Wendland-Cook Program in Religion and Justice at Vanderbilt University Divinity School.[52] In the big picture, this emerging agency will need to be explored in relation to nonhuman agency, picking up Karl Marx's notion (a topic developed in the seventeenth century by economist William Petty), expressed in somewhat outdated language, that labor is the father and nature the mother of wealth. The productive and reproductive labor of people and the planet may well be at the roots of revolutionary agency in our time.

REVOLUTIONARY AGENCY

Ecological economics resists extreme inequalities through shared productivity and shared ownership of economic and ecological means of production. At the core is a new productive base of the economy, composed of new kinds of agency emerging in small-scale green enterprises, cooperative businesses, and popular access to capital. This brings together three concerns: production of wealth, restoration of ecosystems, and local empowerment. In this model, production changes hands from being organized by dominant capitalist interests to being organized by communal interests, a shift that is significant in various ways: Most importantly, power is relocated into the hands of those who are actually doing the work (in conjunction with nonhuman nature) and whose interest is tied to their local communities and the natural environment where they live. This relocation of power has implications also for the correction of the dramatic maldistribution of wealth and of inequalities along the lines of race, ethnicity, gender, and sexuality.[53]

This is the place of worker organizing and of worker cooperatives, in the sense of what economist Richard Wolff has called worker self-directed enterprises.[54] Such business models, based on the cooperation of workers, are not merely reforms of capitalist business models, as the basic concern is no longer the increase of profits for a privileged group of shareholders as opposed to the welfare of workers. Neither are worker self-directed enterprises not non-profits that tend to function well within capitalist economies as they are often just as hierarchically structured than for-profits and do not necessarily allow for broad-based agency. Instead, worker self-directed enterprises distribute profits among all who work and empower all who work, thus benefiting the broader communities rather than the elite few. Such efforts do not belong to the realm of theory alone, as there are growing networks of worker cooperatives all around the world, including a long and substantial history of cooperatives in African American communities in the United States.[55] Worker cooperatives provide fundamental alternatives to the way the economy functions in the Capitalocene, with implications for politics, culture, and religion.

Ecological concerns are central in this alternative economic model in another way as well because, according to Schor, the basic principles of the new economy are the reduction of production and consumption, that is, working less and spending less, as well as creating and connecting more, which is enhanced by new communication technologies. In this context, Schor talks about "true materialism," which develops a new appreciation for material things and pushes beyond dominant materialisms that are interested in material things primarily for symbolic qualities.⁵⁶ Such true materialism is also linked to providing opportunities for economically struggling communities. In theology, materialism is currently being reclaimed as well, based on an understanding that the Abrahamic religions share a strong concern for the flourishing of life on this earth.⁵⁷ In fact, in most of the ancient Jewish traditions and several of the Christian traditions, the idea of salvation is not about going to heaven after death but about leading a happy and productive life.⁵⁸

Economic models that take their cues from emergent ecological thinking can also develop a deeper appreciation of diversity and difference. While diversity and difference are also employed to the benefit of neoliberal capitalism—diversifying production and consumption by employing a diversified (and therefore often less expensive) workforce and marketing and selling to nontraditional customers—things change when working people reclaim diversity and difference for their own interests. The result is alternative economies based on alternative production/reproduction and consumption patterns, embodied for instance in the growing networks between worker and consumer cooperatives. In this context, the capitalist concern for production and productivity is fundamentally transformed. Placing ecological modernization in this context could be promising, as it would fundamentally reshape the thrust and the meaning of modernization.

These new ways of accounting for diversity and difference also account for new forms of resilience and adaptability, along with a different kind of efficiency. In this way, diversity undergirds what Schor and Thompson have called a "networked revolution" and what some of us (with Kwok Pui-lan and Rosemarie Henkel-Rieger) have called "deep solidarity."⁵⁹ Deep solidarity is based on the collective revolutionary agency and resiliency of working people in contexts of exploitation, not only appreciating but also putting to work differences and diversity along the lines of race, ethnicity, gender, and sexuality in constructive fashion. This creates alternatives to dominant models of solidarity that emphasize unity to the exclusion of diversity.

Journalist Naomi Klein has argued for the formation of networks of resistance, drawing connections between seemingly disparate struggles because "the logic that would cut pensions, food stamps, and health care before increasing taxes on the rich is the same logic that would blast the bedrock of the earth to get the last vapors of gas and the last drops of oil."⁶⁰ This serves as another reminder of why economics is so crucial when discussing large-scale ecological exploitation and climate change. While conservatives have long used economic arguments to stop climate action, Klein challenges progressives to use economic arguments in order to fight climate change.⁶¹ Leaving aside fundamental economic transformation because experts in various academic fields worry that this might be unrealistic turns out to be the option that is unrealistic: Hoping that things will fundamentally change without fundamentally changing the roots of the problem equates with an often-quoted definition of insanity attributed to Albert Einstein.[62] If climate change is indeed a matter of survival, it needs to be addressed by all means possible.

The perspective of ecologically informed economics also broadens the sense of the importance of the resistance that is building. Organizing opposition to fracking or high-risk pipelines, for instance, is not merely a matter of environmental concern but also of participation in the decision-making process in both politics and economics, as Klein has noted.[63] This opposition embodies the meaning of deep solidarity by being intersectional, interracial, and intergenerational, uniting people at the local level as well as at the global. Like many progressive theologians of the present, Klein finds hope in social movements that address the unfinished business of the liberation movements of the past two centuries, noting that victories on the legal (and we might add political) front were mostly lost on the economic front.[64]

The good news is that the utter urgency of climate change can provide energy for transformation. In a reversal of Klein's account of the so-called shock doctrine that is used by capitalism to further its causes, the impending disasters can be used to advance the status quo and add urgency, pushing beyond easily ignored appeals to ethics and morality as the primary motivation.[65] This matches some of the underlying sensitivities of liberation theologies, where God-talk is focused not so much on morality and ethical appeals (a widespread misunderstanding not only in theological circles) but on broader economic, social, and cultural-religious developments that produce the energy and motivation for transformation. In other words, God is found not first of all in the world of ideas but in the tensions of life where alternative forms of production and agency are emerging. This matches the experience of prominent figures revered in the Abrahamic religions, like Moses, Jesus, and Mohammed, but it can also be observed in the lives of grassroots religious communities through time, like the Franciscans, the Anabaptists of the sixteenth-century Reformation in Europe, the early Methodists in England, the communities of African American enslaved people, and the Base Ecclesial Communities in Latin America.

Klein is right that solidarity is less and less an abstract moral ideal when it comes to matters of climate change, because the pressures of climate change bring people together so that many of us are less isolated than a decade ago. The beginnings of such solidarity are already embodied in social media, worker co-ops, farmer's markets, and neighborhood sharing banks.[66] Let us not forget the profound solidarity that shapes up in the agency of working people in concert with the planet. A growing sense of solidarity is emerging in theology as well, pushing beyond the limitations of certain forms of identity politics that have kept progressives in silos for the past fifty years.

CONCLUSION

In the fight against ecological destruction and climate change, a good deal of synergy has been emerging between ecology, economics, and theology. What is part of the problem, it seems, can also become part of the solution. This takes us back to the fundamental problems in both economics and theology, with which this chapter began.

Theological approaches can add a critique of economics that pushes beyond the approaches of environmental sociologists and economists, which could be useful in further conversations with ecology. Parallel to White's critique of Christianity as disconnected from nature, there is broad agreement among all theorists discussed in this chapter that capitalist economics throughout its history has been disconnected as well, both from nature and from people. Things are only getting worse in neoliberal capitalism. As economist Robert Nelson has observed, the task of top neoliberal economists is to keep the big ideas of neoliberalism before people, with little concern for empirical studies and for analyzing data. In this way, he argues, economics comes to resemble a certain kind of religion that is also mostly about disembodied ideas.[67] This kind of religion is also characteristic of much of North Atlantic Christianity, which may be the reason why neoliberal economics and conservative Christianity display certain affinities, like faith in an intangible future and a firm belief in the work of divine providence in capitalism, no matter how severe its failures are.

However, things do not need to be this way, and alternatives already exist: Instead of relegating itself to the promotion of disembodied ideas (that have rarely materialized), economics can be reconstructed from the ground up, in touch with the ecological, sociological, and political dynamics described in this chapter. The same is true for religion. Instead of relegating itself to the promotion of disembodied ideas and troubled images of the divine that have done and continue to do tremendous damage (much resistance against climate science is currently supported by religion), religion can also be reconstructed from the ground up. Unexpected experiences of the divine involved in alternative ways of being in the material world and in liberation communities—particularly in struggles for survival and flourishing—are motivating people not only to resist but also to engage in alternative ways of life.

The theological battle is, thus, not merely fought about ideas and images of the divine but also about engagements with the divine in places where life is promoted, be it in nonhuman nature's resilience or in people's resistance and production of alternatives. Similar challenges can be posed to the academy as a whole: What if the major task is neither the formulation of big ideas—the perennial dream not only of religion but also of many of the humanities—nor its opposite, the seemingly neutral collection of data, the proliferation of descriptive empirical studies, or technocratic solutions, but the engagement with emerging levels of resistance to the status quo and the concomitant forms of productivity and agency, both human and nonhuman? Future engagements of climate change might bear some promise when they move from the realm of big ideas and efforts to accommodate the dominant status quo to the kinds of actual struggles on the ground that mark our age.

NOTES

1. For an extended version of the argument in this chapter, see Joerg Rieger, *Theology in the Capitalocene: Ecology, Identity, Class, and Solidarity* (Minneapolis: Fortress Press, 2022), chapter 1. Used with permission by Fortress Press.

2. Mark Lynas, Benjamin Z. Houlton, and Simon Perry, "Greater than 99% Consensus on Human Caused Climate Change in the Peer-Reviewed Scientific Literature," *Environmental Research Letters* 16 (October 19, 2021). https://iopscience.iop.org/article/10.1088/1748-9326/ac2966.

3. See the discussion of the problematic role of ideas in the debates around climate change in Laurel Kearns, "Climate Change," in *Grounding Religion: A Field Guide to the Study of Religion and Ecology*, second ed., eds. Whitney Bauman, Richard Bohannon, and Kevin J. O'Brien (London: Routledge, 2017), 141–46.

4. Paul Griffin, "The Carbon Majors Database: CDP Majors Report" (July 2017), https://cdn.cdp.net/cdp-production/cms/reports/documents/000/002/327/original/Carbon-Majors-Report-2017.pdf?1501833772, reporting on the percentage of CO_2 emissions today and since 1988. See also the related fact check: https://fullfact.org/news/are-100-companies-causing-71-carbon-emissions/. Brett Clark and Richard York, 2005, *IPCC Second Assessment: Climate Change* (1995), 21, also report that, according to the Intergovernmental Panel on Climate Change, the amount of CO_2 in the atmosphere has risen by 31 percent since the onset of industrialization, and half of that increase happened between 1965 and 1995. Regarding meat consumption, see Frank M. Mitloehner, "Yes, Eating Meat Affects the Environment, but Cows Are Not Killing the Climate," *The Conversation*, October 25, 2018, https://theconversation.com/yes-eating-meat-affects-the-environment-but-cows-are-not-killing-the-climate-94968.

5. Rebecca Solnit, "Big Oil Coined 'Carbon Footprints' to Blame Us for Their Greed: Keep Them on the Hook," *Guardian*, August 23, 2021, https://www.theguardian.com/commentisfree/2021/aug/23/big-oil-coined-carbon-footprints-to-blame-us-for-their-greed-keep-them-on-the-hook.

6. Raj Patel and Jason W. Moore, *A History of the World in Seven Cheap Things: A Guide to Capitalism, Nature, and the Future of the Planet* (Oakland: University of California Press, 2017).

7. "The Rise of Cheap Nature," in *Capitalocene or Anthropocene? Nature, History, and the Crisis of Capitalism*, ed. Jason W. Moore (Oakland, CA: PM Press, 2017),

79, Jason W. Moore wrote, "Backed by imperial power and capitalist rationality, it mobilized the unpaid work and energy of humans—especially women, especially the enslaved—in the service of transforming landscapes with a singular purpose: the endless accumulation of capital."

8. The Blog of the Rainforest Action Network, https://www.ran.org/the-understory/how_much_old_growth_forest_remains_in_the_us/.

9. See Justin McBrien, "Accumulating Extinction: Planetary Catastrophism in the Necrocene," in *Capitalocene or Anthropocene?*, 120–21.

10. Ibid., 124.

11. Lynn White Jr., "The Historical Roots of Our Ecologic Crisis," *Science* 155:3767 (March 1967): 1205.

12. Brett Clark and Richard York, "Carbon Metabolism: Global Capitalism, Climate Change, and the Biospheric Shift," *Theory and Society* 34 (2005): 393. Already Karl Marx, engaging the work of soil chemists like Justus von Liebig, talked about the "metabolic interaction" between humans and the earth. Ibid., 398.

13. Sallie McFague, *The Body of God: An Ecological Theology* (Minneapolis: Fortress Press, 1993).

14. For White, there does not even seem to be a qualitative difference between the economics of the early Middle Ages and later capitalist developments.

15. The term has been coined by various authors; https://wiki.p2pfoundation.net/Capitalocene. Jason Moore, in "The Rise of Cheap Nature," 81, notes the organic relation of capital, power, and nature, and later he talks about capitalism as a new way of organizing the relations between nature, work, reproduction, and "the conditions of life." Ibid., 85.

16. I would like to thank PhD student in environmental sociology Annika Rieger, of Boston College, for her collaboration on the camps of EM and the ToP. For our coauthored work on the topic, see Joerg Rieger and Annika Rieger, "Working with Environmental Economists," in *T&T Clark Handbook of Christian Theology and Climate Change*, eds. Ernst Conradie and Hilda Koster (London: T&T Clark Bloomsbury, 2020).

17. Allan Schnaiberg, *The Environment: From Surplus to Scarcity* (New York: Oxford University Press, 1980).

18. Udo Ernst Simonis, "Ecological Modernization of Industrial Society: Three Strategic Elements," *International Social Science Journal* 121 (1989): 347–61; Gert Spaargaren and Arthur P. J. Mol, "Sociology, Environment, and Modernity: Ecological Modernization as a Theory of Social Change," *Society & Natural Resources* 5:4 (1992): 323–44.

19. Spaargaren and Mol, "Sociology, Environment, and Modernity," 334–36.

20. Frederick H. Buttel, "Ecological Modernization as Social Theory," *Geoforum* 31 (2000): 57–65. Suggestions for policy are important to most EM studies, either to help mitigate current damage or to prevent future destruction. Spaargaren and Mol, "Sociology, Environment, and Modernity," 338–41.

21. See, for instance, Brent Waters, *Just Capitalism: A Christian Ethic of Economic Globalization* (Louisville, KT: Westminster John Knox, 2016).

22. Allan Schnaiberg, "Sustainable Development and the Treadmill of Production," in *The Politics of Sustainable Development: Theory, Policy and Practice within the European Union*, eds. Susan Baker et al. (London: Routledge, 1997), 75.

23. Allan Schnaiberg, David N. Pellow, and Adam Weinberg, "The Treadmill of Production and the Environmental State," in *The Environmental State under Pressure*, eds. Arthur P. J. Mol and Frederick H. Buttel (London: JAI/Elsevier, 2000), 15–32.

24. Richard York, "The Treadmill of (Diversifying) Production," *Organization & Environment* 17:3 (2004): 358, 360.

25. See, for instance, from a Christian perspective, John B. Cobb Jr. and Herman E. Daly, *For the Common Good: Redirecting the Economy toward Community, the Environment, and a Sustainable Future*, second ed. (Boston: Beacon Press, 1994), and, from a Buddhist perspective, E. F. Schumacher, *Small Is Beautiful: Economics as if People Mattered* (San Francisco: Harper&Row, 1973).

26. Cobb and Daly, *For the Common Good*.

27. Schnaiberg, "Sustainable Development and the Treadmill of Production," 76–77.

28. Richard York and Eugene A. Rosa, "Key Challenges to Ecological Modernization Theory," *Organization & Environment* 16:3 (2003): 280–81.

29. Spaargaren and Mol, "Sociology, Environment, and Modernity," 324. Buttel, "Ecological Modernization as Social Theory," 39.

30. York and Rosa, "Key Challenges," 382.

31. Arthur P. J. Mol and Gert Spaargaren, "Ecological Modernisation Theory in Debate: A Review," *Environmental Politics* 9:1 (2000): 39.

32. Buttel, "Ecological Modernization as Social Theory," 60–61.

33. Mol and Spaargaren, "Ecological Modernisation Theory in Debate," 334–38.

34. In *Gefahr und grosser Not bringt der Mittel-Weg den Tod* (English translation mine). Friedrich von Logau, *Sämmtliche Sinngedichte*, ed. Gustav Eitner (Tübingen, Germany: Litterarischer Verein, 1872), 421, #89.

35. Sallie McFague, *Life Abundant: Rethinking Theology and Economy for Planet in Peril* (Minneapolis: Fortress Press, 2001), xi, 33. The works of ethicists Cynthia Moe-Lobeda and William T. Cavanaugh emphasize consumption in different ways as well.

36. Joerg Rieger, *No Rising Tide: Theology, Economics, and the Future* (Minneapolis: Fortress Press, 2009), chapter 4.

37. York and Rosa, "Key Challenges," 274.

38. Gould, Pellow, and Schnaiberg, *The Treadmill of Production*, 19–24; Rieger, *No Rising Tide*, chapter 4.

39. Leonardo Boff, *Cry of the Earth, Cry of the Poor* (Maryknoll, NY: Orbis Books, 1997); Ivone Gebara, *Longing for Running Water: Ecofeminism and Liberation* (Minneapolis: Fortress Press, 1999).

40. Gebara, *Longing for Running Water*, 103–4, identifies God in terms of "relatedness as a continual presence that is made explicitly in different ways in different beings," uniting immanence and transcendence (reference to Sallie McFague). For a critique of Boff, Gebara, and McFague, see Joerg Rieger, "Reenvisioning Ecotheology and the Divine from the Margins," *Ecotheology* 9:1 (April 2004): 65–85.

41. Kwok Pui-lan and Rieger, *Occupy Religion: Theology of the Multitude* (Harrisburg, PA: Rowman and Littlefield, 2012); Joerg Rieger and Rosemarie Henkel-Rieger, *Unified We Are a Force: How Faith and Labor Can Overcome America's Inequalities* (St. Louis, MO: Chalice Press, 2016).

42. Moore, "The Rise of Cheap Nature," 93.

43. Ibid., 94.

44. John B. Cobb, "Christianity, Economics, and Ecology," in *Christianity and Ecology*, eds. Dieter T. Hessel and Rosemary Radford Ruether (Cambridge, MA: Harvard, 2000), 508.

45. See the critiques of Jung Mo Sung, *Desire, Market, and Religion: Horizons of Hope in Complex Societies* (New York: Palgrave McMillan, 2011), 78–84.

46. Juliet B. Schor and Craig J. Thompson, "Cooperative Networks, Participatory Markets, and Rhizomatic Resistance: Situating Plenitude within Contemporary Political Economy Debates," in *Sustainable Lifestyles and the Quest for Plenitude: Case Studies of the New Economy*, eds. Juliet B. Schor and Craig J. Thompson (New Haven, CT: Yale University Press, 2014), 240–41.

47. Schor and Thompson, "Cooperative Networks, Participatory Markets, and Rhizomatic Resistance," 245, with reference to Gilles Deleuze and Félix Guattari.

48. Whitney A. Bauman, *Religion and Ecology: Developing a Planetary Ethic* (New York: Columbia Press, 2014), 155, also referencing Deleuze and Guattari.

49. This is how the difference between panentheism and pantheism is often explained, although pantheism may not have to be understood literally, as identifying God with everything.

50. See the case studies in Schor and Thompson, *Sustainable Lifestyles*. See also Kelsey Ryan-Simkins and Elaine Nogueira-Godsey, "Tangible Actions toward Solidarity: An Ecofeminist Analysis of Women's Participation in Food Justice," in *Valuing Lives, Healing Earth: Religion, Gender, and Life on Earth*, vol. 3, eds. Lilian Dube et al. (Leuven, Belgium: Peeters, 2021), 203–22.

51. Schor and Thompson, "Introduction: Practicing Plenitude," 7.

52. Bauman, *Religion and Ecology*, 165. On the agency of working people, see Rieger and Henkel-Rieger, *Unified We Are a Force*. This theme is rarely developed by other theologians, but see the short passage in Daly and Cobb, *For the Common Good*, 298–314. See also www.religionandjustice.org.

53. See also Joerg Rieger, *Theology in the Capitalocene: Ecology, Identity, Class, and Solidarity* (Minneapolis: Fortress Press, 2022), chapter 4.

54. Richard Wolff, *Democracy at Work: A Cure for Capitalism* (Chicago: Haymarket Books, 2012).

55. Jessica Gordon Nembhard, *Collective Courage: A History of African American Cooperative Economic Development and Practice* (University Park: Pennsylvania State University Press, 2014).

56. Schor and Thompson, "Introduction," 10, 13; see also Juliet Schor, *Plenitude: The New Economics of True Wealth* (New York: Penguin Press, 2010).

57. See, for instance, Joerg Rieger and Edward Waggoner, eds., *Religious Experience and New Materialism: Movement Matters* (New York: Palgrave Macmillan, 2016).

58. This is true even for some of the more recent Christian traditions, in particular the so-called holiness movements. The founder of Methodism, John Wesley, makes a strong effort to tie salvation in the here-and-how. See his sermon, "The Scripture Way of Salvation," in *The Works of John Wesley*, vol. 2, the Bicentennial Edition, ed. Albert C. Outler (Nashville, TN: Abingdon, 1985), 153–69.

59. Schor and Thompson, "Introduction," 22. Networks were, for instance, not yet on the horizon in Ernst F. Schumacher's *Small is Beautiful*. For the term "deep solidarity," see Rieger and Henkel-Rieger, *Unified We Are a Force*, and Rieger and Kwok Pui-lan, *Occupy Religion*.

60. Naomi Klein, *This Changes Everything: Capitalism vs. the Climate* (New York: Simon and Schuster, 2014), 61.

61. Ibid., 125.

62. "Doing the same thing over and over again and expecting a different result."

63. Klein, *This Changes Everything*, 295.

64. Ibid., 458. See also Rieger and Kwok, *Occupy*.

65. See Naomi Klein, *The Shock Doctrine: The Rise of Disaster Capitalism* (New York: Metropolitan Books, 2007); Klein, *This Changes Everything*, 406, 417.

66. Klein, *This Changes Everything*, 466.

67. Robert H. Nelson, *Economics as Religion: From Samuelson to Chicago and Beyond* (University Park: Pennsylvania State University Press, 2001). See also the critique of economics in Rieger, *No Rising Tide*.

REFERENCES

Bauman, Whitney A. *Religion and Ecology: Developing a Planetary Ethic*. New York: Columbia Press, 2014.

Boff, Leonardo. *Cry of the Earth, Cry of the Poor*. Maryknoll, NY: Orbis Books, 1997.

Buttel, Frederick H. "Ecological Modernization as Social Theory." *Geoforum* 31 (2000): 57–65.

Clark, Brett, and Richard York. "Carbon Metabolism: Global Capitalism, Climate Change, and the Biospheric Shift." *Theory and Society* 34 (2005): 391–428.

Cobb Jr., John B. "Christianity, Economics, and Ecology." In *Christianity and Ecology: Seeking the Well-Being of Earth and Humans*, edited by Dieter T. Hessel and Rosemary Radford Ruether, 497–511. Cambridge, MA: Harvard, 2000.

Cobb Jr., John B., and Herman E. Daly. *For the Common Good: Redirecting the Economy toward Community, the Environment, and a Sustainable Future*, second ed. Boston: Beacon Press, 1994.

Cook, John. "Consensus on Consensus." *Environmental Research Letters* (April 13, 2016). Accessed at https://iopscience.iop.org/article/10.1088/1748-9326/11/4/048002/meta.

Gebara, Ivone. *Longing for Running Water: Ecofeminism and Liberation*. Minneapolis: Fortress Press, 1999.

Griffin, Paul. "The Carbon Majors Database: CDP Majors Report" (July 2017). Accessed at https://cdn.cdp.net/cdp-production/cms/reports/documents/000/002/327/original/Carbon-Majors-Report-2017.pdf?1501833772.
Kearns, Laurel. "Climate Change." In *Grounding Religion: A Field Guide to the Study of Religion and Ecology*, second ed., edited by Whitney Bauman, Richard Bohannon, and Kevin J. O'Brien, 137–57. London: Routledge, 2017.
Klein, Naomi. *This Changes Everything: Capitalism vs. the Climate*. New York: Simon and Schuster, 2014.
Klein, Naomi. *The Shock Doctrine: The Rise of Disaster Capitalism*. New York: Metropolitan Books, 2007.
McBrien, Justin. "Accumulating Extinction: Planetary Catastrophism in the Necrocene." In *Capitalocene or Anthropocene? Nature, History and the Crisis of Capitalism*, edited by Jason W. Moore. Oakland, CA: PM Press, 2017.
McFague, Sallie. *The Body of God: An Ecological Theology*. Minneapolis: Fortress Press, 1993.
Mitloehner, Frank M. "Yes, Eating Meat Affects the Environment, but Cows Are Not Killing the Climate." *The Conversation*, October 25, 2018. Accessed at https://theconversation.com/yes-eating-meat-affects-the-environment-but-cows-are-not-killing-the-climate-94968.
Moore, Jason W. "The Rise of Cheap Nature." In *Capitalocene or Anthropocene? Nature, History, and the Crisis of Capitalism*, edited by Jason W. Moore, 78–115. Oakland, CA: PM Press, 2017.
Nelson, Robert H. *Economics as Religion: From Samuelson to Chicago and Beyond*. University Park: Pennsylvania State University Press, 2001.
Patel, Raj, and Jason W. Moore. *A History of the World in Seven Cheap Things: A Guide to Capitalism, Nature, and the Future of the Planet*. Oakland: University of California Press, 2017.
Rieger, Joerg. "Reenvisioning Ecotheology and the Divine from the Margins." *Ecotheology* 9:1 (April 2004): 65–85.
Rieger, Joerg, and Rosemarie Henkel-Rieger. *Unified We Are a Force: How Faith and Labor Can Overcome America's Inequalities*. St. Louis, MO: Chalice Press, 2016.
Rieger, Joerg, and Kwok Pui-lan. *Occupy Religion: Theology of the Multitude* Lanham, MD: Rowman & Littlefield Publishers, 2012.
Rieger, Joerg, and Annika Rieger. "Working with Environmental Economists." In *T&T Clark Handbook of Christian Theology and Climate Change*, edited by Ernst Conradie and Hilda Koster, 53–64. London: T&T Clark Bloomsbury, 2020.
Rieger, Joerg, and Edward Waggoner, eds. *Religious Experience and New Materialism: Movement Matters*. New York: Palgrave Macmillan, 2016.
Schnaiberg, Allan. *The Environment: From Surplus to Scarcity*. New York: Oxford University Press, 1980.
Schnaiberg, Allan. "Sustainable Development and the Treadmill of Production." In *The Politics of Sustainable Development: Theory, Policy and Practice within the European Union*, edited by Susan Baker et al., 72–88. London: Routledge, 1997.
Schnaiberg, Allan, David N. Pellow, and Adam Weinberg. "The Treadmill of Production and the Environmental State." In *The Environmental State under*

Pressure, edited by Arthur P. J. Mol and Frederick H. Buttel, 15–32. London: JAI/Elsevier, 2000.

Schor, Juliet B. *Plenitude: The New Economics of True Wealth*. New York: Penguin Press, 2010.

Schor, Juliet B., and Craig J. Thompson, eds. *Sustainable Lifestyles and the Quest for Plenitude: Case Studies of the New Economy*. New Haven, CT: Yale University Press, 2014.

Simonis, Udo Ernst. "Ecological Modernization of Industrial Society: Three Strategic Elements." *International Social Science Journal* 121 (1989): 347–61.

Solnit, Rebecca. "Big Oil Coined 'Carbon Footprints' to Blame Us for Their Greed: Keep Them on the Hook." *Guardian* (August 23, 2021). Accessed at https://www.theguardian.com/commentisfree/2021/aug/23/big-oil-coined-carbon-footprints-to-blame-us-for-their-greed-keep-them-on-the-hook.

Spaargaren, Gert, and Arthur P. J. Mol. "Sociology, Environment, and Modernity: Ecological Modernization as a Theory of Social Change." *Society & Natural Resources* 5:4 (1992): 323–44.

Sung, Jung Mo. *Desire, Market, and Religion: Horizons of Hope in Complex Societies*. New York: Palgrave McMillan, 2011.

Waters, Brent. *Just Capitalism: A Christian Ethic of Economic Globalization*. Louisville, KT: Westminster John Knox, 2016.

Wesley, John. "The Scripture Way of Salvation." In *The Works of John Wesley*, vol. 2, the Bicentennial Edition, edited by Albert C. Outler, 153–69. Nashville, TN: Abingdon, 1985.

White, Lynn, Jr. "The Historical Roots of Our Ecologic Crisis." *Science* 155:3767 (March 1967).

York, Richard. "The Treadmill of (Diversifying) Production." *Organization & Environment* 17:3 (2004).

Chapter 5

Capitalism's Incompatibility with Christianity

The Churches' Deep Solidarity with Labor

Jeremy Posadas

In most of the webinars from which this volume originated, the conversation among the panelists began with this question: From what do people and the planet need to be liberated? The answer I foregrounded then, as the COVID-19 pandemic was overtaking day-to-day life across the planet, and now, is capitalism. Capitalism is certainly not the only thing from which all of humankind and more-than-human nature must be liberated. But I foreground it because it has a special structuring relationship with all other inequities from which people and the planet cry out for liberation: Capitalism is the "-ism" that funds all the other -isms and keeps them in business, from one day and one generation to the next. The very systems that make racism, patriarchy (including cis- and hetero-normativity), colonialism, ableism, environmental degradation, and related apparatuses *systemic* injustices are not self-funding; rather, their ongoing operations are funded through the workings of capitalism, which has co-opted them so that they advance capitalism's aim in confederacy with it.

Thus, this chapter begins by examining how capitalism works, not from capitalism's own perspective, but from the perspective of people and the planet. Understanding capitalism in this way makes clear that capitalism is inherently incompatible with Christianity. Such incompatibility means that Christian congregations have a common cause with labor unions, which inherently have the potential to contest capitalist power: Labor's fight is the body of Christ's fight. Despite differences in what constitutes Christian congregations and labor unions as communities, I contend that Christian congregations must cultivate deep solidarity with labor unions in their shared fight against capitalism's ruthless, inexorable exploitation of people and the planet.

HOW CAPITALISM WORKS

Capitalism is usually defined in terms of goods and services, trade and markets, supply and demand. While the trading of goods and services on markets that set prices through the dynamics of supply and demand certainly is a key mechanism through which capitalism operates, markets functioned long before capitalism. What distinguishes capitalism as such is the basis on which its markets are founded—the particular societal structures that make markets act specifically in capitalistic ways. To perceive the societal structures specific to capitalism, we first need to remember how all of human life, in a capitalist or any other kind of society, depends on the relationship between the human *web of care* and the more-than-human *web of life*.[1]

The only way human communities and humankind as a whole are able to stay alive is through interpersonal care, which is sustained on an ongoing basis through the structures of collective life.[2] People are brought into the world by and from other people, and their physical-survival needs must be met by other people unless and until they have the physical capacities and have been taught how to do so for themselves. And, even when people are able to develop these physical and mental capacities, they must still rely on others to some degree for help in obtaining what they need to stay alive from one day to the next. In addition, throughout all our lives there is a minimum level of emotional care we need in order to stay alive. And these are just the basic forms of care needed to stay alive; in order for people to not only survive but also thrive, many more complex structures of care must be maintained, which together constitute the web of care.

The web of care that is necessary in order for humans to thrive is wholly dependent on a vastly broader and denser web: the web of life, comprised of all living organisms (of which humans are but one component) and their habitats. All living matter comes from and is eventually recycled into nonliving matter, from which new living matter will come, and gets the physical energy necessary for biological processes from nonliving matter, chiefly the sun, or other living matter. Thus, the web of life ultimately consists of all the "biogeochemical cycles" (to use the ecological term), many driven by the sun's energy, that constantly transform matter from nonliving to living and back again. Each human life along with the myriad interactions that constitute the web of care are but brief moments in the planetary cycling of carbon atoms, water molecules, and other elements and compounds from life to nonlife to new life. The human web of care exists only within and from the more-than-human web of life, upon which we are entirely, inescapably dependent.[3] The only reason there are people on the planet at all is because of the relationship between the web of care and the web of life: This is why capitalism, which fundamentally seeks to remake that relationship wholly into exploitation, is above all what people and the planet must be liberated from.

To understand what capitalism does to this relationship, we can start by considering how people in the present-day United States get access to the things necessary for basic survival.[4] With very few exceptions, almost all the material resources necessary for survival—from food, water, and electricity to clothing, housing, transportation, and more—must be purchased with money.[5] And where do people get this money? The vast majority must get it either by doing work for (and in exchange being paid by) an employer or by being economically dependent on someone who does paid work.[6] Some people are forced to work without getting paid, being held captive through violence and receiving their basic necessities directly from their captors; such enslaved labor is not a precapitalist relic but, confederated with racism, has been a key mechanism of the capitalist system for all of its history. Today, there are estimated hundreds of thousands of enslaved workers in the United States plus tens of millions more around the world who produce goods used by US people.[7] Those who have been physically or mentally disabled by societal structures so that they cannot perform paid employment must rely on public welfare aid and private charity, which provide only minimal support, do not permit thriving, and often impose significant intrusions on dignity and autonomy.

People who must work for a living, both employed and enslaved, people who depend on them economically, and societally disabled people constitute nearly all of a capitalist society such as the United States. However, there is a small fraction of society who do not need to work for a living; instead, they obtain money for purchasing basic necessities and much else through returns on their investment portfolios (in other words, their personal wealth). Banks and other corporations pay fees to use their money, and corporations or families pay rent to use land or buildings they own; these portfolio-holders can also use land or other highly priced physical assets they own as collateral for credit. They may have inherited their investment portfolio or amassed it through paid employment, but, when it becomes large enough that its returns can permanently pay for basic necessities, then the money is not coming from their own efforts, but from others' use of the things they own—that is, work that others are doing. Not everyone with investment portfolios reaches this point where they no longer have to work for a living, but those who do gain qualitatively different kinds of freedom and power than what is possible for people who must work for a living: freedom to pursue whatever activities they enjoy and power to control those who wish to use their money or real estate, along with all the social and political power that flows from this.

The fact that the vast majority of people in a capitalist society must work for a living (or be economically dependent on someone who does) is the key to the process that gives capitalism its name. Employed and enslaved workers produce goods and provide services that are sold on the market, but they do not get to set the prices for these goods and services. Instead, the prices are set by those who own the corporations for whom they work or, more often, the executives to whom owners delegate their power.[8] Within the market's dynamics of supply and demand, these prices are set so that the corporation brings in more money than it paid for the raw materials, tools, and facilities needed to produce goods and provide services and had to pay workers (or, for enslaved workers, the living necessities it had to supply) in order to keep them working. Thus, corporations are highly motivated to keep worker pay as low as possible. Racism and patriarchy (including cis- and hetero-normativity) are essential tools for this, by both segmenting people of color and women and feminine-identified people disproportionately into lower-paying occupations and discriminating against their pay within various occupations.

The excess beyond the cost of materials, tools, facilities, and worker pay is, of course, a corporation's profit, which is not distributed to workers (except for the occasional profit-sharing plan). Instead, it is used to expand either the corporation's capacities to make further profit or the owners' and executives' personal wealth, held in their investment portfolios.[9] These portfolios are then invested in other corporations, allowing them to expand their business and ultimately their capacities to make profit. When money cycles from *pay* for workers to produce goods and provide services to *profit* made from selling those goods and services and then to *investment* that expands profit-making capacities, it is known as *capital*. Capital*ism*, then, is the pursuit of the goal of getting ever more money in circulation as capital; this is achieved by maximizing profits, which are then distributed to owners and executives as their personal wealth, which in turn becomes capital when it is invested.

The need for money to purchase the necessities for living compels most people into work (or economic dependence on a worker). Yet, as discussed above, material resources are not the only things people need in order to survive: people need various forms of care throughout their lifetimes, beginning with the care that brings a new generation of people into the world.[10] Capitalist societies are built on the assumption that most of this care—which includes homemaking, child-rearing, emotional support, and much more—should and will be provided by family members and friends without being paid for, for the sake of love and/or duty. Capitalism could not persist without all this caring or domestic labor being provided for free, because it is also what renews workers from one day to the next so that they can continue toiling for their employers' profit.[11]

This, too, is shaped by patriarchy (including cis- and hetero-normativity), which promotes the stereotype that women and feminine-identified people are naturally more inclined toward caring for others, so they are explicitly or implicitly expected to do much more caring and domestic labor than men. Concurrently, racism not only ensures, through discrimination in the job market, that families and communities of color will have less money to afford necessities for living and less time and energy for providing care but also sustains patterns of residential segregation that unequalize access to community safety, nutritious food, unpolluted environments, and adequately resourced schools. These gender- and race-based inequalities amplify the inequality between the vast majority who must rely on the unpaid caring and domestic labor of family and friends and those who can pay others to do such labor. When caring and domestic labor are done as paid employment, it is mostly done by women and disproportionately by women of color, receives low pay and little respect, and exposes workers to multiple forms of mistreatment and violence.

The way capitalism treats caring or domestic labor is closely related to how it treats more-than-human nature: as something of which it has a limitless, free supply to use for its needs. It does so in three senses. First, it freely takes matter and energy out of ecosystems to use them as raw materials. Other than areas legally protected as nature reserves (a relatively recent phenomenon over capitalism's six centuries), capitalism has ravenously converted both nonliving and living material into profit-making goods or tools for profit-making services.[12] Second, it freely dumps wastes from both work processes and consumer use into ecosystems, resulting in everything from landfills to contaminated water supplies to pollutant-filled air. Third, as a consequence of the first two, the capacities of ecosystems to regenerate themselves and their species are degraded over the long term, as one can see in soil that is slowly turning into desert from decades of monoculture farming and lakes and seas that are fishless because of depleted oxygen levels.[13] Just as the exploitation of paid employment and unpaid domestic or caring labor is indispensable for capitalist profit making and thereby the swelling of investment portfolios that can supply ever more capital, so too is capitalism absolutely dependent on devastating the environment while repeatedly deferring payment of any real price to later generations (climate change being the prime example).

To encapsulate these harms to workers, their families, friends, and communities, and the more-than-human environments that give them life—harms without which capitalism could not achieve its overarching goal—let us return to the relationship between the web of care and the web of life.

Capitalism severely degrades the life-sustaining capacities of both the web of care and the web of life and deforms the holistic integration of the web of care *within* the web of life into the subordination of the web of life to the web of care. It tightly restricts how connections form within the web of care and the resources available for forming them, making the web of care conform to multiple structures of inequality. By imposing its logic of unlimited profit making on an earth-system containing a fixed amount of matter, it cuts the circle of earth's natural cycling of matter back and forth between nonliving and living and warps it into an exponential curve of decline from life-diversifying to life-diminished or even lifeless.[14] And because the web of life is the ultimate source for all the energy and matter humans need to survive, yet capitalism only makes these available in the form of products made by ecologically devastating methods, it positions the web of care as a tapeworm winding pervasively throughout the web of life, steadily draining away its capacities to sustain diverse communities of living organisms, including humans.

The wholesale degradation of both the web of life and the web of care and deformation of their natural relationship are not unfortunate accidents of capitalism; nor are they incidental to only some, less perfected versions of capitalism: they are intrinsic to capitalism itself. This is true theoretically, because of the contradiction between the "planetary boundaries" that maintain Earth as a human-habitable planet and the limitless accumulation of capital (requiring endless maximization of profits) that is capitalism's raison d'être.[15] And it has been repeatedly verified empirically, since every instance of capitalism over its six centuries of operation has perpetuated massive social inequity and left behind a net degradation of life-sustaining capacities in the environments it has occupied.[16] Despite upbeat prognostications of a "better" version of capitalism that avoids this manifold eco-social harm—usually offered by people whose investment portfolios stand to benefit from the pursuit of this ever-elusive version of capitalism—there is no way to reconcile the limitless accumulation of capital with widespread social equity and the laws of thermodynamics.

IS CAPITALISM COMPATIBLE WITH CHRISTIANITY?

Given that capitalism inherently operates by severely damaging both the web of life and the web of care and distorting their relationship, the question urgently arises whether it is compatible with Christianity. And the creation myths in Genesis, which provide a framework for understanding the relationship between the web of life and the web of care, are a major resource for answering this question. In Genesis, both accounts are sequenced according to the same principle: Creation provides enough for all living things to thrive together. Before each new group of living things begins to live, God ensures that the structure of the created world is fully able to provide their sustenance. Rather than creating, at one stroke, all of the living things that will ever exist, God fashions a complex structure that is capable of generating new life on an ongoing basis.

Plants need sunlight, air, rainfall, and soil in order to thrive, and, in the first account, God ensures these things are in place before bringing plants to life. These plants, in turn, are alive before God makes the animals that will rely on them for nourishment. The humans, created last, are likewise meant to get their nourishment from plants, though later God will permit them to also eat animals for nourishment (9:3–4). While the second account's sequence is different, it reflects the same principle: first the soil, then water to prepare the soil, then the human formed from the soil and enlivened by God's breath. Before placing the human on Earth, God plants the fruit-bearing trees that will be the human's food. And, because the second account assumes that humans have a necessary role in maintaining God's creation (2:5), only after the first human is made do animals and plants come into being. God then creates multiple human beings so that they can sustain each other's lives. Given that the second account strongly implies that God did not create humans to live forever and also that it emphasizes the similarity between the Hebrew words for soil and human, human death means a return to the soil, where humans will nourish plants on which they feed, thus completing the circle of creation, in which all living things mutually sustain each other.

Much has been made of God's intention for humans to "have dominion" (KJV) or "hold sway" (Robert Alter's translation of the Hebrew verb *radah*) over the created world (1:26, 28), which over the centuries has often been interpreted to mean that the rest of creation is merely an object that humans can use however they wish. But the only model given in the creation myths of what it means to rule (*radah*) is God's providing sustenance for all living beings; this is the kind of rule humans observe God performing, and, since they hadn't yet eaten from the Tree of Knowledge of Good and Evil, they would only have been conscious of ruling as providing for all. Moreover, in each account they are explicitly instructed as to how they are permitted to use creation in certain ways but forbidden from using it in other ways—that is, they are not given unlimited use of creation. So, God's intention for the created world is for humans to live in balance with the rest of life—and not only that, but to live together and take care of the created world so that the principle of life mutually sustaining life is upheld. The theological vision of creation revealed in the Bible, it turns out, greatly aligns with the ecological understanding of the web of life (including the web of care) established by modern Western science.[17]

What, then, is the theological and moral status of capitalism from a Christian standpoint? The time is right for the body of Christ to unconditionally, unambiguously, and univocally teach and confess: *Whereas capitalism per se is constituted through the wholesale degradation of both the web of life and the web of care and deformation of their natural relationship, therefore, we hold that capitalism violates God's holy purposes in creation and is intrinsically disordered against the created world. Wherever capitalism operates, by its constitutive structure it undermines and prevents the realization of the justice God desires for all of creation: thus, capitalism is repugnant to the Gospel and a scandal to the faith. This means it is impossible for Christians to promote capitalism and still remain consistent with the Gospel. Nor is it sufficient to pursue the least harmful form of capitalism, because the practices of capitalist power are inherently incompatible with Christian living. Rather, Christians have a sacred duty to resist, dismantle, and supplant capitalism in every way possible and to strive endlessly to eradicate it from the earth.*[18] And, since doctrinal declarations are often named geographically, let us call this the Madeira Declaration, given the island's role in the history of capitalism.

Such a doctrinal declaration will likely strike many church-going readers as unnecessarily strident or tendentious. But what would be a more appropriate Christian response to a force that actively causes death, disease, and emotional anguish for millions of people around the world every day and devastates every ecosystem it touches, decade by decade—and has done so for hundreds of years? Concurrently with any good that capitalism achieves, it systematically diminishes the very capacities that make human life possible and operates by degrading the dignity of many persons in order to protect the dignity of some: hence, capitalism is fundamentally incompatible with a theological stance of being pro-life or respecting human dignity. Moreover, capitalism by its very structure makes it impossible for humankind either to live in harmony with the rest of creation or to eradicate racism, patriarchy (including cis- and hetero-normativity), colonialism, ableism, and myriad other social inequities. It is, thus, just as strongly incompatible with theological commitments to stewardship of or care for creation and to human liberation. The integrity of life, the dignity of every person, the liberation of all people, the wholeness of creation—a Christian who has heard God's call to hold fast to any of these things will find that capitalism repeatedly obstructs and obviates them, at which point the memory of Jesus's counsel regarding God and Mammon (Luke 16:13; Matthew 6:24) and Amos's vision of justice as an unpolluted river (Amos 5:23–24) make the choice clear.

Because capitalism is incompatible with Christianity, Christians must dismantle and supplant capitalism in every way possible. For such dismantling and supplanting to be effective, however, Christian churches must partner with labor unions—and both must motivate each other to focus on dismantling and supplanting capitalism, not merely ameliorating its worst effects. And why are labor unions the churches' indispensable partner? The labor movement is the primary bulwark against capitalist power. As Joerg Rieger and Rosemarie Henkel-Rieger discuss in their book *Unified We Are a Force*, workers organized in labor unions have the potential to fight against capitalist power at its very core: profit-making work processes.[19] They can impact capitalist power in ways churches cannot, so they rightly lead the struggle against capitalist power. Churches by their very nature share in this struggle, a fact that can be obscured by differences in how churches and labor unions are constituted as communities, which we examine next.

DON'T LABOR AND THE CHURCHES HAVE DIFFERENT PURPOSES?

Labor unions are local and constitutive units of the labor movement just as congregations are the local and constitutive units of the several churches. At first glance, congregations and labor unions are quite different as organizations. A labor union is an association of workers who work for the same employer or industry and have organized themselves in order to create collective power to change their working conditions. Labor unions enable workers to demand and negotiate changes in their working conditions because it is more difficult for an employer to ignore or fire a whole group of workers supporting one another than to ignore or fire a single worker. Generally, membership in a labor union is limited to those who work for a given employer or set of employers; that is, people cannot join just any labor union they wish, but only a union with others who work for the same employer. However, working for the same employer is, in principle, the only necessary qualification for membership in a labor union. And, although the workers of large employers may be divided into different unions based on the nature of their occupations, the principle still holds that membership in a union is a consequence of an antecedent relationship, the worker-employer relationship. (It must also be recognized that various unions have at times resisted being inclusive toward demographic shifts—especially in terms of race, national status, and gender—in the workforces they organize.)[20]

Congregations are similar to unions in that their members' relationships to and shared identity with each other is based on their relationship with someone else: in unions, members' relationship with the employer; in congregations, members' relationship with God. However, whereas a worker must already have entered the employment relationship as a condition for becoming a member of a union, most congregations are open to anyone participating in much of worship along with other activities even if they do not already have a relationship with God or are only exploring one. While there is always the hope that participation in congregational activities will lead to a public commitment to a relationship with God—and certain activities are off-limits until such a commitment is made—there is in principle no set duration for how long one may participate prior to making it. Moreover, whereas a worker-employer relationship permits membership only in the union of others who work for the same employer, a Christian's relationship with God is not intrinsically limited to any particular congregation; while Christians typically only join congregations belonging to their specific confessional tradition, it is generally permissible to change traditions within Christianity, although familial or other social pressures often create barriers.

Although membership in a union or in a congregation is based on each member having a relationship with the same entity, the role that relationship plays in the lives of members is very different. Congregations generally aspire for a member's relationship with God to shape every aspect of the member's life, from the personal and interpersonal to the sociopolitical and global. In other words, congregations typically promote a totalizing relationship with God. By contrast, unions resist a totalizing relationship with the employer. Despite many employers' attempts to permeate and control more and more of workers' lives, even during nonwork time, unions strive to limit employers' reach. For example, when unions fight for their members to be scheduled in less fragmented shifts, they are seeking to minimize the amount of nonwork time that must be sacrificed in the transition to, between, and from shifts. By definition, unions promote a highly circumscribed relationship with the employer, in order for members to transform the work process itself in ways that are more life-giving and creative and to pursue the fullness of whatever nonwork relationships they want, whereas congregations assume that the relationship with God should guide how one acts in all relationships.

The fact that congregations promote a totalizing relationship with God while unions promote a strictly circumscribed relationship with the employer points to a deeper difference: Unions foster a relationship between workers and their employer that is inherently antagonistic, while congregations foster a relationship between members and God that can be characterized as mutualistic, although this mutualism is framed theologically in diverse ways. More conservative theologies often conceptualize the relationship as one in which humans are to obey God while God actively hears humans' needs through prayer and responds to them lovingly yet justly. More liberal theologies, by contrast, tend to emphasize human partnership and/or co-creativity with God to realize a loving and just order in human life. In both cases, humans and God engage one another in ways that bring fulfillment and joy proper to each.

By contrast, unions necessarily work to resist and decrease the employer's power over workers. As discussed above, the capitalist market constantly pressures employers to be as profitable as possible, and working conditions are a major factor employers can manipulate in order to maximize profit. Even if an employer is committed to creating pleasant working conditions, these must still be conducive to making a profit or else the employer will not be able to stay in business. As Elizabeth Anderson documents in *Private Government: How Employers Rule Our Lives (and Why We Don't Talk about It)*, the capitalist worker-employer relationship grants the employer near-absolute power over workers during work time: what they must do, how they must do it, what they are forbidden from doing.[21] Legal regulations concerning workplace safety, maximum work hours, the minimum wage, and so on—which, in fact, exist largely because workers organized against their employers—provide workers a bare minimum of protection against abusive employer practices, but their effectiveness is dependent on whether there is effective, regular government enforcement. And these regulations leave plenty of room for perfectly legal abusive and degrading working conditions, as Emily Guendelsberger has recently documented in her book *On the Clock*, based on her experiences working in low-wage retail, logistics, and service work.[22]

Unions by definition aim to build a countervailing force to this largely unrestricted employer power.[23] They do so through a mass effect: Since it is more difficult and costly for an employer to discipline or fire a large number of workers than an individual worker, by organizing together, unionized workers make it more likely that an employer will have to respond constructively to their complaints and demands. What gives this mass effect concrete power, however, is unionized workers' willingness to collectively interrupt the work process, whether by slowing down on the job or engaging in a complete work stoppage, known as a strike. These are blunt tools, and their actual use is less frequent than the threat of their use, which can pressure an employer to negotiate with workers.[24] Along with these blunt tools, unions must develop a whole repertoire of ways to pressure an employer, from mobilizing community support to pressuring shareholders to changing policy legislatively. (Longtime union organizer Jane McAlevey's *A Collective Bargain: Unions, Organizing, and the Fight for Democracy* is the best contemporary introduction to how unions build this repertoire of power.) Through all of these, unions reconfigure the worker-employer relationship from one of unilateral power of the employer over workers to one in which workers have multiple ways of refusing to obey the employer. This antagonism is inherent in the fact that the ultimate goal demanded by the market—maximizing profit—conflicts with a union's goal of securing the well-being of workers both within and outside of their work for the employer.

The fact that unions promote a circumscribed and inherently antagonistic relationship between workers and their employer while congregations promote a totalizing and mutualistic relationship between members and God means that union members' basic relationship with each other is constituted very differently from congregation members' basic relationship with each other. Union members' relationship with each other begins transactionally: Each member gains more impact by choosing to organize with other members. The purpose of the relationship is to be an effective means of improving each member's well-being by changing the behavior of their common employer. Many unions foster a sense of relationship among members that goes beyond the transactional, so that membership in the union displaces identification with the employing corporation; over time, this can even lead union members to regard their fellow members as extended family. But this does not change that the underlying purpose of the relationship and what justifies its continuation is the pursuit of a shared goal.

The relationship between congregation members, by contrast, first arises not from what they can do for one another, but from a shared identity as members of (or people interested in exploring) the overall Christian community, commonly called the body of Christ. Even though participating in congregational life and thereby cultivating a relationship with fellow congregation members does, in many cases, enhance members' relationship with God, that is not the reason for cultivating the relationship with fellow members.[25] Rather, for nearly all practicing Christians, to be a practicing Christian at all entails relationship with fellow congregation (or analogous community) members, a necessary manifestation of being in relationship with God. So, membership in a congregation is the default assumption for nearly all Christians, whereas unions must convince workers and continually demonstrate that it is more advantageous to be a members of the union than not to be.

LABOR UNIONS AND CONGREGATIONS EXPAND THE WEB OF CARE TOGETHER

Although I have been emphasizing the major differences between unions and congregations, when we consider how they both strive to expand people's capacities to care we find crucial convergence that is the basis for solidarity and partnership against capitalism's predation on care. We discussed above how capitalism coerces the vast majority of people to work by making it impossible for them to adequately care for themselves and those they love without submitting to the power of the corporations that employ them, receiving in exchange the money necessary for care activities: Most people work above all else because they want to take good care of themselves and those they love. Moreover, capitalism relies on interpersonal networks to provide the care necessary to replenish its workforce from one day to the next and one generation to the next, yet this care is unpaid (or, at best, inadequately paid). In this way, capitalism colonizes our capacities to care and forces them to be instruments for the continuous accumulation of profit and increase of investment portfolios; capitalism is a parasitism that infects the web of care.

Labor unions seek to break capitalism's stranglehold over our care capacities. Many of the demands they fight for expand workers' capacities to care for themselves and their loved ones. For instance, for many workers, demands for things like paid time off and more reasonably scheduled shifts are attempts to free up more nonwork time to care for loved ones or care for themselves. Demands for better wages or retirement income are, for the most part, demands for financial resources that workers need in order to pursue their diverse visions of thriving, for themselves and those they love. Demands for safer work processes and better health-care coverage and educational opportunities seek greater care for bodies and minds. Yet demands that aren't strictly for material resources for care, such as demands for a greater say in workplace decisions, are often related to care, because workers want to secure less degrading and more creative working conditions, a way of caring for themselves and one another and preserving more of their capacities to care for loved ones outside of work.

Being able to more fully care for themselves, one another, and their loved ones is not the only thing that motivates workers' demands of the corporations that employ them. Workers can also demand these things because they want to be able to buy nicer goods, or because it doesn't feel fair for employers to enjoy so much more of the profits, or because they value extrinsic marks of success, or because of many other motivations. People do many things that matter to them for multiple reasons simultaneously. But I contend that, for most workers, most of the time, the strongest motivator of most demands they fight for through their union is the desire to take good care of themselves, their fellow workers, and their loved ones. And the leading edge of the labor movement is unions that pursue care not only for workers and their loved ones but also for the whole community—the communities they live in, the communities of people for whom they provide services, the communities environmentally impacted by the profit-making work they are ensnared in.

This paradigm of union organizing is often referred to as "social-justice unionism," and it is vibrant both in the United States and throughout the world.[26] Some of the most effective recent US instances of it are actions by nurses and teachers (whose occupations, not coincidentally, are care-centered). For example, for over a decade starting in the 1990s, the California Nurses Association organized to codify in law a maximum nurse-to-patient ratio for hospital care. Such a ratio, they argued repeatedly, would allow them to better care for their patients because their attention would not be overly fragmented. In 1999, having organized with patient-advocacy organizations against the hospital lobby, the nurses succeeded in getting this law passed, so far the only one in the nation.[27]

In 2012, when the Chicago Teachers Union was negotiating a new contract with Chicago Public Schools, it fought not only for better pay and benefits but also for goals that would improve the educational experience of students, such as smaller classrooms, more music and art classes, and fewer high-stakes exams. Under new leadership, the union reached out to parents throughout the city, particularly working-class parents, on the basis of a shared interest in good education for all children. After a weeklong strike, the union made progress on a number of these demands; more importantly, it demonstrated how unions can fight for the good of the whole community, not just their worker-members. And, in 2018, when teachers and other school workers in all fifty-five of West Virginia's school districts went on strike, leading half the state's students to lose access to the free or reduced-price breakfast and lunch for which they depended on schools, the union organized its own food distribution to help feed students.[28] In examples like these and many others, we see unions acting as a force to care for the whole community—unions as multipliers of collective capacities to care.

Again, in a capitalist society, most people cannot access the resources they need to care for themselves and others without doing (or being dependent on someone who does) paid employment: paid employment is the point where capitalism most directly colonizes people's capacities to care and subordinates them to the maximization of profit and wealth. Labor unions, especially those motivated by social-justice unionism, organize workers at this point of colonization to actively resist and push back against it.[29] Where employers continually claim more and more of workers' time, energy, attention, and skills for as low a wage as workers will accept—leaving less of these things available for caring for oneself and others outside of work—labor unions press to secure more of all these things for workers, primarily so that they can more fully care for themselves, those they love, and their communities without the requirement of profitability. Thus, labor unions are groups of workers fighting to protect their care capacities against capitalism's predation and to constantly enhance their care capacities by making more time, energy, attention, skills, and money and other material resources available for care.

The perspective of the web of care likewise gives us a fuller sense of how congregations are also a countervailing force against capitalism's parasitism on care. Activities of care, both for members and for the broader community, are central to Christian congregations' existence.[30] (It must be acknowledged, though, that these activities of care are often marred by prevailing social inequalities as well as patterns of emotional dysfunction.) To begin with the most prominent examples, baptism, preaching, and Eucharist are fundamentally acts of care: bathing, teaching, and feeding.[31] Functionally, these three care activities play key roles in constituting Christian congregations in the first place. In most congregations, baptism is the basis for membership, while the sermon or the Lord's Supper or both are the focal points of the structure of weekly worship. Moreover, the life of a congregation is sustained by many practices of care alongside these liturgically enacted ones. The teaching that sermons provide is part of a whole matrix of activities that form members' minds and spirits across the life span; such activities range from Sunday School, Bible study, small groups, and other formal programs to informal actions such as intergenerational role modeling and conversations to think through moral issues. The practices labeled by scholars as pastoral and congregational care provide ongoing emotional support to congregation members. And congregations foster networks of friendship in varying intensities, both through intentional social occasions like fellowship hours or attending cultural events together and through the accumulation of shared activities—attending or leading worship, cooking together for church events, serving in leadership positions, and so on—over many years. Congregations continue to exist because their members care for one another, year after year and generation to generation.

But congregations *also* care for their communities, in diverse ways and on the basis of diverse theological understandings of the relationship between church and society.[32] Many congregations regularly do service projects that temporarily alleviate a symptom of a societal problem, everything from food and clothing drives and holiday meals to neighborhood or park clean-ups to building low-cost homes (domestically or internationally). Many congregations also maintain ongoing programs to alleviate symptoms, such as operating food pantries or emergency shelters, regularly hosting social-service providers, or even themselves directly providing social services, such as support groups or assistance getting access to housing, income, and employment. Beyond trying to lessen the impact of societal problems, some congregations engage in advocacy to increase public awareness and encourage action on issues such as homelessness, health inequity, racial discrimination, immigration, and many others. Some congregations go even further and organize to pressure politicians or other community leaders to change practices and policies that promote injustice, such as the Moral Mondays that began in North Carolina. The movement known as faith-, congregation-, or broad-based community organizing is one of the longest-running and best-known forms of this kind of congregational social action. More recently, some congregations have started to establish or incubate cooperatives that foster an alternative economy.[33]

Although congregations make diverse theological sense of these various efforts based on their respective traditions, a common thread is that these efforts expand a congregation's care capacities so that they impact not only its own members but also the community in which it is embedded. Moreover, they expand the care capacities within the community itself by redistributing resources and/or reconfiguring power in ways that empower marginalized members of the community to more fully care for themselves and their loved ones.[34] Congregations expand care in these ways because they understand it to be intrinsic to Christian life, often explained as the "horizontal" dimension that is inseparable from the "vertical" dimension, that is, relationship with God. This understanding, shaped by centuries of biblical interpretation and social teaching, is framed theologically in diverse ways, from evangelism to service to liberation. And, while there are a few congregations that shun social ministry, in most congregations caring for the community is seen as a natural outgrowth of God's care for them.

Acknowledging that congregations expand their own and their broader community's care capacities motivated by Christian faith but not necessarily an anti-capitalist commitment, we can nevertheless detect how, by expanding the web of care, congregations have the potential to act against capitalism's parasitism on it. Congregations activate care that, by definition, is not intended to serve the capitalist drive for profit; they generate and incubate care capacities that cannot be wholly instrumentalized by capitalism, because they are pursued for their own sake, as an extension of the relationship with God. Certainly, there are congregations that pursue care in ways that support capitalism, whether intentionally, as in a congregation that proclaims the moral goodness of capitalism, or implicitly, as in a congregation whose members are mostly in the executive class (and whose care for each other thereby reinforces class inequalities of power and wealth) or whose advocacy focuses on ameliorating effects of capitalism. But, as I argued above, this is inconsistent with the Gospel. Instead, congregations are called by God, as part of ongoing dismantlement and supplanting of capitalism, to promote, support, and protect networks of care among their members and in the broader community that contest capitalism's endless drive to instrumentalize everything for the maximization of profit.

Among the various networks of care that congregations can promote, support, and protect as part of dismantling and supplanting capitalism, unions are foremost because they can directly challenge capitalist power at the point where its vulnerability is most concentrated, the work processes that profitably produce goods and services. There are numerous ways congregations can actively partner with unions, which, for most congregations, would be an important growing edge.[35] They can, for example, make their facilities available for groups of workers who are trying to form a union to meet in, extending hospitality that can be a comfort amid an exhausting process. Safe spaces where workers can meet privately are a crucial resource for the conversations by which workers educate and encourage each other. When workers are initially organizing to form a union or when already-unionized workers are negotiating a new contract, congregations can be active supporters by hosting workers to educate the congregation about the organizing effort, publicly expressing solidarity with the workers, attending or hosting union rallies, and volunteering to assist as needed. Efforts like these are even more urgent if employers push workers to the point where workers must strike in order to increase their leverage. By publicly demonstrating support for workers, congregations validate them in the eyes of community members who see the congregation as a morally credible organization.

During all these key phases of union organizing, congregations can serve as conduits to community leaders, both those who are members and those who are friends of members. Direct personal contacts such as these can be highly effective at moving community leaders to support union efforts, which is especially important if community leaders control hinge points of power that can influence employers' behavior. Outside of high-intensity phases such as initial organizing, contract negotiations, and strikes, congregations can foster ongoing support by continually educating members of both the congregation and the broader community about the challenges workers and unions are facing, the basic purpose and function of unions, and labor issues more generally. Congregations can also join or help establish a local faith-labor coalition to address problems that affect a wide range of marginalized groups in their community.[36] On a larger scale, congregations can mobilize to seek the enactment of laws and policies that promote justice for workers and protect their right to form unions.

Concurrent with all these strategically oriented activities, congregations can invite unions to social and fellowship events for the sake of encouraging friendship between members of the union and the congregation. (Moreover, in congregations whose membership also includes [potential] union members, especially in the southern United States, building deeper relationships between congregation and union members can also be a form of enhancing relationships within the congregation.) This is essential in order for a congregation to cultivate the sensibility of being in partnership *with* a union rather than doing kindly service *for* a union—that is, to cultivate solidarity instead of mere charity.

Although congregations need to follow unions' lead in breaking capitalism's hold over our care capacities, the relationship is one of mutual improvement; congregations are junior partners, not silent partners. Because congregations draw their members from and are thereby integrated within the broader communities in which unions are embedded, they can encourage unions to pursue the good of the whole communities in which union members live as well as communities that are affected by the corporations that employ them—the social-justice unionism described above. A major aspect of this is challenging unions to continually become more intersectionally inclusive, recognizing the various ways multiple, interlocking oppressions target many of their members, and shaping their agendas to transform both work and broader community in ways that dismantle all of these oppressions. (This, however, is a matter of mutual accountability. For unions in a number of sectors are vibrantly practicing intersectional inclusivity, while many congregations at various points within demographic and theological axes have yet to begin or are struggling to achieve it.)

Even as a number of unions, especially those with more demographically diverse membership bases, have made noticeable progress in intersectional justice making, for those that have not, congregations can be an important partner for improving in this way. Because congregations, like only a few other societal institutions, seek to engage members' whole lives (based on the totalizing relationship with God discussed above), they have the capacity—*if* they have been adequately mobilized for justice making in the first place—to be involved in multiple movements, for example, movements for racial justice, reproductive justice, disability justice, and immigration justice. As congregations themselves deepen solidarity with these movements, they can invite unions that do not already have relationships with these movements to join them in these efforts. Moreover, congregations can foster connections across movements by convening both strategic and social gatherings of leaders of unions and other movements.

In linking unions with other justice movements, some of the greatest capitalism-dismantling impact congregations can have is facilitating union solidarity with ecological justice, that is, justice between the human and more-than-human components of nature.[37] Recall that capitalism not only degrades the web of care but also degrades the web of life *and* deforms the relationship between the two. As we have discussed, unions are constituted to protect and expand the web of care; however, this does not automatically entail protecting and expanding the web of life or restoring right relationship between the two webs. In fact, too often unions have accepted the capitalist framing of a choice between economic security through employment within capitalism versus ecological justice. Congregations, however, have a sacred obligation to protect and expand both webs and restore right relationship between them. As they build solidarity with unions, therefore, they must steadily call on unions to be, in environmental scholar Jason Moore's evocative phrase, "comrades in arms with the web of life."[38] While a number of unions have made steps in this direction, many Christian church bodies have gone farther than the majority of labor unions, so their congregations have a number of resources to encourage unions, from moral frameworks integrating humans with nature to spiritual practices of connecting with the earth to participation in networks for ecological justice.

Yet, even as intersectionally engaged congregations can encourage unions to pursue justice in a more intersectionally comprehensive way, they must also be open to reconsidering and transforming, under unions' influence, their own labor practices, both paid employment and unpaid caring or domestic labor. As employers, congregations must intentionally refuse to exploit workers in the ways capitalism normalizes. For instance, congregations must not pay wages or create working conditions for their own employees that would be unacceptable to unions with whom the congregation partners. And unions can guide congregations in creating employment structures that guarantee congregational employees have power to challenge working conditions that inhibit their capacities to care for their loved ones and communities or are unjust in other ways.

Congregations typically rely on unpaid caring and domestic labor ("domestic" here meaning cooking for congregational meals, cleaning church spaces and vestments, and the like) as much or more than on the labor of paid employees, and dismantling capitalist patterns of exploiting this kind of labor may likely be more difficult. The problem is not that congregations rely on members volunteering to do various kinds of caring or domestic labor, but how that labor is structured: especially whether this labor is acknowledged and valued (and, if so, how), who does this labor and whether it is equitably shared among members, and whether those who do this labor have power in the congregation commensurate with the indispensability of this labor for the congregation's survival. To bring up the most common instance: Many congregations replicate capitalism's patriarchal structures in which women are expected to do most of the necessary caring or domestic labor but are assigned subordinate status in the congregation's power structures. The Christian obligation to dismantle capitalism in all its forms means transforming these patterns, both by teaching members of all genders to share in caring and domestic labor and by ensuring that members of all genders can participate as equals in all congregational power structures.[39] In a more abstract vein, there needs to be a wholesale theological reassessment of why congregational practices of care outside of worship, like in education and fellowship, are not considered sacred to the same degree and in the same way that liturgically performed acts of care are.

CONCLUSION

By one reckoning, capitalism is now as old as Noah was when God told him to build the ark.[40] Over that entire span, capitalism, the "-ism" that keeps all the other -isms in business, has been degrading the planet and all life on it (including human life), breaking cycles that, for geological eons, have transformed energy and matter from life to nonlife to new life. By inexorably speeding up portions of those cycles—in large part by constantly pressing workers to speed up production—capitalism is threatening to cause, by means of air, even more damage than the flood did by means of water. In less time than capitalism has been in existence, humankind may not be able to continue existing on this planet. This is written into capitalism's basic operating code; there is no version of it that can avoid this fate. Yet, for Christians, there can be no doubt that this fate is not the fate God wants for creation. "In the beginning," say the creation myths by which Christians remember and affirm the ecological cycles of life, a whole world is called into being by divine desire, teeming with living things that sustain one another's life and that, in dying and returning to the earth and sea, bring forth new life. This world has no need for capital and its voracious conversion of nearly all life into death. Christians everywhere, therefore, are called to dismantle capitalism and root it out from all the earth, so that all life may have life abundantly and in peace with all other life. And, for this sacred task, congregations are right to regard labor unions as prophets and partners.

NOTES

1. The account that follows is distilled from a broad literature of contemporary ecological, feminist, and anti-racist critiques of capitalism. Good entry points for general audiences are Raj Patel and Jason Moore, *A History of the World in Seven Cheap Things: A Guide to Capitalism, Nature, and the Future of the Planet* (Berkeley: University of California Press, 2018), and Fred Magdoff and Chris Williams, *Creating an Ecological Society: Toward a Revolutionary Transformation* (New York: Monthly Review Books, 2017). The scholarly literature is exemplified by Nancy Fraser, "Behind Marx's Hidden Abode: For an Expanded Conception of Capitalism," *New Left Review* 86 (March/April 2014), 55–72; Jason Moore, *Capitalism in the Web of Life: Ecology and the Accumulation of Capital* (New York: Verso, 2015); Alyssa Battistoni, "Bringing in the Work of Nature: From Natural Capital to Hybrid Labor," *Political Theory* 45 no. 1 (2017), 5–31; Tithi Bhattacharya, ed., *Social Reproduction Theory: Remapping Class, Recentering Oppression* (London: Pluto Books, 2017); Sophie Lewis, *Full Surrogacy Now: Feminism against Family* (New York: Verso, 2019); Kathi Weeks, *The Problem with Work: Feminism, Marxism, Antiwork Politics, and Postwork Imaginaries* (Durham, NC: Duke University Press, 2011); Silvia

Federici, *Re-enchanting the World: Feminism and the Politics of the Commons* (Oakland, CA: PM Press, 2018); Gargi Bhattacharya, *Rethinking Racial Capitalism: Questions of Reproduction and Survival* (Lanham, MD: Rowman & Littlefield, 2018).

2. The journey to this paragraph began with Pastor Heidi Neumark's proclamation that "connection is everything: relationship to God and one another is life itself." And the journey to the next paragraph was catalyzed by my ecology teacher, Dr. Jessica Healy, who exemplifies a Christian dual commitment to liberating people and the planet. With love and in awe, I dedicate this chapter to both of them, and I give thanks to Union Theological Seminary, where I first learned liberation theologies, and to the Wendland-Cook Program in Religion and Justice at Vanderbilt Divinity School, where a faculty fellowship allowed me to pull together the ideas presented here. Neumark, *Breathing Space: A Spiritual Journey in the South Bronx* (Boston, MA: Beacon Press, 2003), 2.

3. Joerg Rieger applies Friedrich Schleiermacher's notion of "absolute dependence" to the relationship between human and nonhuman labor in *Theology in the Capitalocene: Ecology, Identity, Class, and Solidarity* (Minneapolis: Fortress Press, 2022).

4. The experience in wealthy Western nations at capitalism's core sometimes differs markedly from that in capitalism's colonial or neocolonial periphery, where most of the world lives. Nonetheless, many of the features and dynamics I describe here are true to a large degree outside capitalism's core, and they steadily increase the more a nation "develops" in capitalism. For an overview of capitalism's hierarchy of nations, see Jason Hickel, *The Divide: Global Inequality from Conquest to Free Markets* (New York: Norton, 2018).

5. The reason these things must be purchased with money is because capitalism was initiated with acts of theft by wealthy Europeans, stealing land away from people for whom it had supplied basic necessities for centuries or millennia or stealing people away from this land; the former is colonization (and its domestic twin, enclosure), and the latter is enslavement. See Kris Manjapra, *Colonialism in Global Perspective* (Cambridge, UK: Cambridge University Press, 2020); Ellen Meiksins Wood, *The Origin of Capitalism: A Longer View*, new ed. (New York: Verso, 2017); and Edward Baptist, *The Half Has Never Been Told: Slavery and the Making of American Capitalism* (New York: Basic Books, 2016).

6. Michael Zweig, *The Working Class Majority: America's Best Kept Secret*, second ed. (Ithaca, NY: Cornell University Press, 2012).

7. See the International Labor Organization's website on forced labor, modern slavery, and human trafficking: https://www.ilo.org/global/topics/forced-labour/lang--en/index.htm.

8. While self-employed workers do set the prices for their goods and services, they must do so in a market largely shaped by large corporations that produce comparable goods and services, corporations that charge prices based on their pursuit of profit.

9. Although not-for-profit corporations use any profit they make differently from how for-profit corporations do, such profit is nonetheless generally not distributed to employees. Moreover, much support for not-for-profit corporations comes from

donations by those whose investment portfolios are large enough that they do not need to work for a living.

10. The scholarly concept for all of this care is "social reproduction." See Bhattacharya, *Social Reproduction Theory* (cited above, note 1).

11. According to one of the most comprehensive studies of unpaid domestic labor (which, unfortunately, leaves out some of the costs of care provided by family and friends for older adults), the total value of unpaid domestic labor—itself only one large portion of the total unpaid caring and domestic labor on which society depends for its survival—was $3.3 *trillion* (13 percent of gross domestic product) in 2017, a year when total corporate profits after taxes were $1.9 trillion. Three years later, in the first year of the pandemic, its value increased 20 percent, to $3.9 trillion. Data are from the "Household Production" section of the Bureau of Economic Analysis website, https://www.bea.gov/data/special-topics/household-production; and the FRED database of the Federal Reserve Bank of St. Louis, https://fred.stlouisfed.org/series/CP#0.

12. Although most matter and energy taken out of ecosystems—and capitalism defines all ecosystems as simply "natural resources" for production—must nowadays be purchased from whoever owns the land on or water in which they're located, again, the chain of ownership did not begin by being paid for, but by theft, from both its indigenous inhabitants (colonialism) and those who held it in common up until then (enclosure, colonialism's domestic twin). See note 5 above as well as Peter Linebaugh, *Stop, Thief! The Commons, Enclosures, and Resistance* (Oakland, CA: PM Press, 2014), and Andro Linklater, *Owning the Earth: The Transforming History of Land Ownership* (New York: Bloomsbury, 2013).

13. The practices of regenerative/restorative agriculture and aquaculture and the science of agroecology demonstrate that environmental devastation is not necessary for feeding the global human population. See David Montgomery, *Growing a Revolution: Bringing Our Soil Back to Life* (New York: Norton, 2018); Bren Smith, *Eat Like a Fish: My Adventures as a Fisherman Turned Restorative Ocean Farmer* (New York: Knopf, 2019); United Nations Food and Agriculture Organization, *The 10 Elements of Agroecology: Guiding the Transition to Sustainable Food and Agricultural Systems*, FAO report #I9037EN/1/04.18 (New York: United Nations, 2018); The Nature Conservancy, *Global Principles of Restorative Aquaculture* (Arlington, VA: The Nature Conservancy, 2021), https://www.nature.org/content/dam/tnc/nature/en/documents/TNC_PrinciplesofRestorativeAquaculture.pdf.

14. Even though earth is a system containing a fixed amount of matter, it is continuously receiving more energy in the form of sunlight. This energy is stored over the short term in the chemical bonds that convert nonliving matter into living matter; what maintains the circular balance is the long-term storage (for millions of years) of previously living matter deep underground as fossil fuels. But, since the Industrial Revolution, capitalism has broken open these stores and moved that matter from underground to the atmosphere much faster than earth can naturally process while maintaining a climate livable for human beings. See Andreas Malm, *Fossil Capital: The Rise of Steam Power and the Roots of Global Warming* (New York: Verso, 2016).

15. Will Steffen, Katherine Richardson, Johan Rockström, et al., "Planetary Boundaries: Guiding Human Development on a Changing Planet," *Science* 347 no. 6223 (2015): 736–47, https://doi.org/10.1126/science.1259855.

16. While the beginning of capitalism as such is often dated to the start of the Industrial Revolution or the European conquest of the Americas, I follow Patel and Moore in seeing European colonization of the Atlantic island of Madeira in the early 1400s as the point when and place where capitalism's particular constellation of techniques for exploiting (enslaved) people and the planet were, arguably, first practiced all together. See the introduction in Patel and Moore, *History* (cited above, note 1).

17. This makes sense given the agricultural basis of the creation myths and is only unexpected because capitalism has suppressed indigenous understandings of nature's holism throughout its realm. See Ellen Davis, *Scripture, Culture, and Agriculture: An Agrarian Reading of the Bible* (Cambridge, UK: Cambridge University Press, 2008), and United Nations Food and Agriculture Organization, *10 Elements of Agroecology* (cited above, note 13).

18. Discerning readers will recognize some of the categories of moral theology here from their misapplication by many church polities to same-gender relationships and gender-expansive people. Separately, on Madeira's role in the history of capitalism, see note 16, above.

19. Joerg Rieger and Rosemarie Henkel-Rieger, *Unified We Are a Force: How Faith and Labor Can Overcome America's Inequalities* (St. Louis, MO: Chalice Press, 2016); see especially chapter 1. See also Erik Olin Wright, "How to Be an Anticapitalist Today," *Jacobin* magazine website, December 2, 2015, https://www.jacobinmag.com/2015/12/erik-olin-wright-real-utopias-anticapitalism-democracy.

20. See Jane McAlevey, *A Collective Bargain: Unions, Organizing, and the Fight for Democracy* (New York: HarperCollins, 2020).

21. Elizabeth Anderson, *Private Government: How Employers Rule Our Lives (and Why We Don't Talk about It)* (Princeton, NJ: Princeton University Press, 2019).

22. Emily Guendelsberger, *On the Clock: What Low-Wage Work Did to Me and How It Drives America Insane* (New York: Little, Brown, 2019).

23. Worker cooperatives (co-ops), in which the workers themselves own the corporation on an equal basis with one another, can be seen as the furthest horizon of the labor movement. See, for example, Richard Wolff, *Democracy at Work: A Cure for Capitalism* (Chicago: Haymarket Books, 2012).

24. Employers do have many ways of undermining the threat of a strike. And, as McAlevey notes, these tools are only effective if union leaders have sufficiently mobilized members to use them. McAlevey, *Collective Bargain*, 157–60 (cited above, note 20). Also see the film *The Hand That Feeds*, directed by Rachel Lears and Robin Blotnick (Brooklyn, NY: Jubilee Films, 2014).

25. Moreover, congregation members whose identities are marginalized by theological traditions (for instance, queer Christians in most congregations) must cultivate a relationship with God despite the obstacles thereto raised by fellow congregation members.

26. Kim Scipes, "Social Movement Unionism or Social Justice Unionism? Disentangling Theoretical Confusion within the Global Labor Movement," *Class, Race and Corporate Power* 2 no. 3 (2014), https://doi.org/10.25148/crcp.2.3.16092119.

27. National Nurses United, "Ratios: Learning from the California Experience," National Nurses United website, https://www.nationalnursesunited.org/ratios-california-experience.

28. Micah Uetricht, *Strike for America: Chicago Teachers against Austerity* (New York: Verso, 2014); Eric Blanc, *Red State Revolt: The Teachers' Strike Wave and Working-Class Politics* (New York: Verso, 2019); Michael Moore, director, *Fahrenheit 11/9* (Midwestern Films, 2018). While it's easy to think that contention over remote instruction during the COVID-19 pandemic is a repudiation of teacher-parent solidarity, we must remember that the ultimate cause for this contention is that capitalism's normal mode is to stretch families and schools to their (under-resourced) limits in nurturing children and youth.

29. Again, worker cooperatives are the furthest development of the labor movement, and, when they commit themselves to serve the common good, they turn the entire work process into something that contributes to caring for the community.

30. As used in this section, *care* as a congregational practice includes but is much broader than what in practical theology is typically categorized as pastoral or congregational care.

31. Gordon Lathrop, *Holy Things: A Liturgical Theology* (Minneapolis: Fortress Press, 1993).

32. Rieger and Henkel-Rieger's distinctions between charity, advocacy, and deep solidarity are particularly important; see Rieger and Henkel-Rieger, *Unified*, chapter 3 (cited above, note 19).

33. William Barber with Jonathan Wilson-Hartgrove, *The Third Reconstruction: Moral Mondays, Fusion Politics, and the Rise of a New Justice Movement* (Boston: Beacon Press, 2016); Alexia Salvatierra and Peter Heltzel, *Faith-Rooted Organizing: Mobilizing the Church in Service to the World* (Downers Grove, IL: InterVarsity Press, 2014); Southeast Center for Cooperative Development, *Churches and Cooperatives Toolkit* (Nashville, TN: Southeast Center for Cooperative Development, 2021), https://www.co-opsnow.org/tool-kit.

34. Some of the most compelling accounts of how congregations do this are Heidi Neumark, *Breathing Space* (cited above, note 2) and *Sanctuary: Being Christian in the Wake of Trump* (Chicago: Eerdmans, 2020).

35. This section is drawn in part from my own experiences (admittedly brief, about half a year) as an organizer with Service Employees International Union (SEIU) Local 32BJ. See also chapter 6 in Rieger and Henkel-Rieger, *Unified* (cited above, note 19).

36. The Interreligious Network for Worker Solidarity is currently emerging to continue the work of the organization Interfaith Worker Justice (originally the National Interfaith Committee for Worker Justice), which for a quarter-century organized faith-labor coalitions and mobilized them for local and national action around multiple labor issues. Also see Francisco Garcia, "Faith Needs Labor to Respond to this Moment," Wendland-Cook Program in Religion and Justice website, May 21,

2020, https://www.religionandjustice.org/blog/faith-needs-labor-to-respond-to-this-moment-xx3jh-hgk32.

37. Although the terms *environmental justice* and *ecological justice* are often used as synonyms and are inherently connected, it is important to distinguish the two: Environmental justice pertains to how the consequences of environmental degradation are disparately imposed on some human communities (chiefly nonwealthy and non-White ones) but not others, while ecological justice pertains to how the consequences of environmental degradation are imposed on the more-than-human rest of nature and on ecosystems as a whole. Nicholas Low and Brendan Gleeson, *Justice, Society, and Nature: An Exploration of Political Ecology* (London: Routledge, 1998), 2.

38. Tom Gann, josie sparrow, and Jason W. Moore, "Comrades in Arms with the Web of Life: A Conversation with Jason W. Moore," *New Socialist* 2 (October 2021), http://newsocialist.org.uk/be-comrades-web-life-conversation-jason-w-moore.

39. The primary basis for ending the restriction of ordained and/or other church leadership to cisgender men is, of course feminist and queer theology, to which Christian anti-capitalism adds reinforcement.

40. See the introduction in Patel and Moore, *History* (cited above, note 1).

REFERENCES

Anderson, Elizabeth. *Private Government: How Employers Rule Our Lives (and Why We Don't Talk about It)*. Princeton, NJ: Princeton University Press, 2019.

Baptist, Edward. *The Half Has Never Been Told: Slavery and the Making of American Capitalism*. New York: Basic Books, 2016.

Barber, William, with Jonathan Wilson-Hartgrove. *The Third Reconstruction: Moral Mondays, Fusion Politics, and the Rise of a New Justice Movement*. Boston: Beacon Press, 2016.

Battistoni, Alyssa. "Bringing in the Work of Nature: From Natural Capital to Hybrid Labor." *Political Theory* 45, no. 1 (2017): 5–31.

Bhattacharya, Gargi. *Rethinking Racial Capitalism: Questions of Reproduction and Survival*. Lanham, MD: Rowman & Littlefield, 2018.

Bhattacharya, Tithi, ed. *Social Reproduction Theory: Remapping Class, Recentering Oppression*. London: Pluto Books, 2017.

Blanc, Eric. *Red State Revolt: The Teachers' Strike Wave and Working-Class Politics*. New York: Verso, 2019.

Bureau of Economic Analysis. "Household Production." Accessed at https://www.bea.gov/data/special-topics/household-production.

Davis, Ellen. *Scripture, Culture, and Agriculture: An Agrarian Reading of the Bible*. Cambridge, UK: Cambridge University Press, 2008.

Federal Reserve Bank of St. Louis. "FRED Database." Accessed at https://fred.stlouisfed.org/series/CP#0.

Federici, Silvia. *Re-enchanting the World: Feminism and the Politics of the Commons*. Oakland, CA: PM Press, 2018.

Fraser, Nancy. "Behind Marx's Hidden Abode: For an Expanded Conception of Capitalism." *New Left Review* 86 (March/April 2014): 55–72.

Gann, Tom, josie sparrow, and Jason W. Moore. "Comrades in Arms with the Web of Life: A Conversation with Jason W. Moore." *New Socialist* 2 (October 2021). http://newsocialist.org.uk/be-comrades-web-life-conversation-jason-w-moore.

Garcia, Francisco. "Faith Needs Labor to Respond to This Moment." Wendland-Cook Program in Religion and Justice website, May 21, 2020. https://www.religionandjustice.org/blog/faith-needs-labor-to-respond-to-this-moment-xx3jh-hgk32.

Guendelsberger, Emily. *On the Clock: What Low-Wage Work Did to Me and How It Drives America Insane*. New York: Little, Brown, 2019.

Hickel, Jason. *The Divide: Global Inequality from Conquest to Free Markets*. New York: Norton, 2018.

International Labor Organization. "Forced Labor, Modern Slavery, and Human Trafficking." Accessed at https://www.ilo.org/global/topics/forced-labour/lang--en/index.htm.

Lathrop, Gordon W. *Holy Things: A Liturgical Theology*. Minneapolis: Fortress Press, 1993.

Lears, Rachel, and Robin Blotnick. *The Hand That Feeds*. Brooklyn, NY: Jubilee Films, 2014.

Lewis, Sophie. *Full Surrogacy Now: Feminism against Family*. New York: Verso, 2019.

Linebaugh, Peter. *Stop, Thief! The Commons, Enclosures, and Resistance*. Oakland, CA: PM Press, 2014.

Linklater, Andro. *Owning the Earth: The Transforming History of Land Ownership*. New York: Bloomsbury, 2013.

Low, Nicholas, and Brendan Gleeson. *Justice, Society, and Nature: An Exploration of Political Ecology*. London: Routledge, 1998.

Magdoff, Fred, and Chris Williams. *Creating an Ecological Society: Toward a Revolutionary Transformation*. New York: Monthly Review Books, 2017.

Malm, Andreas. *Fossil Capital: The Rise of Steam Power and the Roots of Global Warming*. New York: Verso, 2016.

Manjapra, Kris. *Colonialism in Global Perspective*. Cambridge, UK: Cambridge University Press, 2020.

McAlevey, Jane. *A Collective Bargain: Unions, Organizing, and the Fight for Democracy*. New York: HarperCollins, 2020.

Montgomery, David. *Growing a Revolution: Bringing Our Soil Back to Life*. New York: Norton, 2018.

Moore, Jason. *Capitalism in the Web of Life: Ecology and the Accumulation of Capital*. New York: Verso, 2015.

Moore, Michael. *Fahrenheit 11/9*. Midwestern Films, 2018.

National Nurses United. "Ratios: Learning from the California Experience." National Nurses United website. https://www.nationalnursesunited.org/ratios-california-experience.

The Nature Conservancy. *Global Principles of Restorative Aquaculture*. Arlington, VA: The Nature Conservancy, 2021. Accessed at https://www.nature.org/content/dam/tnc/nature/en/documents/TNC_PrinciplesofRestorativeAquaculture.pdf.

Neumark, Heidi. *Breathing Space: A Spiritual Journey in the South Bronx*. Boston: Beacon Press, 2003.

———. *Sanctuary: Being Christian in the Wake of Trump*. Chicago: Eerdmans, 2020.

Patel, Raj, and Jason Moore. *A History of the World in Seven Cheap Things: A Guide to Capitalism, Nature, and the Future of the Planet*. Berkeley: University of California Press, 2018.

Rieger, Joerg, and Rosemarie Henkel-Rieger. *Theology in the Capitalocene: Ecology, Identity, Class, and Solidarity*. Minneapolis: Fortress Press, 2022.

———. *Unified We Are a Force: How Faith and Labor Can Overcome America's Inequalities*. St. Louis, MO: Chalice Press, 2016.

Salvatierra, Alexia, and Peter Heltzel. *Faith-Rooted Organizing: Mobilizing the Church in Service to the World*. Downers Grove, IL: InterVarsity Press, 2014.

Scipes, Kim. "Social Movement Unionism or Social Justice Unionism? Disentangling Theoretical Confusion within the Global Labor Movement." *Class, Race and Corporate Power* 2, no. 3 (2014). https://doi.org/10.25148/crcp.2.3.16092119.

Smith, Bren. *Eat Like a Fish: My Adventures as a Fisherman Turned Restorative Ocean Farmer*. New York: Knopf, 2019.

Southeast Center for Cooperative Development. *Churches and Cooperatives Toolkit*. Nashville, TN: Southeast Center for Cooperative Development, 2021. Accessed at https://www.co-opsnow.org/tool-kit.

Steffen, Will, Katherine Richardson, Johan Rockström, et al. "Planetary Boundaries: Guiding Human Development on a Changing Planet." *Science* 347, no. 6223 (2015): 736–47. https://doi.org/10.1126/science.1259855.

Uetricht, Micah. *Strike for America: Chicago Teachers against Austerity*. New York: Verso, 2014.

United Nations Food and Agriculture Organization. *The 10 Elements of Agroecology: Guiding the Transition to Sustainable Food and Agricultural Systems*, FAO report #I9037EN/1/04.18. New York: United Nations, 2018.

Weeks, Kathi. *The Problem with Work: Feminism, Marxism, Antiwork Politics, and Postwork Imaginaries*. Durham, NC: Duke University Press, 2011.

Wolff, Richard. *Democracy at Work: A Cure for Capitalism*. Chicago: Haymarket Books, 2012.

Wood, Ellen Meiksins. *The Origin of Capitalism: A Longer View*, new ed. New York: Verso, 2017.

Wright, Erik Olin. "How to Be an Anticapitalist Today." *Jacobin* magazine website, December 2, 2015. https://www.jacobinmag.com/2015/12/erik-olin-wright-real-utopias-anticapitalism-democracy.

Zweig, Michael. *The Working Class Majority: America's Best Kept Secret*, second ed. Ithaca, NY: Cornell University Press, 2012.

Chapter 6

Christian Animist Economics

The Intimate Re-enchantment of Creation for a Regenerative Eco-Socialism

Timothy Reinhold Eberhart

> The human ecosystem has lost its equilibrium and is on the way to the destruction of the earth and hence to its own destruction. The slowly spreading crisis is given the name "environmental pollution," and people are seeking technological solutions for it. But in my view it is in actual fact a crisis of the whole total project of modern civilization . . . Unless there is a fresh orientation of this society's fundamental values, we shall not succeed in finding a new practice in our dealings with nature; unless human beings arrive at a new way of understanding themselves, and at an alternative economic system—then an ecological collapse of the earth can easily be extrapolated from the facts and trends of the present crises.
>
> —Jürgen Moltmann[1]

The facts and trends of present biospheric crises continue to reveal the imperative for this generation to take up the epochal task of transitioning beyond capitalism to an alternative economic system based in a fundamental reorientation of society's valuation of the more-than-human natural world. Calls for such a revolutionary change in political economy in this kairos time of contracted emergency and opportunity[2] are mounting in response to ongoing and increasingly dire reports regarding climate destabilization; biodiversity collapse; land, water, and air despoliation; and more. Thomas Berry spoke of this as the *Great Work* of integrating all human activities into the rhythms and limits of the biosphere.³ David Korten calls it the *Great Turning* in shifting from an industrial growth society to a life-sustaining, equitable civilization.⁴ The Stockholm Environment Institute describes this as the *Great Transition* to a future marked by environmental resilience, human solidarity, and life's flourishing.⁵ Among the more prominent ecocentric political-economic proposals to replace capitalism, we can name Herman Daly's *Ecological Economics*, Vandana Shiva's *Earth Democracy*, Charles Einstein's *Sacred Economics*, Kate Raworth's *Doughnut Economics*, and John Cobb and Philip Clayton's *Ecological Civilization*. What they all share is a fundamental recognition that neither "market ecology," through which consumers are provided "green" products and services through the extractivist logics and mechanisms of capitalism, nor "productivist socialism," which in varied collectivist social forms similarly ignores the limits and needs of the biosphere, is capable of averting the ecological collapse of the earth. Instead, they each insist on what *The Belem Ecosocialist Declaration (2009)* describes in its call for "a transformed economy founded on the non-monetary values of social justice *and* ecological balance."⁶ Moreover, in the wake of profound damage to earth's biodiverse life forms and systems—a "human-caused biotic holocaust"⁷—such a new economy must go beyond simply sustaining present planetary conditions to playing a more active role in regenerating biospheric health. The choice is stark: either regenerative eco-socialism or social barbarism and eco-catastrophe.

Central among the tasks theology has to contribute to the upbuilding of a regenerative eco-socialism are critical and constructive engagements with foundational cosmological assumptions undergirding modern political economy. As environmental historian and historical geographer Jason Moore argues, capitalism's basic strategy of accumulation rests on an implicit society/nature hierarchical dualism, in which human life is seen as both separate from and superior to more-than-human life, thereby rendering nonhuman nature cheap. "For capitalism, Nature is 'cheap' in a double sense: to make Nature's elements 'cheap' in price; and also *to cheapen*, to degrade or to render inferior in an ethico-political sense, the better to make Nature cheap in price."⁸ As such, efforts to transition beyond capitalism for the sake of a more egalitarian and regenerative future will be stymied, he says, so long as our political imaginations, even those stretching in radical directions, remain captive to modernity's basic society/nature organization of reality.⁹

Of course, the formation of the Western imagination underlying capitalism's cheapening of nonhuman nature cannot be understood apart from its Christian theological foundations. The task of worldview deconstruction and reconstruction needed to replace the society/nature binary, therefore, which is work for all the world's wisdom traditions today, bears uniquely on those responsible for the ongoing formation of the Christian theological imagination. For over five decades now, this has been central to the work of those engaged in Christian ecological theology. While this chapter is aligned with the general aim of the world's re-enchantment through critical and constructive theological reimagination, I will be emphasizing the particular contributions of Christian animist perspectives, articulated most clearly by eco-theologian Mark Wallace. Wallace's intimate focus on humanity's relations with our other-than-human neighbors, grounded in his creative understanding of God's double incarnation in the humanity of Jesus and the elemental animality of the Holy Spirit, provides a compelling holistic theological vision through which Christians might see and embrace the flourishing of all humans within a much broader flourishing web of all our relations. Such a deep re-enchantment of socio-ecological imagination, leading to deep socio-ecological solidarity, is fertile ground on which a regenerative eco-socialist economy might yet emerge.

The cheapening of human and more-than-human life within capitalism operates through the processes of commodification and exploitation, which lead to the degradation of both. The "great transformation," which took place in the emergence of modern market societies, as Karl Polanyi argued, was the transition to a social order in which all aspects of life, including especially land and labor, were made into commodities.[10] Commodities, as Marx described, are objects or persons whose values are determined, not by their inherent worth or dignity, practical usefulness, or niche contributions within broader dynamic systems, but by the amount of abstract money they might garner through the dynamics of market exchange. In the transition to capitalist societies, human persons were converted into labor power and more-than-human nature into either free energy (e.g., a river, a waterfall) or raw materials, with both transformations facilitating the accumulation of financial profit through the ongoing processes of increasing productivity and consumption. The result, as Polanyi saw, was the inevitable disintegration of both human society and more-than-human nature. For "to allow the market mechanism to be the sole director of the fate of human beings [labor] and their natural environment [land]" inevitably leads, he argued, to the "demolition of society" and the "defilement of landscapes."[11]

The inevitability of socio-ecological deterioration within capitalist economies is bound up with the inextricable connection between the transformation of human and more-than-human life into commodities and the exploitation of both in order to maximize financial accumulation. Exploitation is the process by which the agents of productivity, whether human workers or nonhuman nature, are denied a full return for the value of their productive contributions as well as the particular conditions they need for continued generativity. In relation to workers, the most common form of exploitation involves laborers receiving wages below the value their productivity contributes to any given enterprise, with surplus value going to the managerial and ownership classes, while the needs of workers for rest, dignity, stability, creativity, and more are continually and often progressively undermined. As Marx saw, this same dynamic is at work in capitalism's exploitation of the land. "All progress in capitalist agriculture is a progress in the art, not only of robbing the worker, but of robbing the soil . . . Capitalist production . . . only develops . . . by simultaneously undermining the original sources of all wealth—the soil and the worker."[12] To be more specific, the exploitation of more-than-human nature in capitalism involves (1) the extraction of natural resources like forests and fish at rates faster than they are being naturally regenerated; (2) the consumption of nonrenewable resources like fossil fuels, oil, coal, natural gas, and minerals at rates far faster than they are being replaced by the discovery of renewable substitutes; and (3) the externalizing deposit of wastes like carbon emissions into the atmosphere at rates faster than they can be safely assimilated.[13] In both cases, the cumulative effects of exploitation over time, in which value, energy, or power disproportionately flows upward and away from the originating sources of generativity, destroys the human and more-than-human grounds on which the perpetual growth system of capitalism depends.

While Polanyi rightly characterizes the commodification of land and humans as a novel transformation by which the logics of capitalist exchange came to govern all social and ecological relations within modern market societies, the hierarchical human/nature dualism undergirding and justifying the uniquely capitalist forms of exploitation has deeper roots in the dominant Western intellectual tradition from which capitalism emerged. One sees this, for example, in Immanuel Kant's determination that human beings have no direct moral duties toward animals, for animals, he argued, "are not self-conscious and are there merely as a means to an end."[14] Only rational beings are worthy of our moral consideration, as ends in themselves, and only human beings, he believed, are rational. Similarly, in relation to what he deemed "inanimate objects," humans are under no obligation to pay heed to the elements of nature in and for themselves but only to how their use or misuse might impact one's human neighbor.[15] Kant here was following René Descartes, who had written a century before that "brutes not only have a smaller degree of reason than men, but are wholly lacking in it," which thereby justifies a moral universe in which "human beings have absolute dominion over all the other animals."[16] Two centuries later, in his essay "On Nature," John Stuart Mill defined the meaning of Nature as, in one sense, the collective name for everything that exists, but, in a narrower sense, "not everything which happens, but only what takes place without the agency, or without the voluntary and intentional agency, of man."[17] This clear boundary between human and nonhuman nature, for Mill, led him to conclude that "the ways of Nature are to be conquered" by the draining of marshes, the excavation of wells, the mining of deep earth minerals, and the taming of the oceans. In fact, nature's powers are to be seen as an enemy, "from whom [humanity] must wrest, by force and ingenuity" what we are able for our own benefit and use.[18]

Though such "enlightened" thinkers, representative of the modern Western imagination, believed their foundational assumptions had broken free from Christian dogmatic influence, their dualistic-hierarchical understandings of human and nonhuman nature were in fact derived from the dominant theological conceptions of reality that preceded them. In fact, the prevailing Christian cosmology in both ancient and medieval Europe of a divinely created order arranged in a grand hierarchy of being is arguably the root source of modernity's—and modern capitalism's—underlying society/nature dualism. In this "Great Chain of Being," humanity was affirmed to hold a prominent position, above that of all other life forms and just below that of the supernatural order of angels and God, the Supreme Being. The ranked order proceeded something like the following: God / supernatural beings || humans / vertebrate animals / invertebrate animals / plants / simple microorganisms || inanimate matter. Within this basic schema, the purpose of any given lower order was to serve the orders above, whereas the purpose of those higher was to govern the orders below and to use them for their benefit. Moreover, among natural beings, a firm ontological divide between human and all other life forms below was upheld by the belief that only human beings possess rational capacities and are thus capable of functioning as principal agents, whereas all other creatures, being incapable of rational action, were understood to exist solely for the sake of human well-being. Thomas Aquinas is representative here, in arguing that only the rational creature, the human, "has dominion over its own act, is free in its action, because he is free who is cause of himself," whereas "every other creature is naturally under slavery," for "the intellectual nature alone is free." Therefore, "it is clear," he concludes, "that God cares for all things *for the sake of* intellectual substances," and thus "is refuted the error of those who said it is sinful for a man to kill dumb animals: for by divine providence they are intended for man's use in the natural order. Hence it is not wrong for man to make use of them, either by killing or in any other way whatever."[19]

As ecofeminists have long noted, the Great Chain of Being has functioned historically to undergird social hierarchical dualisms as well. Ecofeminist philosopher Karen J. Warren describes an "oppressive conceptual framework" as a basic set of beliefs, values, attitudes, and assumptions that explains and justifies social relationships of domination and subordination. She argues there are three basic features: (1) value-hierarchical thinking, which assigns greater value to whatever is deemed "above" than to that which is designated "below"; (2) value-dualisms, which sees reality through a series of oppositional binaries; and (3) a logic of domination, which serves as the ideological justification for the subjugation of whatever is deemed subordinate.[20] Alongside the human/nature binary, dominant Western thought has upheld a range of related hierarchal dualisms—male/female, mind/body, reason/emotion, free/slave, white/Black, civilized/savage—each sanctioning or maintaining various manifestations of social oppression. The ongoing impact of an implicit cosmological hierarchy of being is evident, in particular, in the way proximity to nature has been used as a primary ideological justification for social domination. Women, dark-skinned peoples, and Indigenous communities, for example, have each been identified as being more closely associated with the nonhuman natural realm, depicted as being less rational, more emotive, and/or uncivilized, with such characterizations sanctioning a subjugated status of service to, exploitation for, and even disposal of by those deemed superior.

The present socio-biospheric consequences of global capitalism's commodification, exploitation, and degradation of more-than-human and human persons, grounded in an implicit cosmological chain of hierarchical command and control, are staggering. The result of a global economic order in which animate and inanimate life forms are deemed unworthy of moral consideration (Kant), such that the mass of organized human activities operate free from any underlying ethical duty toward them, is a world in which the variety and variability of planetary life forms are rapidly collapsing, with present rates of global diversity loss several hundred times higher than at any point over the last ten million years.[21] In treating the earth's "dumb" creatures as if their sole purpose is to be used for human benefit, by killing them or in any other way whatsoever (Aquinas), and by attempting to rule over nonhuman nature with absolute dominion (Descartes), the underlying logics and resultant operations of capitalism are in fact undermining the very conditions of healthy, biodiverse habitats, biomes, and earth systems on which all of human society is fundamentally dependent.[22] And, by having wrested from Nature through brute force and ingenuity, in particular by "dragging to light what she has buried at immense depths of the earth" (Mill) for human use, the machinations of capital accumulation are directly responsible for accumulating carbon-dioxide emissions in the atmosphere, leading to runaway climate change. A 2018 Global Sustainable Development report commissioned by the United Nations secretary-general concluded that the dominant capitalist economic theories, approaches, and models that drive global governance "almost completely disregard the energetic and material dimensions of the economy" and are thereby wholly unprepared to address the upcoming era of "rapid climate change, biodiversity loss, and other environmental hazards."[23] This is to say nothing of capitalism's historical and ongoing record of intra-human domination, exploitation, and violence, based in the same "oppressive conceptual framework" of hierarchical dualism, a record that includes the maintenance and sanctioning of chattel slavery, colonial violence, genocide, workplace exploitation, gender/orientation discrimination, communal fragmentation, political destabilization, psychological distress, and more.

Among the many tasks required to transition beyond the capitalist operations of commodification, exploitation, and degradation toward a regenerative eco-socialism, therefore, the work of cosmological reconstruction must play a vital role. As Jason Moore argues, precisely because modernity's nature/society hierarchical binary "is complicit in the violence of modernity at its core," the articulation of new methodological approaches, narrative strategies, and conceptual languages, which "comprehend the irreducibly dialectical relation between human and extra-human natures in the web of life," is necessary to the upbuilding of a more socially *and* ecologically egalitarian political economy.[24] What's needed, in other words, is the promotion of cooperative, interconnected, and mutualistic conceptual frameworks aligned with and supportive of a political economy of deep social *and* ecological solidarity.

Of course, cosmological reconstruction has been central to nearly every major Christian eco-theological contribution over the last half century. As early as 1961, Joseph Sittler was articulating the need for Christian doctrine to extend beyond a primary focus on the human soul and human history to the grace-filled, salvific presence of God within nature. Such a vision of the "Cosmic Christ" seen in *ta panta* ("the whole" or "all things"), he argued, was needed "to diagnose, judge, and heal the ways of men as they blasphemously strut about this hurt and threatened world as if they owned it."[25] Following his mentor Teilhard de Chardin, Thomas Berry called for a "New Story" in which human beings are to be understood as coequal participants within the grand symphony of the cosmos, invited to treat all others as subjects to be revered rather than objects to be used, since modernity's cosmological story, he said, has led us to where "we now find ourselves on a devastated continent where nothing is holy, nothing is sacred."[26] Arguing that humanity's "misuse and exploitation of the natural world have caused nature to be the new poor," Sallie McFague urged theological experimentation with new conceptual models and metaphors of God's relationship to the earth, proposing in particular that we affirm the "World as God's Body" in order to emphasize that "the world is our meeting place with God."[27] Similar constructive approaches aimed at affirming the deep immanence of God in the whole of nature can be seen in Jürgen Moltmann's *God in Creation*; Karen Baker-Fletcher's *Sisters of Dust, Sisters of Spirit*; and Catherine Keller's *Cloud of the Impossible*.

As one of the most creative ecological theologians writing today, Mark I. Wallace draws upon the contributions of these broader perspectives while providing a much-needed turn to the more intimate level of humanity's relations with our other-than-human neighbors. In particular, Wallace's work "fleshes out" the implications of the basic eco-theological affirmation that divinity is present and embodied in both human and more-than-human nature by exploring the particularly animalistic and elemental nature of God. He does so by adeptly engaging the wisdom of humanity's oldest religious tradition—animism—which Indigenous peoples, past and present, have maintained through beliefs, stories, ceremonies, and practices respectful of the vivifying spirit or soul (animus) within *all* our relations, whether human, animal, rock, plant, air, water, or fire. Precisely because Christianity, especially in the West, bears particular responsibility for humankind's exploitative orientation toward more-than-human nature, he argues—such that "it is oftentimes the Christian religion *itself* that is the primary obstacle to recognizing . . . the sanctity of all beings"[28]—Christianity's role remains a crucial one in articulating more ecologically curative symbolic frameworks to help resituate humanity's place within the broader web of all living beings. In particular, his affirmation that Christian doctrine implies a double incarnation of God in the humanity of Jesus *and* in the elemental animality of the Holy Spirit, alongside his recognition of the emotional implications of such belief, holds tremendous promise to foster the kind of perspectival and affective changes required to support the regenerative eco-socialist projects that are urgently needed today.

Wallace contends that Christianity's scriptural, incarnational, and Trinitarian belief systems are fundamentally aligned with *animotheism* or "the belief that all beings, including nonhuman animals, are imbued with divine presence."[29] He argues that Christianity's centuries-long "Babylonian captivity" to the Neoplatonic graded hierarchy of being, "in which plants and animals, rocks and rivers, are denigrated as soulless matter, while human beings are elevated as godlike, intelligent creatures,"[30] in fact represents a radical departure from Christianity's inherently—but almost entirely forgotten—animistic orientation. The dominant understanding of divinity within historic Christianity has therefore been that of the *Sky God*, imaged as an immaterial, unmoved, unaffected, disembodied being inhabiting an ethereal, timeless, and unearthly heavenly realm far removed from the interwoven terrestrial elements of mud, water, blood, matter, and bodies. But the primordial image of God hidden within biblical religion and the central affirmations of Christian theology, according to Wallace, is instead that of an Earth God, who indwells landscapes, invigorates bodies, flows through natural processes, and animates every planetary life-form with deific presence.[31]

Central to Wallace's vision of Christian animism is his interpretation of the third person of the divine communion, the Holy Spirit, as the "green face" or the "animal face" of God. In the same way that Christian doctrine affirms God's incarnation in the human person of Jesus, he says, the scriptural narratives also support belief in God's elemental-animistic incarnation in the Spirit. Throughout the Bible, he demonstrates, the Spirit is depicted elementally as *living water* (John 4:14), *animating breath* (Genesis 1:2), *healing wind* (Judges 6:34), and *cleansing fire* (Acts 2:1–4).[32] In this way, "the biblical texts stand as a stunning counter-testimony to the conventional mindset," for these traditional elements of earthly life "are constitutive of the Spirit's biblical reality as an enfleshed being who ministers to the whole creation God has made for the refreshment and joy of all beings."[33] The most common scriptural image of God's earthly incarnation through the Spirit, for Wallace, is that of a bird. Much like the "winged bird-God" of Genesis 1:1–2, he notes, who hovers over the expanse of creation like a mother bird brooding over her nest egg to give birth to flora and fauna, the Spirit Bird is present at Jesus's baptism—"descending like a dove, and alighting on him" (Matthew 3:16)—as the avian embodiment of God's life-giving favor. "Gently alighting on Jesus' person," he writes, "the Gospels' heaven-sent dovey pigeon is God enfleshing Godself in carnal form, but now not only in human flesh in the person of Jesus (God's Son) but also in animal flesh in the person of the Spirit (God's Spirit)."[34]

Through his animistic interpretation of the scriptural accounts of God's triune nature, Wallace is led to affirm not only the double incarnation of God as human and more-than-human but also the double crucifixion of divine life through both social and ecological degradations, which lead to death. For, if divinity is to be affirmed as the animating power of and for life within not just human beings but all life forms, then, wherever the earth is despoiled, wounded, and discarded, he maintains, the Spirit too suffers exploitation and loss.

> Jesus suffers because he bears the sins of the world in his human flesh. The Spirit, as coeternal and coparticipatory with Jesus in the eternal Godhead, also experiences this suffering (even as does God the Father, for that matter). But the Spirit also suffers in a way distinctive of her role in creation because she feels the pain of a degraded earth in her more-than-human body. The Spirit is the bird God. The Spirit is the earthen God who indwells all things . . . Whenever, then, these life forms suffer loss and pain, the Spirit suffers loss and pain. Whenever these life forms are threatened and destroyed, the Spirit feels threatened and experiences death and trauma in herself.[35]

An important aspect of Wallace's articulation of a Christian animist perspective is his understanding that the biospheric crises we face due to the exploitation and destruction of the nonhuman natural world must be addressed at both the conceptual *and* affective levels. He explicitly identifies the commodification of nature via market exchange as a main culprit, but, in doing so, he argues that, in order to counter the instrumentalization of nature, we must find ways of *"re-enchanting* Earth as an animate being" in order to "empower our collective desire to heal Earth's suffering by rekindling a spiritual vision of our biotic and abiotic kinfolk as revered members of a unified, blessed family."[36] He quotes evolutionary biologist Stephen Jay Gould in noting that we will not fight to save species, habitats, and earth systems apart from an emotional bond with them. And, because a large majority no longer feel a sense of common kinship with our more-than-human neighbors, he argues, we must find ways of nurturing deep emotional reattachments with our plant and animal relations. "This is the religious and ethical promise of Christian animism: a new vision of a world in which all things are steeped in God's presence and thereby deserving of our solicitude, or even better, our love."[37] For, if God's incarnate presence is with us, not just among exploited and crucified human persons but also among our degraded and dying landed, aquatic, and avian kin, then God as the "wounded," "groaning," and "crucified" Spirit confronts us not only biologically but also religiously, spiritually, and affectively. At the same time, precisely because it is *God* who suffers the death and dying of nature and *God* who is groaning out of divine forbearance and love for the victims of both social *and* ecological crucifixion, our hope for the healing and renewal of the earth can and should be embraced as an active longing that flows from and joins with God's own heart.

Several broad ethical implications emerge, according to Wallace, from a Christian animist perspective. All of life, he argues—as ensouled or animated with God's life-giving and suffering presence—now deserves our deepest care, reverence, protection, affectionate concern, and respect. No longer viewed as soulless, inert, passive matter, available solely for human instrumental use and benefit, the more-than-human natural world—the whole and every member—becomes for us "a breathing, feeling, conscious" Other(s), such that "all of reality slowly evolves into a hallowed grove of sentient animals, cherished plants and trees, and much revered landscapes, mountains, rivers, and seas."[38] In place of what he calls the species chauvinism inherent to the anthropocentric, dualistic, and hierarchical cosmological imagination of the modern West, he proposes instead a biocentric position, which recognizes that "the interdependence we share with all creation is the primary fact that should ground human moral choices" and which in fact demands we give priority status to more-than-human nature, if we are to preserve the web of life on which human existence is entirely dependent.[39]

In an age of multiple, overlapping biospheric crises that are rapidly worsening, the protection and sustainment of society and more-than-human nature demand a rapid transition beyond capitalism toward a socially just and ecologically regenerative political economy. Neither personal lifestyle shifts, local-communal efforts, nor even aggressive state regulatory interventions will be sufficient, by themselves, to address the unfolding calamities of climate chaos, biodiversity collapse, ecosystem devastation, and the resultant societal consequences, *if* the commodifying logics and exploitative operations of capitalism continue to govern both human and ecological relations worldwide. At the same time, amid the promising resurgence of Marxist, democratic socialist, and kindred communitarian-collectivist traditions and movements today, it is imperative that whatever models of egalitarian ownership, decision-making, production, distribution, compensation, and so forth, we might envision, propose, and fight for be as radically and thoroughgoingly *ecological* as they are social. Worker-owned and -governed cooperative enterprises, state- and/or municipality-run utilities, socially oriented community banks, and related manifestations of economic democracy—while crucial instruments in our striving to achieve social equality—might still uncritically depend upon comparable dualistic and exploitative relationships between human society and nonhuman nature. As such, although "it may be tempting . . . to devise policies addressing each one of the planetary and social boundaries in turn," as Kate Raworth writes, "their interconnectedness demands that they each be understood as part of a complex socio-ecological system and hence be addressed within a greater whole."[40]

I have argued that, among the many tasks needed to transition toward a regenerative eco-socialist political economy, Christian theology can and must contribute not only by critiquing the cosmological dualistic hierarchy at the center of the Western imagination but also by articulating and nurturing conceptual frameworks of *deep socio-ecological solidarity*[41] as well. Certainly, this is work for all the world's religious, philosophical, and wisdom traditions, but, because Christianity has served historically as the primary "host body" of the Grand Hierarchy of Being justifying social domination and ecological despoilment, those of us presently stewarding the Christian tradition are especially responsible for reframing our own vision before we'll be of any cooperative worth to neighbor traditions (Matthew 7:5). Toward this end, Mark Wallace's Christian animism builds upon earlier eco-theological contributions by articulating a theology of God's fleshly presence incarnate in both human and more-than-human persons within the dynamic interconnected whole of created life. Although Wallace himself does not provide a substantive account of the political-economic implications entailed in a Christian animist worldview, I believe his work offers important contributions toward the upbuilding of an eco-socialist economy.

If the process of commodifying people and land was central in the transition from precapitalist to capitalist societies, resulting in the exploitation of both, then developing cultural strategies to de-commodify human and more-than-human persons is crucial in liberating the entire web of life from the unrelenting necro-grind of market exchange. To be a commodity is to have been made into an object whose value is abstract, instrumental, and unworthy, ultimately, of direct moral consideration. Historically, the commodity emerged out of a theological process of *de-sacralization*. As such, I would argue that, among the various strategies we might adopt to de-commodify people and land today, theological efforts aimed at their *re-enchantment* or *re-sacralization* can and ought to play a central role. Most eco-socialists follow Marx in juxtaposing "exchange-value," or the amount of money a commodity might garner through a market transaction, with "use-value," usually defined as the practical, material usefulness of a person or thing within a particular context. Although helpful as a descriptive concept—despite its dependence on the logic of instrumentality—"use-value" isn't particularly compelling at the affective level of human motivation and concern. Like all political economies, regenerative eco-socialism must align with an orienting mythos—or multiple, mutually aligned symbols, stories, languages, and rituals—that can inspire and sustain a radically new relationship between human and more-than-human nature. Here is where I believe Christian animism, alongside the deeper animist traditions indigenous to all the earth's places and cultures, can contribute to the perspectival and emotive changes needed, not just at a generalizable level of "divine immanence" or even the Earth as "God's Body" but also at the most intimate level of everyday human interactivity with more-than-human nature. If, with Wallace, we affirm that the God of Jesus and the Holy Spirit is incarnate not just within human life but also within our immediate plant, mammal, avian, aquatic, wind, water, fire, and earth neighbors, then we ought to speak of their possessing not just use-value but *divine-value* or *sacred-value* as well.

Such a cosmological revolution—all the world filled with persons animated with divine presence and significance—would provoke a radical transformation of the primary motivations and purposes driving our political-economic institutions and systems. Within capitalism, perhaps the primary question that governs nearly all social and ecological relations is, "How might individual human beings use, organize, manipulate, put to work, and relate to others—nonhuman and those deemed less-than-fully-human—for the sake of maximizing financial profit?" The flow is a one-way system that at present is degrading and degenerating the social and ecological sources from which value is extracted through exploitation for the benefit of those atop the value hierarchy—to the point of impending global socio-ecological collapse. In a regenerative eco-socialist political economy rooted in an animist worldview, Christian or otherwise, the motivating questions around which human and more-than-human life might be organized would be profoundly different. For example: Who are these sacred Others with whom we are sharing our existence? What of the divine nature, or what divine-value is uniquely present, *in the flesh*, among them? What do these holy Others need to flourish or to serve their purpose within the broader, mysterious web of relations of which we are a part? How might we enter into synergistic relationships with one another? And what are the appropriate dispositions, behaviors, and responses—of reverence, of gratitude, of repayment—when the sacrifice of any members of the web of life is required to sustain the lives of others? Here, the flow of social and ecological relations, as well as accrued benefits, are neither hierarchical, exploitative, nor abstract but, rather, circular, mutually beneficial, and thoroughly biocentric. A Christian animist enterprise, then, would be one in which *all* who labor for the sake of sustaining the common life we share and enjoy—including all our nonhuman relations—are accounted for in decision making, are justly "compensated" for the particular contributions they provide, are never overworked to the point where their existence and contributions are depleted past capacities for natural regeneration, and are harmonized such that needs, assets, and "wastes" are integrated in ways that benefit the whole of human and more-than-human society.

There is no question that the task of transitioning beyond capitalism toward a political economy of deep socio-ecological solidarity is immense. What an animist perspective offers is the conviction that divinity, though wounded and crucified, is nonetheless on the side of the earth's regeneration. In and through the Spirit of God, the birds of the air, the microorganisms in the soil, the pollinators in the fields, the fish in the sea, the leaves on the trees, and the winds and rains in the sky have always been united for the sake of life's continuation. The urgent question we now face is this: Will we humans, especially those struggling to throw off the shackles of capitalism, unite with our more-than-human comrades in a truly worldwide solidarity?

NOTES

1. Jürgen Moltmann, *Ethics of Hope* (Minneapolis: Fortress Press, 2012), 133.

2. Catherine Keller, *Political Theology of the Earth: Our Planetary Emergency and the Struggle for a New Public* (New York: Columbia University Press, 2018), 2–5.

3. Thomas Berry, *The Great Work: Our Way into the Future* (New York: Broadway Books, 2000).

4. David Korten, *The Great Turning: From Empire to Earth Community* (San Francisco: Berrett-Koehler Publishers, Inc., 2006).

5. P. T. Raskin, G. Banuri, P. Gallopín, A. Gutman, R. Hammond, and R. Swart Kates, *Great Transition: The Promise and Lure of the Times Ahead*, SEI PoleStar Series Report no. 10 (Boston: SEI Publications, 2002).

6. Michael Löwy, *Ecosocialism: A Radical Alternative to Capitalist Catastrophe* (Chicago: Haymarket Books, 2015), appendix 2.

7. Norman Myers, "What We Must Do to Counter the Biotic Holocaust," *International Wildlife* 29, no. 2 (March-April 1999): 30–39.

8. Jason W. Moore, ed., *Anthropocene or Capitalocene? Nature, History, and the Crisis of Capitalism* (Oakland, CA: PM Press, 2016), 2–3.

9. As ecofeminist scholars have long emphasized, and as Moore rightly notes, the society/nature binary is inextricably bound up with capitalism's cheapening of human labor, especially the work of those deemed closest to nature, as well as a host of associated binaries related to race, gender, geography, and more, each "directly implicated in the modern world's colossal violence, inequality, and oppression," Moore, 2.

10. Karl Polanyi, *The Great Transformation: The Political and Economic Origins of Our Time* (Boston: Beacon Press, 2001), 71.

11. Ibid., 73.

12. Karl Marx, *Capital* vol.1 (London: Penguin, 1976), 637–38.

13. See Herman Daly, *Beyond Growth: The Economics of Sustainable Development* (Boston: Beacon Press, 1997).

14. Immanuel Kant, *Lectures on Ethics* (London: Taylor and Francis Books, 1930), 239.

15. Ibid., 241.

16. René Descartes, "Discourse on the Method Part V," in *The Philosophical Writings of Descartes*, vol. 1, ed. and trans. John Cottingham, Robert Stoofhoff, and Dugald Murdoch (Cambridge, UK: Cambridge University Press, 1965).

17. John Stuart Mill, *On Nature* (New York: AMS Press, Inc., 1970), 9.

18. Ibid., 20–21.

19. Thomas Aquinas, *The Summa Contra Gentiles, Part II, Book 3,* Chapter CXII (London: Burns, Oates & Washbourne Ltd., 1928), 88–92.

20. Karen J. Warren, "The Power and the Promise of Ecological Feminism," in David. R. Keller, *Environmental Ethics: The Big Questions* (Oxford, UK: Wiley-Blackwell, 2010), 282.

21. Inter-governmental Platform on Biodiversity and Ecosystem Services (IPBES), *Summary for Policymakers of the Regional Assessment Report on Biodiversity and Ecosystem Services for the Americas of the Intergovernmental Science-Policy Platform on Biodiversity and Ecosystem Services* (Bonn, Germany: IPBES Secretariat, 2018), 35.

22. See, for example, "Biodiversity Loss Is Endangering Food Security, UN Warns," *Yale Environment 360* E360 Digest (February 22, 2019), https://e360.yale.edu/digest/biodiversity-loss-is-endangering-food-security-un-warns.

23. Paavo Järvensivu, Tero Toivanen, Tere Vadén, Ville Lähde, Antti Majava, and Jussi T. Eronen, *Global Sustainable Development Report 2019 Drafted by the Group of Independent Scientists; Invited Background Document on Economic Transformation, to Chapter; Transformation: The Economy*, accessed on June 14, 2019, bios.fi/bios-governance_of_economic_transition.pdf.

24. Jason W. Moore, *Capitalism in the Web of Life: Ecology and the Accumulation of Capital* (London: Verso Books, 2015), 4–5.

25. Joseph Sittler, "Called to Unity," in *Evocations of Grace: The Writings of Jospeh Sittler on Ecology, Theology, and Ethics*, ed. Steven Bouma-Prediger and Peter W. Bakken (Grand Rapids, MI: Eerdmans, 2000), 45–46.

26. Thomas Berry, "The World of Wonder," in *Thomas Berry: Selected Writings on the Earth Community*, ed. Mary Evelyn Tucker and John Grim (Maryknoll, NY: Orbis Books, 2014), 33.

27. Sallie McFague, *The Body of God: An Ecological Theology* (Minneapolis: Fortress Press, 1993), xii, vii.

28. Mark I. Wallace, *When God Was a Bird: Christianity, Animism, and the Re-enchantment of the World* (New York: Fordham University Press, 2019), 168.

29. Ibid., 2.

30. Ibid., 4.

31. Mark I. Wallace, *Finding God in the Singing River: Christianity, Spirit, Nature* (Minneapolis: Fortress Press, 2005), 4–6.

32. Ibid., 8.

33. Ibid., 36.

34. Wallace, *When God Was a Bird*, 31.

35. Wallace, *Finding God*, 124.

36. Wallace, *When God Was a Bird*, 144–45.

37. Ibid., 48.

38. Ibid., 61.

39. Wallace, *Finding God*, 91–93.

40. Kate Raworth, *Doughnut Economics: 7 Ways to Think Like a 21st Century Economist* (White River Junction, VT: Chelsea Green Publishing, 2017), 43.

41. My articulation of this phrase is an extension of what Joerg Rieger and Kwok Pui-lan mean by "deep solidarity." See Joerg Rieger and Kwok Pui-lan, *Occupy Religion: Theology of the Multitude* (Plymouth, UK: Rowman & Littlefield Publishers, Inc., 2012).

REFERENCES

Aquinas, Thomas. *The Summa Contra Gentiles, Part II, Book 3, Chapter CXII*. London: Burns, Oates & Washbourne Ltd., 1928.

Berry, Thomas. *The Great Work: Our Way into the Future*. New York: Broadway Books, 2000.

———. "The World of Wonder." In *Thomas Berry: Selected Writings on the Earth Community*, edited by Mary Evelyn Tucker and John Grim, 33. Maryknoll, NY: Orbis Books, 2014.

"Biodiversity Loss Is Endangering Food Security, UN Warns." *Yale Environment 360*. E360 Digest (February 22, 2019). https://e360.yale.edu/digest/biodiversity-loss-is-endangering-food-security-un-warns.

Daly, Herman. *Beyond Growth: The Economics of Sustainable Development*. Boston: Beacon Press, 1997.

Descartes, René. "Discourse on the Method Part V." In *The Philosophical Writings of Descartes, Vol. 1*, edited and translated by John Cottingham, Robert Stoofhoff, and Dugald Murdoch. Cambridge, UK: Cambridge University Press, 1965.

Inter-Governmental Platform on Biodiversity and Ecosystem Services (IPBES). *Summary for Policymakers of the Regional Assessment Report on Biodiversity and Ecosystem Services for the Americas of the Intergovernmental Science-Policy Platform on Biodiversity and Ecosystem Services*. Bonn, Germany: IPBES Secretariat, 2018.

Järvensivu, Paavo, Tero Toivanen, Tere Vadén, Ville Lähde, Antti Majava, Jussi T. Eronen. *Global Sustainable Development Report 2019 Drafted by the Group of Independent Scientists; Invited Background Document on Economic Transformation, to Chapter; Transformation: The Economy*. Accessed on June 14, 2019, bios.fi/bios-governance_of_economic_transition.pdf.

Kant, Immanuel. *Lectures on Ethics*. London: Taylor and Francis Books, 1930.

Keller, Catherine. *Political Theology of the Earth: Our Planetary Emergency and the Struggle for a New Public*. New York: Columbia University Press, 2018.

Korten, David. *The Great Turning: From Empire to Earth Community*. San Francisco: Berrett-Koehler Publishers, Inc., 2007.

Löwy, Michael. *Ecosocialism: A Radical Alternative to Capitalist Catastrophe*. Chicago: Haymarket Books, 2015.

Marx, Karl. *Capital*, vol.1. London: Penguin, 1976.

McFague, Sallie. *The Body of God: An Ecological Theology*. Minneapolis: Fortress Press, 1993.

Mill, John Stuart. *On Nature*. New York: AMS Press, Inc., 1970.

Moltmann, Jürgen. *Ethics of Hope*. Minneapolis: Fortress Press, 2012.

Moore, Jason W., ed. *Anthropocene or Capitalocene? Nature, History, and the Crisis of Capitalism*. Oakland, CA: PM Press, 2016.

Moore, Jason W. *Capitalism in the Web of Life: Ecology and the Accumulation of Capital*. London: Verso Books, 2015.

Myers, Norman. "What We Must Do to Counter the Biotic Holocaust." *International Wildlife* 29, no. 2 (March-April 1999): 30–39.

Polanyi, Karl. *The Great Transformation: The Political and Economic Origins of Our Time*. Boston: Beacon Press, 2001.

Raskin, P. T., G. Banuri, P. Gallopín, A. Gutman, R. Hammond, and R. Swart Kates. *Great Transition: The Promise and Lure of the Times Ahead*. SEI PoleStar Series Report no. 10. Boston: SEI Publications, 2002.

Raworth, Kate. *Doughnut Economics: 7 Ways to Think Like a 21st Century Economist*. White River Junction, VT: Chelsea Green Publishing, 2017.

Rieger, Joerg, and Kwok Pui-lan. *Occupy Religion: Theology of the Multitude*. Plymouth, UK: Rowman & Littlefield Publishers, Inc., 2012.

Sittler, Joseph. "Called to Unity." In *Evocations of Grace: The Writings of Joseph Sittler on Ecology, Theology, and Ethics*, edited by Steven Bouma-Prediger and Peter W. Bakken, 45–46. Grand Rapids, MI: Eerdmans, 2000.

Wallace, Mark I. *Finding God in the Singing River: Christianity, Spirit, Nature*. Minneapolis: Fortress Press, 2005.

———. *When God Was a Bird: Christianity, Animism, and the Re-enchantment of the World*. New York: Fordham University Press, 2019.

Warren, Karen J. "The Power and the Promise of Ecological Feminism." In David. R. Keller, *Environmental Ethics: The Big Questions*, 282. Oxford, UK: Wiley-Blackwell, 2010.

Chapter 7

Planetary Economies

Whitney Bauman

It is a tricky business to claim, as many Western types have, that humans are made in the image of God. What is that image, and which part is "like" us? And "who" are those humans? For many Western Christians, this imago has been the source of equality among humans or the basis for human dignity or even human rights. The United Nations Universal Declaration of Human Rights may not have been conceptually possible without such ways of thinking.[1] On the other hand, as Lynn White and others have pointed out, this imago may also be a basis for anthropocentrism and contemporary environmental ills.[2] Also, as some have argued, who counts as human and who does not has always been tied up in colonial racial and patriarchal discourse.[3] In other words, the drawing of the boundary between the human and the animal is the site at which many women, people of color, and/or colonized people have become "animal." Is the logical outcome of the imago the Anthropocene era? Perhaps. This brief chapter argues that the omni-God of the Christian imago, the "power papa" as Catherine Keller calls Him,[4] and the current fossil-fueled era that we are commonly calling the Anthropocene are mutually reinforcing.[5] In other words, might the theology of an omni-God help to underwrite the fossil-fueled economics of colonialism, racism, sexism, and capitalism? If so, what types of eco-theological anthropologies might help reintegrate all humans back into the humus? If the primary divide is that which separates some humans from the rest of nature and then treats nature as pure resource, while the use of fossil fuels accelerates this extractive, racist, and colonial project, then, rather than merely extending something like "human rights" to all humans, we need to acknowledge the value and agency of the entire evolving, planetary community. I start here with a brief overview of the times and places of fossil-fueled capitalism and then move on to how the COVID-19–pandemic period helped to open us back onto our emergent planetary bodies. What types of common grounds,[6] along with the other bodies of the planetary community, might we build future worlds on that will promote planetary economics, which are always and already home economies and queer economies? This will be the guiding question of the final section of this chapter. In the end, this is an attempt to take Sallie McFague's advice and make home (or planetary) economics the context for all human thinking.[7]

THE TIMES AND PLACES OF FOSSIL-FUELED CAPITALISM

Life under pressure, especially under fossil-fueled pressure, will always rupture when the pressure becomes too great. The gravity of the situation is that too much gravity, or perhaps the result of the stuff gravity buried deep within the earth's surface, leads to the crushing of life on the surface and in the depths of this planet. Releasing all that gravity-induced pressure into the atmosphere has now led to a situation in which the planetary systems that have been intact since the last ice age, allowing for all known human civilizations on this planet to emerge, are now bursting apart.[8] The pace of fossil-fueled capitalism simply puts too much pressure on earthly bodies and systems and on some bodies and systems more than others.

Since the mid-twentieth century, the modern Western world has experienced what sociologists are calling a "great acceleration."[9] This acceleration, marked by an increase in the speed of production, transportation, and communication technologies, is in large part the result of a fossil-fueled neoliberal capitalism spreading across the planet. Such speed also has correlates with an increase in reproduction, though unequally, with those benefiting from fossil-fueled worlds having fewer children while those impoverished by them having more children. Such a distinction is, of course, not entirely accurate, as we are all impoverished by fossil-fueled speed in some way (climate change, anxieties, cancers, and other mental and physical disorders). However, when looking at the uneven contributions to environmental and social ills, it is still important to look at the equation: population x technology x consumption.[10] A person born in the United States will consume way more than a person born in another place whose economy is less fossil-fuel based.

The more speed one has is positively correlated to one's capital and fueled in large part by fossil fuels (and some nuclear energy). In other words, the more capital you have, the more you are likely to be what Zygmunt Bauman calls a "global mobile," rather than an "immobile local."[11] According to some estimates, global energy sources come from about 70 percent fossil fuels (coal, oil, and gas).[12] This doesn't even account for all the petroleum-based products that our lives depend on, including plastics. Prior to nuclear energy, the energy-use number was even more, but I think we can still define this era as a fossil-fueled one. Not to mention, the promise of nuclear energy does nothing to address the problem of the speed at which the modern Western project advances; rather, it maintains or accelerates it. The more capital one has, the more access to fossil fuels (and fossil fuel products) one has, the more one has "freedom from" the consumptive consequences of one's daily habits of production, transportation, and communication.

The myth of radical individualism, or the neoliberal individual, gains more credence the wealthier one is precisely because one can move at speeds that disregard connections to the rest of the planetary community. However, as we know from many critical theories, this transcendent growth that understands some human individuals to live "out of this world," without regard to bodily or biotic constraints, is lived at the expense of many other earth bodies. The 1 percent versus the 99 percent of the Occupy Movement,[13] the global mobiles and immobile locals mentioned above, the "least of these" in liberation theologies (including intersectional analyses), and the famous image of the champagne-glass economy[14] all point to the issues of environmental degradation and social injustice being exacerbated by fossil-fueled speed.

Sadly, this fossil-fueled speed, supported by a theological anthropology of a god that creates (some) humans in his image and in a place over and above the rest of the planetary community, has begun to outstrip the carrying capacity of planetary processes. Some earth scientists have argued that we simply have to find the green technologies to "ratchet up" the planet to the next level.[15] This type of thinking, to my mind, is just a continuation of an elite salvation narrative in which the few are saved by fossil-fueled realities at the expense of the many (both human and nonhuman). This is the vision of the so-called Ecological Modernists as well as of those promoting geo-engineering and of many so-called transhumanists.[16] It is also the view of the über-wealthy Elon Musk and Jeff Bezos, who both sent rockets from the earth in 2021.[17] I am no Luddite, but I do think that too much faith in human technological progress is folly and, at best, anthropocentric. It reflects a hope that all others will "rise with the rising tides" of innovation, and this hope doesn't seem to be borne out in human histories. True, there are life extensions and other such benefits of modern medicine and other technologies. But, there is also an increasing "gap" between the wealthiest and the poorest, and most of the earth's planetary systems are in decline. The same old thinking projected onto the future will not get us out of anything, and, in fact, maybe the problem is that we have tried much too hard to get ourselves out of the messiness of living within a planetary community. The COVID-19 pandemic, if nothing else, may be able to teach us a thing or two about staying with the messy times and places of the planetary community.

PANDEMICS AND CLIMATE CHANGE

Many of us moderns who are caught up in fossil-fueled capitalism, though not all of us, have experienced time differently because of the COVID-19 pandemic. Transportation on land, sea, and air all slowed down and nearly came to a halt. Indeed, the decrease in global emissions of CO_2 was seen during the global financial crisis of 2008 and during the pandemic years of 2020–2021.[18] Our daily sped-up lives, moving from one point to the next as fast as we could to accomplish as much as is possible in one day, came to a halt. Or, in the case of essential workers of all stripes, the pandemic became one, very long day: Many worked multiple shifts at a time, with too few people to do what needed to be done. In both cases, time was not just the incremental, mechanical standard Greenwich Mean Time made up of sequential seconds, minutes, hours, days, weeks, months, and years. Such a time is fossil-fueled in that the speed provided by use of fossil fuels allows one to move through the world at such a pace that one doesn't have regard for any cycles of seasons or planets or for any given place. For many, this fossil-fueled mechanical clock time, a time that has little regard for different experiences in the world but rather takes one out of their relationships with the rest of the natural world, began to break down. This failure of fossil-fueled time provided openings for many different experiences of time.

For some, this meant, again, working to the point of exhaustion for no other purpose than to deal with the immediate crisis, now, then now, then now. For others, it meant unemployment or working from home in ways that allowed for the recognition of different aspects of daily life. From my own privileged situation, I (stereotypically) began to watch more birds from my windows and bake sourdough bread. Both of these things are linked to different understandings of time outside the efficient movement of fossil-fueled time. With fossil-fueled time, one is rewarded for moving faster throughout the day with more future possibilities: What one can do in one day or one year increases (sometimes) exponentially with time. However, there is a backgrounding (a creation of an under-commons) of all the social and ecological ills that result from the speeding up of a form of linear time. One has to ignore a lot of life in order to live at the pace of progress.

Time that is spent bird-watching and baking bread unfolds at its own pace and in its own place. For others, biking, walking, and running have enabled them to pay more attention to the ways in which our cities and human-built environments have been structured around cars and fossil-fueled vehicles. This pandemic has given some people glimpses of a new way to think about moving through time and space. In addition, due to this slowdown in daily life and in transportation, many began to notice just how many other planetary bodies we share life with. Migrating birds, bees and insects of various types, wild foxes and other nonhuman animals that inhabit urban spaces on the regular, and the usual urban nonhuman suspects, such as rodents, have been noticed more by many and have "taken back" their own space in our worlds as the hustle and bustle of daily fossil-fueled life has calmed.[19]

As the decrease in CO_2 emissions mentioned above (which has now increased again), this pandemic "slow down" gave space for the rest of the planetary community to breathe. Indeed, many species of birds and insects saw a "comeback" in 2021, due at least in part to the slowdown of fossil fuel use. In addition, it gave the very grounds on which we stand a bit of release from the everyday pressure of fossil-fueled reality. One seismologist that studies the vibrations of rush-hour traffic in London noticed a significant decrease in seismic activity during the economic shutdowns in the United Kingdom.[20] The pandemic allowed modern fossil-fueled humans (a group I am a part of) to take note of the "backgrounded" collateral damage incurred by the rest of the planetary community due to our fast-paced living.[21]

At the same time, a critical eye has been placed on the breath that fossil fuel use takes away from so many. During the pandemic period, we moderns all had more time to pay attention to the injustices perpetuated by the racist hetero-patriarchal structures of fossil-fueled capitalism. "I can't breathe" became the slogan for the Black Lives Matter (BLM) movement, and it is important to understand that the same breath stolen by racism, sexism, heterosexism, and xenophobia is also polluted by fossil-fueled capitalism. The cruelty of racism and of sexism, in other words, steals the life breath of certain bodies in a way that is similar to how the pumping of CO_2 into the atmosphere steals the life breath of many nonhuman earth bodies. In addition, environmental racism means that the sacrificial pollution zones are most often placed in poor communities of color.[22] This is a point that the environmental-justice movement has been making for decades and that intersectional environmentalism is now beginning to address, but there is so much more to be done.[23]

Perhaps if we could live into these cracks in fossil-fueled times—the ones highlighted by movements such as BLM, pointing out the fragility caused by systemic racisms, and the ones caused by the pandemic, which have stressed labor, education, medicine, and democratic institutions in the United States—there might be potential to open onto a more just and sustainable way of organizing our bodies together within the planetary community. Then, we might be able to live through the current world's end and foster the growth of new worlds to come. In order to do this, we need a bit of monkey wrenching to help break down destructive, racist, hetero-patriarchal fossil-fueled systems of time. We might also need to take a page from the queer art of failure and learn how to fail that same oppressive system spectacularly. If we can live into the creative spaces that the failures of modernity creates, then we might also learn to think about possible futures while, as Donna Haraway suggests, "staying with the trouble."[24] It is only in staying with the messy bodies and multiple realities and times of the planetary community that we can begin to live in different ways and organize our lives according to something other than the dominant global model of fossil-fueled capitalism.

COMMON GROUNDS FOR PLANETARY BECOMING

Fossil-fueled capitalism depends upon the smooth spaces of certainty, foundations, and universals to function. Only these ways of experiencing the world and organizing our experiences and bodies within the world are efficient enough to keep up with such great speeds. Anything uncertain, multiple, and complex just gunks up the works of fossil-fueled modernity. However, the pressures that have built up under the veneer of certainty have burst open during the global pandemic. Economic inequities, sexisms, racisms, and ethnocentrisms have all come to a head and can no longer be covered over. Rather than reinstituting a unified foundation from which to build new worlds, we may instead want to search for common grounds from which to build multiple worlds. Such grounding of multiple worlds can allow for a pluriverse to emerge at any given moment of planetary becoming.

Common grounds might include basic needs: We humans all need shelter, food, oxygen, and water to live (as do most other animals). What institutions and systems aid in supporting this common ground and which ones work to undermine this common ground? In terms of our animality, we might be able to agree that we humans are all Homo sapiens and mammals and that we are but one species among many other species with whom we share the planet's air, water, earth, and fire. Even if some of us think we are "special" within the planet, we can surely agree that we are not the only animal-type things on this planet. Rather than having an *imago dei* that suggests humans are "above nature," perhaps having a more relational understanding of the entanglement of our humanity with all of creation, such as Ivone Gebara and Jürgen Moltmann have called for, would support this creatureliness of a planetary reality from a Christian perspective. As earthlings, we can agree that we are beholden to gravity and that we need the biosphere provided by the planet, as do all other living things on this planet. Again, these are all grounds and not universal foundations: There was not always a planet Earth and thus there was not always planetary gravity, there were not always human beings or other species of plants and animals that now inhabit this planet. And what we have here now, these common grounds, will not always exist. But we may be able to agree that, "for a time," we dwell in and on these common grounds.[25]

In constructing such "common grounds" for possible worlds within the planetary community, we should always also pay attention to the "under-commons."[26] What is beneath the common grounds on which we stand? What bodies, systems, and species have made up the common ground that we don't even take note of on a daily basis? We must include the under-commons, both human and nonhuman, that contribute to the very grounds on which we stand instead of taking them for granted, ignoring them, or backgrounding them.

It is also always important to keep in mind the fluidity of these common grounds, much like the fluidity of the oceans and waters. If anything, fossil-fueled modernity has, ironically, built its ideas and systems upon notions of solid ground. Even though the very fluid that fuels its visions, institutions and dreams, oil, is as unstable as it gets, the rest of fossil-fueled modernity assumes solidity.[27] But, in reality, if we trust in geology and its multiple analytical maps, tectonic and oceanic plates are always shifting; the deeper you get in the dirt, the more fluid things get. So, perhaps we need a more liquid understanding not just of modernity[28] but also of our knowledge, ethics, and aesthetics. We are much more fluid than solid.

PIRACY, THE PLURIVERSE, AND FLUID HUMANITIES

One problem with the globalization of neoliberal capitalism is that it is a continuation of a form of colonial center-periphery thinking. The entire planet and all therein are liquidated as consumables for the "solid" center. What we have here is a contemporary example of the "hungry ghosts" from Buddhist lore.[29] The problem with thinking of anything, including the self, as stable is that it is then abstracted from its underlying relationality: the flow of things. Everything else then becomes food for the empty self, hence the hungry ghosts. Other stories, such as the Yoruba *Palm Wine Drinkard*, describe giant, hungry, insatiable babies that also speak to this type of self-centered greed. And, of course, vampires and zombies have often been associated with fossil-fueled consumption. Zombies of colonial and capitalist making are particularly relevant for issues of race and class that arise with neoliberal globalization.[30] Perhaps this is why evil, ghostlike children, vampires, and zombies continue to populate the imaginations of many modern Western cultures: it is a working out of these deep consumeristic, capitalist, and colonial affects, especially as these are found in the white, modern Western male. The only colonial subject (historically and for the most part still)—the elite, white, able-bodied, straight male—treats all others as objects for consumption. In other words, all else is liquidated to maintain the illusion of solidity and separation of the colonial individual (the hard phallus of phallogocentrism).[31]

If we want to highlight the liquid nature of all things and challenge the solidity of the colonial self—that paradoxically liquefies all others to bring them into its solid center—then pirates and piracy might be a helpful source to draw from. They function to challenge capitalism, progress, and foundations. They also highlight interconnectedness and multiplicity. Let me explain. Historically, pirates have challenged the colonial expansion of mercantile capitalism. They were (and are) a threat to the continual liquidation of assets that move from the periphery to the center because they halt the flow of products and redistribute them.[32] Contemporary internet hacking and information piracy does the same. Stealing copyrights, making knockoffs, providing generic but equal brands of more expensive drugs—these are all instances of the redistribution of wealth and goods. Granted, not all piracy is Robin Hood-ish; plenty of struggling artists and indigenous peoples get pirated by larger corporations (think Urban Outfitters and pharmaceutical companies). Perhaps I should say here that the piracy I speak of is not of the continued corporate theft kind, which they just call "business as usual," but of the theft from corporations already at the center of power and wealth. The latter type of piracy has deeply religious justifications: Jesus hanging out with beggars and thieves, the redistribution of wealth that is suggested by many religions, the critique of both extreme wealth and extreme poverty in Buddhism, communalisms found in many indigenous traditions, the focus on "the poor" and "the least of these," in liberation strands of religious thought. All of these might justify an ethic of piracy to some degree. Again, I'm not saying the motivation of all pirates historically and at present is the end of capitalism, corporate power, and the redistribution of wealth, but I am arguing that that could be one justification for piracy: Let's call it piracy for the planet to distinguish it from the type of intellectual and biological piracy that is committed to keep the wealthy and powerful, wealthy and powerful.

Pirates are a challenge to the idea that the spread of neoliberal capitalism is coterminous with progress. They challenge us to ask "progress for whom and for what?" Certainly not the local peoples from whom resources and ideas are stolen. Certainly this is not progress for those impoverished by the green revolution in agriculture or the extraction of oil in Nigeria. Certainly this is not progress for planetary creatures going extinct or those already experiencing the destruction of global climate change. Pirates remind us that life on the fluid sea doesn't allow for a single narrative of progress but rather that all progress comes at the expense of something else. So, can we talk instead about what types of progress we want to promote and for which planetary creatures? At sea, we must continuously think together about our values and goals that are always on the move. And, as humans on the move, we are also meaning-making creatures that place value and goals onto our daily movements. This is part of being a healthy human (those who find life meaningless or who can't move on from things we often say have some sort of psychological issue). We must make decisions about which directions to go in, what needs redistributing and to whom, and these decisions are made based upon the values, narratives, hopes, and dreams we have as we are interpolated with the worlds around us.

In this sense, piracy and some sort of oceanic or fluid ethic helps us think about our interconnectedness and the multiplicity of perspectives and values that makes up the planetary community. An ethic is much more like a ship that carries us across certain thresholds but, as Thomas Tweed argues, "only for a time."[33] Ethics are not universal, a priori, or eternal. The nature of living in an entangled and ever-shifting and moving planetary community means that our thinking, imagining, and ethics must also be open to these contexts. For this, I argue for what I have elsewhere called an epistemology and ethic of viable agnosticism and a polyamory of place.[34]

An epistemology and ethic of viable agnosticism means that we hold open the ends of our identities, lives, and thoughts for the unknown other. We can think back to a time when we were little, but not before birth; our awareness and memories trail off. We can think forward into the future of our lives only so far, and, at some point, the world will move on without us. Similarly, we can see only so far back in time even with the aides of evolutionary science and cosmology. Our knowledge of the universe shades off into a "singularity." What is before or outside that is a mystery: nothing? a multiverse? And we can see only so far through modern satellite imagery out to the edges of the universe until we reach the microwave background radiation, or the edge of the universe: Again, is there another universe beyond that or nothing? We just don't know. This also goes for the gap between our ideas of the world and the world in itself or the self and the other. A viable agnosticism holds open the spaces of mystery and uncertainty at beginnings and endings rather than closing them off with projections of a full-blown theism or atheism. Instead of projecting everything or nothing, both certain projections, in order to live in a fluid world, with multiple perspectives and paths into the future, we must hold open the space for mystery, wonder, awe, and uncertainty. These spaces allow porous bodies and porous moments the space to breathe and move from one to the other.[35] When these porous spaces of mystery are sealed off or reified, bodies begin to suffocate, atrophy, and die. As Catherine Keller has suggested, certainty has caused more violence on the planet than uncertainty ever will.[36] So, here at the end of this chapter, I'd like to reflect on what an economics based upon the flourishing of the open, evolving planetary community might look like.

HOME ECONOMICS ARE QUEER ECONOMIES

If human beings are not the Homo economicus assumed by fossil-fueled neoliberal thought, and we are instead planetary creatures, then we must begin to think of humans as of the humus, of the earth, as planetary creatures. As such, we are terrestrial sapiens (wise earthlings). We share this wisdom with most living things and even living systems. There is a lot of wisdom distributed throughout the planetary community. All things human must account for our embeddedness in the planetary community, including economics. Home economics, as McFague argued decades ago, should be the ultimate framework of all human economics (the home being the earth, terra).[37] However, this is not a patriarchal hetero-normative home economics that we might be familiar with from high school in the United States. Rather, a system of rules for the *oikos* (house) or terra (earth) must take into account the queerness of the fluid life that we all emerge from and affect. I use the term *queer* not just in the sense that what we think of as stable genders, sexes, and sexualities are actually co-constructed differently in different places over time. I mean that, but I also mean that all of nature (including the universe) is co-constructed over time and through relations. Life is much queerer than the certainties we project onto it. At the end of this chapter, then, I want to expand a bit on three components that should be included in a queer home economics: rules of ecosystems, economies of desires, and economies of abundance and flourishing.

RULES OF ECOSYSTEMS

Just as a single time cannot be imposed over all entities across the entire planet without violence, so with economic systems. The times and places of things matter. Fossil-fueled time demands the efficiency of a neoliberal system: isolated individual humans, starting from an equal ground, acting rationally, with the nonhuman world understood as stuff for use toward human ends. This economic system externalizes those things that are inefficient, such as unpaid work; the fact that we don't start equally and that we are born with unearned privileges that depend on our race, gender, sex, sexuality, and ability; the costs and benefits for the rest of the natural world; fair labor practices; and the costs of climate change and extinction events—just to name a few. All of these are backgrounded by the imposition of a neoliberal mentality over the face of the entire planet.

What if, instead, we started from the places in which we live our daily lives and the interaction between places on a planetary scale? What if we acknowledge that we humans are all nodes of exchanges of energy, information, and materials, just as all other biotic and abiotic life-forms are, as are ecosystems and bioregions and the planet itself. If we start with an ecosystemic approach—what are healthy exchanges that help a given ecosystem and all therein to flourish the most?—and move out toward how this issue applies in bioregions and then at the planetary level, perhaps we would begin to base our human economies on the economies of the ongoing planetary communities of which we are a part.

Of course, many in the field of environmental economics and policy are beginning to flesh out how we might materialize these more theoretical ideas.[38] Some argue for putting a price on those things which have been externalized in the market. In other words a "green capitalism" is what is needed.[39] Others argue that what we need is a stronger understanding of the commons and that capitalism is inherently environmentally destructive. Some form of green socialism is what is called for.[40] While the "true costs" of production and consumption and some sort of redistribution of wealth, resources, and evils are necessary, I don't think they are sufficient for re-placing humans within a home economics of the planet.

Erotic Economies

As terrestrial creatures, our primary identification in the world is through our sensing bodies. As Merleau-Ponty might argue, and more recently Mayra Rivera expanded upon, we are entangled with all other flesh on the planet.[41] Far from being rational, skin-encapsulated egos that judge all things from atop a tower, above the fray, we are always and already in the mix. Furthermore, as affect theorists have pointed out, there is a lot of affect, deep emotions, and habits that goes into the formation of what we think of as Western, objective reason.[42] Most economic theories are built upon rational-choice theories that assume individuals can look at all the information and make a purely "rational" decision about what to consume and how to spend money and labor. This just simply is not the case. First, there is no way to get "all the information." Never mind the greenwashing and brownwashing that companies do, the persuasion and lobbying on the part of advertisers and companies, and the inability to predict how one decision will ripple out into the future: No single person can even grasp all information that does exist at once. Second, we are embodied creatures that don't act on "reason" alone, and "reason" itself is yet another way of feeling that shapes and orders the world in certain ways. I'm not suggesting that we do away with reason, but that we put reason in its embodied context. Third, not all bodies are treated equally, and there are years and years of direct and institutional racism, sexism, heteronormativity, cis-genderism, and ableism. This means that we don't all start out from an equal beginning.

Just those three major points should be enough to nail the coffin closed on rational choice–based theories and economics. However, there is a fourth and final point that I want to argue: Human beings are just as much about desires, dreams, fears, and deep-seated habits as about using individual agency to make rational decisions. In fact, given our embeddedness in ecological, evolutionary, and sociocultural contexts, we probably have much less agency than we think. And we depend upon the wisdom found in these other entities and systems. We are channeled into a future that has largely nothing to do with us. Our hopes and dreams are way more about what has been constructed at the moment that we are thrown into the world than about what we as individuals choose. Yes, our choices matter, and, yes, we have some freedom, but not the type of "freedom from" that the liberal individual self is based upon. We cannot escape our fleshy enmeshment. We are drawn together by attraction, eros, the primary attraction, as David Abrams notes, being gravity.[43] Thus, the type of freedom we have is an erotic freedom, based upon our entangled planetary becoming, a "freedom for" working toward this or that type of future for the flourishing of planetary communities and bodies therein.

Economies are perhaps even more about desires, hopes, and dreams than they are about rational accounting, work, and labor. Building economies based upon a liberal, rational, individual understanding of the self continues to force bodies into that image. This forcing causes much violence to bodies that have been systematically discriminated against throughout the histories of our various cultures. Indeed, the Homo economicus is only attainable for those who have the power to take full advantage of fossil-fueled speed. One's fast pace of life is achieved at the expense of others we are entangled with. In order to keep moving, many relations must be backgrounded to avoid the friction of planetary entanglement. This, in part, is why there are environmental-justice movements, the BLM movement, the Me Too movement, and queer movements. These are the friction points, the cracks, the sites of violence that reveal what happens when we ignore what the pace of fossil-fueled living is doing to the planetary community. Continuing to cocreate economies in the image of the hetero-patriarchal understanding of "Homo economicus" will do nothing but create more destruction to the entire planetary community. Thus, I think it is important to feel our way into new ways of being and becoming that upset the Homo economicus and all its deep habits of becoming.

Flourishing of Planetary Bodies

The queerness of our embodiment, once we begin to really sense our enmeshment, requires us to rethink many of our human institutions. Any sort of home economics must consider the blurry boundaries between the self and the other (human and other than human) and the ways in which we are both subjects and objects, how we are made up of multiple subjects, and also how we make up other subjects (ecologically and evolutionarily). We are hybrids (Haraway), assemblages (Deleuze and Guattari), hyperobjects (Morton), societies of entities (Whitehead), ecosystems, and parts of other ecosystems. This queering of boundaries between self–other, human–animal, animal–plant, plant–mineral, and biotic–abiotic requires a different, queer home economics.

It is no coincidence that queer communities, such as the Radical Fairies and lesbian separatists, experimented with new ways of living together in community outside of nuclear families and in ways that were more ecologically sound. As Rosemary Ruether points out well in *The Making of the Modern Family*, following Foucault and others, the nuclear family and capitalism go hand in hand.[44] Tinkering with gender and sexuality also leads to tinkering with economic assumptions. Early Jesus followers of the first couple hundred years knew this as well and were gender bending and living in different understandings of chosen family.[45] Monastic communities of all sorts also had queer understandings of family. And, of course, the more communal life of most indigenous communities around the world had room for multiple genders prior to the colonization by Western monotheists (and, in some cases, these are still being embraced or revived). I'm not arguing that communism has fared better in terms of accepting multiple genders, sexes, and sexualities; the communism of China and Russia in particular are built upon the basic division of humans and the rest of the natural world and the ranking of humans toward an ideal within humanity. Until the human community is queered within and with its relationship to the rest of the natural world, then new possible ways of becoming cannot be released.

Planetary flourishing requires what I have called a polyamory of place: the love of multiple places and the exchanges between materials, energy, and information between them. As humans, we are limited in our ability to love: We can't love the whole planet, not even all humans, at any one given place in time. Such love is abstract. However, we can recognize the eros that draws us all together with all other life on the planet and create habits that honor that embodied love in the places we do inhabit, and in the interactions with other places that we affect in different ways. This queer, planetary economy of erotic connections should favor more those things that lead to planetary flourishing and penalize those that lead to violence. The same home economics will not apply to every place equally but should emerge from the unique set of relations in a given place. Such home economics has no place for externalities; not even our waste can be thrown "away."[46] Rather, we must constantly measure our economic interactions and attune toward habits and ways of becoming that support planetary flourishing.

NOTES

1. Gaymon Bennett, *Technicians of Human Dignity: Bodies, Souls, and the Making of Intrinsic Worth* (New York: Fordham University Press, 2016).
2. Lynn White, "The Historical Roots of Our Ecological Crisis," *Science* 155 (1967): 1203–7.
3. Aph Ko, *Racism and Zoological Witchcraft: A Guide to Getting Out* (Brooklyn, NY: Lantern Books, 2019).
4. Catherine Keller, *God and Power: Counter-Apocalyptic Journeys* (Minneapolis: Fortress, 2005).
5. Terra Rowe, *Of Modern Extraction: Experiments in Critical Petro-Theology* (London: T&T Clark, 2022).
6. Laurel Kearns and Catherine Keller, "Introduction: Grounding Theory—Earth in Religion and Philosophy," in *EcoSpirit: Religions and Philosophies for the Earth*, edited by Laurel Kearns and Catherine Keller (New York: Fordham University Press, 2007), 1–20.
7. Sallie McFague, *Life Abundant: Rethinking Theology and Economy for a Planet in Peril* (Minneapolis: Fortress, 2001).
8. See, e.g., Emily Sohn, "Climate Change and the Rise and Fall of Civilizations," on the NASA website, "Global Climate Change: Vital Signs of the Planet," January 20, 2014, last accessed July 26, 2022, https://climate.nasa.gov/news/1010/climate-change-and-the-rise-and-fall-of-civilizations/.
9. J. R. McNeill and Peter Engelke, *The Great Acceleration: An Environmental History of the Anthropocene since 1945* (Cambridge, MA: Harvard University Press, 2014).
10. Herman E. Daly and John Cobb, *For the Common Good: Redirecting the Economy toward Community, the Environment, and a Stable Future* (Boston: Beacon, 1989).
11. Zygmunt Bauman, *Globalization: The Human Consequences* (Cambridge, UK: Polity Press, 1998).
12. See, e.g., The Environmental and Energy Study Institute 2021 report, last accessed July 26, 2022, https://www.eesi.org/topics/fossil-fuels/description.
13. Joerg Rieger and Kwok Pui-Lan, *Occupy Religion: Theology of the Multitude* (Lanham, MD: Rowman & Littlefield, 2012).
14. See, e.g., Laura Noren's graphic, "Champagne Glass Distribution of Wealth," on The Society Pages, May 27, 2009, last accessed July 26, 2022, https://thesocietypages.org/graphicsociology/2009/05/27/champagne-glass-distribution-of-wealth/.
15. Ruth DeFries, *The Big Ratchet: How Humanity Thrives in the Face of Natural Crisis* (New York: Basic Books, 2014).
16. See "An EcoModernist Manifesto," on www.ecomodernism.org, April 2015, last accessed July 26, 2022, https://static1.squarespace.com/static/5515d9f9e4b04d5c3198b7bb/t/552d37bbe4b07a7dd69fcdbb/1429026747046/An+Ecomodernist+Manifesto.pdf.
17. Mary-Jane Rubenstein, *Astrotopia: The Dangerous Religion of the Corporate Space Race* (Chicago: University of Chicago Press, 2022).

18. Zeke Hausfather, "Global CO2 Emissions Have Been Flat for a Decade, New Data Reveals," CarbonBrief (April 11, 2021), https://www.carbonbrief.org/global-co2-emissions-have-been-flat-for-a-decade-new-data-reveals.

19. See, e.g., the story on the BBC website, "Coronavirus: Wild Animals Enjoy Freedom of a Quieter World," April 29, 2020, last accessed July 26, 2022, https://www.bbc.com/news/world-52459487.

20. Thomas Lecoco, Stephen P. Hicks, Kasper van Wijk, et al., "Global Quieting of High-Frequency Seismic Noice Due to COVID-19 Pandemic Lockdown Measures," *Science* 369.6509 (July 23, 2020): 1338–43.

21. On the concept of "backgrounding," see Val Plumwood, *Environmental Culture: The Ecological Crisis of Reason* (New York: Routledge, 2002): 27–58.

22. See the updated "Toxic Wastes and Race and Toxic Wastes and Race at Twenty," on the United Church of Christ website, last accessed July 26, 2022, https://www.ucc.org/what-we-do/justice-local-church-ministries/justice/faithful-action-ministries/environmental-justice/environmental-ministries_toxic-waste-20/.

23. See the nonprofit started by Leah Thomas, Intersectional Environmentalist, last accessed July 26, 2022, https://www.intersectionalenvironmentalist.com/.

24. Donna Haraway, *Staying with the Trouble: Making Kin in the Chthulucene* (Durham, NC: Duke University Press, 2014).

25. Laurel Kearns and Catherine Keller, *EcoSpirit*.

26. Sefano Harney and Fred Moten, *The Undercommons: Fugitive Planning and Black Study* (Brooklyn, NY: Autonomedia, May 1, 2013).

27. Terra Rowe, *Of Modern Extraction*.

28. Zygmunt Bauman, *Liquid Modernity* (Cambridge, UK: Polity Press, 2000).

29. In Buddhist mythology, in particular Chinese Buddhism, "hungry ghosts" are a form of rebirth after one has led a life of greed. More broadly, I understand it as a metaphor for consumer culture or the insatiable desire to consume more and more. See, for example, David Landis Barnhill, "Good Work: An Engaged Buddhist Response to the Dilemmas of Consumerism," *Buddhist-Christian Studies* 24 (2004): 55–63.

30. In addition to the more negative understanding of zombies created by capitalism and the metaphor of capitalism that is "vampire capitalism," Franz Fanon talks about how zombies, other mythical creatures, and the idea of possession played a positive role in helping the colonized hold on to some space outside of the colonizer's world in *The Wretched of the Earth* (New York: Grove Press, 1963), 18–20.

31. Jacques Derrida, "Plato's Pharmacy," in *Dissemination* (Chicago: University of Chicago Press, 2004), 67–186.

32. Of course, not all pirates throughout history have been rouge or anti-colonial. There are many that worked for corporations and nations. For an interesting history of the complexities of piracy, see Mark G. Hanna, *Pirate Nests and the Rise of the British Empire, 1570–1740* (Chapel Hill: University of North Carolina Press, 2014).

33. Thomas Tweed, *Crossing and Dwelling: A Theory of Religion* (Cambridge, MA: Harvard University Press, 2006).

34. Whitney Bauman, *Religion and Ecology: Developing a Planetary Ethic* (New York: Columbia University Press, 2014).

35. Mayra Rivera, *Poetics of the Flesh* (Durham, NC: Duke University Press, 2015).

36. Keller, *God and Power*.

37. McFague, *Life Abundant*.

38. Including Daly and Cobb, *For the Common Good*.

39. Hartmut Berghoff and Adam Rome, *Green Capitalism: Business and the Environment in the Twentieth Century* (Philadelphia: University of Pennsylvania Press, 2017).

40. John Bellamy Foster, *The Return of Nature: Socialism and Ecology* (New York: Monthly Review Press, 2020).

41. Rivera, *Poetics of the Flesh*.

42. Donovan Schaefer, *Wild Experiment: Feeling Science and Secularism after Darwin* (Durham, NC: Duke University Press, 2022).

43. David Abram, *Becoming Animal: An Earthly Cosmology* (New York: Vintage Books, 2010).

44. Rosemary Radford Ruether, *Christianity and the Making of the Modern Family: Ruling Ideologies, Diverse Realities* (Boston: Beacon Press, 2000).

45. Erin Vearncombe and Brandon Scott, eds., *After Jesus; Before Christianity: A Historical Exploration of the First Two Centuries of Jesus Movements* (New York: HarperCollins, 2021).

46. Kenneth Worthy, *Invisible Nature: Healing the Destructive Divide between People and the Environment* (Amherst, NY: Prometheus Books, 2013).

REFERENCES

Abram, David. *Becoming Animal: An Earthly Cosmology*. New York: Vintage Books, 2010.

Barnhill, David Landis. "Good Work: An Engaged Buddhist Response to the Dilemmas of Consumerism." *Buddhist-Christian Studies* 24 (2004): 55–63.

Bauman, Whitney. *Religion and Ecology: Developing a Planetary Ethic*. New York: Columbia University Press, 2014.

Bauman, Zygmunt. *Globalization: The Human Consequences*. Cambridge, UK: Polity Press, 1998.

———. *Liquid Modernity*. Cambridge, UK: Polity Press, 2000.

BBC. "Coronavirus: Wild Animals Enjoy Freedom of a Quieter World." April 29, 2020. Last accessed July 26, 2022. https://www.bbc.com/news/world-52459487.

Bennett, Gaymon. *Technicians of Human Dignity: Bodies, Souls, and the Making of Intrinsic Worth*. New York: Fordham University Press, 2016.

Berghoff, Hartmut, and Adam Rome. *Green Capitalism: Business and the Environment in the Twentieth Century*. Philadelphia, PA: University of Pennsylvania Press, 2017.

Carbon Brief. "Global CO2 Emissions Have Been Flat for a Decade, New Data Reveals." https://www.carbonbrief.org/global-co2-emissions-have-been-flat-for-a-decade-new-data-reveals.

Daly, Herman E., and John Cobb. *For the Common Good: Redirecting the Economy toward Community, the Environment, and a Stable Future.* Boston: Beacon, 1989.

DeFries, Ruth. *The Big Ratchet: How Humanity Thrives in the Face of Natural Crisis.* New York: Basic Books, 2014.

Derrida, Jacques. "Plato's Pharmacy." In *Dissemination.* Chicago: University of Chicago Press, 2004: 67–186.

"An EcoModernist Manifesto." April 2015. Last accessed July 26, 2022. www.ecomodernism.org. https://static1.squarespace.com/static/5515d9f9e4b04d5c3198b7bb/t/552d37bbe4b07a7dd69fcdbb/1429026747046/An+Ecomodernist+Manifesto.pdf.

The Environmental and Energy Study Institute 2021 report. Last accessed July 26, 2022. https://www.eesi.org/topics/fossil-fuels/description.

Fanon, Franz. *The Wretched of the Earth.* New York: Grove Press, 1963.

Foster, John Bellamy. *The Return of Nature: Socialism and Ecology.* New York: Monthly Review Press, 2020.

Hanna, Mark G. *Pirate Nests and the Rise of the British Empire, 1570–1740.* Chapel Hill: University of North Carolina Press, 2014.

Haraway, Donna. *Staying with the Trouble: Making Kin in the Chthulucene.* Durham, NC: Duke University Press, 2014.

Harney, Stefano, and Fred Moten. *The Undercommons: Fugitive Planning and Black Study.* Wivenhoe, NY: Minor Compositions, 2013.

Hausfather, Zeke. "Global CO2 Emissions Have Been Flat for a Decade, New Data Reveals." CarbonBrief, April 11, 2021. https://www.carbonbrief.org/global-co2-emissions-have-been-flat-for-a-decade-new-data-reveals.

Kearns, Laurel, and Catherine Keller, eds. *EcoSpirit: Religions and Philosophies for the Earth.* New York: Fordham University Press, 2007.

Kearns, Laurel, and Catherine Keller. "Introduction: Grounding Theory—Earth in Religion and Philosophy." In *EcoSpirit: Religions and Philosophies for the Earth*, edited by Laurel Kearns and Catherine Keller, 1–20. New York: Fordham University Press, 2007.

Keller, Catherine. *God and Power: Counter-Apocalyptic Journeys.* Minneapolis: Fortress, 2005.

Ko, Aph. *Racism and Zoological Witchcraft: A Guide to Getting Out.* Brooklyn, NY: Lantern Books, 2019.

Lecoco, Thomas, Stephen P. Hicks, Kasper van Wijk, et al. "Global Quieting of High-Frequency Seismic Noise Due to COVID-19 Pandemic Lockdown Measures." *Science* 369.6509 (July 23, 2020): 1338–43.

McFague, Sallie. *Life Abundant: Rethinking Theology and Economy for a Planet in Peril.* Minneapolis: Fortress, 2001.

McNeill, J. R., and Peter Engelke. *The Great Acceleration: An Environmental History of the Anthropocene since 1945.* Cambridge, MA: Harvard University Press, 2014.

Noren, Laura. "Champagne Glass Distribution of Wealth." The Society Pages. May 27, 2009. Last accessed: July 26, 2022. https://thesocietypages.org/graphicsociology/2009/05/27/champagne-glass-distribution-of-wealth/.

Plumwood, Val. *Environmental Culture: The Ecological Crisis of Reason.* New York: Routledge, 2002: 27–58.

Rieger, Joerg, and Kwok Pui-Lan. *Occupy Religion: Theology of the Multitude*. Lanham, MD: Rowman & Littlefield, 2012.

Rivera, Mayra. *Poetics of the Flesh*. Durham, NC: Duke University Press, 2015.

Rowe, Terra. *Of Modern Extraction: Experiments in Critical Petro-Theology*. London: T&T Clark, 2022.

Rubenstein, Mary-Jane. *Astrotopia: The Dangerous Religion of the Corporate Space Race*. Chicago: University of Chicago Press, 2022.

Ruether, Rosemary Radford. *Christianity and the Making of the Modern Family: Ruling Ideologies, Diverse Realities*. Boston: Beacon Press, 2000.

Schaefer, Donovan. *Wild Experiment: Feeling Science and Secularism after Darwin*. Durham, NC: Duke University Press, 2022.

Sohn, Emily. "Climate Change and the Rise and Fall of Civilizations." NASA website, "Global Climate Change: Vital Signs of the Planet." January 20, 2014. Last accessed July 26, 2022. https://climate.nasa.gov/news/1010/climate-change-and-the-rise-and-fall-of-civilizations/.

Thomas, Leah. "Intersectional Environmentalist." Last accessed July 26, 2022. https://www.intersectionalenvironmentalist.com/.

"Toxic Wastes and Race and Toxic Wastes and Race at Twenty." United Church of Christ website. Last accessed July 26, 2022. https://www.ucc.org/what-we-do/justice-local-church-ministries/justice/faithful-action-ministries/environmental-justice/environmental-ministries_toxic-waste-20/.

Tweed, Thomas. *Crossing and Dwelling: A Theory of Religion*. Cambridge, MA: Harvard University Press, 2006.

Vearncombe, Erin, and Brandon Scott, eds. *After Jesus; Before Christianity: A Historical Exploration of the First Two Centuries of Jesus Movements*. New York: HarperCollins, 2021.

White, Lynn. "The Historical Roots of Our Ecological Crisis." *Science* 155 (1967): 1203–7.

Worthy, Kenneth. *Invisible Nature: Healing the Destructive Divide between People and the Environment*. Amherst, NY: Prometheus Books, 2013.

PART III

Practical Engagements

Chapter 8

Resistance as Healing

Disrupting the Spiritual Foundations of Capitalism

Gabriella Lettini

[W]ading in blood and dripping with filth, thus capitalist society stands . . . as a pestilential breath, devastating culture and humanity.

—Rosa Luxemburg, *The Junius Pamphlet*, 1915

The development of the COVID-19 pandemic, in which we were fully immersed as I[1] started writing this chapter in the fall of 2020, has been reflecting an image of who we are as a society.[2] The picture is bleak, and, while this is not unexpected, it is heartbreaking.

The narrative of what has been happening during these difficult times depends on whose voices and experiences we choose to center. In the spring of 2020, as we faced the brutal effects of an unknown virus, a large part of the world population had to adapt quickly to ways of living that were new to many of us: wearing a mask in public, living in lockdown, socially distancing, working from home and homeschooling, and, eventually, creating community pods to have a minimum of interaction. Social media were progressively flooded with pictures of people embarking on new hobbies to pass the time and deal with the anxiety for their health and their loved ones' well-being. However, for others, the challenges were of a completely different kind, mostly a dramatic exacerbation of the economic and safety issues they had already been facing in their daily lives. Centering the narrative of this pandemic on essential workers like nurses and delivery personnel and also on undocumented farmworkers and people in prisons, homeless shelters, and immigration detention centers forces the more privileged to face with new urgency the dramatic realities that were already embedded in our societies and that some could never forget for a moment. Our societies are not only marred by profound inequalities but also intentionally built on them and on the exploitation of the masses, in particular the masses of Black people, indigenous people, and people of color. Western societies are not organized for the survival and thriving of communities but for the immoral accumulation of wealth by the few that results from the exploitation of natural resources and human labor. The COVID-19 pandemic has not merely shown the limitations of the neoliberal capitalist system but also clarified its true nature. The system is not flawed but indeed works only for the people that it is supposed to work. Nevertheless, during these pandemic times, even the privileged 1 percent at the top of the pyramid of inequality have had glances of the fact that, in an interconnected world, safety is not guaranteed as lack of care for their caretakers can ultimately result in their own illness, and, even in places of privilege, nature is responding to the massive violation it has suffered. In the state of California, for instance, the pandemic has been lived along with the reality of massive fires, unbreathable air, and almost constant fire emergency alerts.

COVID-19 AND CAPITALISM

This pandemic is both rooted in capitalism and rendered much more catastrophic and deadly by it. The COVID-19 virus can be ultimately traced back to the way capitalist society has thought of nature as a resource to be exploited without regard for the consequences. As the environmental sustainability activist-scholar Anitra Nelson points out, while the West was quick to blame the new coronavirus on the Chinese population's eating habits, it is large-scale industrial agriculture that incubates most new pathogens.[3] The whole food production by large multinational corporations is organized from start to finish around unhealthy and unsustainable practices that not only produce new pathogens but also quickly disseminate them. Additionally, industrial deforestation pushes people to live in close proximity to animals that had previously no human contact. In a capitalist world that devalues natural and human resources as disposable, people's safety keeps being secondary to profit and access to health care is still seen as a privilege instead of a basic human right. At the same time, occasions for animal-human contamination multiply, rendering human communities much more vulnerable to new diseases. Scientists have been warning heads of state and decision makers that a pandemic, most likely affecting the respiratory systems, was on the horizon. In January 2017, Anthony Fauci, then director of the National Institute of Allergy and Infectious Diseases (NIAID), during a forum on pandemic preparedness at Georgetown University, affirmed that the Trump administration was probably going to experience an infectious-disease outbreak.[4] Nevertheless, adequate funding was not directed to research in this area. Hospitals and senior centers, even in large cities, were not properly equipped for the basic protection of their staff and patients. We were repeatedly lied to about the severity of the situation and the dismal level of preparation for it. In the early days of the pandemic, even medical professionals were often disciplined for wearing a mask during their shifts to cover for the fact that it was a basic necessity. Similar examples can be found around the world, where most countries were unprepared to deal with this pandemic.

It is not by chance that the United States, which can be seen as the epicenter of global capitalism, is currently the country with the highest numbers of deaths,[5] ten months into this pandemic, even with plenty of advanced notice about what was happening in other countries and time to prepare between waves of contagion. It is also not by chance that, during this pandemic, the United States has witnessed so many human-caused natural disasters, so many killings of Black people by police, and a disproportionately high COVID-19 death toll in the communities of Black people, indigenous people, and people of color. What we experience is not the result of unlucky chances but the results of centuries of systemic settler colonialism, racism, and exploitation of natural resources.

Capitalism is a system of relationships based on exploitation, where a few can become wealthy at the exploited masses' expense. It is an economic system that justifies unequal power relationships and the trampling of fundamental human rights for the profit of very few and the illusion of relative safety and well-being for a larger number of privileged people, mainly white. In the last decades, the number of people who genuinely benefited from capitalism has been shrinking dramatically, as the former middle class manages to survive while being immersed in debt and a few medical crises away from bankruptcy and possible houselessness.

Capitalism has always been perpetrated by the constructions of self-serving myths and the perpetuation of lies, supported by religious and cultural ideologies. While Max Weber saw the origins of capitalism in Protestantism, it can be argued that many earlier forms of Christianity already had offered a solid underpinning for it when they nurtured ideologies that justified economic inequality and the exploitation of the natural world and other human beings or supported the building of economic and political power of imperial entities, such as the Roman Catholic Church after the Emperor Constantine's era. At its core, the myth of capitalism is that one's wealth is a well-deserved recognition of hard work and a sign of God's favor. The wealth of the few becomes more important than the state of most human beings and the planet, more valuable than justice, fair relationships, and healthy living. It interprets the wealth of the few as something he or she has earned by divine mandate because of industriousness, rather than as theft, the misappropriated fruit of the labor of others.

One of the lies of capitalism is that anyone could become successful if he or she worked hard enough. This is the myth that fuels the American Dream. If people do not make enough money or are poor, houseless, or jobless, it is their fault and it reflects on their moral fiber and value as human beings. The spirituality of capitalism is based on individualism and egoism, masquerading as self-sufficiency and business acumen and justifying exploitative actions as needed by the market.

In the United States, we can still not think that access to health care, sustainable living wages, housing, education, and work safety are fundamental human rights. Anyone fighting for it is still labeled negatively, as a danger to society and a supporter of totalitarian forms of communism. Wealth is supposed to be the fruit of hard work and good morals, while it is most often inherited and built on exploitation. The myth of solitary self-made individuals who lifted themselves by their individual bootstraps persists. Eli Zaretsky wrote about the long process that, from the times of slavery, created the reality of today in the United States:

> Also important in managing a herd is to destroy all forms of critical thinking, in particular anything that challenges the supremacy of private property. The multitude was taught to react with instinctive, even ferocious, negativity to any idea that could be described as "socialist" or "communist." Not only did this render the herd more submissive, it created a feeling of narcissistic superiority that helped its members accept the drastic loss of long-established rights. The master class, which had lived in fear of herd uprisings until it quelled the rebellions of the 1960s, was amazed at how easily the herd gave up the belief that it was entitled to jobs, housing and good schools. Also helpful, as with poultry and cattle, was the use of drugs (heroin, cocaine, methamphetamine). Most fundamental, however, was convincing the masses that they had little or no right to medical care.[6]

Once again, during the COVID-19 pandemic, those already most exploited and marginalized in US society have been disproportionally affected by the pandemic while also being asked to bear most of the responsibilities to keep society functioning as essential workers. They have been treated like sacrificial herds. Medical personnel had to work without adequate protection and resources to support their patients, working in grueling shifts. People with the lowest-paying jobs, like farmworkers, and members of the so-called gig economy, like Uber drivers, were not able to work from home. People were forced to choose between paying their bills and safety for themselves and their family, while others lost their sources of income without support networks, savings, or access to governmental grants.

In this context, the people who have always been the foundation of the functioning and wealth of the country were suddenly put in the public spotlight as "essential workers," and some of them have been praised as heroes. Yet, while we saw children's drawings and big signs thanking the essential workers posted on people's windows, we have not witnessed the same kind of impetus to make sure they receive justice, are paid a fully sustainable wage, can work with safe protective gear, and can afford health care. In effect, praising the "essentials" is an easy way out from dealing with the fact that, in this society, they are really treated as disposable, the ones who have to put their lives in jeopardy because they cannot afford to do otherwise, and who can be easily replaced. Essential workers are disproportionately Black, indigenous, or people of color and are part of the working poor. Undocumented immigrants comprise a large number of them. They are called heroes now but treated as disposable and sacrificial beings. The capitalist society feigns to elevate them only to disguise that it is sending people to the slaughter. This mechanism has been well studied in the past and has been typically embedded in the ideology of war.

The ideology of capitalism elevates essential workers now so they can better be exploited as willing sacrificial heroes while also showing its utmost disdain for those who cannot be productive according to its logic. During this pandemic, it has become even clearer who is considered disposable: the elderly with little to no economic means, people with disabilities and chronic issues, and people living in prisons, on the street, or in ICE detention centers. There has been little concern for their safety and well-being, while the for-profit prison and immigration systems gain revenue from systemic suffering.

Economic losses related to the pandemic have also forced more people who were previously able to hide under the cover or delusion of being middle class to admit that they were only a paycheck away from food insecurity and houselessness. However, this rise in poverty has not directly been caused by the virus but by an inadequate social system where workers are exploited and left on their own if, for any reason, they can no longer perform their roles; where welfare support programs are seen as undeserved entitlements or handouts. Additionally, Joerg Rieger pointed out what he calls "the ugly truth of the pandemic": Most people never recovered from the 2008–2009 recession; they were not bailed out while corporations and banks were.[7]

During this pandemic, we have also kept promoting the false dichotomy between concern for safety and for the economy, as if saving lives would be a luxury that the capitalist system cannot afford. In Italy, my country of origin, the virus spread especially in the North, with the highest concentration in the area around Milan, Lombardy, which is Italy's business center. In March and early April 2020, we reached peaks of over one thousand deaths a day in a region that is comparable to the Bay Area in the United States. Yet, while people were supposed to be in mandatory lockdown, many factories were still operative, a fact that was being hidden from the general public. Much suffering could have been prevented by putting people before profits and by prioritizing a sustainable income for all above the entitlement to wealth of the very few. Additionally, the veil that disguised the house of cards created by decades of the neoliberal Berlusconi regime suddenly was pulled away; it became painfully clear that the Italian public health-care system had been almost fully dismantled in favor of the private sector. This is why public hospitals did not have enough ventilators to deal with the number of people with respiratory crisis and struggled to find the means to test even medical workers for COVID-19. Zaretsky summarized, "When the coronavirus presented them with a choice between letting people die and closing down 'the economy,' there was no question which the masters would choose."[8]

Physical safety and economic survival should never be seen as alternative choices. We should be able to imagine and create systems where communities, instead of allowing the accumulation of absurd wealth, store resources for the common good to be used in situations of personal and collective crisis, recessions, and climate disruptions, such as the fires that are frequent in California. These need to be sustainable resources, not crumbs that are insufficient for people to survive and thrive. We need a system of real social solidarity and equity instead of pretending to believe that bailing out corporations and banks will help everyone. It never happened.

MORAL INJURY AND CAPITALISM

In recent months we have started seeing, even in mainstream media, multiple articles and news items addressing the moral injury of health-care workers facing this pandemic. Moral injury is a concept more often discussed in relation to military personnel. There are different ways to understand it. In Jonathan Shay's approach, it refers to the spiritual outcome of having to deal with situations of betrayal by people in positions of authority.[9] Alternatively, it may refer to having perpetuated, failed to prevent, or been a witness to acts of violence and great harm, like in the work of Brett Litz.[10] My definition encompasses both understandings, focusing on the systemic causes of moral injury and the need to address justice issues as part of the process of healing or soul repair.[11]

Studies have found that even hearing about acts of violence and injustice can cause moral injury. One can feel at the same time to be a victim of a system of injustice and also be a part of upholding this very system. One can also feel guilty for not being able to make enough of a difference.

The effects of moral injury can be many and are experienced on a spectrum of severity. They are deep spiritual despair, guilt, unworthiness, a sense that one can no longer see oneself and the world as good, a lack of trust, rage, and a deep sense of void and meaninglessness. In some cases, this spiritual despair leads to suicide. Moral injury has been often described as the hidden wound of war. Today, it is also one of the hidden, less obvious wounds caused by this pandemic on individuals and on whole societies at large.

While I have appreciated and even been part of some work supporting the healing of individuals and groups through spiritual approaches and practices, my focus has been on the systemic causes of moral injury and the need to address systemic justice issues as part of the process of collective healing or soul repair. Repair not as a return to a past state but a sort of imperfect mending so one can keep living in the present and struggle for a more equitable and sustainable future.

Moral injury is not new to health-care workers. They have always faced difficult decisions every day, witnessed tragic situations, and functioned in societies where people often did not have access to the health care they needed and deserved. The COVID-19 pandemic made their situations even harder. As new waves of the pandemic were hitting the United States and Europe, not enough was done to secure the safety and well-being of the people who care for the sick; there was a failure to create adequate structures of work and support due to a lack of understanding of what health-care workers were (and are) going through. Clinicians, scholars, and chaplains have been working hard to understand what learning and protocols that proved useful to support military personnel can also be effective with medical workers. When they struggle, they are not experiencing an individual failure but are having a very human reaction to system injustice, failures of governments, and heartbreaking situations. This kind of learning will not only ensure the resilience of our health-care workers now but also will be beneficial for the future of health care in general.

As we speak about the moral injury of health-care workers, I want to mention again all others who are treated as disposable and sacrificial beings in this pandemic. There will be no special healing programs for them, and the kind of betrayal and harm experienced during the pandemic is not something that could be addressed and healed with such programs alone. No amount of mindfulness training or resilience protocols will be enough to address the depth of harm caused by centuries of systemic injustice. Nothing will be different after the pandemic if we do not address the structural issues that affect us. In order to address the harm done, we need to name it in its greater complexity and challenge systems, institutions, and people to accountability. This process of truth telling, accountability seeking, and justice making is necessary for any healing process in our society in the aftermath of the pandemic. There should be no moral bailout, but processes of restorative justice.

Moral injury should be addressed as a redirecting of personal and collective beliefs and values and therefore should be a spiritual response to a system that has failed most of us and that has systemically violated Black people, indigenous people, and people of color. This response, when understood not as a personal failure to cope with the world but as a healthy moral response based on care for each other and the web of existence, can generate and nurture collective resistance. While, through our spiritual practices, we can learn to better cope with the stress associated with living in an oppressive world so that we can be more resilient and adaptive, this should not be equated with healing. Healing moral injury is a process of resistance to the system that must include faith in action, both as measures of harm control such as voting but, more importantly, as political and restorative practices that will transform the way we live, who and what we value, and whose needs we put at the center of our theology, ethics, budgets, and policy decisions.

LIBERATING OUR THINKING AND MORAL IMAGINATION

As we think about liberating ourselves from the capitalist system that has devastated the communities of Black people, indigenous people, people of color, and poor white people, it is necessary to question the spiritual underpinnings of this system of relationships that we may have unintentionally interiorized and may keep perpetuating. What do we need to be liberated from, or to free ourselves of, if we want to bring about a new way of being? What do we need to reimagine?

First of all, I think the demarcation between humans and the planet needs to be challenged and healed. The anthropocentrism of so much of the European and Euro-American traditions, embedded in most white Western Christian theologies, has brought forth an understanding of the natural world as something existing primarily for human consumption. White people need to be liberated from an understanding of human beings as something apart, different from nature, somehow superior to it, and entitled to exploit it and transform it for our benefit, without thinking of the whole. We need to free ourselves from this egocentric, self-serving, misguided point of view, which roots white supremacist thinking, and rethink of ourselves as a part of nature, embedded in an interdependent web, where our well-being depends on the well-being of other beings in ways that we need to understand more deeply. We need to be liberated from any understanding of a hierarchy of beings, which leads to the justification of relationships of exploitation.

The issue is spiritual and political. Capitalism has been thriving on forms of dehumanization that already existed, such as slavery, ethnocentrism, xenophobia, sexism, and patterns of exploitation of the natural world. The rise of capitalism in the Western world is tied to colonization and slavery. In fact, it has been argued that racism is a technology used by the European power elites to maintain the terrible exploitation of African enslaved people in the United States and justify the ongoing colonization of people on other continents, both of which were needed for capitalism to thrive without being truly challenged by a united workers' front. White people's wealth and privileges today are based on this history. This does not mean that all white people have the same privilege and power or that there are not extremely poor and underprivileged parts of the population in the United States and in Europe, but that they are part of a history that created the world as it is now, where the logic of white supremacy and settler colonialism still informs North American and European societies. It means white people often made, or were led to make, choices that put them on the side of the white elites for personal and communal benefits or maybe merely as a survival strategy instead of supporting the liberation of other human beings, which would have eventually supported their own true liberation. It also means that many white poor people may not have much or any economic privilege now, but they still have racial privilege and can still act on ideologies of white supremacy that harm working people who are Black, indigenous, or of color and that hinder communal action.

In *Theology in the Capitalocene*,[12] Joerg Rieger distinguishes between privilege and power and argues that the two are often misunderstood as being one and the same. Rieger recognizes the reality of systemic white racial privilege, which is often still unacknowledged. Yet he does not think that it always translated into systemic power. Many well-intentioned white activists would, therefore, be unintentionally ineffective because they mistakenly think their racial privilege, which also gives them some power, is enough to be the kind of systemic power that can be a true challenge to capitalism and, therefore, to racism. According to Rieger, many people in the white middle class think that they have enough power to enact systemic change regarding racism and sexism and even ecological destruction. This, for Rieger, is believing in another version of the American Dream, a dream that will be squashed as the power differential between the white middle class and global capitalism is abysmal. In other words, without engaging capitalism as a united front of working people whose labor is exploited, we will not be able to make enough of a difference to racism, sexism, and ecological destruction.

Rieger refers to his previous work on deep solidarity, "based not on moral imperatives to well-meaning people (often demonizing the wealthy) but on a clear-sighted analysis of power in relation to privilege."[13] For Rieger, deep solidarity is not a moral imperative for privileged people, as "the true potential for solidarity, by contrast, is rooted in the realities of exploitation and oppression that affect the many, not just the few."[14] Rieger often refers to the experience of the Occupy Wall Street (Occupy) movement to stress his point, as it brought to national mainstream attention the differences between the 99 percent and the 1 percent.

The example of the Occupy movement is useful to understand why the struggle to engage capitalism to be effective and sustainable across time can never be disjointed from addressing the reality of other forms of oppression. The local Occupy movements were stronger when they addressed how they were affected by white supremacy, colonialist mentalities, sexism, and ableism, and sought redirection. When this did not happen, the movement was weakened, as some members experienced deep betrayal and loss of trust, a pattern found in many struggles for justice and that weakens them.[15]

Racism, sexism, and other forms of oppression have consistently weakened and hindered massive coalition attempts of the working classes at the national and transnational level. It is hard to overestimate the divide et impera strategies systematically put in place by capitalism. Yet too many of us in the 99 percent, unfortunately, fail to resist them, destroying the trust necessary to sustain a broad movement of diverse working people or minimizing the common denominator of labor exploitation under capitalism, a concern expressed by Keeanga-Yamahtta Taylor[16] and Annie Olaloku-Teribe.[17]

Subverting the spirituality of capitalism entails tending continuously to the conditions that make deep solidarity truly a possibility, ensuring that the power based on coalition strategy will not easily collapse, and creating the conditions for the sustaining of a broad movement, power based on relationships across different groups. Acknowledging the kind of *power and privilege* the history of white supremacy bestowed on some of us means tending to the quality of the relationships on which we want to base the power of our struggles, struggles that we want to be ongoing even as we address conflicts, misunderstanding, misalignments of priorities, disappointments, and setbacks.

To generate and maintain its power, any mass movement against capitalism needs to simultaneously tend to the ways power is exercised within the movement, or it will become ineffective as people will stop believing they have a common goal across their differences. Dismantling an economic system built on exploitation cannot happen without the power of a large movement of people of all colors (including white) that compose the working class and whose fate is interrelated across continents. Yet this movement cannot exist or be sustained without tending to the ways white supremacy, sexism, and other oppressions still operate within and through it, eroding trust and cohesion. White people need to ask themselves how they may be exercising white privilege within any movement and must relinquish it, following the lead, guidance, and wisdom of the people whose belief systems the capitalist system has most silenced and ignored. This is not equivalent to giving all of one's power up. It is giving up an oppressive way to exercise one's power over others. It is not just a matter of morality; it is also a matter of strategy. The two cannot be disjointed.

In other words, in engaging in processes of liberation from capitalism, we need to engage internalized oppressions and paradigms of liberation that justify the oppression of others. The oppressive ideologies that sustained systemic exploitation, based on the evils of patriarchy, racism, homophobia, xenophobia, and colonialism, have been internalized by most of us, even when we fight against them. Therefore, it is misguided to think that today, we can get rid of any form of systemic oppression without addressing the others and the ways they feed off each other.

Labor movements are most effective when people can have common agendas that do not sell out the needs of the most vulnerable or traditionally underrepresented for the more immediate benefit of some groups, usually composed of white males. The best way to ensure that the needs of the most exploited are addressed is to ensure that such voices are central to movements and not only tokenized. We need to be liberated from the idea that there are expendable people, which lurks even in the movements for justice when the rights of some, whether they are people with disabilities, women of color, transgender queer people, or nonbinary people, are seen as secondary or whose needs are seen as something that "can wait" or that can be sacrificed in the name of the well-being of others.

Creating and sustaining the conditions to fight capitalism includes reflecting on how the logic of capitalism has informed even the way we engage in justice struggles and movement building. For instance, too often, people in justice movements are considered disposable: they are put under enormous strain; blamed for not being committed enough to the struggle if they need to slow down and rest; and then replaced when they burn out. The work by Black activist blogger Tricia Hersey,[18] who founded the Nap Ministry in 2016, challenges Black communities to recognize the connections between capitalism and racism, names lack of rest as a racial-justice issue, and sees rest as a form of resistance and spiritual practice. The work of writer, artist, and activist Jenny Odell in *How to Do Nothing: Resisting the Attention Economy*,[19] explores the ways capitalist productivity has relegated all ways of being and activities that nurture our souls, connect us to the rest of nature, and nurture community to irrelevance, a sort of "doing nothing" that hinders the production of wealth. As we internalize this need to always produce something valuable according to capitalist criteria, we cut ourselves from the sources of spiritual, relational, and communal nurturance that can sustain us in our struggle for justice.

Capitalism also tries to shape the way people think through religious ideas and cultural myths that sustain its ideology. To thrive, capitalism needs the undervaluing of some forms of life and the enslavement of others. It promotes the idea that capitalism creates wealth when the workers are doing so, but not for themselves. It fosters individualism, lack of empathy, entitlement, and toxic resentment toward other workers who may have just a bit more. We need to be freed from the belief that individual wealth is a right. It is not, and it is usually accumulated at the expense of generations of other beings, human and not. We need to think about community resources for living and thriving sustainably and be liberated by wealth and the whole idea that the 1 percent somehow has the right to rob others of their resources and life energies.

Earlier I addressed the way essential workers have been praised as heroes and saviors, while they are treated as expendable people whose struggles and needs are not addressed. This pattern reminds me suspiciously of forms of imperial Christian theology that appropriated and subverted the story of Jesus of Nazareth and his early community. First, the powerful exploit and harm someone, then they declare it sacred, having healing qualities, yet do nothing to change the living conditions of the many others suffering in the same situations. This is the basic structure of patterns of surrogacy. The work of René Girard on scapegoating,[20] Delores G. Williams's writing on atonement theories' relation to slavery,[21] and Rebecca Parker's and Rita Nakashima Brock's work in *Saving Paradise*[22] are important examples of these paradigms at work in different moments in history.

We need to heal from unaddressed historical trauma that generated the justification of more atrocities. We need to understand and avoid scapegoating, the shifting of blame for societally unaddressed issues on to those whom we think of as the "other." We need to be liberated from apathy and despair and also from the ideas that one savior or one quick solution can fix the whole and that experts are only academics with no direct lived experience of an issue. We need complex intersectional community thinking to address a complicated situation. We need to be liberated from isolation and defeatism and lack of imagination so that we may see that some other ways of living and thriving can be possible. They have always been possible.

RESISTANCE AS HEALING

While I painted a very bleak picture of the evils that afflict us under capitalism and in these pandemic times, this is not the only reality. During these times, there is resistance to what causes suffering and oppression: there is love, there are deep care and compassion, there are multiple attempts to live according to a different logic from the capitalist ones. There is the spiritual and political will to transform societies. Liberation and transformation are already happening. In this resistance, we can find ongoing collective healing from the moral injuries perpetrated by capitalism.

We are witnessing multiple forms of sacred resistance to the structures of capitalism that embrace alternative lifestyles, not trying to live perfectly out of capitalism but nurturing new realities so a different world system can be called into being as an organic, everyday transformation. We are witnessing and often embodying the belief that alternative ways of living are possible without the myth of achieving perfect purity and the need to impose it on others.

In such realities, there is a sense of being in relationships of accountability, interdependence, and care. That is what community is. There is an understanding of the sacredness of community, coming from different spiritual and philosophical perspectives instead of the idolatry of one's individual traditions or rights. There is a deep understanding of community care that goes beyond being kind and generous toward one's neighbors; it includes being responsible for their health, saying that we are all interrelated, as we are, and looking at the deeper structural, historical differences that shape our history, realities, and experiences. This is what an intersectional look at reality does. This will lead us beyond the "we are all in this together" to "we are living this pandemic differently, and yet we can act so that in the future we will truly be together in whatever happens." Within this community of struggle for a better tomorrow, there is also a centering of the voices and needs of the most affected by injustice in this society and a willingness to listen directly to their voices and their strategies and follow their lead. This can be seen in the movements supporting Black Lives Matter and partly in the Poor People's Campaign: A National Call for Moral Revival.[23]

Struggling to dismantle capitalism includes trying to embody different ways of living and relating and experimenting with old and new economic systems. People have been experimenting with practices their ancestors and their poorer neighbors already knew as their only mode of survival: sharing; bartering; reusing; repurposing; and using new forms of food production, from urban gardens to community farms.

As US economists Michael Albert and Robin Hahnel contend in their writings on participatory economics, looking for alternatives to capitalism in new models is not utopian—or no more so than expecting wealth to ever trickle down:

> Are we being utopian? It is utopian to expect more from a system than it can possibly deliver. To expect equality and justice—or even rationality—from

capitalism is utopian. To expect social solidarity from markets, or self-management from central planning, is equally utopian. To argue that competition can yield empathy or that authoritarianism can promote initiative or that keeping most people from decision making can employ human potential most fully: these are utopian fantasies without question. But to recognize human potentials and to seek to embody their development into a set of economic institutions and then to expect those institutions to encourage desirable outcomes is no more than reasonable theorizing. What is utopian is not planting new seeds but expecting flowers from dying weeds.[24]

A common new focus in many communities of resistance is understanding and addressing trauma, including the historical and personal trauma stored in our own bodies. Author adrienne maree brown's *Emergent Strategy*[25] and *Pleasure Activism*,[26] inspired by Octavia Butler's work, and Sonya Renee Taylor's *The Body Is Not an Apology*[27] are nurturing new generations of activists and somatic therapists. Their writing and activism challenge the way communities of struggle have engaged in justice work, interiorizing the myths of capitalism and white supremacy: disrespect of bodies or of some bodies, idolatry of productivity and stress as a way of life, the idealization of suffering as a sign of good work, perfectionism, and the trivialization of self-care. It is not by chance that so much of this important work is led by Black women, often queer disabled women. They point out that what leads to their liberation will ultimately liberate everyone.

Suffering under the oppressive realities of capitalism and the joys of bringing forth alternative ways of being do not exist in a simple binary but in complex interconnections, as we are held by a power greater than all of us, that some call love and recognize as the same God of compassionate justice witnessed in the Bible. In this power, when we can keep connected to it, there is hope. Generations and generations before us have resisted different kinds of systemic oppression grounded in it, and now it is our moment to do so. We are not alone in this struggle, as we are in relationships not only with each other but also with generations of resistance fighters before us, human and nonhuman beings, and with the learning they gifted us. May we keep grounded in this knowledge and trust that our collective resistance is also the site of our personal and collective healing.

NOTES

1. While I acknowledge that identity is fluid, ever-changing, and more complex than any definition can encompass, my life has been deeply shaped by the privileges of being a white cisgender straight woman of Italian nationality and the challenges of coming from a poor working-class family traumatized by war, being a woman

living under patriarchy, being the first generation in higher education, being part of a religious minority with a long history of persecution and discrimination (Waldensian), and living with invisible disabilities. In the United States, I am a resident alien who currently lives on Lenape unceded territory.

2. Post-pandemic, it will be possible to reflect on this moment, having assessed more information and with greater critical distance. However, I think it is crucial to start discussing the roots of this catastrophic moment so we can embody a different future.

3. Anitra Nelson, "COVID-19: Capitalist and Postcapitalist Perspectives," *Human Geography* 13, no. 3 (November 1, 2020): 305–309. https://doi.org/10.1177/1942778620937122.

4. George Gallagher, "Fauci: 'No Doubt' Trump Will Face Surprise Infectious Disease Outbreak," *Infectious Disease News*,(January 11, 2017).

5. As I Reddit this essay, over 972,416 people have died in the United States, out of 5,961,788
worldwide deaths. Retrieved February 26, 2022, https://www.worldometers.info/coronavirus/?utm_campaign=homeAdvegas1.

6. Eli Zaretsky, "Culling the Herd: A Modest Proposal," *London Review of Books* (May 14, 2020), https://www.lrb.co.uk/blog/2020/may/culling-the-herd-a-modest-proposal.

7. Joerg Rieger, "The Ugly Truth of a Pandemic and the Logic of Downturn," *Faith and Reason* (April 9, 2020), https://www.religionandjustice.org/interventions-forum-covid19.

8. Zaretsky, "Culling the Herd".

9. See Jonathan Shay, *Achilles in Vietnam: Combat Trauma and the Undoing of Character* (New York: Scribner, 1984); and *Odysseus in America. Combat Trauma and the Trials of Homecoming* (New York: Scribner, 2002).

10. Brett T. Litz, Nathan Stein, Eileen Delaney, Leslie Lebowitz, William P. Nash, Caroline Silva, and Shira Maguen. "Moral Injury and Moral Repair in War Veterans: A Preliminary Model and Intervention Strategy." *Clinical Psychology Review* 29, no. 8 (2009): 695–706.

11. For an overview of my current understanding of moral injury, please see Gabriella Lettini, "Moral Injury and Its Causes, Symptoms and Responses," in *Moral Injury: A Guidebook for Understanding and Engagement*, ed. Brad E. Kelle (New York: Lexington Books, 2020).

12. Jeorg Rieger, *Theology in the Capitalocene. Ecology, Identity, Class and Solidarity* (Minneapolis: Fortress Press, 2022).

13. Ibid., 166.

14. Ibid.

15. Heather McKee Hurwitz, "Gender and Race in the Occupy Movement: Relational Leadership and Discriminatory Resistance," *Mobilization: An International Quarterly* 24, no. 2 (2019): 157–76, https://doi.org/10.17813/1086-671X-24-2-157.

16. Keeanga-Yamahtta Taylor, *From #BlackLivesMatter to Black Liberation* (Chicago: Haymarket Books, 2016).

17. Annie Olaloku-Teriba, "Afro-Pessimism and the (Un)Logic of Anti-Blackness," *Historical Materialism* 26, no. 2 (2018): 96–122.

18. Tricia Hersey, *Rest Is Resistance: A Manifesto* (New York: Little, Brown Spark, 2022).

19. Jenny Odell, *How to Do Nothing: Resisting the Attention Economy* (Brooklyn, NY: Melville House, 2019).

20. René Girard, *The Scapegoat* (Baltimore: Johns Hopkins University Press, 1986) and *Things Hidden Since the Foundation of the World* (Redwood City, CA: Stanford University Press, 1987).

21. Delores S. Williams, *Sisters in the Wilderness: The Challenge of Womanist God-Talk* (Maryknoll, NY: Orbis, 1992).

22. Rita Nakashima Brock and Rebecca Parker, *Saving Paradise: How Christianity Traded Love of This World for Crucifixion and Empire* (Boston, Beacon Press, 2008).

23. Poor People's Campaign: A National Call for Moral Revival, https://www.poorpeoplescampaign.org/.

24. Michael Albert and Robin Hahnel, "Participatory Planning," retrieved November 28, 2020, http://symbioid.com/pdf/Politics/participatory-planning-michael-albert-robin-hahnel.pdf?view=FitH, 22.

25. adrienne maree brown, *Emergent Strategy: Shaping Change, Changing Worlds* (Chico, CA: AK Press, 2017).

26. adrienne maree brown, *Pleasure Activism: The Politics of Feeling Good* (Chico, CA: AK Press, 2019).

27. Sonya Renee Taylor, *This Body Is Not an Apology: The Power of Radical Self-Love* (Oakland, CA: Berrett-Koehler, 2018).

REFERENCES

Albert, Michael, and Robin Hahnel. "Participatory Planning." Retrieved November 28, 2020. http://symbioid.com/pdf/Politics/participatory-planning-michael-albert-robin-hahnel.pdf?view=FitH, 22.

Brock, Rita Nakashima, and Rebecca Parker. *Saving Paradise. How Christianity Traded Love of This World for Crucifixion and Empire*. Boston: Beacon Press, 2008.

brown, adrienne maree. *Emergent Strategy: Shaping Change, Changing Worlds*. Chico, CA: AK Press, 2017.

———. *Pleasure Activism: The Politics of Feeling Good*. Chico, CA: AK Press, 2019.

De Soir, Erik. "Lived Experiences of Nurses in Emergency and Intensive Care Medicine: Post COVID Decompression to Cope with Burden Trauma and Moral Injury?" In *Military Psychology Response to Post Pandemic Reconstruction*, vol. I, edited by Samir Rawat, Ole Boe, and Andrzej Piotrowski. New Delhi: Rawat, 2021.

Dzau, Victor J., Darrell Kirch, and Thomas Nasca. "Preventing a Parallel Pandemic—a National Strategy to Protect Clinicians' Wellbeing." *New England Journal of Medicine* (August 6, 2020). doi: 10.1056/NEJMp2011027.

Frank, Robert. "American Billionaires, Mostly White, Gained More than $400 Billion during the Crisis." CNBC. May 21, 2020.

Gallagher, George. "Fauci: 'No Doubt' Trump Will Face Surprise Infectious Disease Outbreak." *Infectious Disease News,* January 11, 2017.

Girard, René. *Things Hidden since the Foundation of the World*. Redwood City, CA: Stanford University Press, 1987.

———. *The Scapegoat*. Baltimore: Johns Hopkins University Press, 1986.

Haseltine, William A. "The Moral Trauma of COVID-19: How Failures of Our National Leaders Have Torn the Moral Fabric of Our Lives." *Psychology Today* (August 21, 2020).

Hersey, Tricia. *Rest Is Resistance: A Manifesto*. New York: Little, Brown Spark, 2022.

Hurwitz, Heather McKee. "Gender and Race in the Occupy Movement: Relational Leadership and Discriminatory Resistance." *Mobilization: An International Quarterly* 24, no. 2 (2019): 157–76. https://doi.org/10.17813/1086-671X-24-2-157.

Jun, Jin, Sharon Tucker, and Bernadette Mazurek Melnyk. "Clinician Mental Health and Well-Being during Global Healthcare Crises: Evidence Learned from Prior Epidemics for COVID-19 Pandemic." *Worldviews on Evidence-Based Nursing* (June 3, 2020). doi: 10.1111/wvn.12439.

Lettini, Gabriella. "Moral Injury and Its Causes, Symptoms and Responses." In *Moral Injury: A Guidebook for Understanding and Engagement*, edited by Brad E. Kelle. New York: Lexington Books, 2020.

Litz, Brett T., Nathan Stein, Eileen Delaney, Leslie Lebowitz, William P. Nash, Caroline Silva, and Shira Maguen. "Moral Injury and Moral Repair in War Veterans: A Preliminary Model and Intervention Strategy." *Clinical Psychology Review* 29, no. 8 (2009): 695–706.

Malm, Andreas. *Corona, Climate, Chronic Emergency: War Communism in the Twenty-First Century*. London: Verso, 2020.

Mantri, S., J. M. Lawson, Z. Wang, et al. "Identifying Moral Injury in Healthcare Professionals: The Moral Injury Symptom Scale-HP." *Relig Health* 59 (2020): 2323–40.https://doi.org/10.1007/s10943-020-01065-w.

Nelson, Anitra. "COVID-19: Capitalist and Postcapitalist Perspectives." *Human Geography* 13, no. 3 (November 1, 2020): 305–309. https://doi.org/10.1177/1942778620937122.

Odell, Jenny. *How to Do Nothing: Resisting the Attention Economy*. Brooklyn, NY: Melville House, 2019.

Olaloku-Teriba, Annie. "Afro-Pessimism and the (Un)Logic of Anti-Blackness." *Historical Materialism* 26, no. 2 (2018): 96–122.

Paravati, Claudio, ed. COVID19: *Costruire il Futuro. Economia, Ambiente e Giustizia Sociale*. Rome: Com Nuovi Tempi, 2020.

Petterson, Steve, et al. "Projected Deaths of Despair during the Coronavirus Recession," *Well Being Trust* (May 8, 2020). WellBeingTrust.org.

Rajkumar, Ravi Philip. "COVID-19 and Mental Health: A Review of the Existing Literature." *Asian Journal of Psychiatry* 52 (2020). doi:10.1016/j.ajp.2020.102066.

Rieger, Jeorg. *Theology in the Capitalocene. Ecology, Identity, Class and Solidarity.* Minneapolis: Fortress Press, 2022.

———. "The Ugly Truth of a Pandemic and the Logic of Downturn." *Faith and Reason* (April 9, 2020). https://www.religionandjustice.org/interventions-forum-covid19.

Ripp, Jonathan, Lauren Peccoralo, and Dennis Charney. "Attending to the Emotional Well-Being of the Health Care Workforce in a New York City Health System during the COVID-19 Pandemic." *Academic Medicine* 95, no. 8 (August 2020): 1136–39. doi: 10.1097/ACM.0000000000003414.

Schwartz, Rachel, Jina L. Sinskey, Uma Anand, and Rebecca D. Margolis. "Addressing Postpandemic Clinician Mental Health: A Narrative Review and Conceptual Framework." *Annals of Internal Medicine* M20–4199 (August 21, 2020). doi:10.7326/M20-4199.

Shay, Jonathan. *Achilles in Vietnam: Combat Trauma and the Undoing of Character.* New York: Scribner, 1984.

———. "Casualties." *Daedalus* 140, no. 3 (Summer 2011): 179–88.

———. *Odysseus in America. Combat Trauma and the Trials of Homecoming.* New York: Scribner, 2002.

Simon, Joshua. "Society for Sick Societies: The Tiny Hands of the Market." *Social Text* (June 16, 2020).

Talbot, Simon E., and Wendy Dean. "Physicians Aren't 'Burning Out.' They're Suffering from Moral Injury." *STAT* (July 26, 2018).

Taylor, Keeanga-Yamahtta. *From #BlackLivesMatter to Black Liberation.* Chicago: Haymarket Books, 2016.

Taylor, Sonya Renee. *This Body Is Not an Apology: The Power of Radical Self-Love.* Oakland, CA: Berrett-Koehler, 2018.

Taylor, Warren D., and Jennifer Urbano Blackford. "Mental Health Treatment for Front-Line Clinicians during and after the Coronavirus Disease 2019 (COVID-19) Pandemic: A Plea to the Medical Community." *Annals of Internal Medicine* 173, no. 7 (2020): 574–75. doi:10.7326/M20-2440.

Their, Hadas. *A People's Guide to Capitalism. An Introduction to Marxist Economics.* Chicago: Haymarket Books, 2020.

Watkins, Ali, Michael Rothfeld, W. K. Rashbaum, and B. M. Rosenthal. "Top ER Doctor Who Treated Virus Patients Dies by Suicide." *New York Times* 27 (2020).

Williams, Delores S. *Sisters in the Wilderness. The Challenge of Womanist God-Talk.* Maryknoll, NY: Orbis, 1992.

Zaretsky, E. "Culling the Herd: A Modest Proposal." *London Review of Books* (May 14, 2020). https://www.lrb.co.uk/blog/2020/may/culling-the-herd-a-modest-proposal.

Chapter 9

Corporate Confession

The Presbyterian Church (USA) and Fossil Fuels

abby mohaupt

Days into the United Nations' 26th Conference of Parties (COP) in 2021, it was already clear that the decisions made would fail to stem the momentum of climate change. High-level leaders representing governments, science, and civil society gathered in Glasgow, Scotland, to draft agreements for emissions reduction, reparations, and other mitigations to and adaptations for climate change.[1] The fossil fuel industry constituted the largest delegation to the COP. Meanwhile, many grassroots leaders were denied entry. In response, there were daily vigils, public actions, and protests led by and including people of faith from around the world.[2] The formal proceedings proved to be inadequate in responding to the urgency of climate change; just months later, the Intergovernmental Panel on Climate Change reported that unprecedented social and scientific shifts would be needed if the global community could be expected to live through temperature rise.[3] The report is a sobering reminder of the scope and urgency of global action that must happen by 2030. Corporations, governments, and entire industries must change. What the COP's inadequate action showed was that everyday people must organize grassroots movements in order to demand those shifts with more vigils, public actions, and protests.

People of faith have long mobilized in the public square to respond to pressing moral issues. Climate change has been no different. Using a variety of tactics, especially nonviolent resistance, interfaith coalitions in particular have organized to demand a response to climate change by civil society.[4] In this chapter, I focus on one strategy: fossil fuel divestment (or the selling of stocks in the fossil fuel industry), as it is used by one religious community, the Presbyterian Church (USA) or PC(USA). To do so, I draw from an intersectional analysis of economics, social movements, theology, and climate science, beginning first with a brief history of the relationship between the fossil fuel industry and Christianity. Then, I argue that theological commitments and teachings to care for the planet are etched in reformed theology. I explore, then, the PC(USA) and the movement to divest from fossil fuels as an extension of the denomination's responses to climate change. Finally, I argue for the embrace of a confessional divestment from fossil fuels as an authentic and prophetic engagement with the personal-which-is-systemic because we are—each of us—entangled in the fossil fuel industry.

By contextualizing faith-based history alongside the work of fossil fuel corporations, which have manipulated global economies, I argue that bold, *collective* action by the body incorporate must insist and acknowledge—confess—the role that Christianity has played in nurturing climate change. In reformed worship (in which the PC[USA] engages), effective confession moves into collective action—from impossible pardon by a sovereign God to embodying peace between all living things. Divestment from fossil fuels in the PC(USA) acts as a corporate confession—or giving up—of fossil fuels, preparing the way for and connecting to the social movements for climate justice to come. Without this confessional divestment that boldly and publicly holds the fossil fuel industry accountable to its globally dire consequences, it may be impossible for the PC(USA) to retain public moral authority.

A HISTORY OF RELATIONSHIP BETWEEN FOSSIL FUELS AND CHRISTIANITY

The history of the fossil fuel industry—and, specifically, of the petroleum-oil industry—in the United States is connected to Christianity from its beginning. In his book, *Anointed with Oil*, Darren Dochuk describes how early oil hunters attributed their success in finding oil to their faith. They "embraced a high-risk, high-reward entrepreneurialism in hopes of achieving a prosperity that could signal their blessedness and allow them to save society in anticipation of the end times."[5] It was not just the "oil hunters" who saw themselves as blessed when they struck oil. When oil was found near a town, everyone in that town also saw himself or herself as blessed because of the "cascading fortunes" of economic prosperity.[6] New towns sprang up around the oil wells, with side industries like gambling dens and brothels that seemed at odds with any description of the sacred.[7] Still: oil meant a variety of industries and successes for people in many different lines of work.

This description echoes Max Weber's critique of the Protestant work ethic, which he characterized as insisting that more work and more profit meant more of God's favor.[8] Still, oil was often found without the systematic and sustained effort of a work ethic; instead, one could look for years and lose everything without striking oil; one could strike it rich on the first day with a stroke of luck (or God's divine providence). What was found could be lost without warning.[9] In some ways, the uncertainty of oil's whereabouts was a perfect metaphor for God's mysterious grace and favor that the Protestant ministers contemporary to early oilmen preached into the culture.

That sense of economic security and spiritual safety was necessary in the early years of the oil boom, when much of society felt unstable. Petroleum was first struck in the United States in Pennsylvania in 1859, when the economic system of slavery was being dismantled in the shadow of the Civil War and Reconstruction. Over time, the wealth of oil "bankrolled colossal cathedrals, schools, missionary organizations, and foundations, all determined to fashion the United States into a resplendent Christian commonwealth."[10] As the South crumbled economically and formerly enslaved people struggled for real freedom, the North—with oil rigs and oil towns—was growing economically. Oil became a way to recover from the war. The reverend S. J. Eaton wrote that oil came directly from God, saying that it was "a salve for a society rent asunder by war," arguing that the economic boom from oil would help heal the nation.[11] Eaton was just one of many religious leaders who attributed the newly emerging oil industry to God's favor.

Christian faith was entangled in the beginning of the oil industry in the United States in many ways: through society's work ethic, as recipients of oil wealth, and blessings from Christian communities and leaders. A "work ethic" that equated finding oil with divine favor permeated society in the early oil days. For example, Dochuk notes that Standard Oil founder John D. Rockefeller had a "bureaucratic outlook in keeping with the Protestant work ethic Max Weber would famously write about, which assumed godly capitalism would honor the principles of efficiency and control. . . . [Rockefeller] propagated a social gospel that called on Christians to construct a better society by way of their economic and political clout."[12] This meant that Rockefeller implicitly attributed his oil wealth to his faith. He "framed his new found vocation as providential" and saw God's grace in the blessing and "miracle" of oil itself.[13] In 1870, Rockefeller created Standard Oil Company after record profits, money he thought would perpetuate God's favor. In turn, as his oil company spread across the country and then the world, Rockefeller used his wealth to fund churches, schools, missions, and other programs.

At odds with this way of thinking were those drillers around the country who were sometimes driven by a millennialist theology, believing that it was necessary to extract as much as possible from the ground before the second coming of Christ and that, in the meantime, it was the responsibility of Christians to guide and rule American society.[14] In this vein, Lyman Stewart, a Presbyterian, fought in the Civil War just as oil was being discovered and then invested in oil to make enough money to become a missionary after being discharged. He spent his days looking for oil and his evenings preaching.[15] He "shared . . . an unassailable belief that God was guiding him toward earth's bounty and an ordained future."[16] This guidance was for his ability to extract whatever he could find. This belief supported a theological worldview that the earth exists for the dominion of men (in this context, it was always men who had power). Thus, in order to be faithful to this biblical interpretation of someone like Stewart, one needs to find and drill as much oil as possible. Stewart, supported by his church as he went off to search for oil, eventually became vice president of Union Oil Company of California, where he "would wield his authority . . . out of a desire to save a world he feared lost to monopolism and other worldly sins."[17] Later, Stewart envisioned and invested in *The Fundamentals*, a set of religious tracts that explained the foundations of Christianity and was distributed around the world.[18] In his article about the relationship between Stewart's religion and oil work, B. M. Pietsch notes that Stewart's life was at the shifting point of economy and faith—a Victorian-era restrained capitalism and unregulated extraction that "imagined wealth as a product of supernatural blessing instead of a product of labor."[19] If the world was to end, the chief end of man (per the Westminster Catechism) for reformed Christians was to maximize the glory of God in all things.

By the 1890s, other places in the world were starting to drill for oil, but the United States led the industry, which, in turn, solidified its status as an international economic leader. This caused some Americans to view their society as set apart and uniquely loved by God.[20] Meanwhile, the church and the oil industry stayed in close contact: "Catholic [oil] workers in New Jersey and Baptist and Pentecostal laborers in South Texas recruited their contemporaries in the pews with a zeal that blended their faith in God and oil with an undying sense of patriotic responsibility."[21] Further, missionaries and oil companies worked together, with the church going into areas first to "open up regions, supplying the oil drillers with advanced knowledge of terrain and cultures."[22] Here, faith, patriotism, and capital blended together.

The United States became a world economic power because of its oil production. Oil and Christianity have long been at the heart of American power and culture, though not everyone has seen oil as a gift.[23] Indeed, "countless Americans across time have viewed oil's anointing as a threat rather than a grace."[24] One of these early critics, Ida Tarbell, a freelance writer rooted in her Methodist upbringing, took on Rockefeller. She noted the "unequal working conditions of the oil industry" and the "devastation wrought by oil" on places where drilling happened.[25] But Tarbell wasn't saying that fossil fuels should completely go away—instead, she thought the industry should be "cleaned up."[26] Her critique led others, social justice–minded clergymen and scholars, to push back at Rockefeller.[27] In the same way, Washington Gladden, a preacher of the social gospel, thought that Rockefeller was undermining the New Testament by harming the collective social good. He railed against his church (Riverside Church in New York City) taking "tainted money" from Rockefeller.[28] Gladden and Tarbell are premonitions of the later faith-based conversations about church, money, and the fossil fuel industry. Is the industry changeable, as Tarbell argued? Or is it irrevocably without merit and thus people of faith need to distance themselves, as Gladden called for? Can it be possible to have moral authority in the world while investing capital in an industry that is killing that same planet?

All of this history intersects with a theological commitment to care for the planet. If, as many biblical scholars and Christian environmentalists claim, the role of the human is not extraction by care, the church must wrestle with an industry at odds with that mandate. And the fossil fuel industry has been rooted in destruction. Since its inception, the oil industry has contributed significantly to the current climate crisis. According to Nathaniel Rich, in his book *Losing Earth*, the industry spent decades lying to policy makers and the public about whether burning fossil fuels would cause global climate change and catastrophic suffering.[29] In the United States, Christianity legitimized the industry and put its moral authority behind it. This connection between blessing and oil extraction has continued. As it becomes more and more apparent that this industry inflicts global harm on people and the planet, Christianity must collectively respond. In the following sections, I explore the place of divestment as a tactic, how divestment and the liturgical practice of confession interplay, and how any next steps by the church must be bold if it and we have a chance at being faithful, using the PC(USA) as a case study.

DIVESTMENT AS A TACTIC

To understand the particulars of the PC(USA) divestment as a public witness in a time of climate change, we must look at how divestment went from being an economic or a corporate strategy to being a social movement tactic. Moving an institution's money to solidify its identity or commitments is not primarily a social movement tactic; it is first and foremost an economic or a business decision. Companies buy and sell parts of their assets as a way to make money or hone product identity.[30] Divestment of assets by a company is an articulation of an institution's values and identity, almost always used in collaboration with other tactics.

In the mid to late twentieth century, divestment was most notably used as a tactic of nonviolent social action in the movement to end apartheid in South Africa (and has since been used in many other struggles). The anti-apartheid movement, according to Janice Love in her book *The U.S. Anti-Apartheid Movement: Local Activism in Global Politics*, was based on the belief that "people can effectively use institutions locally available to respond to international issues."[31] Those years of struggle required activists to persevere in the face of difficulty and to engage in a variety of creative strategies, including divestment. In the decades of struggle, the "anti-apartheid movement [was] a multiracial, worldwide movement consisting of governmental and nongovernmental actors operating at international, national, and subnational levels in an attempt to end racial oppression in southern Africa."[32] A call for divestment with the purpose of showing solidarity through financial investments was a global sanction, to which Protestant Christians in the United States responded. Divestment as a tactic was part of the larger context of sanctions, protests, United Nations' policies, international speaking tours, and sports boycotts. It was a call for schools, municipalities, faith communities, and individuals to direct their money and investments in solidarity with the work for liberation from apartheid in South Africa.[33] In this larger context of a decades-long movement to dismantle apartheid, grassroots activists called allies around the world to divest. The response took place in solidarity with the heart of the movement: people from the region itself. This kind of global solidarity has happened in other struggles: in Palestine as activists have responded to calls to divest from companies doing business with and in the state of Israel and—very recently—the move by North America and Europe to divest from Russian oil.[34]

These examples show how, in the US religious world, the tactic of divestment has primarily been used by majority-white denominations because of their historic wealth (which stems from white supremacy, colonialism, and privilege). In the past, these wealthy denominations have been called upon by grassroots movements to use that wealth in solidarity with communities of color. While divestment has been connected to climate justice movements (which owe their start to the environmental justice movement led by Robert Bullard and others), the conversation on divestment in majority-white spaces can often devolve into a discussion about "stewardship of money" rather than stewardship of the earth. Instead, these conversations could focus on an intersectional approach to the injustices caused by the fossil fuel industry and the power of financial capital to make a statement with its presence or absence. Majority-white denominations, then, can use their historic privilege and access to wealth to drive company and industry change. This power-leveraging is done through shareholder activism and engagement, when resolutions are brought to company boards demanding that policies or procedures within a company be changed. During the fight against apartheid in South Africa, these resolutions called for companies to stop doing business with the South African government until it changed its racist segregation policies.

Divestment from the fossil fuel industry has become a tactic in responding to climate change that allows for what Love suggested about divestment in response to apartheid—a local way to respond to a global issue. In fact, activist and author Bill McKibben attributes the success of the global movement to divest from fossil fuels to ordinary people around the world taking action within their own regions to fight back against the fossil fuel industry.[35] This grassroots achievement was quantified in the 2021 Divest Invest Report, which noted that 1,485 organizations and 58,000 individuals, representing $39.2 trillion in combined assets, have divested from fossil fuels.[36] Each little bit added up to significantly bolster the movement.

The divestment movement echoes what Gladden said in the twentieth century: The fossil fuel industry needs to fundamentally change its entire business plan. It is not reformable. A complete reenvisioning of new structures is now essential for survival. Climate change will cause widespread suffering, and nearly no one will escape the consequences of the fossil fuel industry.[37] The capitalist system that ties Christianity to fossil fuels and suffering must be dismantled.

The PC(USA)'s rich history of connecting theology to earth care preceded its entry into the movement to divest from fossil fuels and insists that the denomination must continue its climate justice work beyond divestment. In the next section, I briefly explore the PC(USA)'s earth care and climate justice work, the campaign to divest from fossil fuels in the denomination, and the role of confession in the tradition. I connect theology and liturgy to the climate crisis and a particular social movement tactic that presses for theological commitment and bold action.

CASE STUDY: THE PRESBYTERIAN CHURCH (USA)

The totality of the problem of climate change and pervasive bad actions of the industry (such as over extraction from the planet and misinformation campaigns) comprise a gap into which faith communities can step as part of the divestment movement. Climate change devastates creation, which Christian doctrine insists is created by God and given to humanity to steward. In particular, reformed theology in Presbyterianism teaches that only God is sovereign over all that is created and that humans are placed on the planet to tend and keep the rest of creation. Though, historically, some of these biblical teachings of humans having power over the rest of the planet have motivated the fossil fuel industry itself, they've also been the foundation of decades of denominational policy, Bible studies, lifestyle changes in personal and ecclesial rhythms, and worship guides created in response to ongoing environmental and climate devastation and injustice. This tension represents a theological wrestling match with capitalism within the denomination—one that ultimately has led to a loss of public moral authority by the denomination.

The PC(USA) has a long history of its own in terms of environmental policies, worship resources, and programming. These programs have been supported and organized by official PC(USA) staff as well as parachurch organizations. The PC(USA) itself was organized in 1983 from the Presbyterian Church US and the United Presbyterian Church in the United States, and the sources below are pulled from that starting point up to the present day. Methodologically, the following findings emerged from focused research done via grounded theory through over fifteen interviews. The sample was drawn from grassroots leaders in the PC(USA)'s environment leadership and denominational leaders from the movement to divest from fossil fuels and then was supplemented by public and communal denominational documents. The PC(USA) website (the most public-facing communication about the denomination), for example, describes the nature of the PC(USA)'s commitment to the environment:

> The Presbyterian Church (USA) has a long history and continues to lead on issues of environmental stewardship and justice. As expressed by the PC(USA) Collaborative Agenda on Environmental Stewardship endorsed by the 222nd General Assembly in 2016, the six agencies of the PC(USA) affirmed a call to prayer, education, advocacy and other forms of direct action to glorify God in our care of creation.[38]

That is, each of the main bodies of the denomination has publicly affirmed the need to act in a variety of ways to connect care for the earth with Presbyterian faith, drawing on a history of similar practices and resources. These resources have been created by national denominational staff based on General Assembly policy, by the passages of Presbyterian policy (via overtures or resolutions at General Assembly), and/or by parachurch organizations like Presbyterians for Earth Care, Presbyterian Peace Fellowship, and Fossil Free PC(USA). Environmental resources include educational resources (resources that teach about environmental or climate issues, build skills, or develop thinking), worship resources (which develop the spirituality of Presbyterians, either individually or corporately), activism or policy changes (that either create a more sustainable or environmentally just denomination or push the secular society to enact policy), and lifestyle changes (both individually through diet or energy use or institutionally through building or purchasing power).

Many educational materials have been created since 1983 (the beginning of the denomination) with the intent to educate Presbyterians about various parts of environmental work and actions. These resources have been developed by the Presbyterian Hunger Program, the Environmental Ministries Office, the PC(USA) Office at the United Nations, and the Washington, DC, office of the Presbyterian Church in terms of official Presbyterian offices, but Presbyterians for Earth Care and the Presbyterian Peace Fellowship have also created educational resources. National conferences have also offered teach-ins through Ecumenical Advocacy Days. These educational resources produced by the denomination cover solar power (panels for which are covered by a low-interest loan from the Presbyterian Foundation), social change, environmental racism and justice, water, and more. The defining resource, however, has been "Restoring Creation: For Ecology and Justice." Approved by the 1990 General Assembly (the highest governing body in the denomination), the report says that "the vision of eco-justice, as a goal toward which to move, lifts up and affirms the church's longstanding commitment to justice and peace and adds a major new insight for our time: that justice and peace among human beings are inseparable from right relationships with and within the natural order."[39] In my larger research on divestment from fossil fuels in the PC(USA), several of my interviews revealed that this document is the defining resource for how the denomination has intentionally engaged ecological and climate justice in the last thirty years.[40] This resource moves from describing the crisis into social policy, building on worship and biblical resources. The intersections of science, social justice, and worship have guided the PC(USA)'s response to climate change ever since.

More recently, resources from the denomination and related entities have taken the form of devotions for Lent and Advent and other worship resources that support advocacy and social witness. Presbyterians for Earth Care has provided devotions almost every year since its beginning in 1995 as a response to the Eco-Justice Report.[41] The Presbyterian Hunger Program regularly produces a Lent devotion on reducing carbon footprints and leads a certification program for congregations. Part of the certification has included the regular addition of earth care in worship (through music, prayers, sermons, offerings).[42] Some of these congregations also engage in advocacy and have social witness policies. Social witness policies have included commitments to carbon offsets and carbon neutrality. In 2006, the PC(USA) agreed to support carbon-neutral goals, "as a bold Christian witness to help combat the effects of climate change," and those goals have been supported by carbon offsetting and tree planting.[43] During Lent, the Presbyterian Hunger Program creates and shares a "Tread Lightly for Lent'" resource that is available on the PC(USA) website and shared with Earth Care congregations. This resource encourages actions such as turning off or changing out light bulbs, buying fair trade coffee and chocolate, and investing in eco-palms for Palm Sunday.[44] Each of these above pieces relies on individual steps or decisions—action that is no longer singularly effective in a season when an industry is systematically affecting the world by manipulating climate. Capitalist climate change has shifted everything and to meet the necessary targets called for by COP and grassroots leaders, challenging capitalism requires bold, collective, faithful action that can replace aggressive corporate action that has historically connected faith and fossil fuels. So, while divestment is a capitalist (meaning based on financial capital being moved between investments) endeavor, it uses the loss of capital to make a moral statement.

The Mission Responsibility Through Investments (MRTI) Committee was established in the 1980s as the first shareholder committee of its kind and has been an example for other denominations: "In recognition of the church's unique opportunity to advance its mission faithfully and creatively through the financial resources entrusted to it, MRTI implements the General Assembly's policies on socially responsible investing (also called faith-based investing) by engaging corporations in which the church owns stock."[45] It is made up of representatives from certain committees of the PC(USA) as well as representatives of the Board of Pensions and the Presbyterian Foundation, two other agencies of the PC(USA).[46] While it does not include anyone from the Presbyterian Hunger Program, the arm of the Presbyterian Mission Agency (PMA) that oversees environmental ministries and concerns in the PC(USA) noted above, MRTI engages companies based on established denominational policies on climate and the environment. MRTI divides its work into "three arms/pillars of faith-based investing, namely—screening, shareholder advocacy, and community investing—to express faithful stewardship of investment resources."[47] It also follows the divestment strategy that was approved by the General Assembly in 1984, which uses divestment as a final tactic in faith-based investment and shareholder engagement.[48] All of this echoes Tarbell, suggesting that bad apples can be changed.

However, when the movement to divest from fossil fuels began in the United States in 2012, early adopters included colleges and universities and then municipalities. Then faith communities joined. The movement has historically called for categorical divestment, effectively saying that no good can come out of the fossil fuel industry.[49] The United Church of Christ was the first faith community in the United States to vote as a faith body in support of divestment in 2012, and, soon after, the national decision-making body of the PC(USA) was tasked with considering divestment from fossil fuels. The movement emerged from grassroots leadership and communities within the denomination.

By 2012, a group of people at First Presbyterian Church in Palo Alto, California, had been meeting for a few years as a climate change group called Cool Planet. Cool Planet organized about twenty people to go hear Bill McKibben speak at one of the local high schools. He was on his "Do the Math" tour, promoting a particular response to climate change, but first laying out the science and math of climate change and the fossil fuel industry. The tour was based on his groundbreaking article in *Rolling Stone*, "Global Warming's Terrifying New Math," which posited that the fossil fuel industry is the enemy of the planet and an apartheid-style divestment movement was needed to hold the industry accountable.[50]

He ended each of these lectures with a call to action, explaining that, because it was wrong to wreck the planet, it was wrong to profit over the wreckage of the planet; thus, it was necessary to divest from the industry that had had the biggest hand in creating climate change: the fossil fuel industry.[51] People in civic and religious communities heard him calling for the creation of "Fossil Free" communities around the United States and the world. Presbyterians in Tennessee and California heard McKibben speak and considered how the PC(USA) could be part of the movement. These Presbyterians created a grassroots movement, one that Rebecca Barnes, who was at the time the national staff person for environmental ministry, described as different from other experiences she'd had in the office. National Presbyterian staff didn't have to call meetings or set agendas; the group of people who were gathering were truly grassroots.[52] The people who wanted the PC(USA) to divest from fossil fuels more formally organized under the name Fossil Free PC(USA) (in order to have solidarity with similarly named and focused groups in other denominations). They wrote an overture, the mechanism in Presbyterian policy that creates new policy once approved by the highest governing body in the PC(USA), the General Assembly. Twelve other presbyteries followed, and the overture was added to the docket at the 2014 General Assembly. It has since been discussed in 2016, 2018, and 2022 (with a referral in 2020 because of the COVID-19 pandemic).

Though the PC(USA) already has decades of environmental policy, resources, and actions to support an immediate response to climate change such as divestment from fossil fuels, and is well known internationally for its worship and theological resources, organizing, and policy statements in favor of faith-based responses to climate change. Still, the denomination has declined to support categorical divestment as a tactic. Instead, the national decision-making body in 2022 approved the recommendation from MRTI to divest from five fossil fuel companies: Chevron, Exxon Mobil, Marathon Petroleum, Phillips 66, and Valero Energy. The denomination thus essentially expressed a Tarbellian opinion of the industry: Some fossil fuel companies are worse than others (which means some are better than others).

How might we make sense of a denomination that has historically supported faith-based responses to earth care refusing to withhold investments from the industry most responsible for the global climate crisis? The call for divestment from fossil fuels first came to the PC(USA) just three years after people who are LGBTQ+ and called to ordination were allowed to be ordained, which caused a seismic break within the denomination. The year that divestment was first discussed at the national level was the same year that gay marriage was affirmed. This was also the year that the denomination voted to divest from three companies that were profiting off of labor in the Gaza Strip. According to some grassroots leaders of the PC(USA) interviewed for the case study, the strain of LGBTQ+ inclusion and the "other divestment movement" stretched the PC(USA)'s limits, both financially and theologically. Churches who were against LGBTQ+ inclusion were leaving the denomination, taking members and money with them. Similar groanings emerged in the face of the movement to divest from the state of Israel. The PC(USA) faced budget shortfalls and declining membership that no longer covers staff salaries and program costs.

Still, the PC(USA) cannot achieve solidarity with climate justice movements as long as it's profiting from the very industry that has shut out and tried to destroy marginalized communities. What a number of the organizers stressed in their interviews is that, in order for the PC(USA) as an institution to have moral integrity in the public square, it must be willing to step further away from power wrought by investments and instead step into the power of people and faith. The case study of the PC(USA) suggests that, if a faith community will not boldly oppose a "sinful" industry, it loses its moral authority because it fails to align its actions with its soul (echoing those early criticisms of taking money from Rockefeller for congregational use). Since the beginning of the movement to divest from fossil fuels, faith communities have led the way, confessing their complicity in climate change by divesting their holdings in the industry most culpable. Still, divestment is just one step in responding to climate change. The world needs renewable energies and more grassroots movements to build a world more in line with the flourishing of all—one that reimagines where and how treasure emerges in the kingdom of God. This imaginative future requires a letting go of—a confession of (a divestment from)—what separates us from the planet, each other, and God.

CONCLUSION: CONFESSION AS LITURGICAL RESOURCE

In the Presbyterian worship tradition, there is a time of confession, when the faithful confess their sins. The prayer is done in unison, usually using the pronoun "we." It is an acknowledgment of collective and social sin, expressing that the individual acts in a system. Along with the unison prayer, there's time for individual confession, done in silence so that each person has the opportunity to connect to God. These prayers are followed by an "Assurance of Pardon," in which the pastor or liturgist reminds the worshippers that, while each of us can attempt to give up the worst parts of ourselves in confession, it is the grace of God that makes us whole. In the same way, divestment acts as a way for practitioners to give up part of the self (investments in fossil fuels), as a way to (re)build identity as a Christian through capital. As Presbyterians proclaim, "Our choices, more than ever, are moral choices, and as the planet grows warmer, our Christian witness must become bolder."[53] As climate crises worsen, people of faith must continue to confess and act to keep their economic choices in line with their theological commitments.

In a time of global climate crisis, economic disparity, and social disconnect, Protestant communities must find ways to grapple with and dismantle systems of oppression and suffering in order to be faithful and relevant in the public sphere. In this chapter, I have argued that in a time of unjust climate change—as described by the most recent International Panel on Climate Change and frontline communities—Christian communities live out their religious leadership through solidarity, using the movement to divest from fossil fuels in the Presbyterian Church (USA) as a case study. If we take the history of the relationship between Christianity and the fossil fuel industry, the Christian theology of responsibility for planet and people, and the responsibility of (US-based, privileged) Christians for the suffering of others, this social movement and liturgical action are the natural steps of solidarity—one that becomes confessional. Divestment as a genre of confession frees the confessor into acknowledging complicity in climate change and imperfection in responding to the suffering of others; it also permits claiming the grace of God to find other ways to build the kingdom of God.

In closing, I offer this prayer of confession, written in the plural because the work to be done still must be done together:

God of Creation, of the environment, of all the diversity of the world, we confess that our ancestors in faith encouraged the destruction of the planet through the overextraction of fossil fuels. Though You call humans to care for the planet, we confess that we have failed in that vocation. We have failed to care for each other, failed to live into the teachings and prayers and actions we have created as resources for ourselves in the work to protect and love You, the planet, and each other. So, dear God, we offer ourselves back to You. Help us be bold and brave as we hold the fossil fuel industry accountable and as we invest our whole selves in a just transition. Amen.

Coming to terms with the scope of confession—the work to be done to build a better world—makes the impossible pardon, the potential for life after all, that much more powerful.

NOTES

1. Ivana Kottasová, Amy Cassidy, Angela Dewan, and Helen Regan, "Overtime for COP26 as Deep Divisions Remain over Key Issues around Money and Markets," CNN (November 23, 2021), https://www.cnn.com/2021/11/12/world/cop26-agreement-climate-intl-hnk/index.html.

2. Matt McGrath, "COP26: Fossil Fuel Industry Has Largest Delegation at Climate Summit," *BBC News,* (November 8, 2021), https://www.bbc.com/news/science-environment-59199484.

3. More nuanced, the report reads that the "growth of global GHG emissions has slowed over the past decade, and delivering the updated NDCs to 2030 would turn this into decline, but the implied global emissions by 2030 exceed pathways consistent with 1.5°C by a large margin, and are near the upper end of the range of modelled pathways which keep temperatures likely below 2°C. Continuing investments in carbon-intensive activities at scale will *heighten the multitude of risks associated with climate change* and impede societal and industrial transformation towards low carbon development. Meeting the long-term temperature objective in the Paris Agreement therefore implies a rapid turn to an accelerating decline of GHG 17 emissions towards 'net zero,' *which is implausible without urgent and ambitious action at all scales*." Grubb, M., et al., "2022: Introduction and Framing," in *IPCC, 2022: Climate Change 2022: Mitigation of Climate Change*, Contribution of Working Group III to the Sixth Assessment Report of the Intergovernmental Panel on Climate Change, eds. P. R. Shukla, J. Skea, R. Slade, A. Al Khourdajie, R. van Diemen, D. McCollum, M. Pathak, S. Some, et al. (Cambridge, UK, and New York: Cambridge University Press, 2022), 1–4. Emphasis mine.

4. This sentiment echoes the framing offered by Ayana Elizabeth Johnson and Katharine K. Wilkerson in "Begin," the introduction to their edited volume *All We Can Save*. They note that, "to address our climate emergency, we must rapidly, radically reshape society. We need every solution and every solver. As the saying goes, to change everything, we need everyone" (New York: Random House, 2020), xxi.

5. Darren Dochuk, *Anointed with Oil: How Christianity and Crude Made Modern America* (New York: Basic Books, 2019), 8.

6. Ibid.

7. B. M. Pietsch, "Lyman Stewart and Early Fundamentalism," *Church History* 82, no. 3 (September 2013), 623.

8. Weber notes that Calvinism is the basis of much of the "spirit of capitalism," one of the reasons I use a Presbyterian denomination (an offshoot of Calvinism) as a case study in the use of capital to respond to climate change. See Max Weber, *The Protestant Work Ethic and the Spirit of Capitalism* (New York: Penguin Books, 2019).

9. For example, Lyman Stewart attributed his wealth to "luck and divine favor," and he first saw his success as short-lived as other investments failed. He later wrote to his children to say that when he lost everything it was because he had ceased tithing (Pietsch, 623).
10. Dochuk, 8–9.
11. Ibid., 33.
12. Ibid., 12.
13. Ibid., 43.
14. Ibid., 17.
15. Ibid., 22.
16. Ibid., 23.
17. Ibid., 66–67.
18. Pietsch, 617.
19. Ibid., 619.
20. Dochuk, 68.
21. Ibid., 377.
22. Ibid., 40.
23. Ibid., 15.
24. Ibid., 16. This particular thread has reemerged in the years since James Hanson and others' testimony before the US Congress in the 1980s, when lobbyists for the fossil fuel industry successfully argued for continued funding even as climate scientists and activists warned against the impending threat of climate change. See Nathaniel Rich, *Losing Earth* (New York: MCD, 2019).
25. Ibid., 148.
26. Ibid., 151.
27. Ibid.
28. Ibid., 152.
29. Rich, *Losing Earth*, 2019, 6.
30. Leonard Vignola Jr., *Strategic Divestment* (New York: Amacom, 1974), 8.
31. Janice Love, *The U.S. Anti-Apartheid Movement: Local Activism in Global Politics* (New York: Praeger, 1985), 245.
32. Ibid., 1.
33. Ibid. As noted above, there were many organizations mobilizing in South Africa.
34. In the months after Russia invaded Ukraine, for example, Dr. Svitlana Romanko, Stand With Ukraine campaign coordinator, wrote on the occasion of a faith-based divestment announcement that "at this decisive and grim moment of modern history, [these faith communities] are way ahead of the world leaders who still allow billions for Russian oil and gas to flow into Putin's war machine. . . . For that, we demand that governments speed up investments in renewable energy, stop funding fossil fuel expansion and put public money where it needs to be: in a peaceful, prosperous and clean energy future for all." From "Global Faith Institutions Announce Divestment as Oil and Gas Companies Threaten 1.5°C Climate Goal with Reckless Expansion Plans," Operation Noah, https://operationnoah.org/featured/press-release

-global-faith-institutions-announce-divestment-as-oil-and-gas-companies-threaten-1 -5c-climate-goal-with-reckless-expansion-plans/.

35. Interview with Bill McKibben, June 2021.

36. Divest Invest Report, October 26, 2021, https://www.divestinvest.org/wp-content/uploads/2021/10/Divest-Invest-Program-FINAL10-26_B.pdf.

37. This was highlighted again in the most recent IPCC report, which said that "growing direct impacts of climate change are unambiguous and movements of protest and activism—in countries and transnational organizations at many levels have grown." Grubb, M., et al., "2022: Introduction and Framing," in *IPCC, 2022: Climate Change 2022: Mitigation of Climate Change*, Contribution of Working Group III to the Sixth Assessment Report of the Intergovernmental Panel on Climate Change, eds. P. R. Shukla, J. Skea, R. Slade, A. Al Khourdajie, R. van Diemen, D. McCollum, M. Pathak, S. Some, et al. (Cambridge, UK, and New York: Cambridge University Press, 2022), 1–61.

38. "Blessed Tomorrow," https://www.presbyterianmission.org/ministries/environment/blessed-tomorrow/.

39. Presbyterian Church (USA), *Restoring Creation for Ecology and Justice* (Louisville, KY: Presbyterian Church [USA], September 1990), https://www.presbyterianmission.org/wp-content/uploads/restoring-creation-for-ecologyjustice.pdf, 12.

40. The subjects of these interviews included a current PC(USA) staff person, a former moderator of the denomination, one of the writers of the report itself, and a former mission coworker.

41. "History," Presbyterians for Earth Care, https://presbyearthcare.org/history/.

42. Presbyterian Church (USA), "Earth Care Congregations," https://www.presbyterianmission.org/ministries/environment/earth-care-congregations/.

43. Presbyterian Church (USA), https://www.pcusa.org/resource/guide-to-going-carbon-neutral-23751/.

44. Presbyterian Church (USA), "Tread Lightly for Lent," January 26, 2021, https://www.presbyterianmission.org/resource/tread-lightly-for-lent/.

45. Presbyterian Church (USA), "Office of Faith-Based Investing and Corporate Engagement," https://www.presbyterianmission.org/ministries/mrti/.

46. Ibid.

47. Ibid.

48. Presbyterian Church (USA), "The Divestment Strategy: Principles and Criteria," https://www.presbyterianmission.org/wp-content/uploads/GA-1984-Divestment-Strategy.pdf.

49. In the weeks before the 2022 PC(USA) General Assembly, MRTI and Fossil Free PCUSA released a joint statement on the calls for divestment from fossil fuels, noting that the capital-based move was not enough on its own. The piece argues that "these divestment recommendations do not go far enough for substantive impact on the ecological crisis. Our Reformed tradition teaches us to use our privilege and leverage it toward a most just world. The Gospel of Jesus prods us to continue across multiple spheres to organize for substantial change that disrupts the status quo and centers God's creation." Effectively, the piece noted that faith-based divestment campaigns

have relied more on the moral impact than the economic use of capital. ("FFPCUSA And MRTI Recommend United Approach to Divestment," *Justice Unbound*, https://justiceunbound.org/ffpcusa-and-mrti-recommend-united-approach-to-divestment.)

50. Bill McKibben, "Global Warming's Terrifying New Math," *Rolling Stone* (July 19, 2012), https://www.rollingstone.com/politics/politics-news/global-warmings-terrifying-new-math-188550/.

51. Fossil fuels are not the only contributor to climate change. They are, however, the largest, and nearly everyone on the planet burns them—either actively (by driving a car) or passively (by participating in a global society that uses fossil fuels for everything). This pervasive and inescapable use of fossil fuels (even though it creates harm) is one of the reasons the movement first wondered if the reformed tradition's understanding of inescapable sin could provide a foundation for divestment as well as a unique way of understanding climate change and a human response to global climate trauma, as noted in several interviews.

52. Interview with Rebecca Barnes.

53. Presbyterian Church (USA), "Blessed Tomorrow," https://www.presbyterianmission.org/ministries/environment/blessed-tomorrow/.

REFERENCES

"Bright Now: Our Divestment Campaign." Operation Noah. https://operationnoah.org/what-we-do/bright-now-our-divestment-campaign/.

Divest Invest Report. October 26, 2021. https://www.divestinvest.org/wp-content/uploads/2021/10/Divest-Invest-Program-FINAL10-26_B.pdf.

Dochuk, Darren. *Anointed with Oil: How Christianity and Crude Made Modern America*. New York: Basic Books, 2019.

"FFPCUSA and MRTI Recommend United Approach to Divestment." *Justice Unbound*. Last modified June 2, 2022. https://justiceunbound.org/ffpcusa-and-mrti-recommend-united-approach-to-divestment.

"Global Faith Institutions Announce Divestment as Oil and Gas Companies Threaten 1.5°C Climate Goal with Reckless Expansion Plans." Operation Noah. https://operationnoah.org/featured/press-release-global-faith-institutions-announce-divestment-as-oil-and-gas-companies-threaten-1-5c-climate-goal-with-reckless-expansion-plans/.

Grubb, M., et al. "2022: Introduction and Framing." In *IPCC, 2022. Climate Change 2022: Mitigation of Climate Change*. Contribution of Working Group III to the Sixth Assessment Report of the Intergovernmental Panel on Climate Change, edited by P. R. Shukla, J. Skea, R. Slade, A. Al Khourdajie, R. van Diemen, D. McCollum, M. Pathak, S. Some, et al., 1–6. Cambridge, UK: Cambridge University Press, 2022.

Johnson, Ayana Elizabeth, and Katharine K. Wilkerson. "Begin." In *All We Can Save*. New York: Random House, 2020.

Kottasová, Ivana, Amy Cassidy, Angela Dewan, and Helen Regan. "Overtime for COP26 as Deep Divisions Remain over Key Issues around Money and

Markets." CNN (November 13, 2021). https://www.cnn.com/2021/11/12/world/cop26-agreement-climate-intl-hnk/index.html.

Love, Janice. *The U.S. Anti-Apartheid Movement: Local Activism in Global Politics*, 245. New York: Praeger, 1985.

McGrath, Matt. "COP26: Fossil Fuel Industry Has Largest Delegation at Climate Summit." *BBC News* (November 8, 2021). https://www.bbc.com/news/science-environment-59199484.

McKibben, Bill. "Global Warming's Terrifying New Math." *Rolling Stone* (July 19, 2012). https://www.rollingstone.com/politics/politics-news/global-warmings-terrifying-new-math-188550/.

Pietsch, B. M. "Lyman Stewart and Early Fundamentalism." *Church History* 82, no. 11 (September 2013): 617–46.

Presbyterian Church (USA). "Blessed Tomorrow." https://www.presbyterianmission.org/ministries/environment/blessed-tomorrow/.

———. "The Divestment Strategy: Principles and Criteria." https://www.presbyterianmission.org/wp-content/uploads/GA-1984-Divestment-Strategy.pdf.

———. "Earth Care Congregations." https://www.presbyterianmission.org/ministries/environment/earth-care-congregations/.

———. "Guide to Going Carbon Neutral." https://www.pcusa.org/resource/guide-to-going-carbon-neutral-23751/.

———. "Office of Faith-Based Investing and Corporate Engagement." https://www.presbyterianmission.org/ministries/mrti/.

———. *Restoring Creation for Ecology and Justice*. Louisville, KY: Presbyterian Church (USA), September 1990. https://www.presbyterianmission.org/wp-content/uploads/restoring-creation-for-ecologyjustice.pdf.

———. "Tread Lightly for Lent." January 26, 2021. https://www.presbyterianmission.org/resource/tread-lightly-for-lent/.

Presbyterians for Earth Care. "History." https://presbyearthcare.org/history/.

Rich, Nathaniel. *Losing Earth: A Recent History*. New York: MCD, 2019.

Vignola Jr., Leonard. *Strategic Divestment*. New York: Amacom, 1974.

Weber, Max. *The Protestant Work Ethic and the Spirit of Capitalism*. New York: Penguin Books, 2019.

Chapter 10

Engaging the Climate Crisis through Spiritual Nonviolence

Daniel Joranko

We are faced with the daunting challenge of transforming into a carbon-free world. Despite attempts at international carbon-reduction frameworks, carbon emissions are still well above where they need to be. There are strong vested interests that resist and impede this move. In the United States, this is coupled with a white nationalist populist movement that dismisses the need for climate action. How are we then to rise to this challenge and shape our spiritual callings so that we may respond in a faithful, sustained, and sufficient manner? What roles might we play in witnessing for a world that cares for the vulnerable among us and in the wider creation and that embeds a greater justice in our social formations? What follows is an attempt to sketch out a basic framework for these roles and for emerging social formations on the ground. It presents a holistic approach to spiritual nonviolence that addresses several of the basic dimensions of our social lives. Four approaches are considered: (1) intentional community; (2) community sustainable development; (3) strategic community organizing; and (4) strategic nonviolence. Each of these addresses a different dimension of life in society. These include the household and the neighborhood, the economy, politics and policy, and the commons as a whole. None of these life dimensions is an entirely separate sphere, of course. Differentiating the spheres, though, can enable them to serve as focal points for practice and reflection. They can also serve as focal points for particular forms of deep vocation.

It should also be noted that none of the four proposed approaches on its own is sufficient to meet the challenges we face. Together, though, it is hoped that they can supplement and complement each other in ways that contribute to fundamental social transformation. This chapter does not attempt to delineate what this transformation might look like when achieved. Nor does it attempt to define comprehensive solutions to the climate problem and current social injustices. Instead, it intends to provide the more modest function of helping to illuminate practice on the ground. Given my experience, much of the focus will be on US cities while recognizing the deep importance of international initiatives.

Spiritual nonviolence contains a repertoire of strategies, tactics, and practices. It can be argued that it also shares a certain ethos, one that allows for considerable differences in understanding and practice. This ethos will tentatively be explored here through the notion of "just-mercy." This notion comes from the restorative justice tradition.[1] It attempts to bring together the two important concerns of justice and mercy. Justice might be broadly defined in a twofold manner—as forming relationships that foster human flourishing and that foster fairness. Mercy also might be broadly defined in a twofold manner—as refraining from retribution and as engaging in care regardless of merit. There is definitely a tension between justice and mercy in both our conceptualizations and in our sentiments. However, in carefully discerned practice, these two concepts can often be blended in a holistic manner.

What follows draws extensively on my experience of over forty years in urban ministry, community organizing, and community development. I have worked the spaces between the streets, the storefront, the sanctuary, the statehouse, and the study. As a younger adult, I was involved in community organizing in Chicago; then in community development in several Michigan cities. In Nashville, I played an extensive support role in one of the nation's longest sit-ins, where affected people challenged substantial health-care cuts by the state of Tennessee. I have been engaged in peace campaigns in the 1980s and the early 2000s. Over the past dozen years, I have focused on organized religious initiatives to address the climate crisis. For about a dozen years, I coordinated and taught inside-out classes at Riverbend Maximum Security Institution through the Vanderbilt Divinity School. I live in an interracial and nonsectarian intentional community in North Nashville, a community whose practices are based in the principles of the Catholic Worker movement. Recently, I have also started to engage in extensive conversations exploring how spiritual nonviolence can best address the climate crisis.

The framework draws upon several streams of tradition that have flowed together over the past century. These include the Gandhian, Catholic Worker, Black Freedom, Peace Church, and Restorative Justice traditions. In his study of the Christian pacifist tradition, Mark Douglas argues for an understanding of tradition that respects a plurality of streams rather than striving for an original purity. He notes that, "we inevitably participate in the problems we are trying to solve."[2] Moreover, emphases and limitations in particular approaches can cause suffering in others despite genuine efforts to avoid causing suffering. Plurality and awareness can help ameliorate these tendencies without eliminating them. There is no perfect practice or approach, but, at the same time, there is also much in certain traditions that can be drawn from and learned from.[3] Moreover, traditions can also provide guidance, focus, and unity among certain participants while providing a place of grounded dialogue with other traditions. If one is to stand in a particular tradition, it helps to be appreciative, critical, and imaginative in one's approach.

These spiritual and ethical traditions will also be brought into dialogue with the theory and practice of sustainability. Sustainability or sustainable development is a broad and often contested umbrella of approaches that brings together considerations of ecology, economics, energy, and equity. It emphasizes both meeting the needs of the present generation without compromising the needs of future generations. It also often places a particular emphasis on the needs of the poor. Such an approach would both emphasize the imperative of carbon reduction while recognizing that energy is fundamental in providing for basic needs of shelter, food, and mobility. Moreover, energy is fully implicated in people's livelihoods, especially in the provision of goods and services, both essential and for enjoyment.

Yet human fossil fuel energy use has forced earth's energy systems out of balance in relation to the flourishing of life. Larry Rasmussen reminds us as follows:

> Energy policy discussions assume that human energy use is primary; then we'll deal with the side effects. (These effects now include climate change.) But *human* primacy and priority "—being useful" is exactly backwards. The first law of energy is preservation of the planet's climate-energy systems as conducive to life. Human energy use is *derivative of the planet's*. This is the energy parallel to [Thomas] Berry's principle that the first law of the human economy is the preservation of the planet's economy. It is also a conviction that flows from creation, or "being," as sacred. The well-being of creation comprehensively is its due, and the starting point for human use of it.[4]

We thus have a sacred duty and social imperative to move out of a fossil fueled economy to bring earth's energy system back into balance. We have the sacred duty to care for the poor and vulnerable in our midst while recognizing that the commons itself has become vulnerable. There is the necessity of satisfying particular human needs while at the same time maintaining the greater ecology that enables these satisfactions. In practice, there is both an imperative to decarbonize and tensions in how this is accomplished.

Spiritual and ethical traditions can bring a real richness to this challenging practice. Moreover, much can be learned from the past practices in the four approaches being considered here. Each of these approaches has evolved as ecological awareness has grown. We both need to recognize the urgency of the climate crisis while taking the time to draw upon the hard-earned wisdom of previous practice. We also need to recognize that the flourishing of the wider creation is not simply another issue in a buffet of issues but, instead, is the foundation for our own flourishing. It needs to be integrated in all of our work and worship.

We will now consider each of the four approaches, starting with intentional community.

INTENTIONAL COMMUNITY

Intentional community focuses at the level of household and neighborhood. The form of service is often radical hospitality. Hospitality in the biblical sense focuses on providing a place for those who have been displaced. Those displaced often come to other people as strangers and can seem a threat to those who are settled. Given this social tendency, there is a need for people who dedicate themselves to genuine hospitality. Members of intentional communities often provide this service. They focus on accompaniment with those in proximity who have been marginalized, displaced, or excluded by the wider society. Vulnerable neighbors can become fellow pilgrims and friends. There is an emphasis on restoration and the provision of space so those accompanied can reclaim dignity. Through these relationships, those who provide service are also often restored through those they serve. Service can become mutual.[5]

We are also increasingly seeing communities where the emphasis is on restoring damaged landscapes. Here, too, spaces are opened where our fellow creatures can reclaim their dignity. The landscapes themselves reciprocate. The patient work in itself is often restorative, and a restored nature provides restoration to the spirits of those whose neighborhoods are served.[6]

The combination of hospitality and concern for the wider creation is exemplified in other ways. Food, for instance, is at the core of hospitality. Care is also shown through growing healthy food in a regenerative manner. Community gardens are one way to foster the sharing of these practices. They also provide a way for the community to provide access to fresh and healthy food to those who would otherwise be deprived.

The provision of direct hospitality will become increasingly necessary as we face the climate crisis. Climate refugees will need to be welcomed into communities. Cooling centers will need to be opened during urban heat waves. Relief and relocation will be increasingly needed in the face of severe storms, flooding, and wildfires.

Many intentional communities are motivated by sacred concerns through their religious traditions. They often maintain a quiet and unobtrusive witness. They also often exemplify an informal gift economy, with an emphasis of sharing of spaces and goods. There is also a focus on living simply so as both not to create undue material social distance and to express care for the wider creation. The Roman Catholic and Orthodox traditions have long organized these communities through orders. Recent years have seen an expansion of less-structured alternatives that reach beyond these traditions. Some of these alternatives have been labeled "The New Monasticism."[7]

Kasturbai and Mohandas Gandhi formed and coordinated ashrams that were at the core of their satyagraha movement. The Gandhian ashrams were intended to provide a place for the spiritual formation seen as necessary to practice a highly disciplined form of nonviolence. Anthony Parel states that Mohandas Gandhi, "attempted to make the Sabarmati Ashram a model of a caste-free society. . . . The members of the Ashram carried out their various responsibilities from a sense of duty, regardless of their original caste background."[8]

Another important example has been the Catholic Worker movement. For a century, it has focused on works of mercy and hospitality with the very vulnerable, particularly the homeless and those in prison. The founder, Dorothy Day, emphasized voluntary poverty, personalist approaches, and radical pacifism. At the same time, she acknowledged the important distinction between the simplicity of voluntary poverty and the oppressiveness and even cruelty of many forms of nonvoluntary poverty. Her cofounder, Peter Maurin, developed alternative economic theories emphasizing useful work, the growing of food, and the sharing of goods.[9] The Catholic Worker movement planted many of the seeds of the Catholic peace movement. The houses continue to grow in number and have begun to reemphasize experiments in local food cultivation and other ecological practices.[10] The contemporary houses are quite flexible and diverse in their approaches to communal living. Victoria Machado states as follows:

> The foundations of a Personalist philosophy and works of mercy are important to the mission of Catholic Worker Houses, but their sustainability also comes from an adaptability and fluidity in how these concepts are implemented. They live the gospel with careful regard to location, each house and farm filling its own niche for the context in which it operates.[11]

My own intentional community—Nashville Greenlands—is a nonsectarian community founded on the principles of the Catholic Worker movement. Some of our members focus on outreach to and accompaniment with the homeless through Open Table Nashville. This has included street chaplaincy and advocacy for affordable housing. Others have provided community meals to low-income people through the Nashville Food Project. Several have been staff organizers with Worker's Dignity, which organizes low-wage and immigrant workers to protect their rights. My own focus has included prison work. We also address concern for the wider creation through our extensive organic gardens and living simply in small spaces.

Living at Greenlands has given me the freedom to help grow the creation care and climate movement across Tennessee over the last fifteen years through projects with limited funding. I have engaged in work in my own denomination (United Methodist), interfaith work through Tennessee Power and Light, and secular work through various environmental organizations. The religious work has included work with congregations in education, service projects, and assistance with decarbonizing. Our coalition work has long challenged the nation's largest utility—the Tennessee Valley Authority—to decarbonize. We also focus on energy justice for low-income people and a just transition for workers. Finally, I have also helped provide leadership in the national United Methodist Creation Justice movement. This included helping found the UMC Earthkeepers program, which, so far, has commissioned over two hundred people to develop creation justice and care projects in their communities.[12]

Richard Rohr has promoted the concept of combining simplicity, contemplation, and social action.[13] He sees a danger in middle-class religion, which may only offer a religion of consolation, rather than commitment, and which is unwilling to confront social injustices. Instead, he calls for both genuine action in the world and spiritual formation through simplicity and contemplation. Much of this formation is in letting go—letting go of unnecessary wants and of unnecessary fears, which cause us both to aggressively compete for security and to withdraw from necessary engagement in the "political and social vocation of Christians." This formation often happens best in some form of community.

Intentional communities can also be important bases for social movements. The ecological crisis will take considerable dedication and courage to confront. Intentional communities can be places to foster both the necessary discipline and celebration along the way. Some may be places of particular but noncoercive forms of spiritual formation. They can be places where people can unlearn the habits of consumer culture, technocratic mentalities, and capital accumulation that Pope Francis sees as at the heart of the climate crisis.[14] They can be homes anchored in particular places that are radically open to learning from one's neighbors. House sharing and other forms of local food production can lead to exemplary models of lowering carbon footprints. By providing lower household costs, they can provide places where activists are freed from some of the financial pressures of the nonprofit sector, and instead be freed to concentrate on the needs of social moments and movements. Finally, they can provide places for community and camaraderie in the struggle.

Works of mercy—providing care regardless of merit—are at the core of this first approach. The person immediately present to us is centered—reminding us of our primary concern for persons as ends and not simply means. For modern life can often reduce persons to their instrumental value. In conventional economics, the person is primarily valued for his or her productivity or purchasing capacity. In politics, people are often manipulated in the service of power. Even in vital causes, people can simply be seen as pieces to be maneuvered. Care on the ground can also continually remind us of the intrinsic value of the other creatures with whom we share our precious planet.

COMMUNITY SUSTAINABLE DEVELOPMENT

While intentional communities can often run on informal gift economies, there is also a need to foster wider and more formal economic formations that enable a greater sharing and justice than the current mainstream economy enables. Such economic formations would provide dignified work, dramatically reduce income inequality, democratize wealth, and decarbonize the economy. There is a need for economic forms that are more consistent with justice than is much of our current economy, which too often extracts wealth from the work and the land in ways that exploit or damage. There is a need to provide avenues to intentionally foster local communities and operate at a human scale where technology can be a tool rather than an often-alienating force.[15] Finally, there is a need to establish enterprises that enable us to become more grounded and attentive to each other and our fellow creatures in the commons of a local landscape.

Leaders in the broad nonviolence tradition have explored the notion of localized economies centered on necessary, dignified, and unexploited labor. Gandhi's constructive work projects and the teachings of Peter Maurin in the Catholic Worker movement immediately come to mind. Outside the explicitly nonviolence tradition, there has also been a considerable history of experimentation in community development. This approach increasingly attempts to incorporate environmental sustainability into the models. There is increasing emphasis on restoration and regeneration of local landscapes. Such initiatives are generally secular in orientation—though the Christian Community Development Association (CCDA) is an example of a more religiously oriented approach. The CCDA orients itself around three Rs. They encourage members to *relocate* to impoverished communities. They focus on racial *reconciliation*. And they foster *redistribution* by founding various community-oriented economic enterprises.[16]

There is considerable literature in local sustainable development and community economic development. There is also considerable practice on the ground. Here we will simply highlight some promising literature and practical examples.

Christopher and Hazel Dunn point to the growing sector of community economic development, which attempts to reclaim capital by capturing social surplus for local communities. Cooperatives and community-development corporations can build assets and capacities in local communities, while reconfiguring ownership patterns. Credit unions, community-development loan funds, and development banks can provide and possibly democratize capital.[17] Thomas Princen explores the potential of substituting both the "logic of sufficiency" and "ecological rationalities" for the logics and rationalities of mechanical and cyber efficiencies.[18] He then explores several case studies of economic initiatives that move in this direction. Paloma Pavel portrays numerous examples that focus on the nexus between economic justice and environmental justice in US urban regions. This includes everything from reclaiming land and green spaces for lower-income communities, policy advocacy for equitable public transportation, farm-to-school initiatives, and community-benefits agreements linked to urban redevelopment.[19]

In the book *Drawdown*, Paul Hawken looks at the one hundred most promising solutions for decarbonizing the economy, both in the mainstream and in local alternative projects.[20] The solutions range across the sectors of energy, food, buildings and cities, land use, transport, and materials to provide a broad spectrum of potential projects that combine good work and draw down the carbon regime. These solutions can become the basis for community sustainable-development initiatives.

Grace Lee Boggs, in her work with grassroots economic development in Detroit, called for the need for transformative organizing that "grows our souls" and contributes to "a great turning" in our approach to economic and ecological well-being.[21] She saw Detroit, in its economic abandonment, as a place and space "to begin anew" in this planetary project.

There are increasing numbers of initiatives in US urban areas that attempt to combine poverty mitigation with carbon mitigation. Some of these train "at-risk" youth for low-income weatherization work. Other examples are Socially Equal Energy Efficient Development (SEEED) in Knoxville, Tennessee, which enhances career readiness through promoting literacy, and Solar Richmond in Richmond, California, which provides free solar systems to income-qualifying homes in low-income communities. Second Chance Baltimore turns the blight of abandoned buildings into assets through deconstruction—which is the process of removing a building by taking it apart in the reverse order of construction. Reclaimed materials are then sold at Second Chance Baltimore's store. This reuses often high-quality materials rather than discarding them in a landfill. Second Chance Baltimore trains local residents in this work; residents thus learn a valuable trade. The funds from the store support the training and work projects. Another example are the Evergreen Cooperatives in Cleveland, Ohio, which are inspired by the Mondragon Cooperatives. They utilize anchor institutions, like local universities and hospitals, to provide capital to start up and support "green worker"–owned cooperatives.

Community sustainable development generally focuses on relatively small-scale enterprises. Scaling up would largely entail enabling such enterprises to become both more widespread and somewhat larger in size. This would necessitate considerably more investment. Green banks, revolving loan funds, and community-development venture funds are possible avenues. Finding ways to pool capital investment, particularly from the middle classes, is essential to mainstreaming this approach. Such initiatives are emerging. For instance, the SEED Commons is a national network of community, with a particular focus on cooperatively owned businesses.[22] Capital funneled through the recently passed Inflation Reduction Act will also provide further opportunities.

Currently, much of the value of community sustainable development stems from enabling those involved to practice a certain moral integrity in their economic lives. Moreover, this approach has a certain liminal character. It both generally participates in markets while foregrounding local communities, democracy, equity, wealth sharing, dignified work, and ecological regeneration. Practitioners often see themselves as prefiguring a more just and sustainable economy. It is an expression and an avenue of hope.

STRATEGIC COMMUNITY ORGANIZING

Community organizing is intended to enable people to effectively participate in the political dimension of their communal lives. Politics can be seen as the means through which people mobilize, maneuver, and negotiate to enable effective governance, which enables communities to flourish and experience fairness. This may include electing representatives, of course, but goes beyond this to emphasize the policies and procedures that are embraced and enacted. This entails a focus on power and the ability of people to participate with power. The United States, as is true of a number of countries, suffers from severe power imbalances. Some communities seem powerless, particularly poorer ones and those impacted by racial injustice. Community organizing begins to rectify this by employing disciplined organizing methodologies that enable communal solidarity, communal deliberation, and well-executed campaigns that are engaged in by people from these communities. Community organizing also navigates and negotiates local identities and interests. In his international study of local urban organizing, Manual Castells sees these identities and interests in terms of "neighborhood, poverty and oppressed ethnic minorities."[23] Community organizations are often formed out of the interplay of these three points of focus, which both intersect and are in tension with each other.

Community organizing is not often closely identified with the nonviolent tradition. However, it shares a considerable degree of tactical repertoire with strategic nonviolence—without necessarily moving into the realm of civil disobedience. Furthermore, nonviolence organizers in the past have sometimes seen themselves as engaging in community organizing. For instance, certain initiatives in the Black Freedom movement come to mind. Finally, this approach contains certain elements that are perhaps necessary for a holistic approach to social transformation. For instance, community organizing keeps the focus on the local and the tangible and on how larger trends affect real communities. It also helps ensure that social movements, such as the climate movement, are shaped by both "ordinary people" and the people ordinarily left out (often many of the same people).

As energy systems are foundational to modern life, it should be evident that injustices within a society are reflected through and exacerbated through these energy systems. There is an increasing focus within the climate movement on how energy policy affects the health of marginalized communities. Michael Mendez explores local climate activism through the lens of "climate embodiment." Climate change and carbonized energy systems have disproportionate effects on marginalized communities. Mendez says this of environmental justice advocates:

> Key to their worldview is an understanding of the human body as a site of intersection between social, political, and environmental dynamics. Activists view climate change as an embodied phenomenon that has multiple impacts on the people who live with it every day. These insights are tied to a keen sense of the ways in which health is determined not just by personal choices or genetic makeup but by a range of social and historical factors that hinge on race and class . . . Through organizing and lobbying efforts environmental justice advocates have been able to disrupt the dominance of the carbon reductionist worldview in climate policy. They have introduced embodied, local forms of knowledge and perspectives into public debate and transformed climate change solutions.[24]

Environmental justice has placed an important focus on the impacts of pollution stemming from facilities that extract and produce fossil fuel–based forms of energy. Energy provision has other important health implications that result from utility shutoffs and high energy cost burdens on the poor. Moreover, poorly weatherized homes have substantial negative health impacts. Poor people often engage with energy issues through the basic need of adequate and affordable shelter—including heat, cooling, and lighting. Campaigns focused on such needs become a struggle for energy justice.

This section of the chapter draws primarily from my experiences as a core organizer in efforts to pioneer energy justice in Chicago nearly forty years ago. Despite the distance in time, these experiences seem particularly pertinent today as they can perhaps be seen as a core part of the beginnings of an organized struggle for energy justice. As noted above, I was a community organizer with the Northwest Community Organization (NCO) in the 1980s. The NCO was formed in 1963 and was centered in the West Town Community of Chicago, with boundaries that stretched some into the surrounding community areas.

In the early 1980s, a campaign originating in the Chicago South Austin community successfully advocated for state legislation that provided utility payment assistance for lower-income households. National legislation was soon modeled on this, which became the Low Income Home Energy Assistance Program (LIHEAP). However, even the LIHEAP was not enough—and Illinois still faced a shutoff crisis for both household gas and electricity. My first campaign as a community organizer was in response to this crisis. Too many families in our community faced the fierce Chicago winter without heat or faced hot summers without any form of cooling. We formed a coalition of several core organizations to propose the first statewide percentage-of-income utility payment program (PIPP) for low-income households in the nation.

We then conducted an intensive campaign. A couple of thousand low- and moderate-income people were mobilized during the course of the campaign. Tactics included community hearings involving the testimony of those directly affected. We focused direct actions on public officials and at Illinois Commerce Commission (ICC) hearings. We engaged in citizen lobbying at the state legislature. We faced stiff opposition from the utility companies and from the state chamber of commerce. Despite this opposition, our legislation passed the state legislature with narrow bipartisan support—and was supported and signed into law by a Republican governor. The original bill that was passed included a provision to develop a plan to weatherize all of the low-income homes in the state, but this was removed from the legislation a year later. However, utility companies came around to support the PIPP as it became successfully implemented. We had also been able to establish several local projects, including one run by the NCO, to weatherize homes for modest-income community residents.

Nearly forty years ago, we waged a successful campaign to effectively counter utility shutoffs and make heating and lighting affordable to the poor. We also focused on weatherization of homes, which provides energy savings and health benefits. Both our policy and the project initiatives were identified as effective strategies through deliberation in low-income communities. Both environmental justice and energy justice have struggled to obtain recognition both in the mainstream of environmental or energy policy and in the respective environmental and climate movements. However, in recent years, both low-income weatherization and PIPPs have increasingly become part of mainstream energy policy that combines equity and carbon reduction. Environmental justice is also experiencing more mainstream recognition.

Winning major community-organizing campaigns can be difficult. One reason our PIPP campaign was successful was that it exhibited the key elements of what Marshall Ganz calls "strategic capacity." Understanding strategic capacity is key to any effective nonviolent approach—whether in community organizing or civil disobedience. With strategic capacity, campaigns can sometimes achieve David-versus-Goliath victories. Ganz notes that "three critical elements of strategy are targeting, tactics, and timing." We were able to creatively deploy these elements. Ganz further identifies three factors that foster such creativity: "motivation, salient knowledge, and learning—or heuristic—practices." Moreover, a fourth factor—sustained collective deliberation—is also necessary. However, this is challenging and "requires leadership with a high tolerance for ambiguity."[25]

Let's briefly consider these factors in relation to this campaign. The first is motivation and commitment. We were highly motivated by our concern for families losing their heat and highly committed to doing what it took to mitigate this crisis. We had intense focus—and lived this campaign for a couple of years. The coalition also contained and combined salient knowledge. Low-income leaders and participants were critical. They were able to identify and speak strongly for what was needed. We had experienced community organizers and leaders who had knowledge both of their communities and of the policy process. They were able to read both the community and the political landscape and respond accordingly. Moreover, over time, they had learned and further developed an effective tactical repertoire. We incorporated policy expertise through the involvement of representatives from the Mandel Legal Aid Clinic at the Law School of the University of Chicago.

Finally, we had the patience to take the time to be highly deliberative. The collective leadership group met weekly to hash out strategy. Tactics emerged in a context of uncertainty—and they were highly responsive. We had a great deal of respect for each other—and discussed, debated, and deliberated until we could come to some common agreement. If I were to identify one of the elements that is most needed—and sometimes missing in current climate organizing—it is this sense of focus and deliberation. In today's landscape, it is easy to let ones' focus become scattered through multiple concerns. There is a need to free up experienced organizers and leaders to intensely focus on a campaign. One needs to also recognize that this level of intensity cannot be sustained over a lifetime—but it can perhaps be sustained for the time necessary for a key campaign.

Community organizing also is confronted with the challenge of scale. Mendez explores this concern. On the one hand, attempted large-scale solutions to the climate crisis—such as the Cap-and-Trade approach—may have negative impacts on marginalized communities (trading of emissions credits can increase localized polluting emissions in already highly impacted communities). A community-organizing approach can recognize and mobilize around these impacts. Localized approaches, though, face the difficulty of having impact over the larger scale of state, national, and global policy.[26] Wider coalitions need to be formed, and wider political landscapes need to be understood. In our PIPP campaign we started with a core coalition and gradually expanded out—including a key organizing initiative in southern Illinois. We also built upon experience with scale, including earlier efforts by our own and affiliated community organizations. For instance, both the Organization for a Better Austin and the NCO had been instrumental in the coalition campaigns limiting redlining through national Community Reinvestment Act (CRA) legislation. Both the PIPP and the CRA campaigns focused on addressing the issue of housing and the larger forces that prevented access to adequate and affordable shelter. Both campaigns were able to build to scale and successfully advocate for policies that addressed concerns at a fundamental level. Studying such current and historical cases of building campaigns to scale seems critical to understanding how community organizing can contribute to fundamental transformation.

My experience at the NCO points to some further ingredients of effective nonviolent organizing. In their study of nonviolent campaigns, Erica Chenoweth and Maria Stephan point to the importance of drawing moderate-minded people into movements.[27] Their presence can help enable the acceptance of fundamental change. In communities such as West Town in the 1980s, these were often modest-income homeowners. Moreover, there is often conflict between the interests of homeowners and lower-income renters in such neighborhoods. The NCO was able to draw both groups into the organization through a blend of attention to both interests and ideals. There was a lot of granular bread-and-butter organizing around the concerns of homeowners, such as their concerns around sanitation, vacant lots, and streets and sidewalks, as well as home mortgages and lending. At the same time, we placed an emphasis on the needs of lower-income people for affordable housing and launched major campaigns such as the PIPP. Through all of this, the NCO attempted to navigate the interplay between neighborhood, poverty, and racial and ethnic oppression. Despite what might be seen as formidable tensions, the NCO was for some time an effective organization that crossed ethnic, racial, and class boundaries. It helped facilitate a degree of residential racial integration that was unusual for Chicago—which, at that time, was the nation's most segregated city. At the NCO's best, one could perhaps taste a form of the "Beloved Community."

We will close this section by briefly considering the question of the ethos of spiritual nonviolence and community organizing. Community organizing is sometimes associated with an abrasive style of action. That was not entirely absent in the NCO. However, the tenor of the PIPP campaign seemed modulated in a way that attempted to draw officials in rather than simply attempting to overcome them. Our cause did become something of a moral concern. I remember one instance, in particular, where the president of the NCO and I guided the chairperson of the ICC in visiting the homes of families of people who had their heat shut off in the midst of the January cold. This seemed to considerably move him, and he fundamentally changed his stance toward our proposed program. One hopes that the potential for moral engagement is not entirely lost in today's cynical political climate. It seems likely that, without some form of moral engagement, we simply do not have the power to force the changes that are needed today.

In regard to ethos, we also seemed to share another important characteristic of the nonviolent approach. I do not want to generalize too much here regarding our diverse participants, but we also seemed to draw on the spiritual commitments present in lower-income communities in the United States. Much of this commitment is found in the laity—sometimes those sitting at the back of the pews. The tenor of this commitment seems to be a somewhat neglected arena of reflection and scholarship. There is an understandable amount of escapism present, given the solidity of the oppression that people face. However, when engaged something seems to crystalize. A certain commitment to just-mercy seems to be embraced and embodied. At least that is my observation.

STRATEGIC NONVIOLENT ACTION

Successful community-organizing campaigns depend to some degree on the potential of legislative bodies to recognize and respond to legitimate interests—however reluctant their response might be. Our PIPP campaign included forms of direct action, but it was never tactically necessary for us to face arrest. However, when inviolable concerns, such as human rights, are routinely violated or when there is a fundamental imperative to alter the foundations of a society, then more robust forms of strategic nonviolent action are also called for. The tactical repertoire associated with this approach can include boycotts, civil disobedience, and direct action that includes sustained nonretaliation to attack. Over the past century, strategic nonviolent action has resulted in considerable impact in addressing seemingly intractable unjust power structures. It therefore seems quite pertinent to the imperative of decarbonizing society despite considerable resistance from powerful sectors of society.

Mohandas Gandhi developed a comprehensive approach to spiritual nonviolence that he called "satyagraha"—truth or soul-force.[28] Here was a renewed understanding of the Hindu tradition that came out of an intense strategic engagement with the deep injustice of imperialism. This understanding came out of a reflection on this practice and a revision of his understanding of the tradition, gained in part through exposure to other sacred traditions: Jain, Sikh, and pacifistic Christian traditions.[29] Other important tributaries flowed, and sometimes contrasted, in the struggle for freedom; these included engaged Buddhism, led by Bhimroa Ramji Ambedkar, and the Moslem nonviolent movement, led by Badshah Khan. Spiritual nonviolence was forged in this struggle in the land considered to be the jewel of the world's first global empire. From this peripheral space in the world system, it eventually deeply impacted the struggles of marginalized people in the core of the world system. As Gandhi hoped, spiritual nonviolence profoundly impacted Christianity—particularly in the engagement of the Black church in the civil rights revolution. These two movements, in turn, deeply impacted the secular civic sphere—through new but imperfect institutionalized formations in a decolonized Indian nation and in the dramatic revisions of civil rights in the United States.

Christians played important roles in several major nonviolent movements in the twentieth century. One was, of course, the Black Freedom movement—much of which was grounded in the Black church. This movement visibly displayed the expressions and symbols, sermons, and songs of the Black church. It also exhibited the dialectics of the secular and the sacred—as these sacred expressions resulted in secular civil rights. It also catalyzed and continues to reverberate through the successful struggle of other marginalized groups for recognition and civil rights.

Another major movement is largely neglected today in the United States. Jim Carroll and Jonathan Schell have highlighted and explored the important role of nonviolence, both in the United States and in Eastern Europe, in the collapse of the Cold War regime and in the confrontation with the world-threatening commitment to nuclear weapons.[30] Roman Catholics, in particular, were often prominent in their witness in this movement. The Solidarity movement in Poland brought unionized working people together to challenge an oppressive empire. They carefully studied nonviolent tactics and deployed them for economic and political justice. Simultaneously, there was a widespread Nuclear Freeze movement in the West that challenged the threat of global extinction through nuclear war between the two powers. Carroll called this the "most successful American grassroots movement of the twentieth century."[31] Together, efforts in the East and the West opened a space for de-escalation and the dismantling of empire.

Several movement organizations are attempting to utilize nonviolent direct-action tactics to confront the climate crisis. These include the Sunrise Movement and Extinction Rebellion. Moreover, the Poor People's Campaign is attempting to follow in the footsteps of Martin Luther King Jr. in challenging entrenched systems of poverty and growing income inequality. They incorporate a serious concern for the climate in their approach. Finally, there have been significant campaigns focused on what Naomi Klein calls "Blockadia"—the civil-resistance efforts in frontline and fenceline communities to block further energy and resource exploitation of their communities.[32] This has included significant efforts by indigenous communities. The most famous of these examples is probably the blockage of the Keystone pipeline.

Given the recentness of these efforts, there has been limited study and documentation of these various initiatives by scholars. Moreover, practitioners are just beginning to step back and deeply evaluate these initial efforts. We will not attempt such an evaluation here. This evaluation needs to begin with conversation with and between practitioners. One can, though, certainly note the dedication and insight that are emerging through these initiatives. However, given the scope and urgency of the climate crisis, it seems that the rich resources of strategic nonviolence still remain underemployed. We need to continue to reflect on the dynamics of strategic nonviolent action in order to deploy these dynamics effectively. To that end, we will briefly examine some of these core dynamics and then conclude with some reflections as to the potential direction of the movement.

The Gandhian approach recognizes the legitimate role of conflict and compromise in addressing interests through normal politics and struggle. However, where compromise on fundamentals is not possible, a satyagraha campaign will be waged. Such campaigns take a deeply strategic approach—satyagraha is employed in escalating tactical steps. It starts with negotiation in good faith. However, when negotiation fails, the campaign will move through carefully prepared escalating steps of confrontation and noncooperation.[33]

The US Black Freedom movement is a paradigmatic example of an escalating strategic campaign that was waged over a number of years. Numerous local campaigns were engaged and successful in leading to fundamental breaks in the segregation regime. There was also an escalation of intensity and risk in the tactics and locations. A list of key campaigns exemplifies this: Montgomery, Nashville, the Freedom Rides, Birmingham, the March on Washington, Mississippi, and the final breakthrough at Selma. This escalating series of campaigns lead to the passage of the fundamental national legislation—the Civil Rights Act and the Voting Rights Act.

Much of the power of strategic nonviolence comes from the staging of real-life moral dramas. The virtuous cause and embodied presence of oppressed protagonists confront the protagonists of an exploitative or oppressive regime. This can be playful and even humorous—the example of the Serbian Otpor! campaigns comes to mind.[34] Or there can be the dignified seriousness of risking arrest or even enduring violence—the march on the Indian salt works or the crossing of the Selma bridge are examples. Music and ritual can play a role. The Catholic peace movement has effectively used ritual, particularly in confronting the nuclear-weapons regime in the 1980s.

Discipline around a code of conduct is often expected of practitioners. Nonretaliation to violence is at the core of this approach. Sacrifice is generally seen as necessary—and both civil disobedience and nonretaliation may result in considerable personal cost. For Gandhi, satyagraha was a deeply spiritual discipline, and he deployed the symbols of his Hindu practice so that they might resonate with others and draw them in. However, he also saw it as a civil practice, which might be engaged in by any sufficiently disciplined person.

Spiritual nonviolence also displays the paradox that putting one's body on the line performs a deeply spiritual practice. It also exhibits a character where what for some is a deep spiritual practice can be effectively joined by many others in a civic endeavor through the practice of mutual discipline. Yet it also transcends common morality. One sacrifices what is seen as a right to immediate self-defense in the practice of nonretaliation. One also may sacrifice the legitimate protections of law through the practice of civil disobedience in the hopes that law might eventually provide a wider protection for many.

Nonviolence attempts to speak to the imagination and the heart in order to open up space for new possibilities.[35] It resonates especially with those groups of people who might be troubled by the excesses and moral pretenses of unjust social systems but who have become accustomed to or feel trapped by these systems. The embodied courage of the witness, the opening of the imagination, and the proposed solution provide a potential way out. Moreover, nonviolent action can embody just-mercy. It can stand firm for justice—at the same time, it can extend a posture of mercy toward the adversary. There seems to be an intangible power in this combination.

Yet dominant social formations do not easily yield. Walter Wink explores the strategic and spiritual dynamics of confronting the dominant social institutions—or, as he puts it, in biblical terms—the principalities and powers.[36] These institutions are intended to serve humanity—but are captured by those who would dominate others and are turned to serve this purpose. Wink also explores the spiritual nature of these principalities and powers. Wink suggests the spirituality of such institutions is in their interiority. He is somewhat unclear in what he means here. A somewhat alternative view is suggested by his consideration of how images and ideologies are deployed to sacralize this domination. Such sacralizing claims can rise to the level of idolatry. These images, ideologies, and incantations can be seen as projections and rationalizations that can enchant people and threaten to capture their spirits and minds. Wink is quite insightful in outlining social movements of spiritual nonviolence that can confront dominating social organizations and puncture the pretentions of these projective illusions.

When confronting these realities, hope may be found in the religious belief that these forms of domination are not ultimate and do not have true sovereignty. Gandhi, for instance, believed that spiritual nonviolence tapped into the dynamics of ultimate reality, which was the source of its power.[37] Christians might see this counter-reality as the Kingdom or Realm of God. No attempt will be made to define this Realm here, other than noting that it refers to the ultimate spiritual destiny of creation, which can be lived through emergent relationships in the present. The notion of the Realm of God reminds us that redemption is social and relational and not simply individual, that it can encompass the wider creation, and that the present powers do not hold ultimate sovereignty.

Several core elements of the dynamics of strategic spiritual nonviolence can be identified from this brief outline. One is the importance of being strategic. Campaigns can be effective through responsive and escalating tactics. Moreover, strategic initiatives can be carefully crafted into a series of escalating campaigns. Second is the importance of speaking to the moral and the spiritual imaginations. Strategic nonviolence can expose the wide gaps in people's complacency with deep harms and their ultimate moral and sacred concerns. Campaigns can also highlight creative and compelling alternatives. Moral and sacred symbols can play a role in opening up this imagination. Third is the importance of dedication and even sacrifice in both persevering and in touching the moral and spiritual imaginations. Finally, there is the importance of discerning both social and spiritual dynamics. Sociological study has demonstrated the effectiveness of strategic nonviolence and helps identify effective tactics.[38] Spiritual practitioners have also explored these dynamics in light of their deepest faith concerns.[39]

What might this all mean for the climate movement? The climate movement faces a number of challenges. One is the increasingly fragmented nature of social movements, which makes coherence difficult. Another is that the climate movement has been overlaid upon existing environmental organizations, which have both considerable institutional strengths and weaknesses. The third challenge is that targets are slippery—energy systems are complex with multiple players—even if a few energy giants seem to rule the roost. Moreover, energy provision is not a direct evil in itself—people rely on it in their current daily lives. One cannot simply turn all of the lights off all of the time. Considering an effective strategy will entail significant conversation and discernment.

I will simply share a few reflections. One regards the potential of the movement to become strategically focused on key leverage points. The nonviolent struggles noted above were often quite strategic in building an escalating series of cohesive campaigns. Key leverage points were identified and focused upon. It is unclear that a genuine strategic vision has coalesced in the climate movement. Moreover, strategic nonviolent action has demonstrated a certain capacity to enable fundamental breakthroughs in terms of the character of social regimes and systems. We currently face the imperative to bring about a foundational commitment to the decarbonization of society. Systems theory suggests that breakthroughs are made in a nonlinear fashion. Concerted pressure is put on certain leverage points, while a new paradigm is being introduced. A phase shift in the system then becomes possible.[40] Strategic nonviolence is intended to accomplish this. How best to develop this strategic focus in the climate movement remains the question. Ganz's concept of "strategic capacity" seems pertinent to developing this focus.

Second, the examples of the peace and solidarity movements at the end of the Cold War are intriguing. These movements found effective ways to confront both localized exploitation and an existential global threat, while incorporating significant religious witness. The potential of spiritual nonviolence to resonate with the religious and moral concerns of our fellow people—even our current adversaries—has not been fully tapped. The potential for symbolic witness here may be one of the greatest opportunities for those of us who bring a faith commitment to this struggle. Yet we are reminded that religion is too often associated in the popular imagination with the wrong side of this struggle. Such a misalignment is nothing new. When deep injustice is deeply embedded there have often been those who use religion as a source of apology for the injustice. Many others find in their religion a source or solace that supports an easy accommodation to deep injustice. However, others find in their religion an imperative and an inspiration for abolishing a deep injustice. The struggles against slavery and then later against the segregation regime are pertinent examples. They were also struggles within religious formations over what true fidelity meant. Today, we too are called to witness in fidelity to a God of justice and mercy who has created and is creating a wide creation where all can flourish. And we are called to witness in a way that reflects God's just-mercy toward all.

CONCLUSION

Given the immensity of the climate crisis, it will take dedicated and disciplined approaches to confront this challenge. Four such approaches have been outlined here. The variety in these approaches enables a plurality of contributing roles that can complement each other. Some people might focus on one approach—and others may combine one or more of them. Strategic nonviolent action might be seen at the heart of the four. Such sustained action may be necessary to obtain national and global commitment to foregoing fossil fuels. The other three approaches, though, can play vital and complementary roles leading up to such a commitment. They, too, would play important roles in finding ways to implement such a commitment. Strategic nonviolence has been effective in fostering fundamental social breakthroughs in the past. However, social follow-through has often faltered. The holistic orientation offered here is intended to provide hope that we might find the way to make a commitment to take the necessary steps to stem the climate crisis and then follow through on this commitment in a just manner. For we have little hope without this hope and this hope is grounded in the Lord.

NOTES

1. I first encountered the locution "just mercy" as the title of the book by Bryan Stevenson on defending those on death row. See Bryan Stevenson, *Just Mercy: A Story of Justice and Redemption* (New York: Spiegel and Grau, 2014).

2. Mark Douglas, *Christian Pacifism for an Environmental Age* (Cambridge, UK: Cambridge University Press, 2019).

3. Ibid.

4. Larry L. Rasmussen, "Creation—Not for Sale," in *Eco-Reformation: Grace and Hope for a Planet in Peril*, eds. Lisa E. Dahill and James B. Martin-Schramm (Eugene, OR: Cascade Books, 2016), 33.

5. For a wonderful personal narrative of accompaniment work, see Lindsey Krinks, *Praying with Our Feet: Pursuing Justice and Healing on the Streets* (Grand Rapids, MI: Brazos Press, 2021).

6. Rachel Kaplan and Stephen Kaplan, "Preference, Restoration and Meaningful Action in the Context of Nearby Nature," in *Urban Place: Reconnecting to the Natural World*, ed. Peggy F. Bartlett (Cambridge, MA: MIT Press, 2005).

7. The Rutba House, ed. *Schools for Conversion: Twelve Marks of a New Monasticism* (Eugene, OR: Cascade Books, 2005).

8. Anthony Parel, *Gandhi's Philosophy and the Quest for Harmony* (Cambridge, UK: Cambridge University Press, 2006), 91.

9. Dorothy Day, *The Long Loneliness: The Autobiography of Dorothy Day* (New York: Curtis Books, 1952) and Dorothy Day, *Loaves and Fishes* (New York: Harper and Row, 1963).

10. Karl Meyer, "Nashville Greenlands," *The Catholic Worker* (May 2003).

11. Victor Machado, "Bioregionalism and the Catholic Worker Movement," in *Watershed Discipleship: Reinhabiting Bioregional Faith and Practice*, ed. Ched Myers (Eugene, OR: Cascade Books, 2016), 169.

12. The program is housed in the Board of Global Ministries of the United Methodist Church.

13. Richard Rohr, *Simplicity: The Art of Living* (New York: Crossroad, 1998).

14. Francis, *Encyclical Letter Laudato Si' of the Holy Father Francis on Care for our Common Home* (Vatican City: Libreria Editrice Vaticana, 2015).

15. Ernest Frederick Schumacher, *Small Is Beautiful: Economics as If People Mattered* (New York: Harper and Row, 1975).

16. John M. Perkins, ed. *Restoring At-Risk Communities: Doing It Together and Doing It Right* (Grand Rapids, MI: Baker Books, 1995).

17. Christopher Gunn and Hazel D. Gunn, *Reclaiming Capital: Democratic Initiatives and Community Development* (Ithaca, NY: Cornell University Press, 1991).

18. Thomas Princen, *The Logic of Sufficiency* (Cambridge, MA: MIT Press, 2005).

19. M. Paloma Pavel, *Breakthrough Communities: Sustainability and Justice in the Next American Metropolis* (Cambridge, MA: MIT Press, 2009).

20. Paul Hawken, *Drawdown: The Most Comprehensive Plan Ever Proposed to Reverse Global Warming* (New York: Penguin Books, 2017).

21. Grace Lee Boggs, *The Next American Revolution: Sustainable Activism for the Twenty-First Century* (Berkeley: University of California Press, 2011).

22. https://seedcommons.org/about-seed-commons/.

23. Manuel Castells, *The City and the Grassroots: A Cross-Cultural Theory of Urban Social Movements* (Berkeley: University of California Press, 1983).

24. Michael Mendez, *Climate Change from the Streets: How Conflict and Collaboration Strengthen the Environmental Justice Movement* (New Haven, CT: Yale University Press, 2020), 34–35.

25. On Ganz's concept of strategic capacity, see Marshall Ganz, *Why David Sometimes Wins: Leadership, Organization in the California Farm Worker Movement* (Oxford, UK: Oxford University Press, 2009), 10–18.

26. Mendez, *Climate Change*.

27. Erica Chenoweth and Maria J. Stephan, *Why Civil Resistance Works: The Strategic Logic of Nonviolent Conflict* (New York: Columbia University Press, 2011).

28. On Gandhi and satyagraha, see, for instance, Bidyut Chakrabarty, *Social and Political Thought of Mahatma Gandhi* (London: Routledge, 2005); and Judith Brown and Anthony Parel, eds., *The Cambridge Companion to Gandhi* (Cambridge, UK: Cambridge University Press, 2006).

29. Veena R. Howard, *Gandhi's Ascetic Activism: Renunciation and Social Action* (Albany, NY: SUNY Press, 2013).

30. James Carroll, *House of War: The Pentagon and the Disastrous Rise of American Power* (Boston: Houghton Mifflin, 2006); and Jonathan Schell, *The Unconquerable World: Power, Nonviolence, and the Will of the People* (New York: Henry Holt, 2003).

31. Ibid., 386.

32. Naomi Klein, *This Changes Everything: Capitalism vs. the Climate* (New York: Simon and Schuster, 2014).

33. Joan V. Bondurant, *Conquest of Violence: The Gandhian Philosophy of Conquest* (Princeton, NJ: Princeton University Press, 1958).

34. Srdja Popovic, *Blueprint for Revolution* (New York: Spiegel and Grau, 2015).

35. Richard B. Gregg, *The Power of Non-Violence* (Philadelphia: J. B. Lippincott Company, 1934).

36. Walter Wink, *The Powers That Be: Theology for a New Millennium* (New York: Galilee Doubleday, 1998).

37. Michael W. Sonnleitner, *Gandhian Nonviolence: Levels of Satyagraha* (New Delhi: Abhinav Publications, 1985).

38. See, for instance, Chenoweth and Stephan, *Why Civil Resistance Works*; and also Peter Ackerman and Jack Duvall, *A Force More Powerful: A Century of Nonviolent Conflict* (New York: Palgrave, 2000); and Gene Sharp, *Waging Nonviolent Struggle: 20th Century Practice and 21st Century Potential* (Boston: Porter Sargent Publishers, 2005).

39. John Dear, for instance, explores the dynamics of spiritual nonviolence and the climate crisis in John Dear, *They Will Inherit the Earth: Peace and Nonviolence in a Time of Climate Change* (Maryknoll, NY: Orbis Books, 2018).

40. Donella H. Meadows, *Thinking in Systems: A Primer* (White River Junction, VT: Chelsea Green Publishing, 2008).

REFERENCES

"About Seed Commons." https://seedcommons.org/about-seed-commons/.

Ackerman, Peter, and Jack Duvall. *A Force More Powerful: A Century of Nonviolent Conflict*. New York: Palgrave, 2000.

Boggs, Grace Lee. *The Next American Revolution: Sustainable Activism for the Twenty-First Century*. Berkeley: University of California Press, 2011.

Bondurant, Joan V. *Conquest of Violence: The Gandhian Philosophy of Conquest*. Princeton, NJ: Princeton University Press, 1958.

Brown, Judith, and Anthony Parel, eds. *The Cambridge Companion to Gandhi*. Cambridge, UK: Cambridge University Press, 2006.

Carroll, James. *House of War: The Pentagon and the Disastrous Rise of American Power*. Boston: Houghton Mifflin, 2006.

Castells, Manuel. *The City and the Grassroots: A Cross-Cultural Theory of Urban Social Movements*. Berkeley: University of California Press, 1983.

Chakrabarty, Bidyut. *Social and Political Thought of Mahatma Gandhi*. London: Routledge, 2005.
Chenoweth, Erica, and Maria J. Stephan. *Why Civil Resistance Works: The Strategic Logic of Nonviolent Conflict*. New York: Columbia University Press, 2011.
Day, Dorothy. *Loaves and Fishes*. New York: Harper and Row, 1963.
Day, Dorothy. *The Long Loneliness: The Autobiography of Dorothy Day*. New York: Curtis Books, 1952.
Dear, John. *They Will Inherit the Earth: Peace and Nonviolence in a Time of Climate Change*. Maryknoll, NY: Orbis Books, 2018.
Douglas, Mark. *Christian Pacifism for an Environmental Age*. Cambridge, UK: Cambridge University Press, 2019.
Francis. *Encyclical Letter Laudato Si' of the Holy Father Francis on Care for our Common Home*. Vatican City: Libreria Editrice Vaticana, 2015.
Ganz, Marshall. *Why David Sometimes Wins: Leadership, Organization in the California Farm Worker Movement*. Oxford, UK: Oxford University Press, 2009.
Gregg, Richard B. *The Power of Non-Violence*. Philadelphia: J. B. Lippincott Company, 1934.
Gunn, Christopher, and Hazel D. Gunn. *Reclaiming Capital: Democratic Initiatives and Community Development*. Ithaca, NY: Cornell University Press, 1991.
Hawken, Paul. *Drawdown: The Most Comprehensive Plan Ever Proposed to Reverse Global Warming*. New York: Penguin Books, 2017.
Howard, Veena R. *Gandhi's Ascetic Activism: Renunciation and Social Action*. Albany, NY: SUNY Press, 2013.
Kaplan, Rachel, and Stephen Kaplan. "Preference, Restoration and Meaningful Action in the Context of Nearby Nature." In *Urban Place: Reconnecting to the Natural World*, edited by Peggy F. Bartlett. Cambridge, MA: MIT Press, 2005.
Klein, Naomi. *This Changes Everything: Capitalism vs. the Climate*. New York: Simon and Schuster, 2014.
Krinks, Lindsey. *Praying with Our Feet: Pursuing Justice and Healing on the Streets*. Grand Rapids, MI: Brazos Press, 2021.
Machado, Victor. "Bioregionalism and the Catholic Worker Movement." In *Watershed Discipleship: Reinhabiting Bioregional Faith and Practice*, edited by Ched Myers. Eugene, OR: Cascade Books, 2016.
Meadows, Donella H. *Thinking in Systems: A Primer*. White River Junction, VT: Chelsea Green Publishing, 2008.
Mendez, Michael. *Climate Change from the Streets: How Conflict and Collaboration Strengthen the Environmental Justice Movement*. New Haven, CT: Yale University Press, 2020.
Meyer, Karl. "Nashville Greenlands." *The Catholic Worker* (May 2003).
Parel, Anthony. *Gandhi's Philosophy and the Quest for Harmony*. Cambridge, UK: Cambridge University Press, 2006.
Pavel, M. Paloma. *Breakthrough Communities: Sustainability and Justice in the Next American Metropolis*. Cambridge, MA: MIT Press, 2009.
Perkins, John M., ed. *Restoring At-Risk Communities: Doing It Together and Doing It Right*. Grand Rapids, MI: Baker Books, 1995.

Popovic, Srdja. *Blueprint for Revolution*. New York: Spiegel and Grau, 2015.

Princen, Thomas. *The Logic of Sufficiency*. Cambridge, MA: MIT Press, 2005.

Rasmussen, Larry L. "Creation—Not For Sale." In *Eco-Reformation: Grace and Hope for a Planet in Peril*, edited by Lisa E. Dahill and James B. Martin-Schramm. Eugene, OR: Cascade Books, 2016.

Rohr, Richard. *Simplicity: The Art of Living*. New York: Crossroad, 1998.

The Rutba House, ed. *Schools for Conversion: Twelve Marks of a New Monasticism*. Eugene, OR: Cascade Books, 2005.

Schell, Jonathan. *The Unconquerable World: Power, Nonviolence, and the Will of the People*. New York: Henry Holt, 2003.

Schumacher, Ernest Frederick. *Small Is Beautiful: Economics as If People Mattered*. New York: Harper and Row, 1975.

Sharp, Gene. *Waging Nonviolent Struggle: 20th Century Practice and 21st Century Potential*. Boston: Porter Sargent Publishers, 2005.

Sonnleitner, Michael W. *Gandhian Nonviolence: Levels of Satyagraha*. New Delhi: Abhinav Publications, 1985.

Stevenson, Bryan. *Just Mercy: A Story of Justice and Redemption*. New York: Spiegel and Grau, 2014.

Wink, Walter. *The Powers That Be: Theology for a New Millennium*. New York: Galilee Doubleday, 1998.

Chapter 11

Distorted Imagination
Land, Food, and Economies

Tim Van Meter

Each day people make small decisions shaping their engagement with larger global ecological issues. These decisions are often loaded with ethical, moral, and theological weight. The mission and context of the Methodist Theological School in Ohio (MTSO) has reshaped public theological questions about food, labor, and human participation in challenging our contemporary ecological destruction. This chapter seeks to detail how campus changes have impacted the voices welcomed to the practices of theological, ethical, and moral decision making in relation to food, land, and farmers.

The MTSO campus was founded in the 1950s on seventy-eight acres of former apple orchard.[1] The campus space in 2009 consisted of about twenty wooded acres, fourteen buildings sitting on twenty-five plus acres, a small pond, about fifteen to twenty acres of fields that were mowed, sprayed, and maintained as grass, as well as other smaller outdoor areas. The campus was groomed to look like the ideal for higher-education campuses throughout the United States.

In my third year of teaching at the MTSO, I designed and taught a course on ecology and religious education. We explored connections between theology, ecology, education, and the land. As part of this course, we read short articles on the concept of the commons, the American addiction to lawns, landscaping, architecture, and the ideals of higher education in addition to longer theological and agrarian texts. Once a month, we took a long walk around our campus and talked about how our school's decisions concerning land and buildings either supported or undercut our mission and declared values. Questions included, "How are we placing our imprint on this land?"; "What myths and tropes are we imitating?"; and "Where do we model transformation and sustainability in our land use?" I would stand in the middle of large, mowed fields and ask students, "How much are we spending to grow grass as our primary outdoor context?"; "How can we reimagine replacing this mono crop with a sustainable or generative land practice?"; "How do we create spaces modeling our commitments to change the world and create communities of faithful change?"; and "How are we in relationship with other creatures we share this space with?"

After teaching the course a couple of times, I began to explore with a group of students and alumni the idea of starting a small intentional community. We explored purchasing land and forming a cooperative for deeper engagement with food, craft, and land. We met several times, searching for shared commitments and beginning to construct a rule for life together. After a few meetings, we did an honest survey of our financial status and realized our cumulative student debt limited our ability to buy land and have the funds to begin the project. We left our discernment together having rethought our understandings of community and possibilities for cooperative action without any place to practice. At about this time, the school president began to think about the possibilities on our campus for starting a farm. I resisted, believing that once an idea is subsumed into an institution, the rules and policies of the institution reshape the vision. During the courses, I'd encourage students to go to the president and dean to lodge complaints about conventional campus land practices. These students were persistent in their requests that we stop spraying, mowing, and so forth, and seek new ways to go forward with an ecological vision. Eventually, I supported the president's desire to start the farm and continue to fully support this initiative. It is easy for a faculty person to stir up interest in a creative, justice-oriented project; it is much rarer to have an administrator who is willing to carry that project to a board of trustees and fight for its implementation from conception to something better than the original vision.

Seminary Hill Farm began in early 2014 with the cultivation of five acres, the building of two eighty-foot by forty-foot hoop houses, and the planting of about 140 varieties of vegetables and fruits for organic production. The farm has since grown to twelve plus acres in rotational, organic production, thirty-two eighty-inch by eight-foot covered beds, bees, and a glass greenhouse in addition to the hoop houses. We have experimented with chickens and a variety of growing practices. Seminary Hill Farm is a teaching facility for local and regional organic farming groups and is currently expanding its educational efforts with young farmers. In 2019, the school purchased an additional eleven acres adjacent to its campus, extending the reach of the farm and its hospitality into the future.

When the farm began, the MTSO committed to preparing and serving local, humane, organic food for on campus meals and large events. Approximately

85 to 90 percent of all food prepared and served by our dining hall is local, humane, and organic. This decision to partner with other local farms and serve locally grown food established the dining hall as a central gathering place for students, faculty, staff, and ecological partners. We support a network of small local farms seeking sustainable thriving for all.

The farm served as the catalyst sparking a larger commitment to partnership with other organizations and institutions working to increase the resilience within local food systems. It also led to other sustainability initiatives on campus, including solar electric panels for administrative and classroom buildings, geothermal wells for heating and cooling, sustainable landscaping, prairie restoration, natural cleaning products, and a reputation that led the Ohio State University's Institute for Food and AgriCultural Transformation (InFACT) to elevate our work as an example for sustainable institutional vision and a key example for a short local food chain.

The sustainability initiatives and, particularly, our agricultural work have shifted my understanding of the research questions underlying faithfully informed relationships to food, land, and climate change. An obvious place of revisioning is the significant difference between offering a student experience through a campus garden and the more substantive institutional shifts occurring by fully engaging a holistic local food system through a working campus farm. While the commitment to organic agriculture is different on twelve acres than it is on a two-thousand-square-foot plot, it is the larger commitments to small farmers, local agriculture (rural and urban), and working to engage communities seeking to thrive and overthrow racist structures underlying food apartheid that set our work apart.

The course that initiated discussions about starting a farm began as the way to bring a minimal opening for ecology into our theological curriculum. When I first proposed a religion and ecology course, faculty colleagues responded that I could teach a religious education course, but not a theology course. I could shape it around ecology, but climate change was too narrow and not very interesting. At the same time I was teaching the course, I was speaking in churches about ecology and climate change. The challenge I faced in these contexts was the politicization of climate change, particularly in religious and farming communities. Questions focused through food and land stewardship were a way to start conversations with farmers and rural people who either denied climate change or understood it as something that did not affect their lives.

There are several key partnerships our work with the land and food have opened. One is with Reverend Heber Brown of the Black Church Food Security Network. Dr. Brown founded an organization committed to leading people of color toward greater food sovereignty. He sees food apartheid as an organizing structure of industrial food, diminishing the possibility of thriving for people of color. This is a radically different idea from that underlying the church's response of charity and from that underlying the industry's support of food banks for addressing hunger in food-insecure neighborhoods. Dr. Brown's work seeks to threaten and overturn the structural underpinnings of racist food policies, intentional and benign.[2]

The campus farm and its ecological practices have offered a nascent space for learning. It has become a place of inquiry and imperfect practice. We have invited scholars and activists to campus for three-day retreats called Seminary Hill colloquies. In these, we have attempted to limit the voices of those who bear the most privilege and open space for voices coerced into silence through unexamined values and imposed limitations. In these colloquies, we have explored the destructive structures linking ecological devastation, racism, genocide of indigenous peoples, and the extractive practices forced upon land and bodies. These conversations have been important for renewal and for opening possibilities for alliances. This practice was interrupted by the COVID-19 pandemic and funding challenges, though there is possibility for renewal. What has arisen from the colloquies is an invitation into the womanist insight that theology is a practice of diverse community.[3] Another is that attention to soil as foundation for understanding land or place opens space for hopeful, renewing engagement with creatures and plants that live through the life of soil. A third is that abundance is at the heart of ecological theology. Each of these openings offers significant space for deeper theological work by the gathered community.

The farm's function as a catalyst also changed institutional dynamics, refocusing how the MTSO understands its place in the world of theological education. Our practices engaging larger questions from a lens of regenerative agriculture have revealed that, often, our questions are too small and our solutions too narrow. We can't speak of a vision for food justice arising out of our commitments without exploring the underlying economic, political, and ethical "solutions" that undercut small farmers and support corporate hegemony. We began to engage questions about food security or access with urban and rural partners. Food banks, community-supported agriculture, and other contemporary easy solutions were inadequate in addressing the systemic structures that undercut possibilities for thriving of people and land. The economic systems privileging industrial agriculture are supported by easy solutions and "realistic" ideas for problems while avoiding exposing broken systems and necrophilic structures. Our farm opened possibilities to think together more carefully about how our commitments to food and wellness could shift long-term relationships with local communities as embodied prophetic partners alongside marginalized peoples, faith communities, educational institutions, and eco-justice organizations.

Colleagues at the Ohio State University and members of InFACT began to meet on our campus and raise us up as a leader in institutional commitments to local food. We entered conversations with a regional coalition of liberal arts universities seeking to shift their commitments to sustainability through campus food sourcing. Our shared commitments to local food and the transformation of farming from extraction to sustainability opened new possibilities for rethinking theological education. We also found that these commitments became internal spaces for conflict, triangulation, and passive resistance to change.

The farm has led us toward intersectional questions as elements in our practice of theological education. Early in the life of the farm we might have asked the following: Can we grow food that models our commitments to sustainability in relation to the places we inhabit? Can we grow food without harming our neighbors, specifically other small farms? As we began to live within the agricultural systems at the heart of farming in North America, questions were revised to include: Who grows food on local and larger scales and who profits from the consumer's food dollars? Who owns land and who works on the land? Who controls the distribution of food from farm to table? We've learned multiple ways that the industrial food complex misleads consumers, from bucolic packaging on factory-farmed meat to the green gaslighting of fake meat funded by major, industrial, agricultural conglomerates. We also learned that growing vegetables, grains, and pulses on an industrial level contains massive extractive costs for land and public health. All ecological solutions that place profits in the hands of the industrial food industry, which is committed to extractive practices, are damaging to the earth. There is no sustainable long-term possibility for people, communities, and our planet to thrive through extractive farming, which relies on fossil fuels, artificial fertilizers, and industrial agricultural conglomerates.

Through our practices, the question, "Who Grows Your Food?" has moved from being a catchy slogan for local food to being a significant economic and ecological question. Shifting power in the food system from a few global conglomerates to a sustainable model that builds resilience in local economies is the only path toward a sustainable future. Eaters are consistently gaslighted to cede their food dollars to the industrial food industry through myths perpetrated around the "green revolution" as a foundation for expanding extractive agricultural practices. In fact, smallholder farmers, defined as farming fewer than five hectares, produce more edible food, with a greater diversity of crops, while maintaining a greater ecological health and species diversity than do large industrial farms.[4] The local farmer is able to limit climate gas emissions and, in many instances, increase soil fertility and sequester carbon through regenerative grazing and integrative growing practices. The most important climate change decision available to most of us is not which diet is best, but who gets our food dollars. In the United States, privileged consumers can choose to pay a bit more to support farmers who facilitate a holistic balance of cover crops, animal inputs, crop rotation, and additional practices that privilege soil health over production. Consumers can also choose to support urban growers and organizations promoting food sovereignty for people who are forced to purchase calories from the industrial hunger system. Prioritizing soil health, community wellness, nutrient-rich food, smallholder farms, and community food sovereignty undermines the industrial food system. Reenvisioning our systems for food production through local lenses, in opposition to the corporate green-revolution lens, can increase biodiversity and community health.[5] Climate, labor, and food activists should see the small regenerative farmer as a core partner for biophilic, sustainable change.

We realized early in our farm's history that we have power that can either help to build or harm the local food system in our communities.[6] On our farm, farmers have health insurance, a pension plan, and a living wage. These are benefits that most small farmers do not have. At the very onset of our farm, it was important that we contract with local farmers to purchase the food we serve in our dining hall and at our events in support of our local food system. Our school dining hall quickly became known as providing an incredible farm-to-table dining experience. Colleagues at the Ohio State University promoted our work as an example of remarkably short distances in our campus food chain. One key supplier is our own farm, and there are just about one hundred meters from our farm to wash and prep to the kitchen. An additional fifteen to twenty-five farms we have regularly purchased from are within fifty miles. We make decisions with our food dollars to support farmers who are building soils, growing healthy food, and engaging in holistic, organic farming practices.

At the 2017 American Academy of Religion in Boston, I sat in on several religion and ecology sessions at which the topic of the food served at the annual conference was the primary topic of discussion. This group wanted to influence the professional organization to adopt food-sourcing principles taking ecological challenges, like climate change, as a core underlying concern. The majority of people present sought to exclude all meat with a strong moral stance that meat was the primary problem, a stance with evidence if meat is industrially sourced. In one session, participants were asked to brainstorm on how to shift the food served to a more sustainable vision. I brought up the possibility of working with caterers who sourced from local farms. This was understood by many to not be possible. The explanation given was that convention centers have contracts that require using their food service without regard to sourcing. The conversation quickly turned to offering only vegetarian and vegan options. We sat in Boston, in November, eating cantaloupe, carrots, cauliflower, celery, strawberries, and other foods along with ranch dressing or a sugary dipping sauce while many in the room argued against any form of locally sourced meat and winter vegetables. We actively participated in supporting a form of green gaslighting supported by industrial food suppliers while many maintained a sense of ethical and moral high ground.

The argument for a plant-based diet has some important elements to consider, and I support anyone who commits to vegan or vegetarian food. However, when the foods in a plant-based diet are purchased from an industrial food supplier, following this diet supports the industrial commitments responsible for the agricultural climate gases.[7] Industrial agriculture is immoral, or at best amoral, while contributing to the destruction of the planet. It is propped up by its use of fossil fuels for growing and transporting food; manufacture of industrial chemicals to artificially enhance production; grotesque practices in factory farming animals; and destroying soils by the application of artificial fertilizers, herbicides, and pesticides as well as other chemical addictions supporting extractive methods.[8] Industrial agriculture has broken the pattern established over thousands of years of using holistic practices to build soil fertility through animal and plant relationships. Industrial and corporate farms break mutually beneficial relationships to deplete soils, requiring artificially created multiple harmful waste streams, promoted as agricultural best modern practices leading a green revolution to feed the world. Vegetarian or vegan diets and partnering with farmers building soil through regenerative practices can be a significant step in supporting local and regional agriculture in resistance to global conglomerates.

Unfortunately, these dietary choices are often perceived as silver-bullet responses addressing climate change. In a 2022 study,[9] vegan and vegetarian diets were found to increase the power of industrial farming at the expense of small farmers. Philip Howard of Michigan State University tracks the concentration of ownership within the industrial food complex.[10] His research illustrates the messiness of the simple dietary solutions that declare that veganism is the most effective way to shift human participation in climate change. Global food conglomerates, such as Tyson, Cargill, ADM, and a few others, control the majority of food produced for consumption in North America and Europe. Depending on the types of foods, these corporations can hold as much as 80 to 90 percent of the total market share for cereals, produce, and proteins. This extensive research offers some insight into the economic systems that punish small farmers while privileging corporate owners. Activists ethically opposing the factory farming of animals by Cargill, ADM, or other entities contribute to the same entities' bottom lines when they advocate for the forms of fake meat these same corporations are heavily invested in.[11] In other words, the industrial food system does not care about the ethics of a particular diet as long as it is able to capture the majority of consumers' food dollars.

A 2021 study from the Food and Water Institute in partnership with *The Guardian* news organization found that consolidation within food processing and distribution has increased over the past decade. "The consolidation runs deep: four firms or fewer controlled at least 50% of the market for 79% of grocery items . . . Ninety three percent of the sodas we drink are owned by just three companies. The same goes for 73% of the breakfast cereals we eat—despite the shelves stacked with different boxes."[12] This illusion of choice is destructive to farms and especially small farmers.

This illusion of choice extends to diets that celebrate the possibility of fake meat solving climate change. The corporations developing fake meats do not have a practice of independent verification of claims or allowing independent researchers to collect data. Manufacture of fake meats, as an industrial process, is more carbon intensive than are regenerative practices that sequester carbon in soils through holistic grazing and organic growing practices. The choice should never be between industrial meat and fake meat, but between regenerative local practices that include meat and industrial, extractive practices that strip life from soils for industrial produce, industrial meat, grains, commodity crops or pea protein (a core ingredient of fake meat). Placing meat-based diets in opposition to plant-based diets, both with industrial sources, is similar to placing coal in opposition to natural gas in the area of energy production. In both cases, both choices are damaging to the long-term health of planet and people, one choice is only slightly less bad, not a sustainable solution.

In June 2022, the US Environmental Protection Agency and the US Department of Agriculture released a report that found that agriculture contributed 11.2 percent of total US climate gases in 2020. This estimate is in line with the United Nations report, which found agriculture is responsible for between 9 and 11 percent of greenhouse gases in the period of 2015–2020. Total agricultural contributions include methane, nitrous oxide as well as carbon dioxide. Our institutional commitments place us in the midst of the conversations about how best to respond to the agricultural contributions to human-driven climate change. There are problematic easy answers at the front of cultural and religious conversations surrounding moral responses to climate change and solutions contributing to thriving for all life. One proposition has been to eliminate meat from our service and only serve vegan or vegetarian food. This has been an ongoing discussion for how our dining service should function. I continue to advocate for serving meat from small farmers where we know both their commitment to humane animal practices and to building the quality of their soils.

There are good reasons to radically shift how animals are understood in the food system. Incomplete ethical and moral statements about the right way to eat or the ethics of plant-based diets are inadequate frameworks for making moral judgements to save the world.[13] However, many of our food decisions place a moral and economic burden on others while ceding food production and distribution to industrial systems. Recent examples include the significant, and well-placed, outrage at the vulnerability of workers in the meatpacking industry, such as those working in chicken and pork processing plants in the Midwest during the pandemic, tying their working conditions to meat in a person's diet. I'm in agreement that industrial agriculture practices of industrial slaughter, industrial meat processing, and centralized animal-feeding operations (CAFOs) result in exploitation of workers, animals, and farmers. Industrial farming, in all forms, is exploitive; the vegetables on our tables that are purchased from large producers exploit workers, land, and farmers. The Coalition of Immokalee workers and other farmworker collectives reported that field workers had higher rates of COVID-19 exposure and illness than those in the meatpacking plants.[14] Exploitation is at the core of our industrial food system.

There are better ways to join in solidarity for food security and sovereignty through cooperative models. Our work with farms, farmers, growing food, and connecting with urban and rural communities to address food apartheid supports linking dietary choices with commitments to small local farms and local cooperatives offering the greatest health for people, animals, soil, and shared vocation. Our farm and food commitments have problematized other ethical and moral considerations. We have commitments to fair wages and benefits for those who work on the farm and in the kitchen. Our institutional privileges allow us to provide to our workers what isn't possible for small farmers. In a recent survey of Ohio farmers, the major stresses undercutting farmers' ability to thrive on their land included the cost of land, the cost of health insurance, market prices, and environmental regulation.[15] All are key areas that threaten the viability of farms and farmers. All of these areas are mitigated in our context by the nature of our institution. Our job isn't to celebrate our exceptions but to work closely with farmers and farm organizations to seek solutions that work for farmers. Can we free up church land for small farm starts? Can we work with denominations to start farm incubators in failed camp properties rather than sell them for development? How might we work with clinics and hospitals founded by churches to offer possibilities for enhanced health care for farmers and farmworkers? These are partners that have worked to remain outside of solutions as they seek profits over care, but a new vision is possible.

These are my neighbors, people that would find the external conversation about what to grow and how to grow it on their farms as offensive as any other intrusion into their lives. Our work has increased my empathy for neighbors that I have little politically, culturally, or spiritually in common with. However, I share their grief over and frustration with a life constrained by systemic biases that undercut our shared thriving while turning us against each other rather than seeking shared solutions for a renewed world.

Soon after the 2016 presidential election, I went to dinner with friends from the university where I earned my graduate degrees. The group was organized by a close friend who hung in with me during my exams and dissertation, a grace that I cherish. One of the people I didn't know as well as others began to talk about how "country ass-backwards" people had screwed the country. He stated that the best thing that could happen would be for rural areas to go bankrupt so that "those people" could move to the city and receive a proper education and "learn about diversity." Others at the table nodded assent or remained in embarrassed silence. I asked about the monetary support for Trump from wealthy people the speaker would find more acceptable, such as his peers in technology. He declared tech as the savior as they developed artificial intelligence and robotic farming as alternatives to people living their lives in relationship to their land. I looked into my beer and had kind thoughts for my rural friends as he dove deeper into the hatred of people he knew nothing about who he blamed for a problem about which he had limited understanding.

I admit, I identify strongly with country ass-backwards people; they have been my people since birth. This identification has become even stronger since I've had the privilege of entering agricultural spaces through our farm. I find myself often defending the existence of my neighbors in response to anti-rural prejudices of learned colleagues. Wendell Berry has written extensively on how cosmopolitan worldviews and predatory economic structures have supported deep-seated prejudices against smallholder farmers and subsequently supported the collapse of small farms and rural communities. The underlying privileging of the city over the rural at the heart of twentieth-century worldviews also supports the destructive practices of industrial agriculture. More food, cheaper prices, and easy access devalue the craft and practices at the center of the human arts of agriculture. The result may ultimately be the end of human craft, stewardship, and practice in relation to food production and other areas that gave rise to the ideas of human culture.

Anti-rural values are easy to see in neoliberal capitalism, but they also underlie Marxist understandings. In these manifestations, the land and agriculture are a romantic fetish, but production and extraction are elevated over craft. The use of farms as a punishment for the intellectual classes did not elevate the respect of rural craft and location-based knowledge. Massive missteps like the disaster of the Aral Sea arose out of a centralized unreal projection for production onto land, water, and the false promises of industrial agriculture in a socialist system.[16]

Environmental philosopher and educator C. A. Bowers wrote a series of critical essays exploring the limits of contemporary political worldviews and educational practices for constructing sustainable cultures. He critiques the unexamined commitments to the myth of infinite progress as essential understanding dooming capitalism and socialism as ineffective systems for addressing the challenges faced in an ecologically challenged world.[17] This is an area very new to my own understanding and research. I point the reader toward critical agrarian theory, which seeks to critique Marxist understandings of the peasant class as inadequate for understanding rural people and their diversity in the participation of creating human cultures.[18] In an essay introducing critical agrarian theory as a response to the limits of peasant studies and Marxism in general, Wolford and Edelman establish the need for this area of study by exploring the limits of Marxism in addressing the realities of rural peoples.[19] These limits include resisting the separation of nature and culture at the foundation of Marx's thought.[20] Referencing Raymond Williams,[21] Edelman and Wolford establish the need for a new critical vision that allows for urban and rural relationship as a foundation for reimagining a shared future. Our imagining of human and more-than-human relationship begins, alongside the Yahwist author of Genesis, in the soil.

Critical agrarianism, like other forms of critical discourse, engages the structural underpinnings of marginalized peoples and seeks to remake power in forms that open space for all to thrive. Human thriving is not a large enough ecological vision within this theoretical framework; thriving is a desire for soil and all that relies upon it for life. Establishing critical agrarian thought, at its beginning, as a framework for exploring the "'life of the soil' with increasing nuance, an issue particularly relevant in the age of what has been called the Anthropocene where changes are taking place, whether because of exogenous climatic conditions or because of more terrestrial designs for development"[22] opens a space for deeper imagination for economic, political, and theological thought that begins with the soil.

It is this place of my work, the work of our ecologically reimagined campus, and the foundations of theological reenvisioning open space for deeper reflections. It all begins in soil, for shared visions renewing of culture, nature, theology as well as reimagining the political, economic, and religious systems sustaining shared life. The Common English Bible articulates this in Genesis 2. The translator brings the text back to its agrarian roots when God calls the human into being by breathing life into soil: "the Lord God formed the human from the topsoil of the fertile land and blew life's breath into his nostrils. The human came to life. The Lord God planted a garden in Eden in the east and put there the human (God) had formed."[23]

There has been excellent theological work[24] in agrarian philosophy and theological imagination. This work takes a deeper meaning in a contextual retrieval of soil as a partnering living entity rather than understood as an empty substance waiting for humans, animals, or plants to bring life. Reflections on the web-of-life–sustaining forests and rangelands state clearly that the diversity of life found in the soil far exceeds that rooted in soils or crawling, walking, flying, or otherwise relying on forest or grasslands for their own existence.[25] Early research[26] is finding similar benefits for lands grazed with regenerative practices, such as White Oak Pastures in Bluffton, Georgia. There, it was found that farmers are sequestering more carbon in their soil than they are producing through their beef, lamb, pork, and chicken, from birth through harvest.[27] Caney Fork Farms in Carthage, Tennessee,[28] Fox Hollow Farm Naturally in Fredericktown, Ohio,[29] and Sister Grove Farm in Grayson County, Texas,[30] are renewing land through regenerative practices in their particular places. Additional research from the Rodale Institute,[31] Savory Global,[32] and other regenerative research stations are finding the necessity of animals as partners for shifting toward carbon sequestration as a signature of agricultural solutions rather than agriculture as the primary problem producing greenhouse gases. The commitment to grazing animals as part of a holistic system brings back into balance the browsing behavior of ruminants prior to the introduction of industrial meat production. The renewed pastures are building soils that teem with life. The pastures host an interdependent web of fungi, bacteria, protozoa, plants, and animals.

Theodore Hiebert writes of the Yahwist's vision of life partnering with God in writing Genesis. Lord God breathes into fertile soil as the initial moment of human being. It is the human as cultivator as well as born out of soil that Hiebert understands as inspiring the writer of Genesis to put into words the holistic vision at the beginning.[33] In this garden, human and animal partner in vocation for the cultivation of soil and all that grows upon it. All have been placed in creative interrelationship for the desired thriving of all life. I'm not certain that we can perceive the creative possibilities without placing our hands in soil and working alongside our fellow creatures.

A theological vision for creaturely thriving starting in soil understands the stewarding of sustainable relationship to Creation and fellow creatures as essential work. Aldo Leopold's ethical framing for engaging ecological challenges states, "A thing is right when it tends to preserve the integrity, stability, and beauty of the biotic community. It is wrong when it tends otherwise."[34] This idea is at the core of Leopold's move into a relational ethics for ecological engagement with land and our fellow creatures. Leopold came to this idea through a lifetime learning about the interactions of biotic communities within their ecological contexts. Though a farm is a constructed entity, it is dependent on the land, neighbors, fellow creatures, crops, and other plant and animal life. A healthy farm will include soil bursting with life, both seen and unseen. Let's return to the image of the holy breathing life into fertile topsoil. The Yahwist's understanding of Lord God is that of a Creator breathing life for the human into living soil. While the Yahwist's understanding of the diversity of life found in fertile soil might not be as rich as what is now understood by those engaging in regenerative farming practices, it is a foundational metaphor for the interconnected hermeneutic essential for reimagining the human in earth relationship.

Leopold's land ethic opens the possibility that life and death are included in the understanding of systemic thriving. I propose that the labor of animals within the holistic vision of a small farm allows for them to fully live into their being by harvesting sunlight while grazing on pasture, depositing nitrogen, phosphorous, and other nutrients in their waste, and contributing to the health of people and fellow animals through their humane death. This understanding of animals as co-laborers with farm and land to construct soils and wellness for all will require a massive reduction in meat consumption. Wendell Berry speaks of this relationship as sacred in "The Gift of Good Land," an essay he writes to build a biblical understanding of the relationship of land and the work of the farmer. He calls for humility in relationship to this gift, to be humble before the land and those who have stewarded the land before the current inhabitant. He also calls for a gratitude and neighborliness, knowing that caring for land requires living into neighborly relationship with other humans and fellow creatures. He also seeks a depth of relationship with mortality. It is an illusion and possibly hubris to believe that anyone can live in relation to our world without committing harm. Berry writes, "we depend upon other creatures and survive by their deaths. To live, we must daily break the body and shed the blood of Creation. When we do this knowingly, lovingly, skillfully, reverently, it is a sacrament. When we do it ignorantly, greedily, clumsily, destructively, it is a desecration. In such desecration we condemn ourselves to spiritual and moral loneliness, and others to want."[35] It is this care for sacred relationship that is broken in industrial agriculture alongside the human reverence for death and life of their fellow creatures and their own.

Any academic paper or presentation responding to our ecological reality must begin with and remain engaged with lament. We are all mired in intellectual commitments, theories, and assumptions that contribute to our end. David Orr prophetically warns that the "crisis we face is first and foremost one of mind, perception, and values; hence, it is a challenge to those institutions presuming to shape minds, perceptions, and values. There isn't a problem with education; the problem is education."[36] His argument isn't to end education but to ally it with the health of the earth rather than the values that are debilitating our shared planet. There is so little space for constructing visionary hope. Agrarian thought is deeply immersed in myths of whiteness, as demonstrated in the sources privileged in this short paper. These primary voices have to be addressed, critiqued, and reframed to make room for those who have both come before settler myths and especially those working to rebuild a world outside those myths. It is one of the attractive elements of critical agrarianism, it is shaped from the beginning by diverse voices from people of the soil critiquing the myths of progress and the myths of the gentle farmer. It is a voice to invite into the room of theological reflection.

I see the above as hints toward a theology, economics, and possible politics arising out of a vision reshaped through regenerative practices in a particular place with embedded, embodied communities. However, I side with any reader who sees the above as inadequate theological construction trapped in narrow worldviews. My narrow intellectual training and physical reality constrain possibilities for hopeful engagement with our ecological realities. I am writing as a white man with all the privileges of an academic middle-class existence. I write from the privilege of an education that is not offered to many. I would hold that this education offers more limitations than possibilities, particularly in trying to address our ecological reality for a possible future of abundance and creaturely thriving. It is the limitations of academic formation and unexamined spiritualities that I fear may be at the heart of comfort with necrophilic structures underlying our parasitic agricultural, industrial, political, and economic systems, which are supported through extractive practices. It is fair to assess our current systems as shaped by a cultural denial of death,[37] and ongoing commitments to comfort deny solidarity and deep relationship with those destroyed to maintain the illusions of progress.

I write acknowledging that a theological construct essential for any sustainable future is hope. In our culture, it is often a cheap practice colonized by the principalities and powers it must resist. I propose that a theological construction opening toward hope must first acknowledge the deep grief at the heart of anyone paying attention. Leopold understands that one of the penalties of ecological knowledge is that a person "lives alone in a world of wounds."[38] I also posit that the infection of predatory economic systems, like capitalism and what has been called "actually existing socialisms,"[39] underlies our economic imagination. In a similar way, contemporary Christianity is an expression poisoned by over a thousand years of marching beside conquerors and colonizers. It is a time for extending the conversation and staying silent in rooms that offer wisdom outside of our governing paradigms. Hope is not something observed or created through the discovery of a silver-bullet technology or diet. Hope is a moral and ethical decision each person makes each day. It is in the small decisions to live toward hope and in deep gratitude for abundance in relationship that humans can begin to mend their relation to our devastated world.

The reflection and practices framed by Seminary Hill Farm at the MTSO must go further. While we have marched with the Immokalee workers for justice, we must move from witness toward justice and construct, in community, a vision for farmworkers shaped by a commitment to wellness and abundance. A critical agrarian perspective holds strong positions for the rights of farmworkers, including smallholder farmers, as well as the desire for plants and animals to thrive within and adjacent to a holistic farm. A regenerative farm is not defined by production of goods, services, or labor. It is an agricultural organism where the farmer seeks to maximize the contributions of all plants and animals to the continuing health and building of soil. Industrial agricultural practices view soil as a medium for amending and extraction of food, not as a living entity upon which all life depends. A critical agrarian perspective places health of soil, water, and air as fundamental values that allow for the thriving of human and more-than-human communities.

I have trusted friends seeking new economic structures through a Christian socialist lens. I am resistant to moving into this economic and political camp. Not because I believe that predatory capitalism can be reformed or has anything much to offer, but because the economic and political visions of socialism, capitalism, Marxism, and other economic and political worldviews conceived without consideration of the limits of resources have no future in a diminished earth. We need theological, political, and economic imagination grounded in Leopold's land ethic and the renewable abundance found in healthy soils, water, and air. An ecological economy includes cooperative models for human thriving but also holds space for cooperation with the more-than-human world. I believe a key next question is the following: What is the vocation of animals and plants in a healing and healthy ecosystem that allows for the possibilities for all life to thrive?

Additional questions need to be held up for long-term contemplation and communal theological reflection. These might include the following: Can human society give up myths of endless human progress and economic growth as a measure of cultural success? Can we elevate health of soil and overall planetary health as the foundation for sustainability and the minimum for ecological engagement? Can creaturely and planetary thriving be centered as the foundation for understanding our political, religious, and spiritual existence? How might every person and our institutions serve as stewards of soil, air, and water? Might we emulate regenerative farmers who enter each season with a desire to build greater soil fertility and farm resilience than that achieved previously? Can our economic systems include metrics centering planetary limits as boundaries for imagining thriving for all life?

Our farm is opening contextual reflective spaces that differ from the manicured campuses common in higher education. It is central to our identity and for theological learning, research, and practice for faculty and students. It is integrated into our tables of hospitality and, increasingly, in our contexts for learning. When colleagues ask what I'm working on or what I've published, my honest answer is that the scholarly work I am most excited about is the community-written texts of Seminary Hill Farm at the MTSO. Come and see, walk with us, sit down in gratitude for food grown by farmers you have met, and leave choosing to live into hope for another day.

NOTES

1. An additional twelve acres were purchased in 2019, to extend the ecological work when an adjacent farm became available.
2. Black Church Food Security Network, https://blackchurchfoodsecurity.net.
3. Dr. Melanie Harris of Wake Forest University Divinity School has been an important conversation partner in shaping these conversations.
4. V. Ricciardi, N. Ramankutty, Z. Mehrabi, L. Jarvis, B. Chookolingo, "How Much of the World's Food Do Smallholders Produce?" *Global Food Security* 17 (2018): 64–72.
5. M. E. Menconi, S. Giordano, D. Grohman, "Revisiting Global Food Production and Consumption Patterns by Developing Resilient Food Systems for Local Communities," *Land Use Policy* 119 (2022).
6. adrienne maree brown, "Emergent Strategy: Shaping Change, Changing Worlds," Compassionate Communities Conference, 2017, lecture, accessed June 9, 2022, https://youtu.be/h-sCy8SzvHY.
7. IPES-Food, "The Politics of Protein: Examining Claims about Livestock, Fish, 'Alternative Proteins' and Sustainability," 2022, www.ipes-food.org
8. I want to state clearly, industrial agriculture, particularly animal agriculture with centralized animal-feeding operations as a profit maximizing tool, is morally and ethically irredeemable.
9. IPES-Food, "The Politics of Protein," 2022.
10. Philip H. Howard, *Concentration and Power in the Food System: Who Controls What We Eat?* rev. ed. (London: Bloomsbury Academic, 2021), accessed July 12, 2022, http://dx.doi.org/10.5040/9781350183100.
11. Philip H. Howard and Mary K. Hendrickson, "The State of Concentration in Global Food and Agriculture Industries," in *Transformation of Our Food Systems: The Making of a Paradigm Shift* (Bochum, Germany: Zukunftsstiftung Landwirtschaft [Foundation on Future Farming], 2020), 89–91.
12. Nina Lakhani, Aliya Uteuova, and Alvin Chang, "Revealed: the True Extent of America's Food Monopolies, and Who Pays the Price," *The Guardian* (July 14, 2021), https://www.theguardian.com/environment/ng-interactive/2021/jul/14/food-monopoly-meals-profits-data-investigation.
13. IPES-Food, "The Politics of Protein," 2022.
14. Peer-reviewed published research is sparse at the time of writing. Substantiating exposure will be important for further research. For the purposes of this paper,

I want to underscore that the privileging of one form of exploitive agricultural labor over another exploitive form of agricultural labor challenges the claim that a plant-based industrial diet is an ecological good.

15. "Health Care and Weather Distressing Farmers," The Ohio State University, College of Food, Agricultural, and Environmental Sciences, accessed June 21, 2022, https://cfaes.osu.edu/news/articles/health-care-and-weather-distressing-farmers.

16. P. P. Micklin, "Desiccation of the Aral Sea: A Water Management Disaster in the Soviet Union," *Science* 241 (2018): 1170–76.

17. C. A. Bowers, *Critical Essays on Education, Modernity, and the Recovery of the Ecological Imperative* (New York: Teachers College Press, 1993).

18. Jan Douwe van der Ploeg, "The Political Economy of Agroecology," *The Journal of Peasant Studies* 48, no. 2 (2021): 274–97, doi: 10.1080/03066150.2020.1725489.

19. M. Edelman and W. Wolford, "Introduction: Critical Agrarian Studies in Theory and Practice," *Antipode* 49, no. 4 (2017): 959–76.

20. Ibid.

21. Raymond Williams, *The Country and the City* (Oxford, UK: Oxford University Press, 1975).

22. Marc Edelman and Wendy Wolford, "Introduction: Critical Agrarian Studies in Theory and Practice," *Antipode* 49, no. 4 (2017): 973.

23. "Genesis 2:7–8," in *Common English Bible*, 2011.

24. Ellen Davis, who wrote *Scripture, Culture, and Agriculture: An Agrarian Reading of the Bible*, is a primary scholar for this connection.

25. S. A. Yarwood, et al. "Forest and Rangeland Soil Biodiversity," in *Forest and Rangeland Soils of the United States under Changing Conditions*, eds. R. Pouyat, D. Page-Dumroese, T. Patel-Weynand, L. Geiser (New York: Springer Publishing, 2022), https://doi.org/10.1007/978-3-030-45216-2_5.

26. G. S. Kleppel, F. Provenza, J. J. Villalba, eds., *Livestock Production and the Functioning of Agricultural Ecosystems*, Volume 1 (Lausanne, Switzerland: Frontiers Media SA, 2021), doi: 10.3389/978-2-88971-218-2.

27. Mariko Thorbecke and Jon Dettling, "Carbon Footprint Evaluation of Regenerative Grazing at White Oak Pastures: Results Presentation," *Quantis* (2019), https://blog.whiteoakpastures.com/hubfs/WOP-LCA-Quantis-2019.pdf.

28. Caney Fork Farms, https://www.caneyforkfarms.com.

29. Fox Hollow Farm Naturally website, https://foxhollowfarmnaturally.com.

30. Sister Grove Farm website, https://www.sistergrovefarm.com.

31. Rodale Institute, "Regenerative Organic Agriculture and Climate Change," https://rodaleinstitute.org/wp-content/uploads/Regenerative-Organic-Agriculture-White-Paper.pdf.

32. The Savory Global website contains examples and cites peer-reviewed research concerning the renewal of grasslands through regenerative grazing, https://savory.global.

33. Theodore Hiebert, *The Yahwist's Landscape: Nature and Religion in Early Israel* (New York: Oxford University Press, 1996): 30–38.

34. Aldo Leopold, "Land Ethic," in *A Sand County Almanac: And Sketches Here and There* (London: Oxford University Press, 1949), 201–26.

35. Wendell Berry, "The Gift of Good Land," in *Essays 1969–1990*, ed. Jack Shoemaker (New York: Penguin Random House, 2019).

36. David Orr, *Earth in Mind: On Education, Environment, and the Human Prospect* (Washington, DC: Island Press, 2004), 27.

37. Ernest Becker's *The Denial of Death* as an early assessment of cultural malaise is but one moment warning as well as the corpus of liberation theologies crying for release from oppressive theologies supported by practices of the Western church. Ernest Becker, *The Denial of Death* (New York: Free Press, 1975).

38. Aldo Leopold, *Round River* (New York: Oxford University Press, 1993), 165.

39. Edelman and Wolford, "Introduction," p. 967. This term was found here in reference to a much larger conversation beyond the scope of this paper and the limited knowledge of the writer.

REFERENCES

Becker, Ernest. *The Denial of Death*. New York: Free Press Paperbacks, 1997.

Berry, Wendell. "The Gift of Good Land." In *Essays 1969–1990*, ed. Jack Shoemaker. New York: Penguin Random House, 2019.

Black Church Food Security Network. https://blackchurchfoodsecurity.net.

Bowers, C. A. *Critical Essays on Education, Modernity, and the Recovery of the Ecological Imperative*. New York: Teachers College Press, 1993.

brown, adrienne maree. "Emergent Strategy: Shaping Change, Changing Worlds." Compassionate Communities Conference, 2017, lecture. Accessed June 9, 2022. https://youtu.be/h-sCy8SzvHY.

Caney Fork Farms. https://www.caneyforkfarms.com.

Davis, Ellen F. *Scripture, Culture, and Agriculture: An Agrarian Reading of the Bible*. Cambridge, UK: Cambridge University Press, 2012.

Edelman, M., and W. Wolford. "Introduction: Critical Agrarian Studies in Theory and Practice." *Antipode* 49, no. 4 (2017): 959–76.

Fox Hollow Farm Naturally website. https://foxhollowfarmnaturally.com.

"Genesis 2:7–8." In *Common English Bible*. Nashville, TN: Christian Resources Development Corporation, 2011.

"Health Care and Weather Distressing Farmers." The Ohio State University, College of Food, Agricultural, and Environmental Sciences. Accessed June 21, 2022. https://cfaes.osu.edu/news/articles/health-care-and-weather-distressing-farmers.

Hiebert, Theodore. *The Yahwist's Landscape: Nature and Religion in Early Israel*. New York: Oxford University Press, 1996.

Howard, Philip H. *Concentration and Power in the Food System: Who Controls What We Eat?* rev. ed. London: Bloomsbury Academic, 2021.

Howard, Philip H., and Mary K. Hendrickson. "The State of Concentration in Global Food and Agriculture Industries." In *Transformation of Our Food Systems: The Making of a Paradigm Shift*, 89–91. Bochum, Germany: Zukunftsstiftung Landwirtschaft (Foundation on Future Farming), 2020.

IPES-Food. "The Politics of Protein: Examining Claims about Livestock, Fish, 'Alternative Proteins' and Sustainability." 2022.

Kleppel, G. S., F. Provenza, J. J. Villalba, eds. *Livestock Production and the Functioning of Agricultural Ecosystems. Volume 1.* Lausanne, Switzerland: Frontiers Media SA, 2021. doi: 10.3389/978-2-88971-218-2.

Lakhani, Nina, Aliya Uteuova, and Alvin Chang. "Revealed: The True Extent of America's Food Monopolies, and Who Pays the Price." *The Guardian* (July 14, 2021). https://www.theguardian.com/environment/ng-interactive/2021/jul/14/food-monopoly-meals-profits-data-investigation.

Leopold, Aldo. "Land Ethic." In *A Sand County Almanac: And Sketches Here and There*, 201–26. London: Oxford University Press, 1949.

———. *Round River*. New York: Oxford University Press, 1993.

Menconi, M. E., S. Giordano, D. Grohman. "Revisiting Global Food Production and Consumption Patterns by Developing Resilient Food Systems for Local Communities." *Land Use Policy* 119 (2022).

Micklin, P. P. "Desiccation of the Aral Sea: A Water Management Disaster in the Soviet Union." *Science* 241 (2018): 1170–76.

Orr, David. *Earth in Mind: On Education, Environment, and the Human Prospect*, 27. Washington, DC: Island Press, 2004.

Ricciardi, V., N. Ramankutty, Z. Mehrabi, L. Jarvis, B. Chookolingo. "How Much of the World's Food Do Smallholders Produce?" *Global Food Security* 17 (2018): 64–72.

Rodale Institute. "Regenerative Organic Agriculture and Climate Change: A Down-to-Earth Solution to Global Warming." Kutztown, PA: Rodale Institute, 2014. https://rodaleinstitute.org/wp-content/uploads/Regenerative-Organic-Agriculture-White-Paper.pdf.

Sister Grove Farm website. https://www.sistergrovefarm.com.

Thorbecke, Mariko, and Jon Dettling. "Carbon Footprint Evaluation of Regenerative Grazing at White Oak Pastures: Results Presentation." *Quantis* (2019). https://blog.whiteoakpastures.com/hubfs/WOP-LCA-Quantis-2019.pdf.

van der Ploeg, Jan Douwe. "The Political Economy of Agroecology." *The Journal of Peasant Studies* 48, no. 2 (2021): 274–97.

Williams, Raymond. *The Country and the City*. Oxford, UK: Oxford University Press, 1975.

Yarwood, S. A., et al. "Forest and Rangeland Soil Biodiversity." In *Forest and Rangeland Soils of the United States under Changing Conditions*, eds. R. Pouyat, D. Page-Dumroese, T. Patel-Weynand, L. Geiser. New York: Springer Publishing, 2022. https://doi.org/10.1007/978-3-030-45216-2_5.

Index

activism: burnout in, 185; ecological, 65, 75–77, 208n37, 216–17, 220; international, 198–99, 207n31; new forms of, 188, 190n26, 231n21

agency: alternative forms of, 8, 97–100, 155; consumer behaviors and, 7, 18; divine views of, 28; indigenous/subaltern communities and, 68; nature and, 86, 140; working people's, 21, 94–95, 105n52

agrarianism: critical approaches in, 59n24, 245–49; politics in, 45–48, 60n31; theological/philosophical views about, 55–56, 246

agroecology, 51, 55, 58

Althaus-Reid, Marcella, 10n4

animals: factory farming of, 239, 241; human contact with, 140, 159, 167, 176, 241, 246–47, 249; theological thinking about, 115, 144–45

animism, 144, 151n28. *See also* Christian animism

anthropocentrism, 88–89, 155, 157, 182

Aquinas, Thomas, 141–42, 150n19

Aristotle, 22–25, 28

Bauman, Whitney, 7, 9, 38n76, 96–97, 102n3, 169n34

Bauman, Zygmunt, 156, 168n11, 169n28

Berry, Thomas, 137, 143, 149n3, 151n26, 213

Berry, Wendell, 244, 247, 252n35

the Bible, 23–24, 115, 123, 145, 188, 245; interpretation of, 124, 144, 196–97, 199–200, 214, 227, 247

Black Church Food Security Network, 237–38

Black freedom movement, 220, 225–26

Black Lives Matter (BLM) movement, 159, 166, 187

Boff, Leonardo, 10n4, 55, 94

Bradshaw, David, 22–24, 35nn24–31, 36nn32–33

Bray, Karen, 6, 11n20, 38n77

Brock, Rita Nakashima, 186, 190n22

brown, adrienne maree, 188, 190nn25–26, 250n6

Buddhism, 104n25, 161–62, 169n29, 225

Buell, Fredrick, 21, 35n17, 35n20

Bullard, Robert, 10n5, 198

capitalism, 110–14; 128n1, 129nn4–5, 131n16; exploitative and extractive practices of, 2–3, 8, 44, 54, 73, 87, 94, 99, 139–40, 147, 177; fossil

255

fuels and, 34n9, 130n14, 156, 199, 202; neoliberal forms of, 65, 71–77, 86–87, 101, 161–62, 244; relationship of Christianity to, 9, 114–16, 177–78; religious character of, 6–7
Capitalocene, 89, 92, 94, 98, 103n15, 183
Carter, J. Kameron, 38n76
the Catholic Church, 44–48, 56–57, 177; environmental advocacy in, 18, 34n6
Catholic Worker Movement, 212, 215, 217
Cavanaugh, William, 12n24, 104n35
Chavis, Benjamin, 4, 10n5
Christian animism, 139, 145–48
Christian Community Development Association (CCDA), 217
Christianity: dominating forms of, 33, 55–56, 88, 101, 144, 147, 196–97, 248; environmentalism and, 4–5, 55; influence of spiritual nonviolence on, 225; liberation movements and, 3, 45, 51. *See also* capitalism
Christian liturgy: corporate confession as a practice of, 126–27, 204–6; economic concerns raised in, 7
Christian pacifism, 212, 215
church: civil rights movement activity in, 225; environmental sustainability practices and, 90, 243; labor alliances and, 9, 109–10, 120–27; ministries/practices of, 122–25
class: analysis of, 46, 128n1; relation of ecology, race, gender, and, 11n15, 55–56, 68, 70, 85–86, 102n1
Cobb, John, 4–5, 10nn9–10, 37n67, 91, 96, 104nn25–26, 105n44, 105n52, 138, 168n10, 170n38
Colombia, 43–45; alternative ecological farming practices in, 54–57; liberation theologies in, 45–48; peasant (Campesinx) farming movements in, 48–51

colonialism, 70, 87, 161, 183; capitalism and settler forms of, 65, 73–74, 76–77, 177; Christian role in, 71, 155; justifications for, 26, 67; racialized forms of, 3, 44
commodification, 71, 76, 139–42
commoning, 75–78
the commons, 66–68
communism, 52–54, 73, 167, 178
community organizing, 211–12, 219–24, 231n25; congregational forms of, 123
Conference of Parties (United Nations COP), 193, 202
consumption, 4, 17, 91, 139–40, 165, 182, 241; consumer behaviors in, 7–8, 247; ethical action toward, 18, 98
consumption vs. production, 90–95, 99, 156
cooperatives, 97, 99, 105n55, 123, 218–19; worker-owned, 7, 98, 131n23, 132n29, 132n33
COVID-19 pandemic, 9, 160, 189n2; capitalism and, 109, 176–79; climate change and, 158–60; essential workers in, 175, 243
Crockett, Clayton, 34n7, 37n69

Daggett, Cara, 29–31, 35n20, 37n59, 37nn61–63, 38n73
Daly, Herman, 4–5, 37n67, 91, 104nn25–26, 105n52, 138, 150n13, 168n10, 170n38
Day, Dorothy, 215, 231n9
Day, Keri, 6, 11n21
decolonization, 56, 70–71, 75; role of indigenous and subaltern communities in, 70–71, 76–77. *See also* colonialism; communing; the commons; indigenous communities
deep solidarity, 78–79, 99–100, 110, 151n41, 184; socio-ecological forms of, 139, 143, 147, 149. *See also* solidarity

Deloria, Vine, Jr., 38n76
divestment, 197–99
Dochuk, Darren, 194–95, 206n5, 207nn10–17, 207nn20–28
Duchrow, Ulrich, 6, 10n4

Eberhart, Timothy Reinhold, 7, 9
ecofeminism, 150n9; philosophical views, 141–42; theological views, 55–56, 94, 167. *See also* Gebara, Ivone; Ruether, Rosemary Radford
ecological modernization theory, 91–95
ecology, vii, 1–9, 17, 55, 56, 74, 89, 94, 96, 97, 101, 129, 138, 201, 213, 235, 237, 240
economic systems: alternative forms of, 91, 95–96, 98, 137, 187–88, 215; dominant forms of, 1, 3, 32, 177, 217, 238, 241, 248; ecological perspectives and, 97–100, 138, 147–49, 164–65, 249; primary paradigms in, 89–93; religion and, 6–7, 100–101, 155. *See also* capitalism
eco-socialism, 137–38, 143; relationship of Christianity to, 148–49
energeia, 22–24
energy: consumption of, 20, 29–32; economics and, 17–18, 21; flux as a concept of, 31–32; religious perspectives on, 18, 27–29
the erotic: decolonization and, 56; planetary flourishing as part of, 165–67
essential workers. *See* COVID-19 pandemic
exploitation: intersection of economic and ecological devastation with, 2–3, 5, 73, 87, 139, 176–77; resistance against, 3, 8–9, 44–45, 73, 99, 110, 226. *See also* capitalism; economic systems
extraction, 2, 3, 7, 8, 10n3, 32, 68, 87, 91, 140, 162, 196, 197, 199, 205, 239, 244, 249

Fals Borda, Orlando, 46–47, 59n9
Federici, Silvia, 56, 61n46 129n1
Finney, Carolyn, 10n6
food production. *See* production: forms of food/meat
fossil fuels, 31–32, 140, 155–57; capitalism and, 140, 155–56, 158–60; Christianity's relationship to, 194–97; divestment from, 193–94, 197–99
Foster, John Bellamy, 170n40
Freire, Paulo, 46–48
Frigo, Giovanni, 34nn5–6

Gandhi, Mohandas, 225, 231n28
Gandhian nonviolence, 226–28
Gebara, Ivone, 10n4, 38n75, 56, 61n45, 94, 104nn39–40, 160
Gottlieb, Roger, 68, 79n3
Gutiérrez, Gustavo, 59n8

Halapua, Winston (archbishop), 71–72, 79n14
Haraway, Donna, 61n41 160, 167, 169n24
Harris, Melanie, 11n15, 250n3
Hau'ofa, Epeli, 70, 79nn11–12
health-care workers, 175, 180–81
Henkel-Rieger, Rosemarie, 99, 105n52, 106n59, 117, 131n19, 132n32
Hernández Vidal, Nathalia, 3, 8, 58n4 60–61nn41–42
Hersey, Tricia, 185, 190n18
Herzog, Frederick, 10n4, 10n8
Hessel, Dieter, 18, 34n4, 105n44
Hinkelammert, Franz, 6
Holy Spirit, 24, 139, 144–45, 148
hope, 100, 146, 166, 188, 219, 228, 230, 238, 247–48
housing, 111, 123, 178, 216, 223

immigrant workers, 175–76, 179, 216
Immokalee workers, 243, 249
indigenous communities: colonialism and, 44, 49, 67, 74; social movement

activity in, 54, 65, 226; theological/religious values in, 72–74, 78, 144. *See also* Colombia; Māori
industrial agriculture, 176, 241–42, 250n8. *See also* production: forms of food/meat
Instituto Mayor Campesino (IMCA), 43–45, 48, 50–54
intentional community, 214–17, 236
Intergovernmental Panel on Climate Change, 30, 86, 102n4, 193, 206n3, 208n37

Jackson, Moana, 72, 79n19
Jennings, Willie James, 10n2
Jesus, 24, 27, 116, 139, 144–45, 148, 162, 167, 186

Kaku, Michio, 20, 34n12
Kant, Immanuel, 140, 142
Kardashev scale, 19–20
Kearns, Laurel, 102n3, 168n6, 169n25
Keller, Catherine, 143, 155, 163, 168n4, 168n6, 169n25
Klein, Naomi, 99–100, 106nn60–61, 106nn63–66, 226, 232n32
Korten, David, 138, 149n4

labor, 94, 95, 97–98, 111–13, 130n11
labor movement, 9, 97, 117, 121, 132n29, 185; interreligious alliances and, 132n36
labor unions, 109–10, 120–22
land, 235–36; commodification/exploitation of, 3, 66, 71, 73, 49, 140, 217, 243; ecological/sustainable practices on the, 55, 218, 237–39, 246
Laudato Si.' See Pope Francis
Leopold, Aldo, 246–47
Lettini, Gabriella, 9, 189n11
liberation theologies, 3, 8, 45, 56, 94, 100, 157; Marxism and, 46–47, 53
local food movement, 9, 215–16, 237, 239

Malm, Andreas, 130n14
Māori, 72–75
Martínez Andrade, Luis, 58n7
Marx, Karl, 50, 139–40, 148
Marxism, 46, 50–53, 103n12, 147, 244–45, 249
Martin-Schramm, Jim, 34n6, 230n4
materialism, 6, 98–99
McAlevey, Jane, 119, 131n20, 131n24
McFague, Sallie, 4–5, 11n12, 12n24, 88, 93, 103n13, 104n35, 104n40, 143, 151n27, 156, 164, 168n7
McKibben, Bill, 199, 203, 208n35, 209n50
Mejia, Francisco Javier ("El cura Mejía"), 44, 51–54
Methodist Theological School in Ohio (MTSO), 235–36, 238, 249–50
Mill, John Stuart, 140–41, 150nn17–18
Mitchell, Timothy, 21, 35n18
Moana eco-theology, 70–72
modernity, 18–19, 49, 53, 88, 138, 141, 159–61
Moe-Lobeda, Cynthia, 5, 11n14, 104n35
mohaupt, abby, 7, 9
Moltmann, Jürgen, 137, 143, 149n1, 160
Moore, Jason, 53, 95, 102–3n7, 103n15, 138, 143, 150n9
moral injury, 180–82, 189n11
Movement of Landless Workers (MST), 48, 94
Mumford, Lewis, 19–20, 34n9

National Network of Free Seeds of Colombia (RSLC), 48, 55. *See also* Colombia
Neumark, Heidi, 129n2, 132n34
Nogueira-Godsey, Elaine, 105n50
nonviolence, 198; spiritual grounding for, 212–13, 232n39; strategic forms of, 224–29

Occupy Wall Street movement, 94, 157, 184
Olaloku-Teriba, Annie, 184, 190n17

oppression, 44, 47, 57, 70, 87, 142; interlocking forms of, 5, 72, 94, 159–60, 184–85

Participatory Action Research (PAR). *See* Fals Borda, Orlando
Patel, Raj, 102n6, 128n1
Paul (the Apostle), 23–24, 29, 35n27
petroculture, 7, 17, 21
pirates and piracy, 162–63
planetary flourishing, 161, 164, 166–67
Polanyi, Karl, 139–40
Poor People's Campaign, 187, 190n23
Pope Francis, 5, 11n16, 12n24, 56, 216
power, 6, 47; contestation to dominant forms of, 94–95, 98, 109–10, 116–17, 198, 219, 227, 239–40; divinity as a source of, 145, 155, 188, 196, 228; energy systems and, 21, 27–28, 32; faith organizing and, 123–24; relations of, 54, 56, 89, 97, 140, 145, 177; relationship of privilege to, 183–85
Presbyterian Church (PC[USA]), 194, 199–204, 206nn39–49
production: capitalist forms of, 2, 128, 140, 156, 176; cooperative/ecological forms of, 98–99, 147; forms of food/meat, 176, 187, 216, 239–43; rural/peasant forms of, 50–51. *See also* consumption vs. production
Pui-lan, Kwok, 99, 105n41, 106n59, 151n41, 168n13

queer home economics, 9, 156, 159 164–67
queer theologies, 33

race, 4, 5, 9, 11, 26, 27, 33, 36, 68, 73, 85, 87, 98, 99, 113, 117, 150, 161, 164, 220, 256
racism, 26, 183, 185; labor and, 111, 113; links to environmental injustice, 2–4, 66, 74, 87, 238
Rasmussen, Larry, 34n6, 213, 230n4

Raworth, Kate, 138, 147, 151n40
regenerative agriculture, 54, 238–39, 246–48
regenerative eco-socialism, 138, 143, 148
religion: Abrahamic forms of, 99–100; alternatives to dominant forms of, 95, 162, 229; critique of, 216, 6–7, 33, 45, 101; ecology and, 2, 68, 88–89, 96–97, 237, 240; intersections between economics, ecology, and, 4–6, 8, 18, 101
religious environmentalism, 68–70
resistance: capitalism and, 184–85; healing forms of, 182, 187–88; movements of, 3–4, 8–9, 73, 76, 99–102, 193
Rich, Nathaniel, 197, 207n24
Rieger, Joerg, 6–8, 11n13, 11n15, 11n19, 12n23, 30, 102n1, 104n36, 104–5nn40–41, 105nn52–53, 105n57, 106n59, 106n67, 117, 129n3, 131n19, 132n32, 132n35, 151n41, 168n13, 179, 183–84, 189n7, 189n12
Rivera, Mayra, 165, 170n35, 170n41
Rockefeller, John, 195–97
Rowe, Terra Schwerin, 6, 8, 11n20, 12n22, 12n25, 33n1, 34n6, 35nn21–22, 61n41, 168n5, 169n27
Rubenstein, Mary-Jane, 168n17
Ruether, Rosemary Radford, 10n4, 38n75, 167, 170n44

sacralization, 18, 228; de-sacralization and, 73, 148
Sagan, Carl, 20, 34n11
Said, Edward, 26, 36n46
Schnaiberg, Allan, 91, 103n17, 104nn22–23
Schor, Juliet, 95–96, 98, 105nn46–47, 105nn50–51, 105n56
Seminary Hill Farm, 236–37
sexism, 94, 159, 183; racism, patriarchy, and, 112–13, 116.

Shiva, Vandana, 138
Singh, Devin, 6, 11n20
Smil, Vaclav, 20–21, 30, 34n14, 35nn15–16
socialism, 138, 165, 245, 248–49
solidarity, 180, 188; ecological practices and, 66, 72, 75, 138, 147, 149, 243, 248; religion and, 5, 8, 94; social movement strategies of, 50, 120, 125–26, 198, 203–5, 220. *See also* deep solidarity
Stewart, Lyman, 7, 12n26, 196, 206n7, 207n9
Sung, Jung Mo, 6, 105n45
sustainability, 5, 90–93, 213; community practices for, 217–19; farming practices, land use, and, 176, 236–37, 239, 249

tangata whenua (people of the land), 72–74. *See also* Māori
Taylor, Dorceta, 10nn5–6
Taylor, Keeanga-Yamahtta, 184, 189n16
Taylor, Sonya Renee, 188, 190n27
Thompson, Craig J., 96, 99, 105nn46–47, 105nn50–51, 105n56
Torres, Camilo, 51, 54

Treadmill of Production (ToP) theory, 91–95

United Church of Christ (UCC), 4, 10nn7–8
United Methodist Church, 216, 231n12

Vaai, Upolu Luma, 71, 79n16
vegan/vegetarian diets, 240–42

Wallace, Mark, 139, 144–48
Wallace, William (Bill), 74, 80n27
Warren, Karen, 141–42, 150n20
Weber, Max, 177, 195, 206n8
White, Lynn, 88, 103n11, 155, 168n2
white supremacy, 69, 72, 74, 77, 183–84, 188, 198
Williams, Delores, 38n75, 186, 190n21
Wolff, Richard, 98, 105n54
womanism, 6, 11n15, 238

xenophobia, 159, 183, 185

York, Richard, 91, 102n4, 103n12, 104n24, 104n28

Zachariah, George, 2, 8, 10n4

Contributor Biographies

Whitney Bauman is professor of religious studies at Florida International University in Miami, Florida. He is also co-founder and co-director of Counterpoint: Navigating Knowledge, a nonprofit based in Berlin, Germany, which holds public discussions over social and ecological issues related to globalization and climate change. His publications include *Religion and Ecology: Developing a Planetary Ethic* (2014); co-authored with Kevin O'Brien, *Environmental Ethics and Uncertainty: Tackling Wicked Problems* (2019); and, co-edited with Kevin O'Brien and Richard Bohannon, the third edition of *Grounding Religion: A Fieldguide to the Study of Religion and Ecology* (2023). He is also the co-editor with Karen Bray and Heather Eaton of *Earthly Things: Immanence, New Materialisms, and Planetary Thinking* (2023). His next monograph is titled, *A Critical Planetary Romanticism: Literary and Scientific Origins of New Materialism* (2024).

Timothy Reinhold Eberhart is the Robert and Marilyn Degler McClean Associate Professor of Ecological Theology and Practice at Garrett-Evangelical Theological Seminary, where he directs a master-of-arts program in public ministry and the Center for Ecological Regeneration. He teaches in the areas of theology and ethics, concentrating on the relation of Christian doctrine to environmental, economic, political, and social-change theory and praxis. His publications include *Rooted and Grounded in Love: Holy Communion for the Whole Creation* (2017); *The Economy of Salvation: Essays in Honor of M. Douglas Meeks* (2015); and chapters on mission, ecclesiology, and eco-theology. He is an ordained elder in the United Methodist Church, a trained permaculturalist, a UMC Earthkeeper, North American Secretary for the Oxford Institute of Methodist Theological Studies, and co-founder of The Institute for Christian Socialism.

Nathalia Hernández Vidal is an assistant professor of sociology at the University of Oregon. Her work examines how indigenous, Black, and

Mestizx communities in Latin America generate place-based forms of dissent and promote forms of living otherwise. Her scholarship has been published in US and Latin American journals and has been supported by the Arthur J. Schmitt Foundation, the University of Hamburg, the Ibero-Amerikanisches Institut, and the Consejo Latinoamericano de Ciencias Sociales (CLACSO), among others.

Daniel Joranko is a climate organizer in the Tennessee Valley region. He is a former adjunct lecturer at the Vanderbilt Divinity School (VDS) and has taught subjects such as religion and ecology, community development, and strategic nonviolence. He also coordinated the VDS Riverbend program, which featured courses inside prisons made up of one half VDS students and one half prisoners. He currently serves as the state coordinator for Tennessee Interfaith Power and Light and the coordinator of the United Methodist Tennessee-Western Kentucky Conference Creation Care Ministry. He is a longtime community organizer, with experience working in Nashville and Chicago.

Gabriella Lettini is Aurelia H. Reinhardt Professor of Theological Ethics, academic dean, and chief academic officer at Starr King School for the Ministry in Oakland, California. Lettini also served as consortial faculty and core doctoral faculty at the Graduate Theological Union in Berkeley, California, and as Visiting assistant professor of theology and culture at Union Theological Seminary in New York City. Lettini was a founding member and co-chair of the Transformative Pedagogy and Scholarship Group and the Moral Injury and Recovery Unit of the American Academy of Religion. In the last decade, Lettini's publications and research have focused on the concept of moral injury.

abby mohaupt is the director of the Garrett Collective at Garrett-Evangelical Theological Seminary in Evanston, Illinois. Ordained in the Presbyterian Church (USA), abby is a sought-after educator, facilitator, organizer, and author on the intersections of faith, climate justice, race, and gender. She is a PhD candidate in religion, culture, and ecology at Drew Theological School.

Jeremy Posadas holds the Hal S. Marchman Chair of Civic and Social Responsibility at Stetson University (in Central Florida) along with a joint appointment in religious studies and gender studies. Prior to this, he taught for over a decade at Austin College (on the rural Texas-Oklahoma border), where he held the John F. Anderson Chair of Christian Thought. His recently published essays have focused on students' emotional labor in religious studies courses; pedagogies for dismantling rape culture; and reproductive justice as a basis for critiquing Christian ethics of work. Posadas created the *United Regions of America* map, which groups all 3,142 counties (and equivalents) of the United States into fourteen regions that calibrate common perceptions with dominant landscapes and industries.

Joerg Rieger (he, him, er) is distinguished professor of theology, Cal Turner Chancellor's Chair of Wesleyan Studies, and director of the Wendland-Cook Program in Religion and Justice at Vanderbilt University. He is author and editor of twenty-six books, including *Theology in the Capitalocene: Ecology, Identity, Class, and Solidarity* (2022); *Jesus vs. Caesar: For People Tired of Serving the Wrong God* (2018); *No Religion but Social Religion: Liberating Wesleyan Theology* (2018); *Unified We Are a Force: How Faith and Labor Can Overcome America's Inequalities* (2016); and *No Rising Tide: Theology, Economics, and the Future* (2009). He lectures frequently nationally and internationally, and his works have been translated into Portuguese, Spanish, Italian, Croatian, German, Malayalam, Korean, and Chinese.

Terra Schwerin Rowe (she/her, settler) is associate professor in the philosophy and religion department at the University of North Texas, a leading program in environmental philosophy, located on land stewarded by and seized from Wichita and Caddo Affiliated Tribes. She received a PhD in theological and philosophical studies from Drew University, is co-director of the AAR seminar on energy, extraction, and religion, is on the steering committee of the academy's religion and ecology unit, and is a member of the Petrocultures Research Group. Her most recent book is *Of Modern Extraction: Experiments in Critical Petro-theology* (2023).

Tim Van Meter is an associate professor at the Methodist Theological School in Ohio (MTSO). He leads ecology and justice specializations in the MDiv, MAPT, and DMin degrees at MTSO. He also directs the Master of Arts in Social Justice and the Master of Arts in Public Theology degrees. He is currently the director for a grant program leading pastoral and lay education exploring climate change, antiracism, trauma-informed responses, and possibilities for resilient communities. In 2023, he led a six-week educational engagement program with young adults exploring the intersections of food sovereignty, antiracism, climate change, and the complex challenges of constructing hopeful vocation and hospitable, resilient communities. Dr. Van Meter serves as the coordinator for ecological initiatives for MTSO, which has established a thirteen-acre organic farm on its one hundred–acre campus. The farm integrated with the dining hall to serve 85 percent of all food from local, organic, and humane sources. MTSO has also committed to use solar energy for electricity and closed-loop geothermal energy for the primary academic buildings.

George Zachariah serves the Trinity Methodist Theological College, Auckland, New Zealand as Wesley Lecturer in Theological Studies.

www.ingramcontent.com/pod-product-compliance
Lightning Source LLC
Chambersburg PA
CBHW020113010526
44115CB00008B/815